Optimization Algorithms: Theory and Applications

Optimization Algorithms: Theory and Applications

Guest Editor

Frank Werner

Basel • Beijing • Wuhan • Barcelona • Belgrade • Novi Sad • Cluj • Manchester

Guest Editor
Frank Werner
Faculty of Mathematics
Otto-von-Guericke University
Magdeburg
Germany

Editorial Office
MDPI AG
Grosspeteranlage 5
4052 Basel, Switzerland

This is a reprint of the Special Issue, published open access by the journal *Mathematics* (ISSN 2227-7390), freely accessible at: www.mdpi.com/journal/mathematics/special_issues/Optimization_Algorithms_Theory_Applications.

For citation purposes, cite each article independently as indicated on the article page online and using the guide below:

Lastname, A.A.; Lastname, B.B. Article Title. *Journal Name* **Year**, *Volume Number*, Page Range.

ISBN 978-3-7258-3160-9 (Hbk)
ISBN 978-3-7258-3159-3 (PDF)
https://doi.org/10.3390/books978-3-7258-3159-3

© 2025 by the authors. Articles in this book are Open Access and distributed under the Creative Commons Attribution (CC BY) license. The book as a whole is distributed by MDPI under the terms and conditions of the Creative Commons Attribution-NonCommercial-NoDerivs (CC BY-NC-ND) license (https://creativecommons.org/licenses/by-nc-nd/4.0/).

Contents

About the Editor vii

Preface ix

Frank Werner
Special Issue: "Optimization Algorithms: Theory and Applications"
Reprinted from: *Mathematics* **2025**, *13*, 175, https://doi.org/10.3390/math13010175 1

Mengnan Chen, Yongquan Zhou and Qifang Luo
An Improved Arithmetic Optimization Algorithm for Numerical Optimization Problems
Reprinted from: *Mathematics* **2022**, *10*, 2152, https://doi.org/10.3390/math10122152 4

Aifen Feng, Xiaogai Chang, Youlin Shang and Jingya Fan
Application of the ADMM Algorithm for a High-Dimensional Partially Linear Model
Reprinted from: *Mathematics* **2022**, *10*, 4767, https://doi.org/10.3390/math10244767 31

Chenyao Zhang, Yuyan Han, Yuting Wang, Junqing Li and Kaizhou Gao
A Distributed Blocking Flowshop Scheduling with Setup Times Using Multi-Factory Collaboration Iterated Greedy Algorithm
Reprinted from: *Mathematics* **2023**, *11*, 581, https://doi.org/10.3390/math11030581 44

Kin Keung Lai, Shashi Kant Mishra, Ravina Sharma, Manjari Sharma and Bhagwat Ram
A Modified q-BFGS Algorithm for Unconstrained Optimization
Reprinted from: *Mathematics* **2023**, *11*, 1420, https://doi.org/10.3390/math11061420 69

José Lemus-Romani, Diego Ossandón, Rocío Sepúlveda, Nicolás Carrasco-Astudillo, Victor Yepes and José García
Optimizing Retaining Walls through Reinforcement Learning Approaches and Metaheuristic Techniques
Reprinted from: *Mathematics* **2023**, *11*, 2104, https://doi.org/10.3390/math11092104 93

Carlos Cobos, Cristian Ordoñez, Jose Torres-Jimenez, Hugo Ordoñez and Martha Mendoza
Weight Vector Definition for MOEA/D-Based Algorithms Using Augmented Covering Arrays for Many-Objective Optimization
Reprinted from: *Mathematics* **2024**, *12*, 1680, https://doi.org/10.3390/math12111680 126

Shuai Wang, Xiaoliang Wang, Yuzhu Tian and Liping Pang
A New Hybrid Descent Algorithm for Large-Scale Nonconvex Optimization and Application to Some Image Restoration Problems
Reprinted from: *Mathematics* **2024**, *12*, 3088, https://doi.org/10.3390/math12193088 165

Aris Magklaras, Christos Gogos, Panayiotis Alefragis and Alexios Birbas
Enhancing Parameters Tuning of Overlay Models with Ridge Regression: Addressing Multicollinearity in High-Dimensional Data
Reprinted from: *Mathematics* **2024**, *12*, 3179, https://doi.org/10.3390/math12203179 181

Miguel Arcos-Argudo, Jesús Lacalle and Luis M. Pozo-Coronado
Cyclic Structure, Vertex Degree and Number of Linear Vertices in Minimal Strong Digraphs
Reprinted from: *Mathematics* **2024**, *12*, 3657, https://doi.org/10.3390/math12233657 194

Kitti Udvardy, Polina Görbe, Tamás Bódis and János Botzheim
Conceptual Framework for Adaptive Bacterial Memetic Algorithm Parameterization in Storage Location Assignment Problem
Reprinted from: *Mathematics* **2024**, *12*, 3688, https://doi.org/10.3390/math12233688 205

About the Editor

Frank Werner

Frank Werner studied mathematics from 1975 to 1980 and graduated from the Technical University of Magdeburg (Germany) with a distinction. He received a Ph.D. degree (with summa cum laude) in Mathematics in 1984 and defended his habilitation thesis in 1989. From this time on, he worked at the Faculty of Mathematics at the Otto-von-Guericke University Magdeburg in Germany, and since 1998, he has worked as an Extraordinary Professor. In 1992, he received a grant from the Alexander von Humboldt Foundation. He has been a manager of several research projects supported by the German Research Society (DFG) and the European Union (INTAS). Since 2019, he has been the Editor-in-Chief of the journal *Algorithms*. He has also been an Associate Editor of *The International Journal of Production Research* since 2012 and *The Journal of Scheduling* since 2014, as well a member of the Editorial/Advisory Boards of 19 other international journals. He has been a Guest Editor of Special Issues in ten international journals and has served as a member of the Program Committee of more than 160 international conferences. Frank Werner is an author/editor of 17 books, including the textbooks *Mathematics of Economics and Business* and *A Refresher Course in Mathematics*. In addition, he has co-edited four proceedings volumes of the SIMULTECH conferences and published more than 300 journal and conference papers, including in *The International Journal of Production Research*, *Computers & Operations Research*, *The Journal of Scheduling*, *Applied Mathematical Modelling*, and *The European Journal of Operational Research*. He has received Best Paper Awards from *The International Journal of Production Research* (2016) and *IISE Transactions* (2021). His main research subjects are scheduling, discrete optimization, graph theory, and mathematical problems in operations research.

Preface

This is the printed edition of a Special Issue published in the *Mathematics* journal. We received 32 submissions for this issue, representing a broad spectrum in the field of optimization. In addition to the editorial, this reprint contains ten research papers focusing on optimization algorithms. Among the subjects addressed in this reprint, one can mention unconstrained optimization, non-convex optimization, multi-objective optimization, graph theory problems, or blocking flow shop scheduling. The authors apply mixed-integer linear programming, metaheuristic techniques, or reinforcement learning, to mention a few.

Finally, we extend our gratitude to all people who have contributed to the success of this issue, including but not limited to authors from nine countries, many referees from all over the world, and the staff of the *Mathematics* journal. I hope that the readers of this Special Issue find many stimulating ideas for their own future research in this challenging field of optimization algorithms, which play an important role in daily life.

Frank Werner
Guest Editor

Editorial

Special Issue: "Optimization Algorithms: Theory and Applications"

Frank Werner

Faculty of Mathematics, Otto-von-Guericke University, 39016 Magdeburg, Germany; frank.werner@ovgu.de; Tel.: +49-391-675-2025

1. Introduction

This Special Issue of the journal *Mathematics* was dedicated to compiling new results in the area of optimization algorithms, and both theoretical works and practical applications have been searched. In comparison with my recent guest-edited Special Issues on Discrete Optimization in mathematics (with 19 papers published between 2018 and 2019) and AIMS Mathematics (22 papers published between 2023 and 2024), as well as a recent Special Issue jointly edited with Alexander Lazarev and Bertrand Lin on Discrete Optimization and Scheduling in mathematics (11 published papers between 2022 and 2024), I have broadened the scope of the current Special Issue.

In the Call for Papers, a wide range of subjects were mentioned, e.g., linear, non-linear, integer and mixed-integer programming; combinatorial optimization; stochastic optimization;, robust optimization; multi-criteria optimization problems; optimization on graphs and networks; scheduling; control-theoretic problems, advanced heuristics and metaheuristics; and machine learning, to name a few. Papers on applications, e.g., in logistics, manufacturing, transportation or healthcare, were also welcome. Such optimization problems are of great relevance and practical importance.

For this Special Issue, 32 submissions were received. After a careful refereeing process, 10 papers with authors from 9 countries were selected for this Special Issue, which represented a broad spectrum of research fields in the optimization area. This corresponds to an acceptance rate of 31.25%. The papers in this Special Issue address topics such as unconstrained optimization, scheduling, graph theory, and multi-criteria optimization. As a rule, all submissions were reviewed by two or more experts from the corresponding research field. Subsequently, the published papers were surveyed in order of their publication dates for this Special Issue.

The first accepted paper, by Chen et al., presents an arithmetic optimization algorithm that is based on a population control strategy. In particular, the population is classified, and the number of individuals is adaptively controlled, which leads to a more effective search in the space. The developed algorithm is tested on six nonlinear systems of equations, 10 numerical integrations, and an engineering problem. The presented algorithm outperforms existing ones.

The second paper in this Special Issue, by Feng et al., deals with a high-dimensional semi-parametric regression model. The authors consider a partially linear model with a restricted profile and use the least squares method to estimate the parameters. By using an augmented Lagrangian function under linear constraints, the problem is transformed into an unconstrained optimization problem. Some numerical simulations are used to underline the effectiveness of the developed algorithm for solving high-dimensional models that are partially linear.

In contribution 3, Zang et al. deal with the distributed blocking flow shop scheduling problem by minimizing the makespan. After presenting a mixed integer linear program-

Received: 29 November 2024
Revised: 12 December 2024
Accepted: 23 December 2024
Published: 6 January 2025

Citation: Werner, F. Special Issue "Optimization Algorithms: Theory and Applications". *Mathematics* **2025**, *13*, 175. https://doi.org/10.3390/math13010175

Copyright: © 2025 by the author. Licensee MDPI, Basel, Switzerland. This article is an open access article distributed under the terms and conditions of the Creative Commons Attribution (CC BY) license (https://creativecommons.org/licenses/by/4.0/).

ming model, an iterated greedy-algorithm-blending multi-factory collaboration mechanism ia derived. For the computational experiments, 270 instances with up to 7 factories, 10 machines, and 500 jobs are used. The developed approach gives better results than the five algorithms used for the comparison.

Then, Lai et al. deal with nonlinear unconstrained optimization and present a modification of the q-BFGS algorithm (q-calculus Broydon–Fletcher–Goldfarb–Shanno method), which is a quasi-Newton approach. For building a q-Hessian, the approach uses only first-order q-derivatives. The presented modification preserves the convergence properties of the q-BFGS method without the convexity assumption of the objective function. Detailed numerical results are given that show that the algorithm can often escape from local optima and can move towards a global minimum.

In the next paper, Lemus-Romani et al. investigate the application of metaheuristic techniques to the retaining wall problem. The two objective functions are cost and CO_2 emissions. In particular, a new discretization technique based on reinforcement learning and transfer function is presented. Finally, extensive experiments are performed to compare the implemented techniques, and they show that the suggested approach is promising.

The sixth published paper, by Cobos et al., deals with many-objective optimization and proposes a new mathematical object, augmenting coving arrays, which allows for better sampling of the intersections of the different objectives by taking the least number of weight vectors based on an a priori-defined interaction level. Their proposed method gives better results compared with the traditional weight vector definition and the NSGA-III approach.

In the next paper, Wang et al. present a new hybrid descent conjugate gradient method based on the strongly convergent property of the Dai–Yuan approach and the Hestenes–Stiefel method. Independent of any line search technique, the new approach has a sufficient descent property. Numerical results are presented for 61 problems with 9 large-scale dimensions and 46 ill-conditioned matrix problems. It turns out that the new approach is more effective, robust, and reliable than the other methods considered.

Contribution 8, by Magklaras et al., investigates the fitness of the ordinary least squares approach for tuning the parameters of overlay models. They propose the application of ridge regression, a widely known machine learning approach. The derived method is applied to perturbed data from a 300 mm wafer fab and results in reduced residuals in comparison with the ordinary least squares algorithm.

Then, Arcos-Argudo et al. deal with a graph-theoretic problem. In particular, they investigate some properties of minimal strong digraphs with the goal of bounding the length of a longest cycle. They present several new results. Among others, they derive a bound for the coefficients of the characteristic polynomial of such digraphs and prove that the computation of a longest cycle is an NP-hard problem.

In contribution 10, the last accepted paper, Udvardy et al. investigate the enhancement of the Storage Location Assignment Problem by using evolutionary algorithms. In particular, they develop a Bacterial Memetic Algorithm and compare it with a traditional genetic algorithm. Although the new algorithm does not yield the expected results, one of the novelties of this paper is the specification of the concept of adaptive parameterization and rules.

It is my pleasure to thank all authors for submitting their recent works, all reviewers for their timely and insightful reports, and the staff of the Editorial Office for their support in preparing this Special Issue. I hope that the readers of this Special Issue will find stimulating ideas that initiate new research works in this interesting research field of great practical importance.

Conflicts of Interest: The author declares no conflicts of interest.

List of Contributions

1. Chen, M.; Zhou, Y.; Luo, Q. An Improved Arithmetic Optimization Algorithm for Numerical Optimization Problems. *Mathematics* **2022**, *10*, 2152.
2. Feng, A.; Chang, X.; Shang, Y.; Fan, J. Application of the ADMM Algorithm for a High-Dimensional Partially Linear Model. *Mathematics* **2022**, *10*, 4767.
3. Zhang, C.; Han, Y.; Wang, Y.; Li, J.; Gao, K. A Distributed Flow Shop Algorithm with Setup Times Using Multi-Factory Collaboration Iterated Greedy Algorithm. *Mathematics* **2023**, *11*, 581.
4. Lai, K.K.; Mishra, S.K.; Sharma, R.; Sharma, M.; Ram, B. A Modified q-BFGS Algorithm for Unconstrained Optimization. *Mathematics* **2023**, *11*, 1420.
5. Lemus-Romani, J.; Ossandon, D.; Sepulveda, R.; Carrasco-Astudillo, N.; Yepes, V; Garcia, J. Optimizing Retaining Walls through Reinforcement Learning Approaches and Metaheuristic Techniques. *Mathematics* **2022**, *11*, 2104.
6. Cobos, C.; Ordonez, C.; Torres-Jimenez, J.; Ordonez, H.; Mendoza, M.: Weight Vector Definition for MOEA/D-Based Algorithms Using Augmented Covering Arrays for Many-Objective Optimization. *Mathematics* **2024**, *12*, 1680.
7. Wang, S.; Wang, X.; Tian, Y.; Pang, L. A New Hybrid Descent Algoritm for Large-Scale Nonconvex Optimization and Application to Some Image Restoration Problems. *Mathematics* **2024**, *12*, 3088.
8. Magklaras, A.; Gogos, C.; Alefragis, P.; Birbas, A. Enhancing Parameters Tuning of Overlay Models with Ridge Regression: Addressing Multicollinearity in High-Dimensional Data. *Mathematics* **2024**, *12*, 3179.
9. Arcos-Argudo, M.; Lacalle, J.; Pozo-Coronado, L.M. Cyclic Structure, Vertex Degree and Number of Linear Vertices in Minimal Strong Digraphs. *Mathematics* **2024**, *12*, 3657.
10. Udvardy, K.; Görbe, P.; Bodis, T.; Botzheim, J. Conceptual Framework for Adaptive Bacterial Memetic Algorithm Parameterization in Storage Location Assignment Problem. *Mathematics* **2024**, *12*, 3688.

Disclaimer/Publisher's Note: The statements, opinions and data contained in all publications are solely those of the individual author(s) and contributor(s) and not of MDPI and/or the editor(s). MDPI and/or the editor(s) disclaim responsibility for any injury to people or property resulting from any ideas, methods, instructions or products referred to in the content.

Article

An Improved Arithmetic Optimization Algorithm for Numerical Optimization Problems

Mengnan Chen [1], Yongquan Zhou [1,2,*] and Qifang Luo [1,2]

[1] College of Artificial Intelligence, Guangxi University for Nationalities, Nanning 530006, China; 2020210812000995@stu.gxmzu.edu.cn (M.C.); 20060043@gxun.edu.cn (Q.L.)
[2] Guangxi Key Laboratories of Hybrid Computation and IC Design Analysis, Nanning 530006, China
* Correspondence: zhouyongquan@gxun.edu.cn; Tel.: +86-136-0788-2594

Abstract: The arithmetic optimization algorithm is a recently proposed metaheuristic algorithm. In this paper, an improved arithmetic optimization algorithm (IAOA) based on the population control strategy is introduced to solve numerical optimization problems. By classifying the population and adaptively controlling the number of individuals in the subpopulation, the information of each individual can be used effectively, which speeds up the algorithm to find the optimal value, avoids falling into local optimum, and improves the accuracy of the solution. The performance of the proposed IAOA algorithm is evaluated on six systems of nonlinear equations, ten integrations, and engineering problems. The results show that the proposed algorithm outperforms other algorithms in terms of convergence speed, convergence accuracy, stability, and robustness.

Keywords: arithmetic optimization algorithm; population control strategy; systems of nonlinear equations; numerical integrals; metaheuristic

MSC: 68T20

Citation: Chen, M.; Zhou, Y.; Luo, Q. An Improved Arithmetic Optimization Algorithm for Numerical Optimization Problems. *Mathematics* **2022**, *10*, 2152. https://doi.org/10.3390/math10122152

Academic Editor: Frank Werner

Received: 28 May 2022
Accepted: 17 June 2022
Published: 20 June 2022

Publisher's Note: MDPI stays neutral with regard to jurisdictional claims in published maps and institutional affiliations.

Copyright: © 2022 by the authors. Licensee MDPI, Basel, Switzerland. This article is an open access article distributed under the terms and conditions of the Creative Commons Attribution (CC BY) license (https://creativecommons.org/licenses/by/4.0/).

1. Introduction

In the practical application calculations of science and engineering, many mathematical problems will be involved, such as nonlinear equation systems (NESs), numerical integration, etc. There are tremendous methods for solving NESs, including traditional techniques and intelligent optimization algorithms. Traditional techniques to solve NESs use gradient information [1], such as Newton's method [2,3], quasi-Newton's method [4], steepest descent method, etc. Due to relying on the selection of initial points and being prone to falling into optimal local one, these methods cannot obtain high-quality solutions for some specific problems. The metaheuristic algorithms, however, have the characteristics of low requirements for the initial point, a wide range of solutions, high efficiency, and robustness. These break through the limitations of traditional methods in solving problems. In recent years, metaheuristic algorithms have made great contributions in solving NESs (Karr et al. [5]; Ouyang et al. [6]; Jaberipour et al. [7]; Pourjafari et al. [8]; Jia et al. [9]; Ren et al. [10]; Cai et al. [11]; Abdollahi et al. [12]; Hirsch et al. [13]; Sacco et al. [14]; Gong et al. [15]; Ariyaratne et al. [16]; Gong et al. [17]; Ibrahim et al. [18]; Liao et al. [19]; Ning et al. [20]; Rizk-Allah et al. [21]; Ji et al. [22]; Turgut et al. [23]).

Numerical integration is a very basic computational problem. It is well-known that, when calculating the definite integral, the integrand is required to be easily given and then solved by the Newton-Leibniz formula. However, this method has many limitations, because in many practical problems, the original function of the integrand cannot be expressed, or the calculation is too complicated, so the definite integral of the integrand is replaced by a suitable finite sum approximation. The traditional numerical integration methods include the trapezoidal method, rectangle method, Romberg method, Gauss method, Simpson's method, Newton's method, etc. The above methods all divide the integral interval into equal parts, and the calculation efficiency is not high. Therefore, it is of great significance to find a new technique with a fast convergence speed, high precision, and strong robustness for numerical integration. Zhou et al. [24], based on the evolutionary strategy method, worked to solve numerical integration. Wei et al. [25] researched the numerical integration method based on particle swarm optimization. Wei et al. [26], based on functional networks, worked to solve numerical integration. Deng et al. [27] solved the numerical integration problems based on the differential evolution algorithm. Xiao et al. [28] applied the improved bat algorithm in numerical integration. The quality of the solution obtained by the above techniques was higher than the traditional methods.

All along, engineering optimization problems have been a popular area of research. Metaheuristic algorithms have been widely applied to engineering optimization problems due to their great practical significance, such as applied to the automatic adjustment of controller coefficients (Szczepanski et al. [29]; Hu et al. [30]), applied to system identification (Szczepanski et al. [31]; Liu et al. [32]), applied to global path planning (Szczepanski et al. [33]; Brand et al. [34]), and applied to robotic arm scheduling (Szczepanski et al. [35]; Kolakowska et al. [36]).

The Arithmetic Optimization Algorithm (AOA) [37] is a novel metaheuristic algorithm proposed by Abualigah et al. in 2021. AOA is a mathematical model technique that simulates the behaviors of Arithmetic operators (i.e., Multiplication, Division, Subtraction, and Addition) and their influence on the best local solution. Some improvements and practical applications of the algorithm have been made by scholars. Premkumar et al. [38] proposed a multi-objective arithmetic optimization algorithm (MOAOA) for solving real-world multi-objective CEC-2021-constrained optimization problems. Bansal. et al. [39] used a binary arithmetic optimization algorithm for integrated features and feature selection. Agushaka et al. [40] introduced an advanced arithmetic optimization algorithm for solving mechanical engineering design problems. Abualigah et al. [41] presented a novel evolutionary arithmetic optimization algorithm for multilevel thresholding segmentation. Xu et al. [42] hybridized an extreme learning machine and a developed version of the arithmetic optimization algorithm for model identification of the proton exchange membrane fuel cells. Izci et al. [43] introduced an improved arithmetic optimization algorithm for the optimal design of controlled PID. Khatir et al. [44] proposed an improved artificial neural network using the arithmetic optimization algorithm for damage assessments.

The basic AOA still has some drawbacks. For instance, it is easy to fall into a local optimum due to the location update based on the optimal value, premature convergence, and low solution accuracy, which need to be solved. Furthermore, in order to seek a more efficient way to solve numerical problems, in this paper, an improved arithmetic optimization algorithm (IAOA) based on the population control strategy is proposed to solve numerical optimization problems. By classifying the population and adaptively controlling the number of individuals in the subpopulation, the information of each individual can be used effectively while increasing the population diversity. More individuals are needed in the early iterations to perform a large-scale search that avoids falling into the local optimum. The search around the optimal value later in the iterations by more individuals speeds up the algorithm to find the optimal value and improves the accuracy of the solution. The performance of the proposed IAOA algorithm is evaluated on six systems of nonlinear equations, ten integrations, and engineering problems. The results show that the proposed algorithm outperforms the other algorithms in terms of convergence speed, convergence accuracy, stability, and robustness.

The main structure of this paper is as follows. Section 2 reviews the relevant knowledge for the nonlinear equation systems, integration, and basic arithmetic optimization algorithm (AOA). Section 3 introduces the proposed IAOA in detail. Section 4 presents experimental results, comparisons, and analyses. Section 5 concludes the work and proposes future research directions.

2. Preliminaries

2.1. Nonlinear Equation Systems

Generally, a nonlinear equation system can be formulated as follows.

$$NES = \begin{cases} f_1(x_1, x_2, \ldots, x_D) = 0 \\ \vdots \\ f_i(x_1, x_2, \ldots, x_D) = 0 \\ \vdots \\ f_n(x_1, x_2, \ldots, x_D) = 0 \end{cases} \quad (1)$$

where x is a D-dimensional decision variable, and n is the number of equations. Some equations are linear; the others are nonlinear. If x^* satisfies $f_i(x^*) = 0$, then x^* is a root of the system of equations.

Before using the optimization algorithm to solve the NES, first is to convert it into a single-objective optimization problem [17] as follows.

$$\min f(x) = \sum_{i=1}^{n} f_i^2(x), x = (x_1, x_2, \ldots, x_i, \ldots, x_D) \quad (2)$$

Finding the minimum of an optimization problem is equivalent to finding the root of the NES.

2.2. Numerical Integration

Definite integrals are very basic mathematical calculation problems as follows.

$$\int_a^b f(x)dx \quad (3)$$

where $f(x)$ represents the integrand function, and a and b represent the upper and lower bounds, respectively.

Usually, firstly, we find the original function $F(x)$ of the integrand when finding a definite integral and then use the Newton-Leibniz formula as follows:

$$\int_a^b f(x)dx = F(b) - F(a), (F'(x) = f(x)) \quad (4)$$

However, in many cases, it is difficult to obtain the original function $F(x)$, so the Newton-Leibniz formula will not be able to be used.

In addition, the rest of the numerical quadrature methods are based on the quadrature formula of equidistant node division and summation or stipulate that the equidistant nodes remain unchanged during the whole process of calculating, as shown in Figure 1a. There need more nodes to obtain a high accuracy. However, the best segmentation is not the predetermined equidistant points, as shown in Figure 1b. Randomly generated subintervals has unequal intervals according to the concave and convex changes of the function curve, so the obtained value has a higher accuracy than the traditional methods. Based on this idea, there is another integral method based on non-equidistant point division [24]. First, generate some points randomly on the integral interval, and then, the algorithm is used to optimize these split points. Finally, a higher accuracy value will be obtained. This not only calculates the definite integral of the function in the usual sense but also calculates the integral of the singular function and the integral of the oscillatory function for this method [27]. The flow of the numerical integration algorithm based on unequal point segmentation is as follows [24].

(1) Randomly initialize the population in the search space S.

(2) Arrange each individual in the integral interval in ascending order. The integral interval has $n(n = D + 2)$ nodes and $n - 1$ segments. Calculate the distance h_i between two adjacent nodes and the function $f(x_k)$ value of each node, then calculate the function value corresponding to the $D + 2$ nodes and the function value of the middle node of each subsection. Find the minimum value w_j and the maximum value W_j ($j = 1, 2, \ldots, D + 1$) among the function values of the left endpoint, middle node, and right endpoint of each subsection.

(3) Calculate fitness value. $F(i) \frac{1}{2} \sum_{j=1}^{D+1} h_j \left| W_j - w_j \right|$.

(4) Update individuals through an optimization algorithm.

(5) Repeat step 4 until reaching the stop condition.

(6) Get the accuracy and integral values.

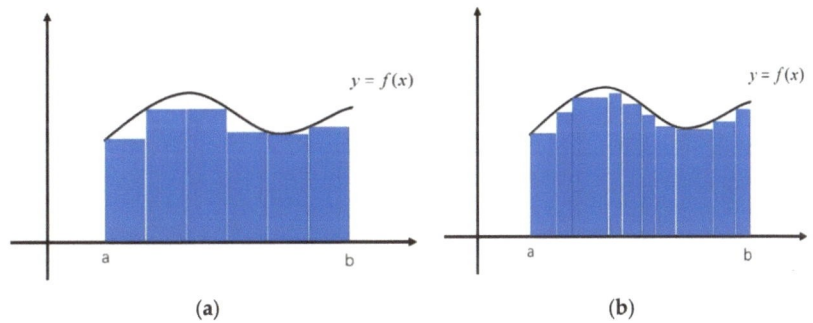

(a) (b)

Figure 1. Two methods of segmentation when solving numerical integrals: (**a**) equidistant division and (**b**) equidistant division.

The numerical integration method based on Hermite interpolation only needs to provide the value of the integral node functions and has high precision. However, this method is based on equidistant segmentation. In this paper, the adaptability of unequal-spaced partitioning and the numerical integration method based on Hermite interpolation are combined to solve the numerical integration problem, and the formula is as follows:

$$\int_a^b f(x)dx = \sum_{k=1}^{n} \frac{h_i}{2}[f(x_k) + f(x_{k+1})] - \frac{\sum_{i=1}^{n-1} \frac{25}{144} h_i [f(a) + f(b)]}{n-1} +$$
$$\frac{\sum_{i=1}^{n-1} \frac{h_i}{3}[f(a+h_i)+f(b-h_i)]}{n-1} - \frac{\sum_{i=1}^{n-1} \frac{h_i}{4}[f(a+2h_i)+f(b-2h_i)]}{n-1} + \quad (5)$$
$$\frac{\sum_{i=1}^{n-1} \frac{h_i}{9}[f(a+3h_i)+f(b-3h_i)]}{n-1} - \frac{\sum_{i=1}^{n-1} \frac{h_i}{48}[f(a+4h_i)+f(b-4h_i)]}{n-1}$$

where n is the number of random split points, h_i is the distance between two adjacent points, and $f(x)$ is the integrand function. The advantage of this method is that it does not need to calculate the derivative value and only needs to provide the node function value. Before using the optimization algorithm to solve the integration, the first step is to convert it into a single-objective optimization problem as follows:

$$\min F(x) = \left| \int_a^b f(x)dx - E \right| \quad (6)$$

where $\int_a^b f(x)dx$ is obtained by Equation (5), and E means the exact value.

Combine the optimization algorithm with Equation (5), and the whole solution process is as follows.

(1) Randomly initialize the population in the search space S.

(2) Arrange each individual in the integral interval in ascending order. The integral interval has n ($n = D + 2$) nodes and $n - 1$ segments. Calculate the distance h_i between two adjacent nodes and the function $f(x_k)$ value of each node and then bring them into Equation (5).
(3) Calculate the fitness value by Equation (6).
(4) Update individuals through an optimization algorithm.
(5) Repeat step 4 until reaching the stop condition.
(6) Get the accuracy and integral values.

2.3. The Arithmetic Optimization Algorithm (AOA)

The AOA algorithm is a population-based metaheuristic algorithm to solve optimization problems by utilizing mathematical operators (Multiplication ("×"), Division ("÷"), Subtraction ("−"), and Addition ("+")). The specific description is as follows.

2.3.1. Initialization Phase

Generate a candidate solution matrix randomly.

$$X = \begin{pmatrix} x_{1,1} & \cdots & \cdots & x_{1,j} & x_{1,n-1} & x_{1,n} \\ x_{2,1} & \cdots & \cdots & x_{2,j} & x_{2,n-1} & x_{2,n} \\ \cdots & \cdots & \cdots & \cdots & \cdots & \cdots \\ \vdots & \vdots & \vdots & \vdots & \vdots & \vdots \\ x_{N-1,1} & \cdots & \cdots & x_{N-1,j} & x_{N-1,n-1} & x_{N-1,n} \\ x_{N,1} & \cdots & \cdots & x_{N,j} & x_{N,n-1} & x_{N,n} \end{pmatrix} \quad (7)$$

After the initialization step, calculate the Math Optimizer Accelerated (MOA) function and use it to choose between exploration and exploitation. The function is as follows:

$$MOA(t) = Min + t \times \left(\frac{Max - Min}{T} \right) \quad (8)$$

where $Max = 0.9$ denotes the maximum and $Min = 0.2$ denotes the minimum of the function value, $MOA(t)$ represents the function value of the current iteration, and T and t represent the maximum number of iterations and current iteration, respectively.

2.3.2. Exploration Phase

During the exploration phase, the operators (Multiplication ("×") and Division ("÷")) are used to explore the space randomly when the $MOA > 0.5$. The mathematical model is as follows:

$$x_{i,j}(t+1) = \begin{cases} best(x_j) \div (MOP + \varepsilon) \times ((UB_j - LB_j) \times \mu + LB_j), & r_2 < 0.5 \\ best(x_j) \times MOP \times ((UB_j - LB_j) \times \mu + LB_j), & otherwise \end{cases} \quad (9)$$

where r_2 is a random number, $x_{i,j}(t+1)$ represents the jth position of ith solution in the $(t+1)$th iteration, $best(x_j)$ denotes the jth position in the global optimal solution, ε is a small integer number that avoids the case where the denominator is zero in division, UB_j and LB_j represents the upper and lower bounds of each dimension, respectively, and μ is equal to 0.5. The Math Optimizer probability (MOP) is as follows:

$$MOP(t) = 1 - \frac{t^{\frac{1}{\alpha}}}{T^{\frac{1}{\alpha}}} \quad (10)$$

where $MOP(t)$ represents the function value for the current iteration, and α is a sensitive parameter and equal to 5.

2.3.3. Exploitation Phase

During the exploration phase, the operators (Subtraction ("−") and Addition ("+")) are used to execute the exploitation. When $MOA < 0.5$, the mathematical model as follows:

$$x_{i,j}(t+1) = \begin{cases} best(x_j) - MOP \times ((UB_j - LB_j) \times \mu + LB_j), r_3 < 0.5 \\ best(x_j) + MOP \times ((UB_j - LB_j) \times \mu + LB_j), otherwise \end{cases} \quad (11)$$

where r_3 is a random number. The pseudo-code of the AOA is as follows (Algorithm 1) [37].

Algorithm 1 AOA
---
1. Set up the initial parameters α, μ.
2. Initialize the population randomly.
3. for t = 1: T
4.   Calculate the fitness function and select the best solution.
5.   Update the MOA (using Equation (8)) and MOP (using Equation (10)).
6.   for i = 1: N
7.   for j = 1: Dim
8.   Generate the random values between [0, 1] (r_1, r_2, r_3)
9.   if $r_1 > MOA$
10.   if $r_2 > 0.5$
11.   Update the position of the individual by Equation (9).
12.   else
13.   Update the position of the individual by Equation (9).
14.   end
15.   else
16.   if $r_3 > 0.5$
17.   Update the position of the individual by Equation (11).
18.   else
19.   Update the position of the individual by Equation (11).
20.   end
21.   end
22.   end
23. end
24. $t = t + 1$
25. end
26. Return the best solution (x).

---

3. Our Proposed IAOA

3.1. Motivation for Improving the AOA

In AOA, the population is updated based on the optimal global solution. Once it falls into the optimal local one, the entire population will stagnate. There is premature coverage, in some cases [33]. In addition, this algorithm does not fully utilize the information of the individuals in the population. Therefore, to make full use of the information of the individuals and address the weakness of AOA, the improved arithmetic optimization algorithm (IAOA) is proposed in this paper.

3.2. Population Control Mechanism

In the basic arithmetic optimization algorithm (AOA), the operators (Multiplication ("×"), Division ("÷"), Subtraction ("−"), and Addition ("+")) are used to wrap around an optimal solution to search randomly in space, and it will lead to a loss of population diversity. Therefore, it is necessary to classify for the population.

3.2.1. The First Subpopulation

Sort the population according to the fitness value and select the first *num_best* individuals as the first subpopulation:

$$num\_best = round(0.1N + 0.5N(1 - t/T)) \qquad (12)$$

where N is the number of individuals, and t and T represent the current iteration and maximum iterations, respectively. Then, these individuals update their position by getting information about each other. The mathematical model is as follows:

$$x_{best\_i}(t+1) = x_{best\_i}(t) + rand \times \left(best(x) - \frac{x_{best\_i}(t) + x_{best\_j}(t)}{2} \times \omega \right) \qquad (13)$$

$$x_{best\_j}(t+1) = x_{best\_j}(t) + rand \times \left(best(x) - \frac{x_{best\_i}(t) + x_{best\_j}(t)}{2} \times \omega \right) \qquad (14)$$

where $x_{best\_i}(t+1)$ denotes the position of *i*th individual in the next iteration, the same as $x_{best\_j}(t+1)$, $best(x)$ represents the global optimum that has been found through individuals after t iterations, x_{best_j} is selected from the first class randomly, and ω means the information acquisition rate and takes the value 1 or 2.

3.2.2. The Second Subpopulation

Select *num_middle* individuals from the population as the second subpopulation.

$$num\_middle = round(0.3 \times N) \qquad (15)$$

These individuals fall between *num_best* and *num_worst* in the population. Then, these individuals update their position, and the updated model is as follows:

$$x_{mid\_i}(t+1) = x_{mid\_i}(t) + Levy \times (best(x) - x_{mid\_j}) \qquad (16)$$

where $x_{mid\_i}(t+1)$ denotes the position of *i*th individual in the next iteration, *Levy* is the Levy distribution function [45,46], and x_{mid_j} is selected from the second class randomly.

3.2.3. The Third Subpopulation

Select *num_worst* individuals from the population as the final subpopulation.

$$num\_worst = N - (num\_best + num\_middle) \qquad (17)$$

In the final class, the individuals update their position by the following equation:

$$x_{worst\_i}(t+1) = x_{worst\_i} + \left(\frac{t}{T} \times best(x) - x_{worst\_j} \right) \qquad (18)$$

where $x_{worst\_i}(t+1)$ denotes the position of *i*th individual in the next iteration, and $best(x)$ represents the global optimum that has been found through individuals after t iterations.

At the early iteration of IAOA, there are more individuals in the first subpopulation for speeding up the update of the global optimum. At the later iterations of the algorithm, the number of individuals in the first subpopulation decreases, which solves the operator crowding problem near the optimum. In addition, the number of individuals in the third subpopulation increases, which effectively prevents the population from falling into the local optimum. The second subpopulation utilizes the Levy flight for small-step updates to find more promising areas. The above strategy can effectively overcome the weaknesses of traditional AOA and improve its performance. The pseudo-code of the IAOA in Algorithm 2 is as follows (Algorithm 2). Figure 2 is the flowchart of the IAOA.

Algorithm 2 IAOA

1. Set up the initial parameters α, μ.
2. Initialize the population randomly.
3. for $t = 1: T$
4.   Calculate the fitness function and select the best solution.
5.   Calculate the number of the first subpopulation by Equation (12).
6.   Update the first subpopulation by Equations (13) and (14).
7.   Calculate the number of the second subpopulation by Equation (15).
8.   Update the second subpopulation by Equation (16).
9.   Calculate the number of the third subpopulation by Equation (17).
10.   Update the third subpopulation by Equation (18).
11.   Update the *MOA* (using Equation (8)) and *MOP* (using Equation (10)).
12.   for $i = 1: N$
13.   for $j = 1:$ Dim
14.   Generate the random values between [0, 1] (r_1, r_2, r_3)
15.   if $r_1 >$ MOA
16.   if $r_2 > 0.5$
17.   Update the position of the individual by Equation (9).
18.   else
19.   Update the position of the individual by Equation (9).
20.   end
21.   else
22.   if $r_3 > 0.5$
23.   Update the position of the individual by Equation (11).
24.   else
25.   Update the position of the individual by Equation (11).
26.   end
27.   end
28.   end
29.   end
30. $t = t + 1$
31. end
32. Return the best solution (x).

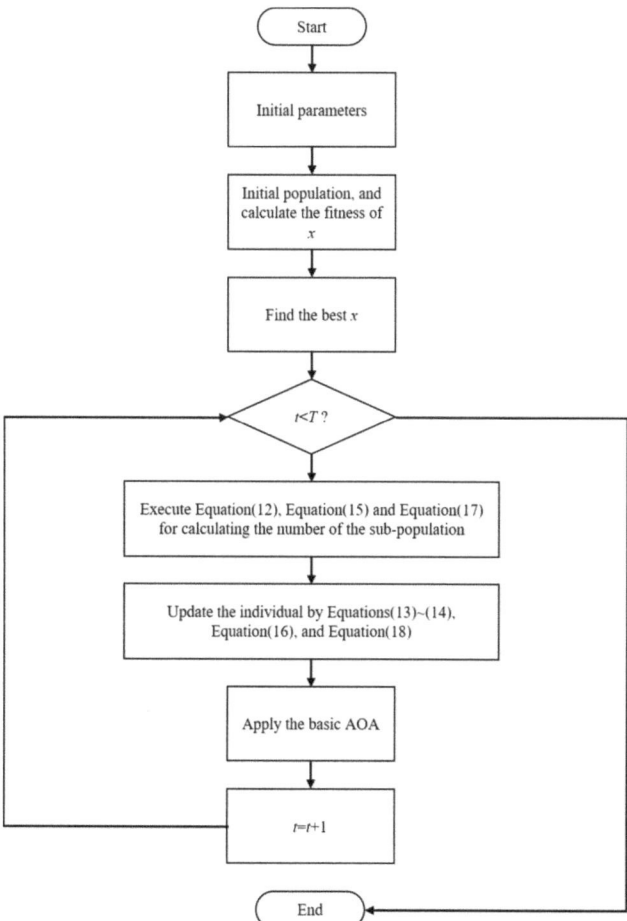

Figure 2. Flowchart of the IAOA.

4. Numerical Experiments and Analysis

4.1. Parameter Settings

Here, six groups of NESs and ten groups of integration have been used to demonstrate the efficiency of the IAOA. The IAOA compares several popular algorithms and two improved arithmetic optimization algorithms (The Arithmetic Optimization Algorithm (AOA) [37], Sine Cosine Algorithm (SCA) [47], Whale Optimization Algorithm (WOA) [48], Grey Wolf Optimizer (GWO) [49], Harris hawks optimization (HHO) [50], Slime mould algorithm (SMA) [51], Differential evolution(DE) [52], Cuckoo search algorithm (CSA) [53], Advanced arithmetic optimization algorithm (nAOA) [40], and a developed version of Arithmetic Optimization Algorithm (dAOA) [42]) for tackling NES. Among them, the parameters of these algorithms are all from the original version. These algorithms are evaluated from four aspects: the average value, the optimal value, the worst value, and the standard deviation. All algorithms are executed on MATLAB 2021a, running on a computer with a Windows 10 operating system, Intel(R) Core (TM) i7-9700 CPU @ 3.00 GHz, 16 GB of Random Access Memory (RAM), and run 30 times independently for all test problems. The flowchart for handling issues by the IAOA is shown in Figure 3.

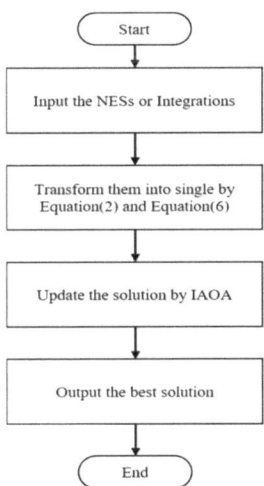

Figure 3. Flowchart for handling issues.

4.2. Application in Solving NESs

Solving nonlinear problems often requires higher-precision solutions in many practical applications. In this section, six nonlinear systems of equations are chosen to evaluate the performance of the IAOA. The characteristics of these equations are different from each other, where problem01 [54] describes the interval arithmetic problem, problem02 [55] describes the multiple steady-states problem, and problem06 [56] describes the molecular conformation. These problems come from real-world applications. For fairness, set the population to 50 and the maximum number of iterations to 200. Tables 1–6 show all the test results of the NES. Best represents the best value, Worst represents the worst value, Mean represents the mean value, Std represents the standard deviation, and p-value stands for the Wilcoxon rank–sum test in Table 7. The Wilcoxon p-value test is used to verify whether there is an obvious difference between the two sets of data.

Table 1. Comparison of the experimental results for problem01.

Variable	Algorithms			
	AOA	IAOA	SCA	WOA
x_1	0.006361583402960	0.257838650825518	0.186732591196869	0.260832096649832
x_2	0.005731653837062	0.381098185347242	0.399818814038728	0.381680691118263
x_3	0.010586282003880	0.278742562628776	0.008959145137085	0.258353295805450
x_4	0.002593989505334	0.200665586275865	0.227237103605413	0.215307146397956
x_5	0.033520558095432	0.445255928027431	0.003829239926320	0.448799960971748
x_6	0.076424218265631	0.149188813621332	0.185905381801968	0.147397359179682
x_7	0.038862694473151	0.432010769672038	0.368813050526818	0.442390776062597
x_8	−0.000004007877210	0.073406152818720	0.037739989370997	0.137586270569043
x_9	0.029054432130685	0.345966262513093	0.206476235144125	0.342058064566263
x_{10}	0.013690425703394	0.427324518269459	0.363350844915327	0.401475021739693
f	$8.45665838921712 \times 10^{-1}$	$4.73405913551646 \times 10^{-10}$	$1.22078391539763 \times 10^{-1}$	$9.59544885085295 \times 10^{-4}$

Table 1. Cont.

Variable	Algorithms			
	GWO	HHO	DE	CSO
x_1	0.256851024248810	0.324317023967532	2.000000000000000	0.089951372914250
x_2	0.383565743620699	0.303967192642514	1.948157453190990	0.309487131659014
x_3	0.278312335483674	0.216191961411362	2.000000000000000	0.456410156556233
x_4	0.198737300040942	0.305260974230829	1.815308511546580	0.356392775439902
x_5	0.446311619177502	0.325255783591842	2.000000000000000	0.476086684751138
x_6	0.145894138632280	0.223020351676054	2.000000000000000	0.078921332097133
x_7	0.145894138632280	0.323185143014029	2.000000000000000	0.499580490394335
x_8	−0.007832029555062	0.327973609353822	1.915762141824520	0.197756675883883
x_9	0.343654620394334	0.333430854648433	2.000000000000000	0.228228833675487
x_{10}	0.425902664080806	0.324142888370713	2.000000000000000	0.470195948900759
f	$1.25544451911646 \times 10^{-3}$	$7.79220329211044 \times 10^{-2}$	$7.96261500819178 \times 10^{-2}$	$6.61705221934444 \times 10^{-2}$

Variable	Algorithms		
	SMA	nAOA	dAOA
x_1	0.249900132290417	0.035430633051580	1.840704485033870
x_2	0.375428314977531	0.053983062784772	1.213421005935260
x_3	0.272448580296318	0.072273530516602	1.203555993641700
x_4	0.199698265955405	0.021399042985613	−0.393935624266822
x_5	0.425934189445810	0.064655913970964	−0.249476549706985
x_6	0.057699959645613	0.012570281350831	0.459915310960444
x_7	0.431865275874618	0.057639809639213	−0.675754718182326
x_8	0.015005640000641	0.005520004765830	−0.895856414267328
x_9	0.347986992756388	0.041229484511092	0.359139808282465
x_{10}	0.415304164782275	0.079595719921909	1.529188120361250
f	$4.47411205566240 \times 10^{-3}$	$6.74563715208325 \times 10^{-1}$	1.91503507134915

Table 2. Comparison of the experimental results for problem02.

Variable	Algorithms			
	AOA	IAOA	SCA	WOA
x_1	0.040781958181860	0.042124781715274	0.000000000000000	0.041561373108785
x_2	0.268625655728691	0.061754610138946	0.266593748985495	0.268697327813652
f	$2.01752031872803 \times 10^{-7}$	$9.24446373305873 \times 10^{-34}$	$8.82826387279195 \times 10^{-5}$	$6.92247231102962 \times 10^{-9}$

Variable	Algorithms			
	GWO	HHO	DE	CSO
x_1	0.265622854930434	0.267855297066815	0.266589101862370	0.266620164671422
x_2	0.178718146817611	0.458749279058429	0.327275026016101	0.178514261126008
f	$1.13985864694418 \times 10^{-7}$	$6.55986405733090 \times 10^{-8}$	$1.31654979128584 \times 10^{-18}$	$1.49504500886345 \times 10^{-9}$

Variable	Algorithms		
	SMA	nAOA	dAOA
x_1	0.021419624272050	0.000000000000000	0.236558250181286
x_2	0.048075232460874	0.719124811309122	0.508933311549167
f	$2.89316821274146 \times 10^{-5}$	$3.07109081317222 \times 10^{-5}$	$3.22387407689191 \times 10^{-4}$

Table 3. Comparison of the experimental results for problem03.

Variable	Algorithms			
	AOA	IAOA	SCA	WOA
x_1	1.990744078311880	−0.947268146986263	−0.225974226141413	−1.424482905343090
x_2	0.220001522814532	−0.785020015568289	1.245763361231140	−0.543544840817441
f	$5.61739095968327 \times 10^{-3}$	$4.02151576372412 \times 10^{-32}$	$7.95691890654021 \times 10^{-4}$	$1.06331568826728 \times 10^{-3}$
Variable	Algorithms			
	GWO	HHO	DE	CSO
x_1	−1.794053112053940	−1.495480498807310	−1.791308474954350	−0.212779003619775
x_2	−0.303905803005920	−0.420394691864127	0.301889327351144	−1.257141525856050
f	$2.77808608355359 \times 10^{-5}$	$6.12298193031725 \times 10^{-5}$	$1.84881969881973 \times 10^{-9}$	$6.26348225916795 \times 10^{-7}$
Variable	Algorithms			
	SMA	nAOA		dAOA
x_1	−1.791387180972800	−1.475077261850100		−1.580085715978880
x_2	−0.302157020359872	−0.454673564762598		0.4651484d76848022
f	$5.47910691165820 \times 10^{-8}$	$2.17709293383390 \times 10^{-4}$		$5.12705019470938 \times 10^{-2}$

Table 4. Comparison of the experimental results for problem04.

Variable	Algorithms			
	AOA	IAOA	SCA	WOA
x_1	−0.000266868453558	−0.000000091835793	−0.120898772911816	−0.310246574315981
x_2	−0.000267036157051	0.000013971597535	0.491167568359585	0.467564824328878
x_3	−0.000267036274281	0.000030454051416	10.000000000000000	1.071469773086650
x_4	0.000000025430197	0.000010000404353	−0.178108600809833	−0.404219784214681
x_5	−0.000267039311495	0.000011275918099	5.423242568753400	3.552125620609660
x_6	−0.000267036127224	0.000000019800029	−0.049710980654501	−1.834136698070800
x_7	0.000000000091855	−0.000000000138437	0.445662462511328	0.286050311387620
x_8	0.000267036101457	−0.000000454282127	−10.000000000000000	−2.931846497771810
x_9	0.000267033832224	0.000000000736505	−0.144419405019169	−4.812450845354100
x_{10}	0.000267043884482	−0.000000002006069864	−0.518105971932846	3.756426716000660
f	$1.08498006397337 \times 10^{-9}$	$7.03339003909689 \times 10^{-16}$	$4.13237426374674 \times 10^{-1}$	$6.47066501369328 \times 10^{-1}$
Variable	Algorithms			
	GWO	HHO	DE	CSO
x_1	0.044653752694561	−0.000047703379713	0.160723693838569	−0.009650846541198
x_2	−0.259567674882923	0.000075691075249	0.431923139718368	0.147278561202585
x_3	−1.777013199398760	−0.000029713372367	0.072922517980119	−3.148557575646470
x_4	0.042606334458592	−0.000050184914825	0.447403957744849	−0.512428980703464
x_5	−4.935286036663600	0.000033675529531	−0.197972459731190	−4.175819684412100
x_6	−8.146156623785810	0.000067989452634	1.490110445009050	−7.123183974281880
x_7	−0.108125274969201	0.000031288762826	0.472265426079125	1.268663892956760
x_8	1.747052457418910	0.000048491290536	0.509493705510866	3.198230908839320
x_9	−0.311997778279745	0.000063892452193	1.142101578993260	−4.763105818868310
x_{10}	8.430357427064680	−0.000123055431652	−2.110335475212350	9.463108408596410
f	$7.56734706927375 \times 10^{-3}$	$6.11971561041781 \times 10^{-10}$	$9.87501536049260 \times 10^{-1}$	2.18295386757873

Table 4. Cont.

Variable	Algorithms		
	SMA	nAOA	dAOA
x_1	-0.000000000028677	0.000020144848903	-0.934997016811202
x_2	0.000014644312649	-0.000060200695401	-1.295640443505010
x_3	0.000038790339140	-0.000020118018817	-5.634966911723890
x_4	-0.000000000221797	-0.000060200956330	-4.825343892476190
x_5	0.000000055701981	-0.000020122803817	0.269511140973028
x_6	-0.000000030051237	-0.000020134693956	-7.253398121182340
x_7	0.000000595936232	0.000020123341500	7.557747336452660
x_8	-0.000000000025333	0.000020925519435	-5.520361069927860
x_9	0.000000799504725	0.000043615727680	-4.709534880735350
x_{10}	0.000000000012983	0.000020120622373	8.954470788407880
f	$1.30095438660555 \times 10^{-10}$	$1.50696700666871 \times 10^{-9}$	$2.07190542503982 \times 10^2$

Table 5. Comparison of the experimental results for problem05.

Variable	Algorithms			
	AOA	IAOA	SCA	WOA
x_1	0.371964486871792	0.500000000000000	0.471178994397267	0.503978268408352
x_2	2.990337880814430	3.141592653589790	3.118271172186020	3.142976305563530
f	$1.89048835343036 \times 10^{-4}$	$1.85873810048745 \times 10^{-28}$	$3.41504906318340 \times 10^{-5}$	$2.00099014478417 \times 10^{-7}$

Variable	Algorithms			
	GWO	HHO	DE	CSO
x_1	0.495722089382004	0.503332577729795	0.299448692445072	0.500482294032500
x_2	3.143566564341090	3.142733305279310	2.836927770362990	3.142098043614560
f	$1.12835512797232 \times 10^{-6}$	$1.16071617155615 \times 10^{-7}$	$6.25300383824133 \times 10^{-23}$	$2.13609775136897 \times 10^{-8}$

Variable	Algorithms		
	SMA	nAOA	dAOA
x_1	0.298949061647857	0.354640044143990	2.956994389007600
x_2	2.835691250750600	2.956994389007600	1.890717921128260
f	$1.05189651760469 \times 10^{-8}$	$1.59376404093113 \times 10^{-4}$	$3.65946616757579 \times 10^{-3}$

Table 6. Comparison of the experimental results for problem06.

Variable	Algorithms			
	AOA	IAOA	SCA	WOA
x_1	0.953663829653960	-0.779548045079158	11.147659127176500	1.516510183032980
x_2	0.663112382731748	-0.779548045079158	0.900762400732728	0.694394649388567
x_3	0.729782844271910	-0.779548045079158	0.919816117314499	10.556407054559600
f	$3.35330112498813 \times 10^{-1}$	$1.00553388370096 \times 10^{-20}$	2.75666643131973	8.65817745834561

Variable	Algorithms			
	GWO	HHO	DE	CSO
x_1	0.781303537791760	-0.782460718139219	-0.779277448448367	-0.765447632695953
x_2	0.777872878718449	-0.789339702437282	-0.779700789186745	-0.784775197498564
x_3	0.779780469890485	-0.766810453292313	-0.780020611467694	-0.735052686517780
f	$5.49159538279891 \times 10^{-4}$	$1.00882211687459 \times 10^{-2}$	$6.71295836563811 \times 10^{-6}$	$2.92512803990831 \times 10^{-1}$

Variable	Algorithms		
	SMA	nAOA	dAOA
x_1	-0.779731780102931	-0.437772635064718	-1.056395480177350
x_2	-0.779371556451744	-7.659741643877890	6.893981344148980
x_3	-0.779303513685515	-2.620897335617900	-1.876924860155790
f	$1.03517116885362 \times 10^{-5}$	1.49720612584788	$2.61017698945353 \times 10^4$

Table 7. Statistical results for the NES.

Algorithms		Systems of Nonlinear Equations					
		problem01	problem02	problem03	problem04	problem05	problem06
AOA	best	7.02711×10^{-1}	1.20198×10^{-8}	8.30574×10^{-12}	2.99534×10^{-10}	5.32587×10^{-6}	1.60969×10^{-8}
	worst	9.05980×10^{-1}	7.47231×10^{-7}	9.55457×10^{-3}	3.58264×10^{-9}	5.96026×10^{-4}	1.00599×10
	mean	8.45666×10^{-1}	2.01752×10^{-7}	3.18486×10^{-4}	1.08498×10^{-9}	1.89049×10^{-4}	3.35330×10^{-1}
	std	4.40686×10^{-2}	1.78065×10^{-7}	1.74442×10^{-3}	8.49280×10^{-10}	1.40374×10^{-4}	1.83668
	p-value	3.01986×10^{-11}	1.01490×10^{-11}	1.07516×10^{-11}	3.01986×10^{-11}	1.49399×10^{-11}	3.01230×10^{-11}
IAOA	best	1.05462×10^{-10}	0.00000	4.93038×10^{-32}	2.97972×10^{-19}	0.00000	1.81191×10^{-30}
	worst	1.25230×10^{-9}	3.08149×10^{-33}	2.09541×10^{-31}	5.52546×10^{-15}	5.57614×10^{-27}	2.98754×10^{-19}
	mean	4.73406×10^{-10}	9.24446×10^{-34}	7.27231×10^{-32}	7.03339×10^{-16}	1.85874×10^{-28}	1.00553×10^{-20}
	std	2.84371×10^{-10}	1.43626×10^{-33}	4.02152×10^{-32}	1.22291×10^{-15}	1.01806×10^{-27}	5.45273×10^{-20}
SCA	best	4.64629×10^{-2}	1.20156×10^{-8}	8.29788×10^{-6}	7.08592×10^{-4}	7.53679×10^{-9}	1.19890×10^{-1}
	worst	2.98744×10^{-1}	8.60445×10^{-4}	3.13588×10^{-3}	2.83503	2.00649×10^{-1}	3.29896×10
	mean	1.22078×10^{-1}	8.82826×10^{-5}	5.47683×10^{-4}	4.13237×10^{-1}	3.41505×10^{-5}	2.75667
	std	5.72692×10^{-2}	2.61875×10^{-4}	7.59630×10^{-4}	6.58494×10^{-1}	4.69615×10^{-5}	6.25475
	p-value	3.01986×10^{-11}	1.01490×10^{-11}	1.07516×10^{-11}	3.01986×10^{-11}	1.49399×10^{-11}	3.01230×10^{-11}
WOA	best	1.87873×10^{-4}	6.72146×10^{-14}	6.18945×10^{-13}	4.04945×10^{-6}	2.16928×10^{-11}	1.76476×10^{-5}
	worst	5.56233×10^{-3}	1.30541×10^{-7}	4.48907×10^{-2}	4.99725	4.78904×10^{-6}	7.91148×10
	mean	9.59545×10^{-4}	6.92247×10^{-9}	4.26773×10^{-3}	6.47067×10^{-1}	2.00099×10^{-7}	8.65818
	std	1.06419×10^{-3}	2.49080×10^{-8}	1.24385×10^{-2}	1.07197	8.71177×10^{-7}	2.24136×10
	p-value	3.01986×10^{-11}	1.01490×10^{-11}	1.07516×10^{-11}	3.01986×10^{-11}	1.49399×10^{-11}	3.01230×10^{-11}
GWO	best	2.65480×10^{-6}	2.31886×10^{-12}	1.77817×10^{-8}	1.01688×10^{-6}	2.21126×10^{-9}	9.05730×10^{-5}
	worst	6.59898×10^{-3}	1.73256×10^{-6}	9.94266×10^{-2}	5.57604×10^{-2}	1.70979×10^{-5}	1.58625×10^{-3}
	mean	1.25544×10^{-3}	1.13986×10^{-7}	3.33932×10^{-3}	7.56735×10^{-3}	1.12836×10^{-6}	5.49160×10^{-4}
	std	2.25868×10^{-3}	4.16137×10^{-7}	1.81481×10^{-2}	1.36923×10^{-2}	3.33417×10^{-6}	3.69947×10^{-4}
	p-value	3.01986×10^{-11}	1.01490×10^{-11}	1.07516×10^{-11}	3.01986×10^{-11}	1.49399×10^{-11}	3.01230×10^{-11}
HHO	best	2.03768×10^{-6}	8.99794×10^{-31}	4.93038×10^{-32}	1.21192×10^{-11}	7.70372×10^{-34}	3.83242×10^{-5}
	worst	1.33302×10^{-1}	1.91904×10^{-6}	5.78702×10^{-4}	1.00491×10^{-9}	3.34700×10^{-6}	7.08247×10^{-2}
	mean	7.79220×10^{-2}	6.55986×10^{-8}	4.12782×10^{-5}	6.11972×10^{-10}	1.16072×10^{-7}	1.00882×10^{-2}
	std	2.90524×10^{-2}	3.50117×10^{-7}	1.19896×10^{-4}	2.78236×10^{-10}	6.10656×10^{-7}	1.45023×10^{-2}
	p-value	3.01986×10^{-11}	1.01490×10^{-11}	5.56066×10^{-8}	3.01986×10^{-11}	1.30542×10^{-10}	3.01230×10^{-11}
DE	best	6.05782×10^{-3}	8.15969×10^{-28}	2.49399×10^{-20}	2.59514×10^{-1}	2.59615×10^{-31}	4.23182×10^{-11}
	worst	9.69921×10^{-1}	1.19322×10^{-17}	5.91181×10^{-7}	2.58615	6.37964×10^{-22}	1.17012×10^{-4}
	mean	7.96262×10^{-2}	1.31655×10^{-18}	3.33313×10^{-8}	9.87502×10^{-1}	6.25300×10^{-23}	6.71296×10^{-6}
	std	2.40157×10^{-1}	2.91169×10^{-18}	1.26981×10^{-7}	6.21653×10^{-1}	1.66035×10^{-22}	2.15862×10^{-5}
	p-value	3.01986×10^{-11}	1.01490×10^{-11}	1.07516×10^{-11}	3.01986×10^{-11}	6.22236×10^{-11}	3.01230×10^{-11}
CSO	best	2.82411×10^{-2}	7.30711×10^{-11}	2.92752×10^{-9}	6.03864×10^{-1}	2.67109×10^{-10}	2.27267×10^{-2}
	worst	1.34962×10^{-1}	7.15408×10^{-7}	2.57784×10^{-6}	4.34942	1.32416×10^{-7}	1.31894
	mean	6.61705×10^{-2}	1.49505×10^{-9}	6.53698×10^{-7}	2.18295	2.13610×10^{-8}	2.92513×10^{-1}
	std	2.71383×10^{-2}	1.66707×10^{-9}	5.69101×10^{-7}	1.05318	3.36401×10^{-8}	3.41112×10^{-1}
	p-value	3.01986×10^{-11}	1.01490×10^{-11}	1.07516×10^{-11}	3.01986×10^{-11}	1.49399×10^{-11}	3.01230×10^{-11}
SMA	best	5.18988×10^{-4}	1.26496×10^{-7}	2.37253×10^{-11}	2.08208×10^{-11}	6.22359×10^{-11}	3.95601×10^{-7}
	worst	1.17331×10^{-2}	2.46549×10^{-4}	5.80093×10^{-7}	2.89907×10^{-10}	5.94920×10^{-8}	4.75099×10^{-5}
	mean	4.47411×10^{-3}	2.89317×10^{-5}	5.98652×10^{-8}	1.30095×10^{-10}	1.05190×10^{-8}	1.03517×10^{-5}
	std	3.00476×10^{-3}	5.64857×10^{-5}	1.28713×10^{-7}	7.25135×10^{-11}	1.30068×10^{-8}	1.04158×10^{-5}
	p-value	3.01986×10^{-11}	1.01490×10^{-11}	1.07516×10^{-11}	3.01986×10^{-11}	1.49399×10^{-11}	3.01230×10^{-11}
nAOA	best	4.73537×10^{-1}	1.16733×10^{-9}	3.11364×10^{-12}	3.28064×10^{-10}	2.13953×10^{-5}	7.56334×10^{-8}
	worst	7.39125×10^{-1}	9.06936×10^{-4}	8.22290×10^{-1}	2.69391×10^{-9}	4.30879×10^{-4}	4.49162×10
	mean	6.74564×10^{-1}	3.07109×10^{-5}	2.77064×10^{-2}	1.50697×10^{-9}	1.59376×10^{-4}	1.49721
	std	5.68300×10^{-2}	1.65502×10^{-4}	1.50077×10^{-1}	6.31248×10^{-10}	7.06193×10^{-5}	8.20053
	p-value	3.01986×10^{-11}	1.01490×10^{-11}	1.07516×10^{-11}	3.01986×10^{-11}	1.49399×10^{-11}	3.01230×10^{-11}
dAOA	best	2.01052×10^{-1}	8.99318×10^{-9}	2.54429×10^{-4}	3.09426×10^{-10}	5.69606×10^{-6}	8.50407×10^{-4}
	worst	6.87872	1.28121×10^{-3}	4.68145×10^{-1}	9.87499×10^{2}	1.56431×10^{-2}	3.78263×10^{5}
	mean	1.91504	3.22387×10^{-4}	6.56368×10^{-2}	2.07191×10^{2}	3.65947×10^{-3}	2.61018×10^{4}
	std	2.16147	3.20053×10^{-4}	1.21675×10^{-1}	2.92259×10^{2}	5.26309×10^{-3}	8.07193×10^{4}
	p-value	3.01986×10^{-11}	1.01490×10^{-11}	1.07516×10^{-11}	3.01986×10^{-11}	1.49399×10^{-11}	3.01230×10^{-11}

Problem 01. The description of the system is as follows [54]:

$$\begin{cases} x_1 - 0.25428722 - 0.18324757x_4x_3x_9 = 0 \\ x_2 - 0.37842197 - 0.16275449x_1x_{10}x_6 = 0 \\ x_3 - 0.27162577 - 0.16955071x_1x_2x_{10} = 0 \\ x_4 - 0.19807914 - 0.15585316x_7x_1x_6 = 0 \\ x_5 - 0.44166728 - 0.19950920x_7x_6x_3 = 0 \\ x_6 - 0.14654113 - 0.18922793x_8x_5x_{10} = 0 \\ x_7 - 0.42937161 - 0.21180486x_2x_5x_8 = 0 \\ x_8 - 0.07056438 - 0.17081208x_1x_7x_6 = 0 \\ x_9 - 0.34504906 - 0.19612740x_{10}x_6x_8 = 0 \\ x_{10} - 0.42651102 - 0.21466544x_4x_8x_1 = 0 \end{cases} \quad (19)$$

There are ten equations in the system, where $x_i \in [-2, 2]$, $i = 1, \ldots, n$, and $n = 10$. The aim was to obtain a higher precision solution x ($x_1, \ldots, x_n$) through the proposed optimization method, and the results are recorded in Table 1. The IAOA is better than others compared with several algorithms. The WOA ranks second, and the rest obtain competitive results. The convergence curve for this problem shows in Figure 4a.

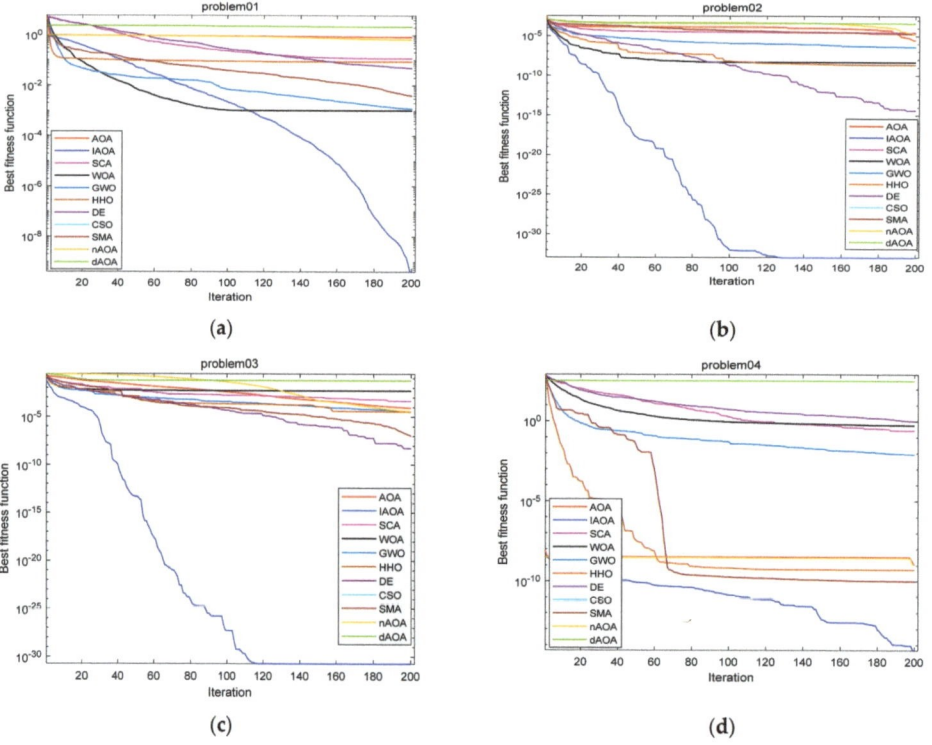

Figure 4. Cont.

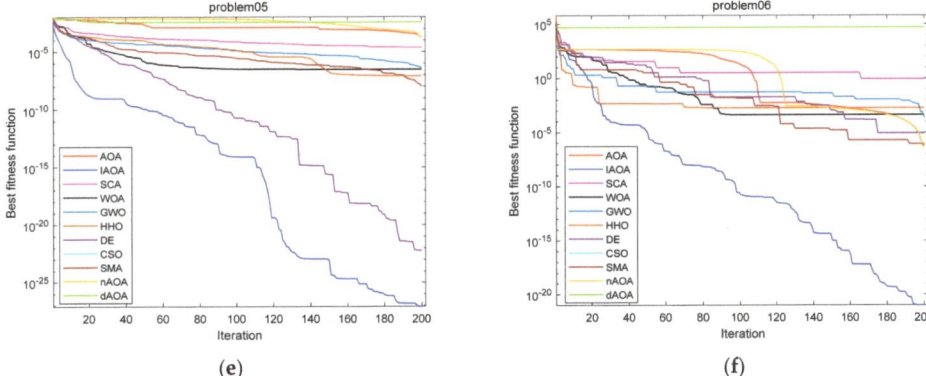

Figure 4. Convergence curve for tackling the NES (problem01–06 (**a**–**f**)).

Problem 02. The description of the system is as follows [55]:

$$\begin{cases} (1-R)\left[\left(\frac{D}{10(1+\beta_1)} - x_1\right) \cdot \exp\left(\frac{10x_1}{1+\frac{10x_1}{\gamma}}\right)\right] - x_1 = 0 \\ (1-R)\left[\left(\frac{D}{10} - \beta_1 x_1 - (1+\beta_2)x_2\right) \cdot \exp\left(\frac{10x_2}{1+\frac{10x_2}{\gamma}}\right)\right] + x_1 - (1+\beta_2)x_2 = 0 \end{cases} \quad (20)$$

There are two equations in system, where $x_i \in [0,1]$, $i = 1, \ldots, n$, and $n = 2$. In Table 2, the experimental results for this problem proved that the proposed IAOA outperforms the other methods. The DE ranks second, and the rest obtain competitive results. The AOA, WOA, GWO, HHO, and CSO are in the third echelon. Furthermore, the rest are in the fourth echelon. The convergence curve for this problem is shown in Figure 4b.

Problem 03. The description of the system is as follows [13]:

$$\begin{cases} \sin(x_1^3) - 3x_1 x_2^2 - 1 = 0 \\ \cos(3x_1^2 x_2) - |x_2^3| + 1 = 0 \end{cases} \quad (21)$$

There are two equations in the system, where $x_i \in [-2,2]$, $i = 1, \ldots, n$, and $n = 2$. The simulation results for this problem are shown in Table 3. It revealed that the IAOA is better than the other algorithms. The DE, CSO, and SMA are in the second echelon. The rest are in the third echelon. The convergence curve for this problem is shown in Figure 4c.

Problem 04. The description of the system is as follows [54]:

$$\begin{cases} x_2 + 2x_6 + x_9 + 2x_{10} - 10^{-5} = 0 \\ x_3 + x_8 - 3 \cdot 10^{-5} = 0 \\ x_1 + x_3 + 2x_5 + 2x_8 + x_9 + x_{10} - 5 \cdot 10^{-5} = 0 \\ x_4 + 2x_7 - 10^{-5} = 0 \\ 0.5140437 \cdot 10^{-7} x_5 - x_1^2 = 0 \\ 0.1006932 \cdot 10^{-6} x_6 - 2x_2^2 = 0 \\ 0.7816278 \cdot 10^{-15} x_7 - x_4^2 = 0 \\ 0.1496236 \cdot 10^{-6} x_8 - x_1 x_3 = 0 \\ 0.6194411 \cdot 10^{-7} x_9 - x_1 x_2 = 0 \\ 0.2089296 \cdot 10^{-14} x_{10} - x_1 x_2^2 = 0 \end{cases} \quad (22)$$

There are ten equations in the system: $x_i \in [-10, 10]$, $i = 1, \ldots, n$, and $n = 10$. Table 4 shows that the IAOA outperforms the others, and AOA, HHO, SMA, and nAOA obtain the competitive results. The convergence curve for this problem is shown in Figure 4d.

Problem 05. The description of the system is as follows [17]:

$$\begin{cases} 0.5\sin(x_1 x_2) - \frac{0.25}{\pi}x_2 - 0.5x_1 = 0 \\ \left(1 - \frac{0.25}{\pi}\right)[\exp(2x_1) - e] + \frac{e}{\pi}x_2 - 2ex_1 = 0 \end{cases} \quad (23)$$

There are two equations in the system, where $x_1 \in [0.25, 1]$ and $x_2 \in [1.5, 2\pi]$. In Table 5, the IAOA obtained the optimal solution, DE obtained the suboptimal solution, and the rest of the algorithms obtained competitive results. The convergence curve for this problem is shown in Figure 4e.

Problem 06. The description of the system is as follows [56]:

$$\begin{cases} \beta_{11} + \beta_{12}x_2^2 + \beta_{13}x_3^2 + \beta_{14}x_2 x_3 + \beta_{15}x_2^2 x_3^2 = 0 \\ \beta_{21} + \beta_{22}x_3^2 + \beta_{23}x_1^2 + \beta_{24}x_3 x_1 + \beta_{25}x_3^2 x_1^2 = 0 \\ \beta_{31} + \beta_{32}x_1^2 + \beta_{33}x_2^2 + \beta_{34}x_1 x_2 + \beta_{35}x_1^2 x_2^2 = 0 \end{cases} \quad (24)$$

There are three equations in the system, where the details about β_{ij} can be found in the literature [56]: $x_i \in [-20, 20]$, $i = 1, \ldots, n$, and $n = 3$. In Table 6, the proposed IAOA outperforms the other algorithms; the GWO, SMA, and DE get competitive results. The convergence curve for this problem is shown in Figure 4f.

The statistical results show that the IAOA outperforms all algorithms on the remaining problems in Table 7. These demonstrate that the IAOA has stronger ability and higher stability than the other methods when solving a nonlinear system of equations. In Figure 4, IAOA's convergence speed is slower than the others before the 110th iteration, but after that, the IAOA still maintains a high convergence speed and achieves the optimum at the 200th iteration for problem01; for problem02 and problem03, the IAOA has the fastest speed throughout the whole process and reaches the optimum at the 120th iteration and before 120 iterations, respectively; for problem04, the IAOA is slower than the other algorithms before 70 iterations; however it continues to converge after that and obtains the optimal value after 200 iterations; for problem05, there is a close convergence rate for the IAOA and DE, but a better value is obtained by the IAOA; for problem06, it has a slower convergence speed than the others before 20 iterations, but after that, the fastest convergence rate is obtained by the IAOA. All the experimental results prove that the algorithm proposed in this paper has the characteristics that include a fast convergence speed, high convergence accuracy, high solution quality, good stability, and strong robustness when dealing with nonlinear systems of equations. The p-values of almost all test functions in the table are less than 0.05, indicating that the IAOA is significantly different from the other algorithms.

4.3. Numerical Integration

The performance of the proposed new method is evaluated in this section using the ten numerical integration problems in Table 8, where F08 is a singular integral and F10 is an oscillatory integral. The IAOA compared with the traditional methods and population-based algorithms in tackling these cases. Tables 9–12 show the best integral values obtained by solving ten problems in 30 independent runs, where the R-method, T-method, S-method, H-method, G32, and $2n \times L5$ represent the traditional methods (rectangle method, trapezoid method, Simpson method, Hermite interpolation method, the 32-point Gaussian formula, and the 5-point Gauss-Roberto-Legendre formula). The rest are swarm intelligence algorithms applied to solve numerical integration problems (evolutionary strategy method [24], particle swarm optimization [25], differential evolution algorithm [27], and improved bat algorithm [28]). The population size and the maximum number of iterations are set to 30 and 200 during the process, respectively. In Table 9, for F01, the solution accuracy of the IAOA is higher than the other methods, and then, the S-method, FN, ES, DEBA, PSO, and DE obtain close results; for F02, the IAOA achieves the best result, and the FN, ES, DEBA, PSO, and DE are in the second echelon; for F03, the

IAOA achieves the better result compared to the FN, ES, and PSO. The MBFES, DEBA, and DE rank third. In Table 10, for F04, the IAOA gets a perfect result, and the FN, ES, DEBA, PSO, and DE obtain similar values; for F05, the IAOA ranks first, and the FN, ES, DEBA, PSO, and DE rank second; for F06, the IAOA, FN, and DE achieve competitive results. For F07–F09, the IAOA obtains the best value, and the FN, ES, and DEBA rank second in Table 11. The traditional methods (R-method, T-method, and S-method) fail to solve F10; therefore, G32 and 2n × L5 are utilized to tackle this problem. In Table 12, the IAOA and DEBA obtain similar values and ranks first. Tables 13 and 14 are statistical results for the numerical integration (F01–F10) are obtained by swarm intelligence algorithms. For F01–F09, the IAOA is better than the other algorithms across all the assessment criteria (the best value, the worst value, mean value, and standard deviation). However, for F10, the IAOA achieves the only optimal result in the best value, and the rest rank second, in which the DEBA obtains the best results. From Figure 5, the method proposed in this paper has the fastest convergence speed and convergence accuracy for all the problems except F10. The above experimental results prove that the IAOA has fast convergence speed, high solution accuracy, and strong robustness. These enable the IAOA to handle numerical integration problems; therefore, it is a worthwhile direction to apply the IAOA to solve the integration solution problems in practical engineering applications.

Table 8. Details of the integrations F01–F10.

Integrations	Details	Range
F01	$f(x) = x^2$	[0, 2]
F02	$f(x) = x^4$	[0, 2]
F03	$f(x) = \sqrt{1+x^2}$	[0, 2]
F04	$f(x) = \frac{1}{1+x}$	[0, 2]
F05	$f(x) = \sin x$	[0, 2]
F06	$f(x) = e^x$	[0, 2]
F07	$f(x) = \sqrt{1+(\cos x)^2}$	[0, 48]
F08	$f(x) = \begin{cases} e^{-x}, 0 \leq x < 1 \\ e^{-x/2}, 1 \leq x < 2 \\ e^{-x/3}, 2 \leq x \leq 3 \end{cases}$	[0, 3]
F09	$f(x) = e^{-x^2}$	[0, 1]
F10	$f(x) = x \cos x \sin xmx, (m = 10, 20, 30)$	[0, 2π]

Table 9. Comparison of the experimental results for F01–F03.

Methods	Integrations		
	F01	F02	F03
R-method	2.000	2.000	2.828
T-method	4.000	16.000	3.236
S-method	2.667	6.667	2.964
H-method	2.830	7.066	3.048
FN [26]	2.667	6.3995	2.95789
MBFES [24]	2.659	6.338	2.956
ES [24]	2.666	6.398	2.9577
DEBA [28]	2.66698573	6.401201	2.958169
PSO [25]	2.666	6.398	2.9578
DE [27]	2.667	6.3995	2.958
AOA	2.61006134	6.20147125	2.94004382
IAOA	2.66661710	6.40000000	2.95788286
Exact	2.66666667	6.40000000	2.95788572

Table 10. Comparison of the experimental results for F04–F06.

Methods	Integrations		
	F04	F05	F06
R-method	1.000	1.683	5.437
T-method	1.333	0.909	8.389
S-method	1.111	1.425	6.421
H-method	1.112	1.452	6.691
FN [26]	1.0986	1.416	6.389
MBFES [24]	1.090	1.419	6.390
ES [24]	1.098	1.416	6.388
DEBA [28]	1.098754	1.416082	6.388921
PSO [25]	1.0985	1.416	6.3887
DE [27]	1.099	1.416	6.389
AOA	1.08923818	1.40101546	6.29531692
IAOA	1.09861229	1.41613957	6.38901606
Exact	1.09861229	1.41614684	6.38905610

Table 11. Comparison of the experimental results for F07–F09.

Methods	Integrations		
	F07	F08	F09
R-method	52.13975183	1.51349542	0.77782078
T-method	62.43737140	1.61179305	0.74621972
S-method	117.61490334	2.48720505	0.74683657
H-method	58.99776108	1.56164258	0.75403569
FN [26]	58.4705	1.54604	0.746823
MBFES [24]	58.48828	1.5455	0.74652
ES [24]	58.47065	1.5459805	0.74683
DEBA [28]	58.470505372351	1.5460388345767	0.7468269544604
PSO	56.80139775	1.52897330	0.74328459
DE	56.04598085	1.52425900	0.74202909
AOA	56.17497970	1.52641514	0.74223182
IAOA	58.47046915	1.54603603	0.74682413
Exact	58.47046915	1.54603603	0.74682413

Table 12. Comparison of the experimental results for F10.

Methods	Integrations		
	F10 (m = 10)	F10 (m = 20)	F10 (m = 30)
G32	−0.6340207	−1.2092524	−1.5822272
2n × L5	−0.55875940	−0.27789620	−0.18508448
H-method	−0.21043575	0.17309499	−0.02945756
MBFES [24]	−0.68134052	−0.37280425	−0.17305621
ES [24]	−0.65034080	−0.30583435	−0.23556815
DEBA	−0.63466518	−0.31494663	−0.20967248
PSO	−1.50150183	−1.33949737	−1.10170197
DE [27]	−0.63982173	−0.31035906	−0.21438251
AOA	−3.07253909	−0.56489050	−0.42642997
IAOA	−0.63466518	−0.31494663	−0.20967248
Exact	−0.63466518	−0.31494663	−0.20967248

Table 13. Statistical results for the numerical integrations (F01–F06).

Algorithms		Integrations					
		F01	F02	F03	F04	F05	F06
AOA	best	5.660532×10^{-2}	1.985287×10^{-1}	1.784189×10^{-2}	9.374106×10^{-3}	1.513137×10^{-2}	9.373918×10^{-2}
	worst	6.785842×10^{-2}	2.466178×10^{-1}	2.112411×10^{-2}	1.103594×10^{-2}	1.827849×10^{-2}	1.105054×10^{-1}
	mean	6.196485×10^{-2}	2.238141×10^{-1}	1.970905×10^{-2}	1.041648×10^{-2}	1.679104×10^{-2}	1.013200×10^{-1}
	std	2.473863×10^{-3}	1.277362×10^{-2}	6.790772×10^{-4}	4.381854×10^{-4}	7.886715×10^{-4}	3.985235×10^{-3}
IAOA	best	4.956295×10^{-5}	0.000000	2.855397×10^{-6}	0.000000	7.267277×10^{-6}	4.004088×10^{-5}
	worst	1.070986×10^{-4}	9.632589×10^{-6}	1.471988×10^{-5}	7.241931×10^{-6}	3.035345×10^{-5}	1.136393×10^{-4}
	mean	7.267766×10^{-5}	9.617999×10^{-7}	6.357033×10^{-6}	1.274560×10^{-6}	1.595556×10^{-5}	7.989662×10^{-5}
	std	1.561025×10^{-5}	2.672207×10^{-6}	2.828416×10^{-6}	1.942626×10^{-6}	5.989208×10^{-6}	2.032255×10^{-5}
PSO [25]	best	3.966996×10^{-2}	1.282142×10^{-1}	1.263049×10^{-2}	6.772669×10^{-3}	1.115352×10^{-2}	6.495427×10^{-2}
	worst	5.467546×10^{-2}	1.880821×10^{-1}	1.614274×10^{-2}	9.112184×10^{-3}	1.385859×10^{-2}	9.718717×10^{-2}
	mean	4.406724×10^{-2}	1.593799×10^{-1}	1.405265×10^{-2}	7.745239×10^{-3}	1.208230×10^{-2}	7.327404×10^{-2}
	std	3.262431×10^{-3}	1.528260×10^{-2}	9.707823×10^{-4}	6.532329×10^{-4}	7.146743×10^{-4}	6.698801×10^{-3}
DE [27]	best	5.444535×10^{-2}	1.776272×10^{-1}	1.740389×10^{-2}	9.410606×10^{-3}	1.537737×10^{-2}	9.229490×10^{-2}
	worst	6.223208×10^{-2}	1.992612×10^{-1}	1.943564×10^{-2}	1.043440×10^{-2}	1.668422×10^{-2}	1.003285×10^{-1}
	mean	5.887766×10^{-2}	1.887098×10^{-1}	1.881844×10^{-2}	1.003350×10^{-2}	1.606658×10^{-2}	9.665791×10^{-2}
	std	1.717478×10^{-3}	5.056921×10^{-3}	4.230737×10^{-4}	2.412656×10^{-4}	3.636407×10^{-4}	1.886442×10^{-3}
DEBA [28]	best	5.858312×10^{-2}	1.958779×10^{-1}	1.797733×10^{-2}	9.632554×10^{-3}	1.541447×10^{-2}	9.078063×10^{-2}
	worst	6.805128×10^{-2}	2.566962×10^{-1}	2.194973×10^{-2}	1.144459×10^{-2}	1.824156×10^{-2}	1.096576×10^{-1}
	mean	6.306158×10^{-2}	2.287206×10^{-1}	2.005007×10^{-2}	1.048558×10^{-2}	1.700868×10^{-2}	1.008133×10^{-1}
	std	2.059708×10^{-3}	1.384008×10^{-2}	8.428458×10^{-4}	4.319549×10^{-4}	7.193521×10^{-4}	4.457879×10^{-3}
ES [24]	best	3.634854×10^{-2}	1.053634×10^{-1}	1.178783×10^{-2}	6.152581×10^{-3}	9.742411×10^{-3}	6.028495×10^{-2}
	worst	3.704455×10^{-2}	1.076016×10^{-1}	1.197536×10^{-2}	6.272540×10^{-3}	9.921388×10^{-3}	6.120127×10^{-2}
	mean	3.662145×10^{-2}	1.064150×10^{-1}	1.189432×10^{-2}	6.206519×10^{-3}	9.813727×10^{-3}	6.070549×10^{-2}
	std	1.618502×10^{-4}	4.726931×10^{-4}	4.687831×10^{-5}	2.718416×10^{-5}	4.560503×10^{-5}	2.303572×10^{-4}

Table 14. Statistical results for numerical integrations (F07–F10).

Algorithms		Integrations					
		F07	F08	F09	F10 (m = 10)	F10 (m = 20)	F10 (m = 30)
AOA	best	2.295489	1.962088×10^{-2}	4.592313×10^{-3}	2.437873	2.499438×10^{-1}	2.167574×10^{-1}
	worst	2.524012	2.400262×10^{-2}	5.421672×10^{-3}	3.611012	3.429053	3.115022
	mean	2.424997	2.226327×10^{-2}	5.031127×10^{-3}	3.225836	1.617425	9.721188×10^{-1}
	std	5.634089×10^{-2}	1.017542×10^{-3}	2.167135×10^{-4}	2.620454×10^{-1}	9.081448×10^{-1}	7.417795×10^{-1}
IAOA	best	0.000000	0.000000	0.000000	0.000000	0.000000	0.000000
	worst	4.285648×10^{-4}	9.665730×10^{-6}	7.650313×10^{-9}	4.941453×10^{-4}	8.932970×10^{-4}	4.121824×10^{-4}
	mean	5.817808×10^{-5}	1.079836×10^{-6}	1.094646×10^{-9}	6.843408×10^{-5}	9.159354×10^{-5}	6.487479×10^{-5}
	std	9.331558×10^{-5}	2.377176×10^{-6}	2.051844×10^{-9}	1.219906×10^{-4}	1.972260×10^{-4}	9.370544×10^{-5}
PSO [25]	best	1.093717	1.499542×10^{-2}	3.212480×10^{-3}	5.688245×10^{-1}	1.024550	8.920294×10^{-1}
	worst	2.077297	2.010782×10^{-2}	4.674802×10^{-3}	1.599995	1.485451	1.953066
	mean	1.669071	1.706272×10^{-2}	3.539538×10^{-3}	8.668366×10^{-1}	1.219538	1.489201
	std	2.419795×10^{-1}	1.205259×10^{-3}	3.409595×10^{-4}	2.759571×10^{-1}	1.216184×10^{-1}	2.065585×10^{-1}
DE [27]	best	2.255785	2.091958×10^{-2}	4.575317×10^{-3}	2.543013	3.461794	3.889322
	worst	2.522405	2.254710×10^{-2}	5.009106×10^{-3}	3.236645	4.684467	5.201887
	mean	2.424488	2.177702×10^{-2}	4.795040×10^{-3}	3.015091	4.242609	4.687029
	std	5.766110×10^{-2}	4.602533×10^{-4}	1.146454×10^{-4}	1.967397×10^{-1}	2.313007×10^{-1}	2.923496×10^{-1}
DEBA [28]	best	2.361570×10^{-1}	2.057410×10^{-2}	4.776881×10^{-3}	6.043389×10^{-14}	1.208677×10^{-13}	5.319404×10^{-13}
	worst	2.468831	2.474051×10^{-2}	5.441200×10^{-3}	6.043389×10^{-14}	1.208677×10^{-13}	5.319404×10^{-13}
	mean	1.163514	2.294436×10^{-2}	5.157892×10^{-3}	6.043389×10^{-14}	1.208677×10^{-13}	5.319404×10^{-13}
	std	6.919695×10^{-1}	9.765442×10^{-4}	1.475304×10^{-4}	3.851264×10^{-29}	7.702528×10^{-29}	3.081011×10^{-28}
ES [24]	best	1.298269	1.319474×10^{-2}	3.051746×10^{-3}	1.460773	1.634373	1.152204
	worst	1.321623	1.341748×10^{-2}	3.121709×10^{-3}	1.665912	2.355153	2.380726
	mean	1.308546	1.331615×10^{-2}	3.081151×10^{-3}	1.568781	1.869004	1.719830
	std	5.523404×10^{-3}	5.640941×10^{-5}	1.521690×10^{-5}	4.627499×10^{-2}	1.831224×10^{-1}	2.898513×10^{-1}

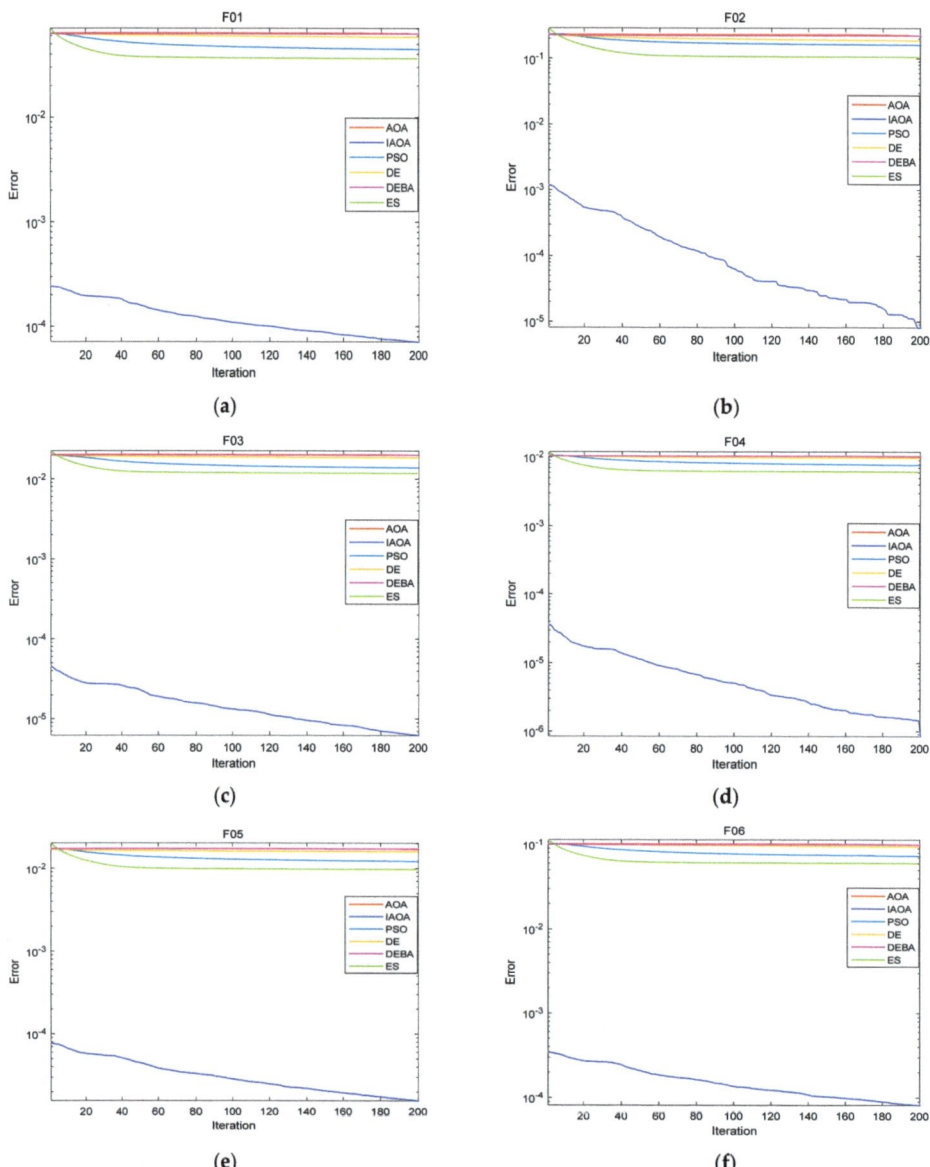

Figure 5. *Cont.*

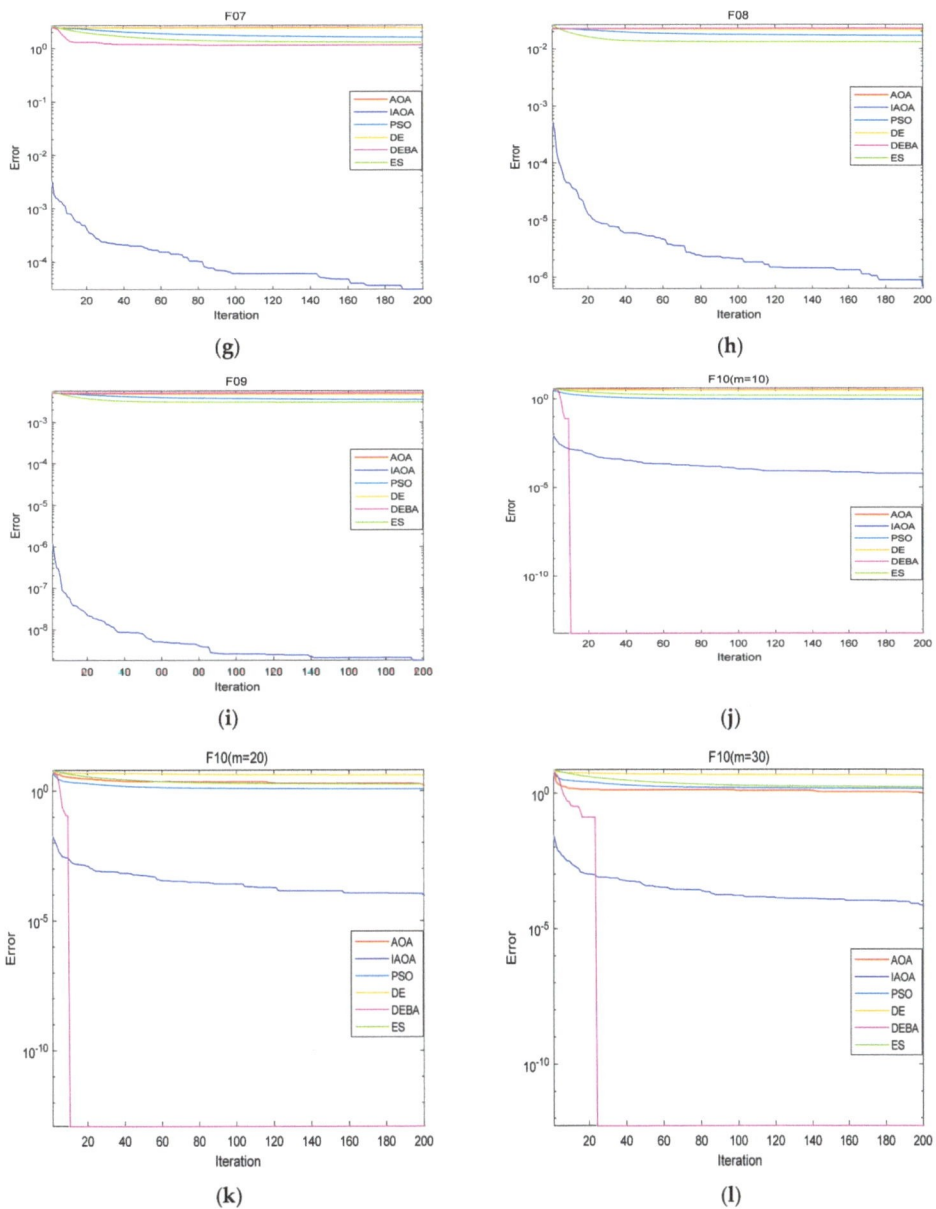

Figure 5. Convergence curve for the numerical integrations (F01–F10 (**a**–**l**)).

4.4. Sovling Engineering Problem

Compared with three-dimensional motion, planar motion restricts the robot to a single plane and is simpler to calculate. However, most robot mechanisms can simplify plane mechanisms or planes for tackling. Now, the robotic arm plays an increasingly important role, which has also attracted the extensive attention of researchers. Improving the working efficiency of the robotic arm under the premise of low energy consumption is a challenging problem facing the industrial field [57]. The kinematics of the robotic arm mainly include forward kinematics and inverse kinematics. One is the pose of the end effector determined according to the rotation angle of each joint based on the base coordinates; the other is taking the end joint as the starting point and, finally, back-to-base coordinates. The inverse kinematics problem is essentially a nonlinear equation problem. The tasks performed by the robotic arm are usually described by its base coordinate system in practical applications. Therefore, the inverse kinematics solution is particularly important in the field of the control. The robotic arm model [58] is shown in Figure 6a, and the mathematical model in coordinates is shown in Figure 6b. The nonlinear equation system for this model is as follows.

$$\begin{cases} 10,000 \times ((a \times \sin(A_2) - b \times \sin(A_2 + B_2) + c \times \sin(A_2 + B_2 + C_2) - X)^2) = 0 \\ 10,000 \times ((h - a \times \cos(A_2) - b \times \cos(A_2 + B_2) + c \times \cos(A_2 + B_2 + C_2) - Y)^2) = 0 \\ |A_2 - A_1| + |B_2 - B_1| + |C_2 - C_1| = 0 \end{cases} \quad (25)$$

where a = 16.5 cm; b = 7.9 cm; c = 5.3 cm; and h = 7.4 cm (A_1 = 150°, B_1 = 132.7026°, and C_1 = 127.0177°) are the initial angles of the three joints; (X = 10 cm, Y = 10 cm) is the coordinate of the end effector; and (A_2, B_2, and C_2) are the aims required to obtain three joint angles in the final stage. The first two equations in the nonlinear equation system find the three joint angles when the end effector reaches the target position (X, Y), and the third equation ensures that the change of the joint angle is the smallest to meet the requirements for saving energy.

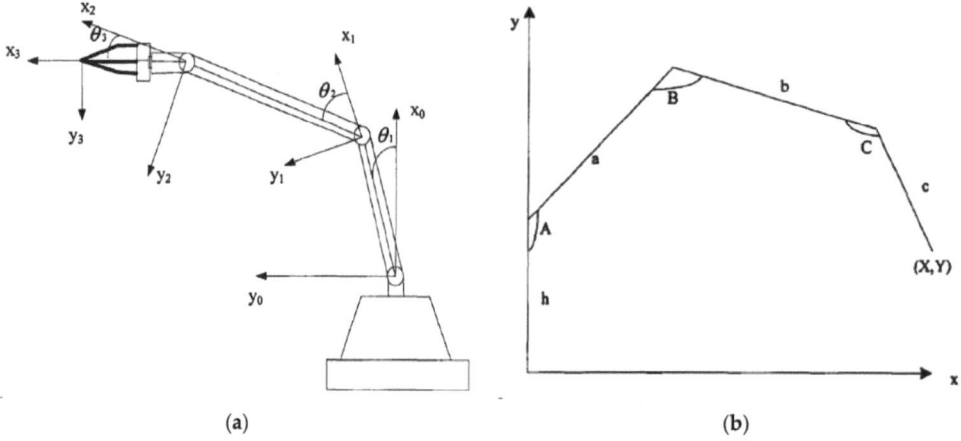

Figure 6. (a) The model of a robotic arm, and (b) a mathematical model for a robotic arm.

Tables 15–18 demonstrate that the IAOA obtains the closest results to the initial angle compared with the PSO, GA and PSSA in solving the inverse kinematics problem of the robotic arm. This shows that the method proposed in this paper allows the robotic arm to consume less energy during movement. In Table 19, f represents the fitness value obtain by Equation (25) and is the difference between the final angle and initial angle of the joint. Obviously, the IAOA achieves the best results for both evaluations. Therefore, it is a great significance to the stability, operation efficiency, operation accuracy, and energy consumption of the robotic arm trajectory control. A new method is provided for the inverse motion solution, which makes up for the deficiency of the traditional method.

Table 15. The results obtained by the IAOA for the engineering problem.

Algorithm		Joint Angles		
		A_2	B_2	C_2
IAOA	initial angle	150	132.7026	127.0177
	Result	145.7291	139.0180	123.9864

Table 16. The results obtained by the PSO for the engineering problem.

Algorithm		Joint Angles		
		A_2	B_2	C_2
PSO	initial angle	150	132.7026	127.0177
	result	139.6534	68.2235	96.4886

Table 17. The results obtained by the GA for the engineering problem.

Algorithm		Joint Angles		
		A_2	B_2	C_2
GA	initial angle	150	132.7026	127.0177
	result	129.8653	118.9625	52.6691

Table 18. The results obtained by the PSSA for the engineering problem.

Algorithm		Joint Angles		
		A_2	B_2	C_2
PSSA [58]	initial angle	150	132.7026	127.0177
	result	147.1015	92.5371	89.5116

Table 19. Comparison of the experimental results for the IAOA, PSO, GA, and PSSA.

Objective Funtions	Algorithms			
	IAOA	PSO	GA	PSSA
f	1.3618×10	3.0608×10^6	3.2329×10^6	2.0199×10^5
$\|A_2 - A_1\| + \|B_2 - B_1\| + \|C_2 - C_1\|$	13.6176	105.3548	118.2234	80.5701

5. Conclusions and Future Works

In this paper, the shortcomings are analyzed of the traditional AOA so that an improved AOA based on a population control strategy is proposed to overcome the weakness. The algorithm can find the best global value faster by classifying the population and adaptively controlling the number of individuals in each subpopulation. This method effectively enhances the information sharing strength between individuals, can better search the space, avoids falling into the local optimum, accelerates the convergence process, and improves the optimization accuracy. The AOA, IAOA, and some other algorithms are compared based on solving 6 nonlinear systems of equations, 10 numerical integrations, and an engineering problem. The experimental results show that the IAOA can solve these problems well and outperform the other algorithms. In the future, the IAOA can be used to solve more nonlinear problems in practical engineering applications. Secondly, it can try to solve multiple integrals. Finally, the algorithm can be further improved and enhanced in its performance.

Author Contributions: Conceptualization and methodology, M.C. and Y.Z.; software, M.C.; writing—original draft preparation, M.C.; writing—review and editing, Y.Z. and Q.L.; and funding acquisition, Y.Z. All authors have read and agreed to the published version of the manuscript.

Funding: This research was funded by the National Natural Science Foundation of China, Grant No. U21A20464 and 62066005.

Institutional Review Board Statement: Not applicable.

Informed Consent Statement: Not applicable.

Data Availability Statement: Not applicable.

Conflicts of Interest: The authors declare no conflict of interest.

References

1. Broyden, C.G. A class of methods for solving nonlinear simultaneous equations. *Math. Comput.* **1965**, *19*, 577–593. [CrossRef]
2. Ramos, H.; Monteiro, M.T.T. A new approach based on the newton's method to solve systems of nonlinear equations. *J. Comput. Appl. Math.* **2017**, *318*, 3–13. [CrossRef]
3. Hueso, J.L.; Martínez, E.; Torregrosa, J.R. Modified newton's method for systems of nonlinear equations with singular Jacobian. *J. Comput. Appl. Math.* **2009**, *224*, 77–83. [CrossRef]
4. Luo, Y.Z.; Tang, G.J.; Zhou, L.N. Hybrid approach for solving systems of nonlinear equations using chaos optimization and quasi-newton method. *Appl. Soft Comput.* **2008**, *8*, 1068–1073. [CrossRef]
5. Karr, C.L.; Weck, B.; Freeman, L.M. Solutions to systems of nonlinear equations via a genetic algorithm. *Eng. Appl. Artif. Intell.* **1998**, *11*, 369–375. [CrossRef]
6. Ouyang, A.J.; Zhou, Y.Q.; Luo, Q.F. Hybrid particle swarm optimization algorithm for solving systems of nonlinear equations. In Proceedings of the 2009 IEEE International Conference on Granular Computing, Nanchang, China, 17–19 August 2009; pp. 460–465.
7. Jaberipour, M.; Khorram, E.; Karimi, B. Particle swarm algorithm for solving systems of nonlinear equations. *Comput. Math. Appl.* **2011**, *62*, 566–576. [CrossRef]
8. Pourjafari, E.; Mojallali, H. Solving nonlinear equations systems with a new approach based on invasive weed optimization algorithm and clustering. *Swarm Evol. Comput.* **2012**, *4*, 33–43. [CrossRef]
9. Jia, R.M.; He, D.X. Hybrid artificial bee colony algorithm for solving nonlinear system of equations. In Proceedings of the 2012 Eighth International Conference on Computational Intelligence and Security, Guangzhou, China, 17–18 November 2012; pp. 56–60.
10. Ren, H.M.; Wu, L.; Bi, W.H.; Argyros, I.K. Solving nonlinear equations system via an efficient genetic algorithm with symmetric and harmonious individuals. *Appl. Math. Comput.* **2013**, *219*, 10967–10973. [CrossRef]
11. Cai, R.Z.; Yue, G.L. A novel firefly algorithm of solving nonlinear equation group. *Appl. Mech. Mater.* **2013**, *389*, 918–923.
12. Abdollahi, M.; Isazadeh, A.; Abdollahi, D. Imperialist competitive algorithm for solving systems of nonlinear equations. *Comput. Math. Appl.* **2013**, *65*, 1894–1908. [CrossRef]
13. Hirsch, M.J.; Pardalos, P.M.; Resende, M.G.C. Solving systems of nonlinear equations with continuous GRASP. *Nonlinear Anal. Real World Appl.* **2009**, *10*, 2000–2006. [CrossRef]
14. Sacco, W.F.; Henderson, N. Finding all solutions of nonlinear systems using a hybrid metaheuristic with fuzzy clustering means. *Appl. Soft Comput.* **2011**, *11*, 5424–5432. [CrossRef]
15. Gong, W.Y.; Wang, Y.; Cai, Z.H.; Yang, S. A weighted bi-objective transformation technique for locating multiple optimal solutions of nonlinear equation systems. *IEEE Trans. Evol. Comput.* **2017**, *21*, 697–713. [CrossRef]
16. Ariyaratne, M.K.A.; Fernando, T.G.I.; Weerakoon, S. Solving systems of nonlinear equations using a modified firefly algorithm (MODFA). *Swarm Evol. Comput.* **2019**, *48*, 72–92. [CrossRef]
17. Gong, W.Y.; Wang, Y.; Cai, Z.H.; Wang, L. Finding multiple roots of nonlinear equation systems via a repulsion-based adaptive differential evolution. *IEEE Trans. Syst. Man Cybern. Syst.* **2020**, *50*, 1499–1513. [CrossRef]
18. Ibrahim, A.M.; Tawhid, M.A. A hybridization of differential evolution and monarch butterfly optimization for solving systems of nonlinear equations. *J. Comput. Des. Eng.* **2019**, *6*, 354–367. [CrossRef]
19. Liao, Z.W.; Gong, W.Y.; Wang, L. Memetic niching-based evolutionary algorithms for solving nonlinear equation system. *Expert Syst. Appl.* **2020**, *149*, 113–261. [CrossRef]
20. Ning, G.Y.; Zhou, Y.Q. Application of improved differential evolution algorithm in solving equations. *Int. J. Comput. Intell. Syst.* **2021**, *14*, 199. [CrossRef]
21. Rizk-Allah, R.M. A quantum-based sine cosine algorithm for solving general systems of nonlinear equations. *Artif. Intell. Rev.* **2021**, *54*, 3939–3990. [CrossRef]
22. Ji, J.Y.; Man, L.W. An improved dynamic multi-objective optimization approach for nonlinear equation systems. *Inf. Sci.* **2021**, *576*, 204–227. [CrossRef]
23. Turgut, O.E.; Turgut, M.S.; Coban, M.T. Chaotic quantum behaved particle swarm optimization algorithm for solving nonlinear system of equations. *Comput. Math. Appl.* **2014**, *68*, 508–530. [CrossRef]
24. Zhou, Y.Q.; Zhang, M.; Zhao, B. Numerical integration of arbitrary functions based on evolutionary strategy method. *Chin. J. Comput.* **2008**, *21*, 196–206.

25. Wei, X.Q.; Zhou, Y.Q. Research on numerical integration method based on particle swarm optimization. *Microelectron. Comput.* **2009**, *26*, 117–119.
26. Wei, X.X.; Zhou, Y.Q.; Lan, X.L. Research on a numerical integration method based on functional networks. *Comput. Sci.* **2009**, *36*, 224–226.
27. Deng, Z.X.; Huang, F.D.; Liu, X.J. A differential evolution algorithm for solving numerical integration problems. *Comput. Eng.* **2011**, *37*, 206–207.
28. Xiao, H.H.; Duan, Y.M. Application of improved bat algorithm in numerical integration. *J. Intell. Syst.* **2014**, *9*, 364–371.
29. Szczepanski, R.; Kaminski, M.; Tarczewski, T. Auto-tuning process of state feedback speed controller applied for two-mass system. *Energies* **2020**, *13*, 3067. [CrossRef]
30. Hu, H.B.; Hu, Q.B.; Lu, Z.Y.; Xu, D. Optimal PID controller design in PMSM servo system via particle swarm optimization. In Proceedings of the 31st Annual Conference of IEEE Industrial Electronics Society, IECON 2005, Raleigh, NC, USA, 6–10 November 2005; p. 5.
31. Szczepanski, R.; Tarczewski, T.; Niewiara, L.J.; Stojic, D. Isdentification of mechanical parameters in servo-drive system. In Proceedings of the 2021 IEEE 19th International Power Electronics and Motion Control Conference (PEMC), Gliwice, Poland, 25–29 April 2021; pp. 566–573.
32. Liu, L.; Cartes, D.A.; Liu, W. Particle Swarm Optimization Based Parameter Identification Applied to PMSM. In Proceedings of the 2007 American Control Conference, New York, NY, USA, 9–13 July 2007; pp. 2955–2960.
33. Szczepanski, R.; Tarczewski, T. Global path planning for mobile robot based on artificial bee colony and Dijkstra's algorithms. In Proceedings of the 2021 IEEE 19th International Power Electronics and Motion Control Conference (PEMC), Gliwice, Poland, 25–29 April 2021; pp. 724–730.
34. Brand, M.; Masuda, M.; Wehner, N.; Yu, X.H. Ant colony optimization algorithm for robot path planning. In Proceedings of the 2010 International Conference on Computer Design and Applications, Qinhuangdao, China, 25–27 June 2010; pp. 436–440.
35. Szczepanski, R.; Erwinski, K.; Tejer, M.; Bereit, A.; Tarczewski, T. Optimal scheduling for palletizing task using robotic arm and artificial bee colony algorithm. *Eng. Appl. Artif. Intell.* **2022**, *113*, 104976. [CrossRef]
36. Kolakowska, E.; Smith, S.F.; Kristiansen, M. Constraint optimization model of a scheduling problem for a robotic arm in automatic systems. *Robot. Auton. Syst.* **2014**, *62*, 267–280. [CrossRef]
37. Abualigah, L.; Diabat, A.; Mirjalili, S.; Abd Elaziz, M.; Gandomi, A.H. The arithmetic optimization algorithm. *Comput. Methods Appl. Mech. Eng.* **2021**, *376*, 113609. [CrossRef]
38. Premkumar, M.; Jangir, P.; Kumar, D.S.; Sowmya, R.; Alhelou, H.H.; Abualigah, L.; Yildiz, A.R.; Mirjalili, S. A new arithmetic optimization algorithm for solving real-world multi-objective CEC-2021 constrained optimization problems: Diversity analysis and validations. *IEEE Access* **2021**, *9*, 84263–84295. [CrossRef]
39. Bansal, P.; Gehlot, K.; Singhal, A.; Gupta, A. Automatic detection of osteosarcoma based on integrated features and feature selection using binary arithmetic optimization algorithm. *Multimed. Tools Appl.* **2022**, *81*, 8807–8834. [CrossRef]
40. Agushaka, J.O.; Ezugwu, A.E. Advanced arithmetic optimization algorithm for solving mechanical engineering design problems. *PLoS ONE* **2021**, *16*, e0255703.
41. Abualigah, L.; Diabat, A.; Sumari, P.; Gandomi, A. A novel evolutionary arithmetic optimization algorithm for multilevel thresholding segmentation of COVID-19 CT images. *Processes* **2021**, *9*, 1155. [CrossRef]
42. Xu, Y.P.; Tan, J.W.; Zhu, D.J.; Ouyang, P.; Taheri, B. Model identification of the proton exchange membrane fuel cells by extreme learning machine and a developed version of arithmetic optimization algorithm. *Energy Rep.* **2021**, *7*, 2332–2342. [CrossRef]
43. Izci, D.; Ekinci, S.; Kayri, M.; Eker, E. A novel improved arithmetic optimization algorithm for optimal design of PID controlled and Bode's ideal transfer function-based automobile cruise control system. *Evol. Syst.* **2021**, *13*, 453–468. [CrossRef]
44. Khatir, S.; Tiachacht, S.; Thanh, C.L.; Ghandourah, E.; Mirjalili, S.; Wahab, M.A. An improved artificial neural network using arithmetic optimization algorithm for damage assessment in FGM composite plates. *Compos. Struct.* **2021**, *273*, 114–287. [CrossRef]
45. Viswanathan, G.M.; Afanasyev, V.; Buldyrev, S.; Murphy, E.J.; Prince, P.A.; Stanley, H.E. Lévy flight search patterns of wandering albatrosses. *Nature* **1996**, *381*, 413–415. [CrossRef]
46. Humphries, N.E.; Queiroz, N.; Dyer, J.R.; Pade, N.G.; Musyl, M.K.; Schaefer, K.M.; Fuller, D.W.; Brunnschweiler, J.M.; Doyle, T.K.; Houghton, J.D.; et al. Environmental context explains Lévy and Brownian movement patterns of marine predators. *Nature* **2010**, *465*, 1066–1069. [CrossRef]
47. Mirjalili, S. A sine cosine Algorithm for solving optimization problems. *Knowl. Based Syst.* **2016**, *96*, 120–133. [CrossRef]
48. Mirjalili, S.; Lewis, A. The whale optimization algorithm. *Adv. Eng. Softw.* **2016**, *95*, 51–67. [CrossRef]
49. Mirjalili, S.; Mirjalili, S.M.; Lewis, A. Grey wolf optimizer. *Adv. Eng. Softw.* **2014**, *69*, 46–61. [CrossRef]
50. Heidari, A.A.; Mirjalili, S.; Faris, H.; Aljarah, I.; Mafarja, M.; Chen, H. Harris hawks optimization: Algorithm and applications. *Future Gener. Comput. Syst.* **2019**, *97*, 849–872. [CrossRef]
51. Li, S.M.; Chen, H.L.; Wang, M.J.; Heidari, A.A.; Mirjalili, S. Slime mould algorithm: A new method for stochastic optimization. *Future Gener. Comput. Syst.* **2020**, *111*, 300–323. [CrossRef]
52. Price, K.V. Differential evolution: A fast and simple numerical optimizer. In Proceedings of the North American Fuzzy Information Processing, Berkeley, CA, USA, 19–22 June 1996; pp. 524–527.
53. Gandomi, A.H.; Yang, X.S.; Alavi, A.H. Cuckoo search algorithm: A metaheuristic approach to solve structural optimization problems. *Eng. Comput.* **2013**, *29*, 17–35. [CrossRef]

54. Grosan, C.; Abraham, A. A new approach for solving nonlinear equations systems. *IEEE Trans. Syst. Man Cybern. Part A Syst. Hum.* **2008**, *38*, 698–714. [CrossRef]
55. Floudas, C.A. Recent advances in global optimization for process synthesis, design and control: Enclosure of all solutions. *Comput. Chem. Eng.* **1999**, *23*, S963–S973. [CrossRef]
56. Nikkhah-Bahrami, M.; Oftadeh, R. An effective iterative method for computing real and complex roots of systems of nonlinear equations. *Appl. Math. Comput.* **2009**, *215*, 1813–1820. [CrossRef]
57. Ding, X. *Robot Control Research*; Zhejiang University Press: Hangzhou, China, 2006; pp. 37–38.
58. Xiang, Z.H.; Zhou, Y.Q.; Luo, Q.F.; Wen, C. PSSA: Polar coordinate salp swarm algorithm for curve design problems. *Neural Process Lett.* **2020**, *52*, 615–645. [CrossRef]

Application of the ADMM Algorithm for a High-Dimensional Partially Linear Model

Aifen Feng *,†, Xiaogai Chang †, Youlin Shang and Jingya Fan

School of Mathematics and Statistics, Henan University of Science and Technology, Luoyang 471023, China
* Correspondence: faf@haust.edu.cn
† These authors contributed equally to this work.

Abstract: This paper focuses on a high-dimensional semi-parametric regression model in which a partially linear model is used for the parametric part and the B-spline basis function approach is used to estimate the unknown function for the non-parametric part. Within the framework of this model, the constrained least squares estimation is investigated, and the alternating-direction multiplier method (ADMM) is used to solve the model. The convergence is proved under certain conditions. Finally, numerical simulations are performed and applied to workers' wage data from CPS85. The results show that the ADMM algorithm is very effective in solving high-dimensional partially linear models.

Keywords: partially linear model; B-spline interpolation; ADMM; variational inequality

MSC: 62J05,90C06,90C25,90C30

1. Introduction

With the rapid development of modern technology, many fields have generated high-dimensional data, such as in biological information, biomedicine, meteorology, geography, econometrics, machine learning, etc. The term "high-dimensional" refers to the fact that the number of variables in data is much larger than the number of samples. In practical situations, the actual structure of a model is often unknown. If only parametric or non-parametric regression models are used for statistical inference, the results will produce large biases and erroneous conclusions. Therefore, semi-parametric regression models came into being in the 1980s, and Engle first proposed semi-parametric regression models, which contain both parametric and non-parametric components. These are more widely used than parametric or non-parametric models. A semi-parametric regression model is a statistical model in which:

$$Y = g(X, \beta) + m(U) + \varepsilon, \quad (1)$$

where Y is a real-valued response variable, $\beta \in R^p$ is a p-dimensional unknown parameter vector, X is a d-dimensional covariate, and $g(\cdot, \cdot)$ is a known and measurable function. $U \in [0, 1]$ is a random variable, $m(\cdot)$ is a smooth unknown function defined on $[0, 1]$, and ε is a random error.

This paper focuses on high-dimensional semi-parametric regression models in which a partially linear model is used for the parametric part. A partially linear model was proposed by Engle [1] in 1986 when he studied weather and electricity problems. The response variables of the model had linear relationships with some covariates and nonparametric relationships with other covariates, so the partially linear model combined the advantages of the interpretability of linear models with the flexibility of non-parametric models. Partial linear models have been studied by many scholars, such as Heckman (1986) [2], Xu (2019) [3], Chen (2020) [4], Auerbach (2022) [5], etc., and they have achieved many results. Among them, Heckman (1986) [2] proposed a partially linear model with a smooth spline and obtained the consistency and asymptotic normality of the parameter estimation based on Bayesian estimation. Härdle (2000) [6] reviewed a series of studies on partially linear models. In the non-parametric part, the B-spline basis function method was used to estimate the unknown function. The B-spline basis function method is a global smoothing method, and its calculation accuracy and efficiency are relatively high. Numerous scholars have studied and achieved many results for high-dimensional data, such as those of Lasso [7–9], SCAD (smoothly clipped absolute deviation) [10–12], and MCP (minimax concave penalty) [13,14], and many scholars have also performed much research on high-dimensional partially linear models. Xie (2009) [10] studied SCAD-penalized regression in high-dimensional partially linear models by using polynomial regression splines to estimate the non-parametric part; Ni (2009) [15] proposed a double-penalty partially linear variable selection method that used smooth splines to estimate the non-parametric part. In the case of parameter dispersion, Chen (2012) [16] studied the variable selection problem for the contour-adaptive Elastic-Net for a partially linear model with high-dimensional covariates; Wang (2017) [17] studied constrained-contour least squares estimation based on contour Lagrange multiplier test statistics with linear constraints and gave the convergence speed and asymptotic normality of the least squares estimation.

Wang considered the following partially linear regression model (PLM):

$$Y = X^T \beta + B^T \gamma + \varepsilon, \tag{2}$$

where Y is a univariate response variable, $X = (X_1, \ldots, X_p)^T \in R^p$, and $Z \in R$ are explanatory variables. We denote $Y = (Y_1, \ldots, Y_n)^T$; $X = (X_1, \ldots, X_n)^T$; $\beta = (\beta_1, \ldots, \beta_p)^T$ is an unknown p-dimensional parameter vector; $\varepsilon = (\varepsilon_1, \ldots, \varepsilon_n)^T$. $B = B(Z) = (B_1(Z), \ldots, B_{m_n}(Z))^T$ is a set of B-spline basis functions of order r, and $\gamma = (\gamma_1, \ldots, \gamma_{m_n})^T$ is a spline coefficient vector.

Let $(Y_1; X_1^T; Z_1) \ldots (Y_n; X_n^T; Z_n)$ be an independent identically distributed sample of the size of the model. We denote $X_i = (X_{i1}, \ldots, X_{ip})^T$; model (2) can be approximated by:

$$Y_i = X_i^T \beta + B(Z_i)^T \gamma + \varepsilon_i. \tag{3}$$

From Equation (3), we can obtain $\varepsilon = Y - X\beta - B\gamma$. By using the least squares method to estimate the parameters β and γ, minimizing the error is equivalent to:

$$\min_{\beta, \gamma} \frac{1}{2} \|Y - X\beta - B\gamma\|^2. \tag{4}$$

In practice, the parameter estimates can also be improved by adding prior information about the regression parameters. The constraint condition is the profile Lagrange multiplier test statistic proposed by Wei and Wu (2008) [18]:

$$R\beta = d, \tag{5}$$

where R is a given $k \times p$ matrix whose rank is k, and d is a known k-dimensional vector.

The study in this paper is equivalent to the solution of the following optimization problem:

$$\begin{aligned} &\min_{\beta, \gamma} \tfrac{1}{2} \|Y - X\beta - B\gamma\|^2, \\ &s.t. R\beta = d. \end{aligned} \tag{6}$$

Wang (2017) [17] studied restricted profile least squares estimation, and a Lagrangian function was constructed based on linear constraints. The parameter estimation was performed by using the Lagrange multiplier method. The results showed that the algorithm was efficient when parameter information was available.

Our study considers the optimization problem in (6) by constructing an augmented Lagrangian function with linear constraints and using the alternating-direction method of multipliers (ADMM) to solve the model. The Lagrange multiplier update is a kind of ascending iteration, and its convergence can only be moderately accelerated. Therefore, the Lagrange multiplier method is more time-consuming. The augmented Lagrange multiplier method is a method that combines the Lagrange multiplier method and a penalty function method in one piece, so it is a simple and effective method. Hestenes [19] and Powell [20] first proposed the augmented Lagrangian function and multiplier method for constrained optimization in the late 1960s. The ADMM [21] is a classical algorithm for solving nonlinear problems that was proposed by Glowinski and Marroco in the 1970s. The ADMM is very suitable for convex optimization [22]. This algorithm has a large number of applications in different fields, such as regularized estimation [23], image processing [24], machine learning [25], optimal control [26], and resource allocation for wireless networks [27]. When the scale of a problem is relatively large, a distributed algorithm is faster. Considering the characteristics of the optimization problem in (6), it can be solved in blocks. This is suitable for the algorithmic framework of the ADMM, so this paper will use the ADMM to solve the high-dimensional partially linear model.

2. Introduction to the ADMM Algorithm

In this part, we summarize some useful content for the following discussion.

Firstly, we briefly review the basic knowledge of the ADMM. Our motivation is to apply the ADMM to solve the model in this paper. Let us start from a general convex minimization problem with a separable objective function and linear constraints:

$$\begin{aligned} \min\ & f(x) + g(z), \\ s.t.\ & Ax + Bz = c, \end{aligned} \tag{7}$$

where $x \in R^m$, $z \in R^n$, $A \in R^{p \times m}$, $B \in R^{p \times n}$, $c \in R^p$, $f: R^m \in R$, and $g: R^n \in R$. x and z are independent variables. The augmented Lagrangian function of the minimization problem is:

$$L_p(x,y,z) = f(x) + g(z) + y^{\mathrm{T}}(Ax + Bz - c) + \frac{p}{2}\|Ax + Bz - c\|_2^2, \tag{8}$$

where y is the Lagrange multiplier and $p > 0$ is a penalty parameter. The minimization problem can be solved with the augmented Lagrange multiplier method. With a given y^0, the iterative scheme of the augmented Lagrangian function for the minimization problem is:

$$\begin{cases} (x^{k+1}, z^{k+1}) := \arg\min\{L_p(x,y,z^k)\}, \\ y^{k+1} := y^k - p(Ax^{k+1} + Bz^{k+1} - c). \end{cases} \tag{9}$$

The iterative scheme is an application of the augmented Lagrangian function method for solving the above iterations, which require the simultaneous polarization of the variables x and z in each iteration. In addition, the ADMM algorithm decomposes the above iteration into two parts [28] and continuously minimizes the variables; it is expressed as follows:

$$\begin{cases} x^{k+1} := \arg\min\{L_p(x, y^k, z^k)\}, \\ z^{k+1} := \arg\min\{L_p(x^{k+1}, y, z^k)\}, \\ y^{k+1} := y^k - p(Ax^{k+1} + Bz^{k+1} - c). \end{cases} \tag{10}$$

The ADMM is widely used, and it is of interest that the subproblem generated by the ADMM must exist in the form of an analytical solution in each iteration.

3. Model and Algorithm

In this section, we will apply the ADMM algorithm to solve the minimization model in this paper and to derive the analytical solution form of each subproblem.

3.1. The High-Dimensional Partially Linear Model

For the optimization problem in (6), by using the augmented Lagrange multiplier method, the constrained programming problem is transformed into an unconstrained optimization problem, and the augmented Lagrangian function is:

$$\min L_\rho(\beta, \gamma, \lambda) = \frac{1}{2}\|Y - X\beta - B\gamma\|^2 + \langle \lambda, R\beta - d \rangle + \frac{\rho}{2}\|R\beta - d\|^2. \quad (11)$$

Using the alternating-direction method of multipliers (ADMM), its n-step iteration starts from a given (β^n, λ^n) with:

$$\begin{cases} \gamma^{n+1} = \arg\min_\gamma L_\rho(\beta^n, \gamma, \lambda^n), \\ \beta^{n+1} = \arg\min_\beta L_\rho(\beta, \gamma^{n+1}, \lambda^n), \\ \lambda^{n+1} = \lambda^n + \rho(R\beta^{n+1} - d). \end{cases} \quad (12)$$

We get the new iteration point at $(\gamma^{n+1}, \beta^{n+1}, \lambda^{n+1})$.

3.2. Solution of the ADMM for High-Dimensional Partially Linear Models

After a simple calculation, the γ-subproblem in Equation (11) can be written as the following equation:

$$\gamma^{n+1} = \arg\min_\gamma \{\frac{1}{2}\|Y - X\beta^n - B\gamma\|^2\}. \quad (13)$$

According to the above method, one can find the partial derivative of γ for any given β:

$$\frac{\partial L_\rho(\beta, \gamma, \lambda)}{\partial \gamma} = -B(Y - X\beta^n - B\gamma) = 0. \quad (14)$$

The analytical solution of γ can be obtained in the form of:

$$\gamma^{n+1} = (B^T B)^{-1} B^T (Y - X\beta^n). \quad (15)$$

For the analytical solution of β, the objective function can be solved by substituting γ into Equation (11):

$$\beta^{n+1} = \arg\min_\beta \{\frac{1}{2}\|Y - X\beta - B\gamma^{n+1}\|^2 + \langle \lambda^n, R\beta - d \rangle + \frac{\rho}{2}\|R\beta - d\|^2\}, \quad (16)$$

with the following partial derivatives for β:

$$\frac{\partial L_\rho(\beta, \gamma^{n+1}, \lambda^n)}{\partial \beta} = (XX^T + \rho RR^T)^{-1}(X^T(Y - B\gamma^{n+1}) + R^T(\rho d - \lambda^n)) = 0. \quad (17)$$

The solutions γ^{n+1}, β^{n+1}, and λ^{n+1} are solved by calculating:

$$\begin{cases} \gamma^{n+1} = (B^T B)^{-1} B^T (Y - X\beta^n), \\ \beta^{n+1} = (XX^T + \rho RR^T)^{-1}(X^T(Y - B\gamma^{n+1}) + R^T(\rho d - \lambda^n)), \\ \lambda^{n+1} = \lambda^n + \rho(R\beta^{n+1} - d). \end{cases} \quad (18)$$

3.3. Algorithmic Design of ADMM for Solving High-Dimensional Partially Linear Models

In summary, the iterative algorithm for solving high-dimensional partially linear models by using the ADMM can be described as follows.

Step 1. Input the variables X, Y, and B, and given the initial variables $(\beta^0, \gamma^0, \lambda^0)$, select the penalty parameter where $\rho > 0$;

Step 2. Input the iteration step $n = 1, 2, \ldots, N$;

Step 3. Update the parameters γ^{n+1}, β^{n+1}, and λ^{n+1} with Equation (18);

Step 4. Iterate through the loop, returning to step 3 until the termination conditions are met, and the algorithm is terminated;

Step 5. Output $(\beta^N, \gamma^N, \lambda^N)$ as the approximate solution $(\beta^*, \gamma^*, \lambda^*)$ of (6).

4. Convergence

In this section, we will use a variational inequality to prove the convergence of the algorithm. The Lagrange function of the model is given by:

$$L(\beta, \gamma, \lambda) = \frac{1}{2}\|Y - X\beta - B\gamma\|^2 + \langle \lambda, R\beta - d\rangle, \tag{19}$$

where λ is the Lagrange multiplier.

The solution of Equation (11) is equivalent to finding $(\gamma^*, \beta^*, \lambda^*) \in S$ such that:

$$\begin{cases} B^T X \beta^* + B^T B \gamma^* - B^T Y = 0, \\ (XX^T + \rho RR^T)^{-1}(X^T(Y - B\gamma^*) + R^T(\rho d - \lambda^*)) = 0, \\ R^T \beta^* - d = 0. \end{cases} \tag{20}$$

Let S^* satisfy Equation (19); then, we define $\omega^* = (\gamma^*, \beta^*, \lambda^*) \in S^*$. Equation (19) is equivalent to a variational problem. We find $(\gamma^*, \beta^*, \lambda^*) \in S^*$ such that the following variational inequality holds:

$$VI(S, F) : (\omega - \omega^*)F(\omega^*) \geq 0, \forall \omega \in S. \tag{21}$$

Here,

$$\omega = \begin{pmatrix} \gamma \\ \beta \\ \lambda \end{pmatrix}, F(\omega) = \begin{pmatrix} B^T X\beta + B^T B\gamma - B^T Y \\ (XX^T + \rho RR^T)^{-1}(X^T(Y - B\gamma) + R^T(\rho d - \lambda)) \\ R^T \beta - d. \end{pmatrix} \tag{22}$$

We need to use the positive definite matrix G:

$$G = \begin{pmatrix} \mu I_p - \hat{X}^T \hat{X} & 0 & 0 \\ 0 & \rho I_p & 0 \\ 0 & 0 & \frac{1}{\rho} I_p \end{pmatrix}, \tag{23}$$

where $\hat{X} = (X^T, \sqrt{\rho}R)^T$. For the positive definite matrix G, the following conditions are satisfied: $\mu > \tau(X^T X + \rho R^T R)$ and $\mu(\cdot)$ is the spectral radius of the matrix.

In order to establish the convergence of the algorithm, the $n+1$th iteration value of the algorithm is taken as a variational inequality problem. The following lemma can be obtained.

Lemma 1. *Let $\{\omega^n\}$ denote the sequence generated by the algorithm; then, for any $\omega' \in S$,*

$$(\omega' - \omega^{n+1})(F(\omega^{n+1}) + M(\beta^n - \beta^{n+1}) - G(\omega^n - \omega^{n+1})) \geq 0,$$

where,

$$M = \begin{pmatrix} -\rho R^T \\ \rho I_p \\ 0_p \end{pmatrix}.$$

Lemma 2. *Let $\{\omega^n\}$ denote the sequence generated by the algorithm; then, for any $\omega^* \in S^*$,*

$$(\omega^n - \omega^*)^T G(\omega^n - \omega^{n+1}) \geq (\omega^n - \omega^{n+1})^T G(\omega^n - \omega^{n+1}) - (\lambda^n - \lambda^{n+1})^T(\beta^n - \beta^{n+1}).$$

Lemma 3. *Let $\{\omega^n\}$ denote the sequence generated by the algorithm; then, for any $\omega^* \in S^*$,*

$$||\omega^{n+1} - \omega^*||_G^2 \leq ||\omega^n - \omega^*||_G^2 - ||\omega^n - \omega^{n+1}||_G^2$$

From Lemmas 1 and 2, it can be proved that the sequence $\{\omega^n\}$ generated by this algorithm shrinks to the solution set S^*. Lemma 3 shows that the sequence $\{\omega^n\}$ generated by the algorithm shrinks to the solution set S, and the following corollary can be obtained from Lemma 3.

Corollary 1. *Let the sequence be generated by the algorithm; then, we get:*
1. $\lim\limits_{k \to \infty} ||\omega^n - \omega^{n+1}||_G = 0$;
2. *The sequence $\{\omega^n\}$ is bounded;*
3. *For arbitrary $\omega^* \in S^*$, the sequence $\{||\omega^n - \omega^*||_G\}$ is non-increasing.*

Theorem 1. *Given any starting point $(\gamma^0, \beta^0, \lambda^0) \in S$, for any $\rho \geq 0$, $\mu > \tau(X^T X + \rho R^T R)$, the sequence $\{\omega^n = (\gamma^n, \beta^n, \lambda^n)\}$ is generated by the algorithm and converges to $\{\omega^\infty = (\gamma^\infty, \beta^\infty, \lambda^\infty)\}$, where $(\gamma^\infty, \beta^\infty, \lambda^\infty)$ is the solution of the model.*

Proof. From Property 1 of Corollary 3, we can get:

$$\begin{cases} \lim\limits_{k \to \infty} ||\gamma^n - \gamma^{n+1}|| = 0, \\ \lim\limits_{k \to \infty} ||\beta^n - \beta^{n+1}|| = 0, \\ \lim\limits_{k \to \infty} ||\lambda^n - \lambda^{n+1}|| = 0. \end{cases} \quad (24)$$

By Property 2 of Corollary 3, let $\omega^\infty = (\gamma^\infty, \beta^\infty, \lambda^\infty)$ be one of the clusters, and let the sequence $\{\omega^{n_j}\}$ converge to the sequence $\{\omega^\infty\}$, so we can obtain:

$$\begin{cases} \gamma^{n_j} \to \gamma^\infty, \\ \beta^{n_j} \to \beta^\infty, \\ \lambda^{n_j} \to \lambda^\infty, \end{cases} \quad (25)$$

and

$$\begin{cases} \lim\limits_{k \to \infty} ||\gamma^{n_j} - \gamma^{n_j+1}|| = 0, \\ \lim\limits_{k \to \infty} ||\beta^{n_j} - \beta^{n_j+1}|| = 0, \\ \lim\limits_{k \to \infty} ||\lambda^{n_j} - \lambda^{n_j+1}|| = 0. \end{cases} \quad (26)$$

It is proved below that the cluster ω^∞ satisfies the optimality condition (19). From Equations (18) and (29), for any $\omega' \in S$, we can obtain:

$$\lim\limits_{j \to \infty} (\omega' - \omega^{n_j}) F(\omega^{n_j}) \geq 0. \quad (27)$$

Then, from Equation (28), for any $\omega' \in S$, the above inequality is transformed into:

$$(\omega' - \omega^\infty) F(\omega^\infty) \geq 0. \quad (28)$$

Therefore, the cluster ω^∞ satisfies the optimality condition (19), i.e., $\omega^\infty \in S^*$. For any $n \geq 0$, by Property 3 of Corollary 3, we can obtain:

$$||\omega^{n+1} - \omega^\infty||_G^2 \leq ||\omega^n - \omega^\infty||_G^2. \quad (29)$$

Through the above proof, we can find that the sequence $\{\omega^n\}$ has a unique clustering point ω^∞. That is, the sequence $\{\omega^n\}$ converges to ω^∞ and has $(\gamma^\infty, \beta^\infty, \lambda^\infty)$ as the solution of the model. The proof is complete.

5. Simulation and Application

5.1. Parameter Settings

The estimation of a high-dimensional partially linear model is performed through a numerical simulation based on a dataset with a sample size of n generated by the model. The random error terms are $\varepsilon \sim N(0, \sigma^2)$, and X obeys the p-dimensional multivariate normal distribution, i.e., $X \sim N(0, \Sigma)$, where $\Sigma = 0.5^{|j-k|}$; j and k are the jth and kth components of the covariance, respectively. The variable Z obeys the uniform distribution of the interval $[0,1]$, i.e., $Z \sim U(0,1)$ and $g(z) = 3\cos(2\pi z)$. The parameter $\beta = (1, 2, 0.5, -1, 0, \ldots, 0)^T$ satisfies the constraint $\beta_5 = \ldots = \beta_p$. The estimation of the smooth function is performed by using cubic spline interpolation and three B-spline basis functions for the numerical simulation. The results are good.

5.2. Simulation Results

According to the above parameter settings, the algorithm proposed in this paper is used, and the specific results are shown in Table 1.

Table 1. Comparison of the mean square errors under different conditions.

n	p	σ	MSEC	MSEW	σ	MSEC	MSEW	σ	MSEC	MSEW
	9		0.0026	0.2853		0.0026	0.3057		0.0026	0.3975
	29		0.0025	0.7691		0.0026	1.0220		0.0031	1.5839
	49		0.002	1.1281		0.0026	1.5182		0.0033	2.6788
	69		0.0035	2.4141		0.0042	3.2338		0.0057	5.2201
100	89		0.0057	34.9406		0.0068	56.5306		0.0111	99.8811
	109		2.5194×10^{-13}	160.7625		3.9866×10^{-13}	126.0699		4.7814×10^{-13}	57.2586
	209		5.2491×10^{-15}	215.5829		5.6079×10^{-15}	247.2301		6.2244×10^{-15}	313.6789
	509		1.7694×10^{-15}	867.2514		1.7710×10^{-15}	789.7276		1.9649×10^{-15}	636.5492
	1009		1.2117×10^{-15}	446.7470		1.3816×10^{-15}	434.2037		1.4950×10^{-15}	429.8142
	9	0.5	0.0025	0.1356	1	0.0025	0.1773	2	0.0025	0.2733
	49		0.0025	0.0025		0.0026	0.8108		0.0030	1.5062
	89		0.0025	0.9857		0.0028	1.4725		0.0032	2.6198
	129		0.0029	1.6449		0.0032	2.1437		0.0042	3.4911
200	169		0.0039	3.1227		0.0052	4.6591		0.0084	8.3544
	209		1.0400e-12	6.8265		7.7886×10^{-13}	16.3884		8.6313×10^{-13}	40.1867
	409		4.2441×10^{-15}	221.4869		4.3281×10^{-15}	228.5344		5.2164×10^{-15}	243.1755
	509		2.2511×10^{-15}	266.5785		2.3479×10^{-15}	284.4385		2.6637×10^{-15}	324.3384
	1009		1.8520×10^{-15}	369.4391		1.7060×10^{-15}	526.3515		1.7332×10^{-15}	843.3223

The simulation's effect is expressed by the mean square error (MSE) of the parameter estimation, MSE = $\|\hat{\beta} - \beta\|^2$, where the sample sizes are $n = 100, 200$ and the dimensions are $p = 9, 29, 49, 69, 89, 109, 129, 169, 209, 509, 1009$. The dimensions are taken from small to large by determining the value of the sample size. This was done, on the one hand, to compare with the results of Wang's [17] study and, on the other hand, to study the simulation's effect in the case of high dimensions ($p \gg n$). The effect of Wang's study is expressed by the MSEW, and the effect of this paper is expressed by the MSEC.

According to the results in Table 1, the mean square error for this paper is slightly better than that of Wang's study in the low-dimensional case, and the mean square error for this paper is slightly lower than that of Wang's. The results are better in the high-dimensional case because the fitting effect of the augmented Lagrange multiplier method is better than that of the Lagrange multiplier method for high-dimensional data. For fixed values of p, the mean square error becomes larger with increasing σ, and the stability of the parameter estimation also becomes worse with the increase in σ. For fixed values of σ, the mean square error decreases with the increase in the dimensions p of the parameter. The method studied in this paper works better for parameter estimation in high-dimensional cases, and the higher the dimensionality, the better the stability of the parameter estimation.

A line plot of the mean square error for different variances was constructed with a sample size of 100 in order to specifically express the effects of this study (Figures 1–3) and to provide a comparison with Wang's results (Figures 4–6).

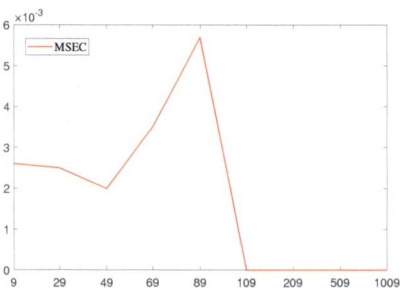

Figure 1. Folding line plot of the mean square error for a variance of 0.5.

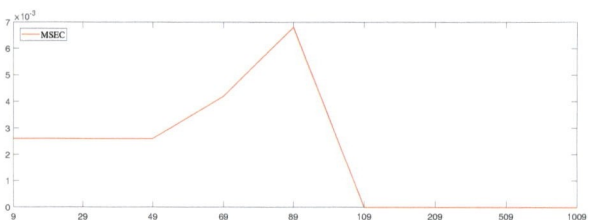

Figure 2. Folding line plot of the mean square error for a variance of 1.

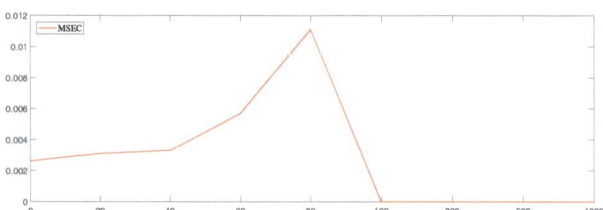

Figure 3. Folding line plot of the mean square error for a variance of 2.

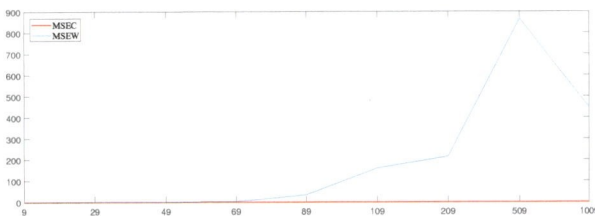

Figure 4. Folding line plot of the compared mean square error for a variance of 0.5.

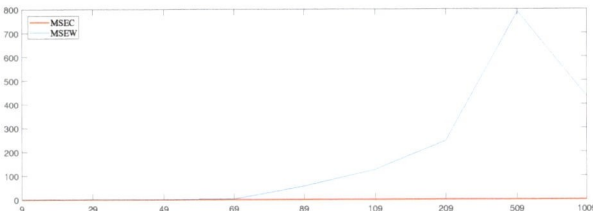

Figure 5. Folding line plot of the compared mean square error for a variance of 1.

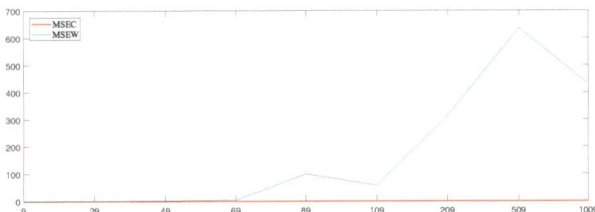

Figure 6. Folding line plot of the compared mean square error for a variance of 2.

Line plots of the mean square errors for different variances were constructed with a sample size of 200 to specifically express the effects of this study (Figures 7–9) and for a comparison with Wang's results (Figures 10–12).

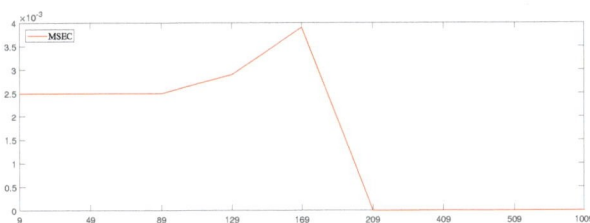

Figure 7. Folding line plot of the mean square error for a variance of 0.5.

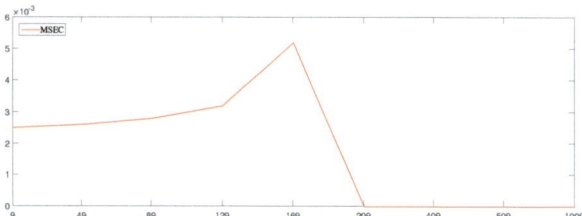

Figure 8. Folding line plot of the mean square error for a variance of 1.

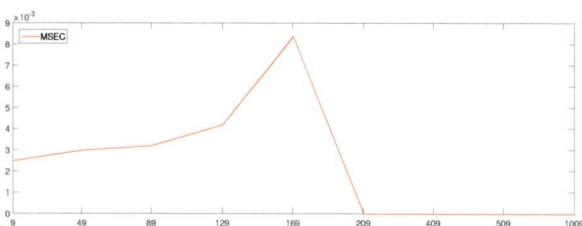

Figure 9. Folding line plot of the mean square error for a variance of 2.

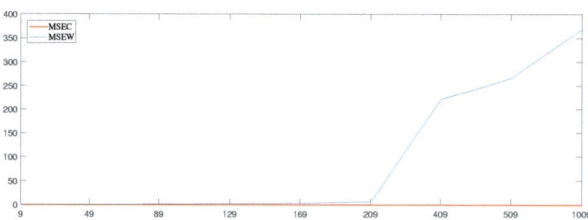

Figure 10. Folding line plot of the compared mean square error for a variance of 0.5.

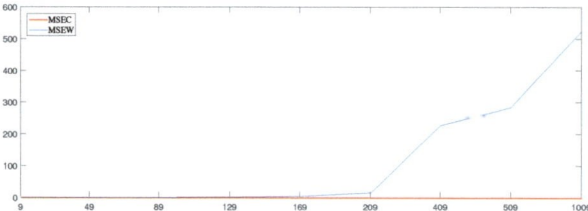

Figure 11. Folding line plot of the compared mean square error for a variance of 1.

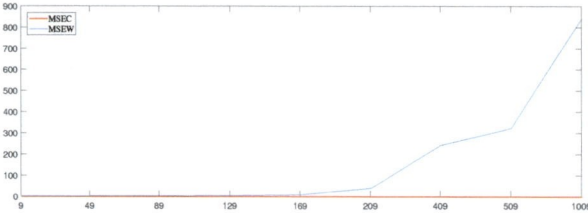

Figure 12. Folding line plot of the compared mean square error for a variance of 2.

In these figures, it can be seen that the mean square error (MSEC) of the method studied in this paper is very small and is very close to zero in high dimensions. Moreover, the mean square error of this method is smaller than that of Wang's method. Therefore, the method studied in this paper is more applicable in the case of high dimensions.

5.3. Application: Workers' Wage Data Analysis

In order to test the algorithm proposed in this paper, we applied the algorithm to the practical problem of the analysis of workers' wage data. The workers' wage data were given by the 1985 Current Population Survey (CPS85) [29]. These data came from reality and are real. Moreover, the indicators of these data contained both quantitative data and classified data, so they were representative. In addition, the data were studied by other authors in the literature to facilitate comparison [30]. The data consisted of 534 samples of CPS85 personnel with 11 variables, which included wages and other characteristics of workers, such as gender, years of education, race, sex, marital status, years of work experience, occupational status, area of residence, and union membership. The wage level did not necessarily have a linear relationship with the years of work experience, so the importance of other variables for wages was mainly considered. The model was built as follows:

$$Y_i = \sum_{j=1}^{10} X_{ij}\beta_j + m(U_i) + \varepsilon_i, \tag{30}$$

where Y_i is the wage of the ith worker, U_i is the number of years of experience of the ith worker, X_{ij} is the jth variable of the ith worker, and $\varepsilon_i \sim N(0, \sigma^2)$.

We describe the use of the method proposed in this paper to study the important factors that affect wages in this section. In order to reduce the absolute differences between wages, avoid the influence of individual extreme values, and satisfy the assumptions of the linear model as much as possible, a logarithmic transformation was required for the variable of wages.

During the experiment, it was necessary to select training samples and test samples. If the proportion of training samples was large, the model may have been closer to a model trained with all samples. However, if the proportion of test samples was small, the evaluation results would not be accurate enough. If the proportion of test samples was large, that could lead to a large difference between the evaluation model and the previous one, thus reducing the authenticity of the evaluation. In all samples, the division ratio for the training samples and test samples was typically 7:3 to 8:2. For large amounts of data, ratios of 9:1 or even 99:1 can be used. Based on the sample size of CPS85, 75 percent of the samples were selected as training samples, and the method in this paper was used for parameter estimation training. The remaining 25 percent of the samples were used as test samples to predict the wages of workers, and the predicted values were expressed in $\hat{y}_i$. The test samples were used to evaluate the prediction ability of the model, and the prediction effect was evaluated with the median absolute error (MAE) and the standard error (SE).

The MAE attenuates the effects of outliers. The loss is calculated by taking the median of all absolute differences between the real and the predicted value.

$$\text{MAE} = medain\{|y_1 - \hat{y}_1|, |y_2 - \hat{y}_2|, \cdots, |y_n - \hat{y}_n|\}. \tag{31}$$

The SE is a measure of the precision of data and reflects the degree of dispersion of a whole sample from the sample's mean.

$$\text{SE} = \sqrt{\frac{\sum (y_i - \hat{y}_i)^2}{n}}. \tag{32}$$

The smaller the SE is, the greater the reliability of the prediction will be; otherwise, the reliability of the prediction is small.

The results are shown in Table 2.

Table 2. The MAE and SE of predictions of workers' wages.

Variables	Variable Description	MAE	SE
edu	Number of years of education	1.9777	0.0429
race	NW=1, W=0	0.7491	0.0861
sex	F=1, M=0	0.7526	0.0860
hispanic	Hisp=1, NH=0	0.7491	0.0861
south	S=1, NS=0	0.7491	0.0861
married	Married=1, Single=0	0.7521	0.0858
union	Union=1, Not=0	0.7491	0.0860
age	Age	1.9885	0.0517
sector	Clerical=1, Const=1, Manag=1, Manuf=1 Prof=1, Sales=1, Service=1, Other=0	0.7569	0.0857

As can be seen from the results in Table 2, the value of the MAE was small, indicating that the loss between the predicted and actual values of workers' wages was lower. The values of the SE were all below 0.09, indicating that the prediction was reliable. In short, the MAE was low and the SE was small, so the parameter estimation method in this paper is relatively efficient.

6. Conclusions

The research in this paper considered a partially linear model with a restricted profile and used the least squares method to estimate the parameters with the purpose of minimizing the error. By constructing an augmented Lagrangian function under linear constraint conditions, the constrained optimization problem was transformed into an unconstrained optimization problem. The model was solved with the ADMM. The ADMM algorithm has the advantage that some large global problems can be solved by decomposing them into several smaller, more easily solvable local subproblems and then coordinating the solutions of the resulting subproblems to obtain the solution of the large global problem. The convergence of the algorithm was obtained by using the method of variational inequality. Through numerical simulations, the results showed that the method of this paper is suitable for parameter estimation in high-dimensional cases. Finally, this paper applied the algorithm to workers' wage data from CPS85 and analyzed the important factors that affected wages.

In this paper, we used the ADMM algorithm to solve a high-dimensional partially linear model, and the effect was very good. The model in this paper is mainly for convex optimization problems. It can be used to solve other optimization problems, such as non-concave penalty optimization SCAD or MCP. This is a subject that will be studied further.

Author Contributions: Conceptualization, A.F. and X.C.; Methodology, A.F. and X.C.; Software, X.C.; Validation, Y.S. and J.F.; Formal analysis, X.C.; Resources, A.F.; Data curation, J.F.; Writing—original draft, X.C.; Writing—review & editing, A.F. and Y.S.; Visualization, X.C.; Supervision, Y.S.; Project administration, A.F. All authors have read and agreed to the published version of the manuscript.

Funding: The research was supported by the National Natural Science Foundation of China (Nos. 12071112, 11971149, 12101195).

Data Availability Statement: Not applicable.

Acknowledgments: We sincerely thank the three anonymous reviewers for their insightful comments, which greatly improved the manuscript.

Conflicts of Interest: The authors declare no conflicts of interest.

References

1. Engle, R.F.; Granger, C.W.J.; Rice, J.; Weiss, A. Semiparametric estimates of the relation between weather and electricity sales. *J. Am. Stat. Assoc.* **1986**, *81*, 310–320. [CrossRef]

2. Heckman, N.E. Spline smoothing in a partly linear model. *J. R. Stat. Soc. Ser. (Methodol.)* **1986**, *48*, 244–248. [CrossRef]
3. Xu, H.X.; Chen, Z.L.; Wang, J.F.; Fan, G.L. Quantile regression and variable selection for partially linear model with randomly truncated data. *Stat. Pap.* **2019**, *60*, 1137–1160. [CrossRef]
4. Chen, W. Polynomial-based smoothing estimation for a semiparametric accelerated failure time partial linear model. *Open Access Libr. J.* **2020**, *7*, 1. [CrossRef]
5. Auerbach, E. Identification and estimation of a partially linear regression model using network data. *Econometrica* **2022**, *90*, 347–365. [CrossRef]
6. Härdle, W.; Liang, H.; Gao, J. *Partially Linear Models*; Springer Science & Business Media: Berlin/Heidelberg, Germany, 2000.
7. Tibshirani, R. Regression shrinkage and selection via the lasso. *J. R. Stat. Soc. Ser. (Methodol.)* **1996**, *58*, 267–288. [CrossRef]
8. Ranstam, J.; Cook, J.A. LASSO regression. *J. Br. Surg.* **2018**, *105*, 1348. [CrossRef]
9. Chetverikov, D.; Liao, Z.; Chernozhukov, V. On cross-validated lasso in high dimensions. *Ann. Stat.* **2021**, *49*, 1300–1317. [CrossRef]
10. Xie, H.; Huang, J. SCAD-penalized regression in high-dimensional partially linear models. *Ann. Stat.* **2009**, *37*, 673–696. [CrossRef]
11. Zeng, L.; Xie, J. Group variable selection via SCAD-L 2. *Statistics* **2014**, *48*, 49–66. [CrossRef]
12. Gao, L.; Li, X.; Bi, D.; Xie, Y. Robust Compressed Sensing based on Correntropy and Smoothly Clipped Absolute Deviation Penalty. In Proceedings of the 2020 IEEE 3rd International Conference on Information Communication and Signal Processing (ICICSP), Shanghai, China, 12–15 September 2020; IEEE: Piscataway, NJ, USA, 2020; pp. 269–273.
13. Zhang, C.H. Nearly unbiased variable selection under minimax concave penalty. *Ann. Stat.* **2010**, *38*, 894–942. [CrossRef] [PubMed]
14. Breheny, P.; Huang, J. Penalized methods for bi-level variable selection. *Stat. Its Interface* **2009**, *2*, 369. [CrossRef] [PubMed]
15. Ni, X.; Zhang, H.H.; Zhang, D. Automatic model selection for partially linear models. *J. Multivar. Anal.* **2009**, *100*, 2100–2111. [CrossRef] [PubMed]
16. Chen, B.; Yu, Y.; Zou, H.; Liang, H. Profiled adaptive Elastic-Net procedure for partially linear models with high-dimensional covariates. *J. Stat. Plan. Inference* **2012**, *142*, 1733–1745. [CrossRef]
17. Wang, X.; Zhao, S.; Wang, M. Restricted profile estimation for partially linear models with large-dimensional covariates. *Stat. Probab. Lett.* **2017**, *128*, 71–76. [CrossRef]
18. Wei, C.H.; Wu, X.Z. Profile Lagrange multiplier test for partially linear varying-coefficient regression models. *J. Syst. Sci. Math. Sci.* **2008**, *28*, 416.
19. Hestenes, M.R. Multiplier and gradient methods. *J. Optim. Theory Appl.* **1969**, *4*, 303–320. [CrossRef]
20. Powell, M.J.D. A method for nonlinear constraints in minimization problems. *Optimization* **1969**, *1*, 283–298.
21. Glowinski, R.; Marroco, A. Sur l'approximation, par éléments finis d'ordre un, et la résolution, par pénalisation-dualité d'une classe de problèmes de Dirichlet non linéaires. Revue française d'automatique, informatique, recherche opérationnelle. *Anal. Numer.* **1975**, *9*, 41–76.
22. Boyd, S.; Parikh, N.; Chu, E.; Eckstein, J. Distributed optimization and statistical learning via the alternating direction method of multipliers. *Found. Trends® Mach. Learn.* **2011**, *3*, 1–122.
23. Wahlberg, B.; Boyd, S.; Annergren, M.; Wang, Y. An ADMM algorithm for a class of total variation regularized estimation problems. *IFAC Proc. Vol.* **2012**, *45*, 83–88. [CrossRef]
24. Yang, Y.; Sun, J.; Li, H.; Xu, Z. ADMM-CSNet: A deep learning approach for image compressive sensing. *IEEE Trans. Pattern Anal. Mach. Intell.* **2018**, *42*, 521–538. [CrossRef] [PubMed]
25. Forero, P.A.; Cano, A.; Giannakis, G.B. Consensus-Based Distributed Support Vector Machines. *J. Mach. Learn. Res.* **2010**, *11*, 1663–707.
26. Glowinski, R.; Song, Y.; Yuan, X.; Yue, H. Application of the Alternating Direction Method of Multipliers to Control Constrained Parabolic Optimal Control Problems and Beyond. *Ann. Appl. Math.* **2022**, *38*, 115–158. [CrossRef]
27. Joshi, S.; Codreanu, M.; Latva-aho, M. Distributed SINR balancing for MISO downlink systems via the alternating direction method of multipliers. In Proceedings of the 2013 11th International Symposium and Workshops on Modeling and Optimization in Mobile, Ad Hoc and Wireless Networks (WiOpt), Tsukuba, Japan, 13–17 May 2013; IEEE: Piscataway, NJ, USA, 2013; pp. 318–325.
28. Gabay, D.; Mercier, B. A dual algorithm for the solution of nonlinear variational problems via finite element approximation. *Comput. Math. Appl.* **1976**, *2*, 17–40. [CrossRef]
29. Berndt, E.R. *The Practice of Econometrics: Classic and Contemporary*; Addison-Wesley Publishing Company: Reading, MA, USA, 1991.
30. Wang, X.; Wang, M. Adaptive group bridge estimation for high-dimensional partially linear models. *J. Inequalities Appl.* **2017**, *2017*, 1–18.

Article

A Distributed Blocking Flowshop Scheduling with Setup Times Using Multi-Factory Collaboration Iterated Greedy Algorithm

Chenyao Zhang [1], Yuyan Han [1,*], Yuting Wang [1,*], Junqing Li [2] and Kaizhou Gao [3]

[1] School of Computer Science, Liaocheng University, Liaocheng 252059, China
[2] School of Computer Science, Shandong Normal University, Jinan 252000, China
[3] Macau Institute of Systems Engineering, Macau University of Science and Technology, Macau 999078, China
* Correspondence: hanyuyan@lcu-cs.com (Y.H.); wangyuting@lcu-cs.com (Y.W.); Tel.: +86-188-6497-4734 (Y.H.); +86-156-6635-1136 (Y.W.)

Abstract: As multi-factory production models are more widespread in modern manufacturing systems, a distributed blocking flowshop scheduling problem (DBFSP) is studied in which no buffer between adjacent machines and setup time constraints are considered. To address the above problem, a mixed integer linear programming (MILP) model is first constructed, and its correctness is verified. Then, an iterated greedy-algorithm-blending multi-factory collaboration mechanism (mIG) is presented to optimize the makespan criterion. In the mIG algorithm, a rapid evaluation method is designed to reduce the time complexity, and two different iterative processes are selected by a certain probability. In addition, collaborative interactions between cross-factory and inner-factory are considered to further improve the exploitation and exploration of mIG. Finally, the 270 tests showed that the average makespan and RPI values of mIG are 1.93% and 78.35% better than the five comparison algorithms on average, respectively. Therefore, mIG is more suitable to solve the studied DBFSP_SDST.

Keywords: blocking; iterated greedy algorithm; distributed flowshop scheduling; multi-factory collaborative strategy; makespan

MSC: 93B28

Citation: Zhang, C.; Han, Y.; Wang, Y.; Li, J.; Gao, K. A Distributed Blocking Flowshop Scheduling with Setup Times Using Multi-Factory Collaboration Iterated Greedy Algorithm. *Mathematics* **2023**, *11*, 581. https://doi.org/10.3390/math11030581

Academic Editor: Ioannis G. Tsoulos

Received: 15 December 2022
Revised: 19 January 2023
Accepted: 19 January 2023
Published: 22 January 2023

Copyright: © 2023 by the authors. Licensee MDPI, Basel, Switzerland. This article is an open access article distributed under the terms and conditions of the Creative Commons Attribution (CC BY) license (https://creativecommons.org/licenses/by/4.0/).

1. Introduction

Industrial intellectualization and informatization are the frontier trends of manufacturing development. Manufacturing is the mainstay of the real economy and the lifeblood of the national economy, and its development is an essential reflection of a country's comprehensive national power. Smart manufacturing is the main research content of the manufacturing system at this stage. In the manufacturing industry, the flowshop scheduling problem (FSP) has been a popular topic of research and is of great practical importance. In FSP, jobs are processed on a series of machines according to a fixed process flow. The ultimate goal is to find the optimal scheduling sequence with optimal value(s) of the single (multiple) objective function(s). As we all know, in the context of globalization, the collaborative production mode between companies is becoming more and more common. The traditional centralized production methods are no longer able to meet market demands. Thus, the centralized manufacturing model is gradually shifted to a distributed manufacturing model [1], which can break geographical restrictions and make full use of the resources of multiple enterprises or factories to achieve a rational allocation, optimal combination, and sharing of resources [2]. Due to the above advantages of the distributed model, researchers have applied the distribution constraint to FSP and proposed the distributed permutation flowshop scheduling problem (DPFSP).

Many works on the DPFSP have been done. Naderi and Ruiz first constructed a MILP model and adopted heuristic of construction, and a variable neighborhood descent method to address this problem [3]. Liu and Gao presented a hybrid variable neighborhood search by combining with the electromagnetism mechanism to optimize the makespan criterion [4]. Since then, a number of constructive algorithms have emerged, i.e., the improved variable neighborhood descent (VND) algorithm [5], the taboo search (TS) algorithm [6], the estimation distribution algorithm (EDA) [7], the scatter search (SS) algorithms [8], and the bounded search iterated greedy (BSIG) algorithm [9]. In addition, Komaki and Malakooti [10] presented a variable neighborhood search (VNS) to solve the DPFSP with a no-wait constraint. In recent years, new scheduling algorithms, i.e., two stage iterated greedy algorithms containing different local search operators [11] and a cooperative co-evolutionary algorithm (CCEA) [12] have been developed to optimize DPFSP and successfully applied to the distributed robotic scheduling problem [13]. To optimize the total flowtime value of DPFSP, Fernandez-Viagas et al. discussed some properties of DPFSP and proposed eighteen construction heuristics to obtain a solution with high quality [14].

Recently, researchers have also taken sequence-dependent setup times (SDSTs) into account in DPFSP, called DPFSP_SDST, and have done some work on DPFSP_SDST. To address this problem, an IG with restart strategy (IGR) is presented [15]. The experimental results have demonstrated that IGR has the best performance among all the compared algorithms, i.e., chemical reaction optimization, differential evolution, evolutionary algorithm, etc. Han et al. designed an iterated greedy (NIG) algorithm that includes swapping of single jobs and job blocks [16]. Furthermore, it shows better performance compared to advanced algorithms. Li et al. also extended the DPFSP by considering a heterogeneous machine with unrelated parallel (forming DHHFSP_SDST) [17]. Next, to further design a good algorithm, the three heuristics based on problem specifics and a discrete artificial bee colony (DABC) algorithm were employed to solve DPFSP_SDST [18]. The study in [19] proposed two mathematical models of DPFSP_SDST, i.e., constraint planning (CP) and MILP. The authors also presented an evolution strategy algorithm based on a self-adaptive mechanism to quickly provide the quality of solutions. In [20], the authors considered DPFSP_SDST with assembly constraints and presented a hyper-heuristic algorithm based on genetic programming.

The above scheduling problems assume that the buffers are infinite between any adjacent machines. However, due to cost constraints, temporary buffers may not be allowed between any adjacent machines. The current machine must be blocked with a job until the next machine is free. In this case, FSP with no buffer is transformed into a blocking flowshop scheduling problem (BFSP). Thus, our article simultaneously considers the above blocking, SDST and distributed constraints and forms a distributed flowshop scheduling problem based on blocking and sequence-dependent setup times (DBFSP_SDST).

DPFSP with more than two machines has been evidenced in the literature [12] as an NP-hard problem. However, DBFSP_SDST, as an extension of DPFSP, adds blocking and sequence-dependent setup time constraints that are more complex than the permutation flowshop scheduling problem (PFSP). This is because, (1) from a distributed perspective, PFSP is a single-factory problem. One issue that needs to be solved is how to generate the optimal scheduling sequence. However, when it comes to DBFSP_SDST, the following two sub-issues must be taken into account. One is to assign the job to factories in a reasonable way, and the other is to arrange the job sequence for each factory [21,22]. (2) The DBFSP_SDST simultaneously considers blocking and SDST constraints in a distributed manufacturing environment in addition to the constraints listed in PFSP.

Regarding DBFSP, Companys and Ribas initially studied this problem and presented ten constructive heuristics based on typical heuristic rules [21]. Ying and Li constructed a MILP model of DBFSP and developed different hybrid IG algorithms [23]. Zhang et al. designed a discrete differential evolution (DDE) method based on problem features to optimize two different mathematical models [24]. Shao et al. employed a fruit fly optimization algorithm incorporating constructive heuristic initialization and an enhanced local search strategy [25]. Next, a mutation strategy combining crossover and insertion operators is employed to obtain a good solution [26]. Recently, Han et al. considered SDST and blocking constraints in DPFSP and developed a variable IG (VNIG) algorithm to optimize energy cost [27].

In the present study, the iterated greedy algorithm (IGA) and its modifications have been successfully applied in many discrete scheduling problems. Ruiz and Stützle proposed IGA to address FSP with the makespan criterion for the first time [28]. Next, Lin et al. modified the IGA by improving initialization, local search, and destruction and reconstruction strategies to optimize DPFSP [29]. Pan and Ruiz proposed an effective IG to solve the mixed no-idle FSP [30]. The study in [31] presented an IG based on a reference (IRG) algorithm to effectively solve no-idle DFSP. Huang et al. designed an enhanced IGA to optimize the assembly DPFSP with total flowtime [32]. Mao et al. presented a multi-stage IGA to address DPFSP with a preventive maintenance constraint [33]. For the scheduling problems with the blocking constraint, IGA also shows superiority. Ribas et al. developed an efficient IGA for optimizing the blocking parallel flowshop scheduling problem with a total tardiness criterion [34]. Qin et al. considered an IG algorithm based on double-level mutation (IGDLM) in solving a hybrid BFSP [35]. For the DBFSP with makespan and total flowtime criteria, Chen et al. used some constructive heuristics in the IGA [36] and a population-based IG [21], respectively, to minimize the above two objectives. In addition, Öztop et al. employed four different IG algorithms for the hybrid flowshop scheduling problem to optimize the objective of total flowtime [37].

From the analysis above, it is found that (1) unlike other population-based algorithms, the iterated greedy algorithm (IGA) is an efficient meta-heuristic algorithm with a simple framework that can be coded and replicated easily. (2) Among the intelligence algorithms for DPFSP discussed above, the iterated greedy algorithm (IGA) exhibits advanced performance. The advantages of the IG algorithm are attributed to the simplicity of the algorithm framework, with few parameters, ease of integration, and good reinforcement and local convergence performance. For the DBFSP_SDST, no relevant research has attempted to solve this problem by using improved IGA. Therefore, to make the IGA more appropriate for DBFSP_SDST, this article has made some adjustments according to the problem characteristics and designed a multi-factory collaborative iterated greedy algorithm.

Our main innovations are that (1) a MILP of DBFSP_SDST with makespan is constructed, and the Gurobi solver is adopted to verify the correctness of this model. (2) According to the characteristics of the problem, a new refresh acceleration calculation method based on job insertion is designed to speed up the calculation of the objective, thereby reducing the time complexity of the algorithm. (3) To enrich the diversity of solutions, *iterative process* I and *iterative process* II strategies are selected by a certain probability. (4) A collaborative strategy between cross-factory and inner-factory is presented.

The remaining parts are listed as follows. Section 2 formulates a MILP model of DBFSP-SDST. Section 3 states the specific details of the mIG algorithm. Experimental results and statistical analyses are performed in Section 4. Section 5 summarizes the research on the problem, algorithm, and future directions of research.

2. Problem-Specific Characteristics

The DBFSP_SDST considered in this article can be characterized as follows. Assume that $F(F > 2)$ identical factories exist. For each factory, J jobs have been processed on M machines. All factories should meet the restrictions in the MILP. The constraints are as follows: (1) A job has been processed continuously in only one factory. (2) Each job should be processed on one machine at a time according to the scheduled order. (3) Each machine can process only a job at a time. (4) No buffer exists between adjacent machines. The current machine must be blocked with a job until the next machine is free. (5) On each machine, the sequence-dependent setup time is taken into account. In addition, the first job on the machine needs to be set with an initial setup time. (6) Jobs cannot be interrupted during processing. Based on the above constraints, the optimization objective of DBFSP_SDST is makespan (unit: seconds).

2.1. Mathematical Model

Notations:
F Number of factories.
J Number of jobs.
M Number of machines in each factory.
j, j' Index of jobs, $j, j' \in \{0, 1, \cdots, J\}$, where 0 denotes a dummy job that starts and ends at each factory.
m Index of machines.
$p_{j,m}$ Processing time of job j on machine m.
$s_{j,j',m}$ Setup time of adjacent job j and job j' on machine m. $s_{0,j,m}$ is a predetermined value when j is the initial job on machine m.
h A positive large number.
Decision Variables:
$C_{j,m}$ Completion time of job j on machine m.
$D_{j,m}$ Departure time of job j on machine m.
$x_{j,j'}$ A decision variable using binary coding, 1 if job j' is a direct successor of job j, 0 otherwise.
Objective:

$$Minimize\ C_{max} \tag{1}$$

Constraints:

$$\sum_{j'=0, j' \neq j}^{J} x_{j,j'} = 1, \forall j \in \{1, 2, \cdots, J\} \tag{2}$$

$$\sum_{j=0, j \neq j'}^{J} x_{j,j'} = 1, \forall j' \in \{1, 2, \cdots, J\} \tag{3}$$

$$\sum_{j'=1}^{J} x_{0,j'} \leq F \tag{4}$$

$$\sum_{j=1}^{J} x_{j,0} \leq F \tag{5}$$

$$\sum_{j'=1}^{J} x_{0,j'} = \sum_{j=1}^{J} x_{j,0} \tag{6}$$

$$D_{j,m} \geq C_{j,m}, \forall j \in \{1, 2, \cdots, J\}, \forall m \in \{1, 2, \cdots, M\} \tag{7}$$

$$C_{j,m} - p_{j,m} = D_{j,m-1}, \forall j \in \{1, 2, \cdots, J\}, \forall m \in \{1, 2, \cdots, M\} \tag{8}$$

$$C_{j',m} - p_{j',m} \geq D_{j,m} + s_{j,j',m} + (x_{j,j'} - 1) \cdot h, \forall j, j' \in \{1, 2, \cdots, J\}, j \neq j', \forall m \in \{1, 2, \cdots, M\} \tag{9}$$

$$C_{j,m} - p_{j,m} \geq s_{0,j,m} + (x_{0,j} - 1) \cdot h, \forall j \in \{1, 2, \cdots, J\}, \forall m\{1, 2, \cdots, M\} \tag{10}$$

$$C_{max} \geq c_{j,M}, \forall j \in \{1, 2, \cdots, J\} \tag{11}$$

Equation (1) is the makespan objective. Constraints (2) and (3) ensure that each job in the scheduling sequence can only have one immediate predecessor and successor, respectively. Constraints (4) and (5) assure that the dummy job has an immediate successor and predecessor, respectively. The dummy job must have an equal number of immediate predecessors and successors, which is assured by Constraint (6). Each job on each machine must have a departure time that is equal to or more than its completion time, as required by Constraint (7). According to Constraint (8), the departure time of each job from the previous machine is equal to the time that started processing on the current machine. Constraint (9) is that the start time of job j' on machine m is larger than the sum of the departure time of job j on machine m and the setup time $s_{j,j',m}$. Constraint (10) considers the initial setup

2.2. Example Instance

The described problem is clearly reflected by considering the example having five jobs ($J = 5$), two machines ($M = 2$), and two factories ($F = 2$). Table 1 gives the processing times for the five jobs, and the SDSTs are shown in Table 2. Processing time and SDST are in seconds. One possible solution is denoted as: $x_{0,1} = 1, x_{1,4} = 1, x_{4,0} = 1, x_{0,5} = 1, x_{5,3} = 1, x_{3,2} = 1, x_{2,0} = 1$; the rest decision variables are equal to 0. The solution corresponds to a sequence {0, 1, 4, 0, 5, 3, 2, 0}, where the dummy job 0 divides it into two sequences {1, 4} and {5, 3, 2}. It means that factory 1 processes jobs 1 and 4, and factory 2 processes jobs 5, 3, and 2. The makespan is 57, and the scheduling Gantt chart as shown in Figure 1.

Table 1. Processing times $p_{j,m}$ of jobs.

$p_{j,m}$	J_1	J_2	J_3	J_4	J_5
M_1	11	3	11	12	9
M_2	25	3	13	5	17

Table 2. The SDSTs $s_{j,j',1}$ and $s_{j,j',2}$ of jobs.

$s_{j,j',1}$	J_1	J_2	J_3	J_4	J_5	$s_{j,j',2}$	J_1	J_2	J_3	J_4	J_5
	7	14	6	21	5		24	1	22	12	10
J_1	-	11	16	10	20	J_1	-	13	18	3	20
J_2	12	-	12	9	23	J_2	8	-	20	19	1
J_3	0	5	-	23	16	J_3	16	3	-	18	23
J_4	4	3	11	-	0	J_4	20	22	15	-	17
J_5	15	23	6	2	-	J_5	9	13	7	5	-

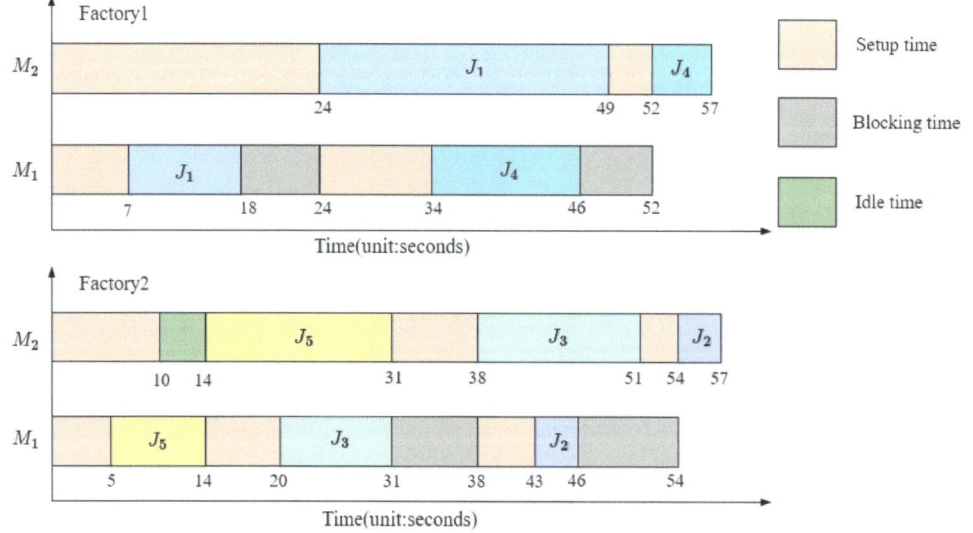

Figure 1. The Gantt chart of the example instance.

2.3. Improved Rapid Evaluation Criteria

A type of acceleration method inspired by Taillard [38] was proposed to save computational effort by combining the characteristics of the problem under study. In the rapid evaluation process, forward and backward calculation methods are adopted. The forward calculation is as follows. (1) Compute the leave time of the first job on the first machine, the second machine, and up to the last machine, respectively. (2) Similarly, the departure times on each machine for the second job, the third job, and until the last job are calculated. See Figure 2a. The backward calculation is as follows. (1) Calculate the departure time of the last job on the last machine, on the penultimate machine, and up to the first machine, respectively. (2) Similarly, the departure times on each machine for the penultimate job, the antepenultimate job, and up to the first job are calculated. See Figure 2b.

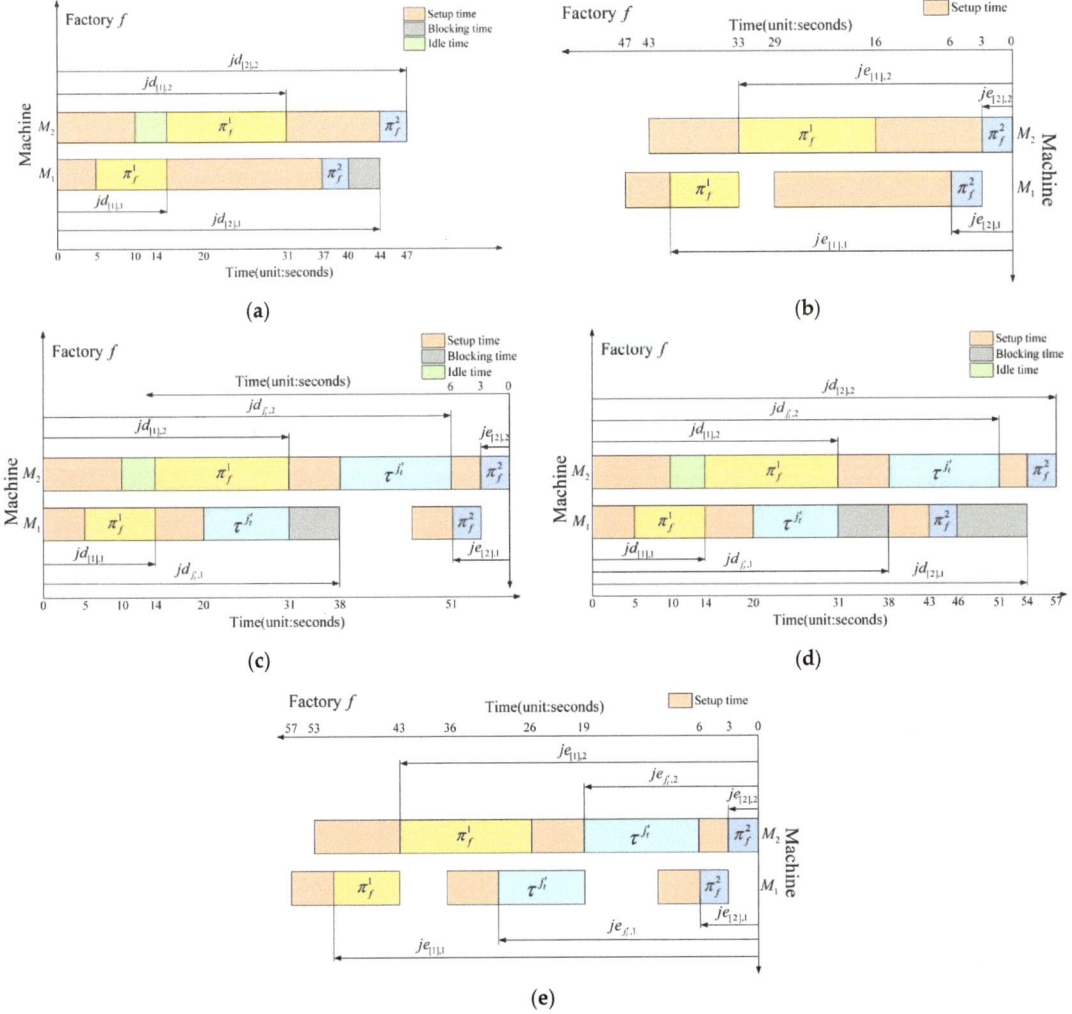

Figure 2. Rapid evaluation criteria. (**a**) Calculate the time $jd_{[j],m}$. (**b**) Calculate the time $je_{[j],m}$. (**c**) Insert job $\tau^{j'}{}_{t}$ into position 2. (**d**) Recalculate $jd_{[j],m}$ of the job after position 2. (**e**) Recalculate $je_{[j],m}$ of the job before position 2 and calculate $je_{j'_t,m}$.

Assume that the factory f consists of η_f jobs processed according to the sequence $\pi_f = \{\pi_f^1, \pi_f^2, \cdots, \pi_f^j, \cdots \pi_f^{\eta_f}\}$, where the job in the factory f is represented as π_f^j, $j \in \{1, 2, \cdots, \eta_f\}$. $[j]$ denotes the index of the jth job. In the forward calculation, $jc_{[j],m}$ and $jd_{[j],m}$ denote the completion time and the leave time, respectively, of π_f^j on m. In the backward calculation, $js_{[j],m}$ and $je_{[j],m}$ denote the completion time and leave time, respectively, of π_f^j on m.

Refresh accelerated calculation for inserting job:

An attempt is made to insert η_s jobs $\tau^{j'_1}, \tau^{j'_2}, \cdots, \tau^{j'_t}, \cdots, \tau^{j'_{\eta_s}}$, $j'_t \in \{1, 2, \cdots, \eta_s\}$ sequentially into the job sequence π_f to minimize the makespan of the factory f.

Step 1: Set $t = 1$ and consider the insertion of the job $\tau^{j'_t}$.

Step 2: Forward calculate $jd_{[j],m}$ for job π_f^j on machine m according to Equations (12)–(14). Please see Figure 2a.

$$jc_{[j],0} = 0, j = 1, 2, \cdots, \eta_f \tag{12}$$

$$jc_{[j],m} = \begin{cases} max(s_{0,[j],m}, jc_{[j],m-1}) + p_{[j],m}, j = 1, m = 1, 2, \cdots, M \\ max(jd_{[j-1],m} + s_{[j-1],[j],m}, jc_{[j],m-1}) + p_{[j],m}, j = 2, 3, \cdots, \eta_f, m = 1, 2, \cdots, M \end{cases} \tag{13}$$

$$jd_{[j],m} = \begin{cases} jc_{[j],m+1} - p_{[j],m+1}, j = 1, 2, \cdots, \eta_f, m = 1, 2, \cdots, M-1 \\ jc_{[j],m}, j = 1, 2, \cdots, \eta_f, m = M \end{cases} \tag{14}$$

Step 3: Backward calculate $je_{[j],m}$ for job π_f^j on machine m according to Equations (15)–(17). Please see Figure 2b.

$$js_{[j],M+1} = 0, j = \eta_f, \eta_f - 1, \cdots, 1 \tag{15}$$

$$js_{[j],m} = \begin{cases} js_{[j],m+1} + p_{[j],m}, j = \eta_f, m = M, M-1, \cdots, 1 \\ max(je_{[j+1],m} + s_{[j],[j+1]}, js_{[j],m+1}) + p_{[j],m}, j = \eta_f - 1, \eta_f - 2, \cdots, 1, m = M, M-1, \cdots, 1 \end{cases} \tag{16}$$

$$je_{[j],m} = \begin{cases} js_{[j],m-1} - p_{[j],m-1}, j = \eta_f, \eta_f - 1, \cdots, 1, m = M, M-1, \cdots, 2 \\ js_{[j],m}, j = \eta_f, \eta_f - 1, \cdots, 1, m = 1 \end{cases} \tag{17}$$

Step 4: The job sequence π_f has a set of $\eta_f + 1$ positions. The job can be tested in these positions. Suppose that the qth position is inserted by job $\tau^{j'_t}$, where $q = 1, 2, \ldots, \eta_f + 1$. Then, $jd_{j'_t,m}$ can be calculated by using Equations (18) and (19), as shown in Figure 2c.

$$jd_{j'_t,0} = 0 \tag{18}$$

$$jd_{j'_t,m} = \begin{cases} max(s_{0,j'_t,m}, jd_{j'_t,m-1}) + p_{j'_t,m}, q = 1, m = 1, 2, \cdots, M \\ max(jd_{[q-1],m} + s_{[q-1],j'_t,m}, jd_{j'_t,m-1}) + p_{j'_t,m}, q = 2, \cdots, \eta_f + 1, m = 1, 2, \cdots, M \end{cases} \tag{19}$$

Step 5: From Equation (20), the makespan of factory f, $C_{max}(j'_t, q)$, can be calculated after inserting job $\tau^{j'_t}$ into the qth position of job sequence π_f, as shown in Figure 2c.

$$C_{max}(j'_t, q) = \begin{cases} \max_{m=1,2,\cdots,M}(jd_{j'_t,m} + s_{j'_t,[q],m} + je_{[q],m}), q = 1, 2, \ldots, \eta_f \\ jd_{j'_t,M}, q = \eta_f + 1 \end{cases} \tag{20}$$

Step 6: Repeat steps 3 and 4 until all positions have been considered. It is assumed that position q^{best} is the best position at which job $\tau^{j'_t}$ can be inserted.

Step 7: After job $\tau^{j'}{}_t$ is inserted into position q^{best}, the $jd_{[j],m}$ ($je_{[j],m}$) of the job before (after) position q^{best} is unchanged. Therefore, we only need to recalculate $jd_{[j],m}$ of the job after position q^{best}, according to Equations (12)–(14), and $je_{[j],m}$ of the job before position q^{best}, according to Equations (15)–(17). It is also necessary to calculate $je_{j'_t,m}$ of job $\tau^{j'}{}_t$, as shown in Figure 2d,e.

Step 8: Set $t = t + 1$, $\eta_f = \eta_f + 1$.

Step 9: Repeat steps 4, 5, 6, 7, and 8 until all η_s jobs have been considered.

With the above steps, we find that the computational complexity of inserting the jobs into the sequence is reduced from $O\left(m\left(\eta_s \eta_f^2 + \sum_{t=1}^{\eta_s}\left(2t\eta_f + t^2\right)\right)\right) \approx O(mn^2)$ to $O\left(m\left((2\eta_s + 1)\eta_f + \sum_{t=1}^{\eta_s}(2t - 1)\right)\right) \approx O(mn)$. The computational cost savings are substantial when dealing with large-scale problems.

3. Proposed IG Algorithm for DBFSP_SDST

First, unlike other population-based algorithms, the iterated greedy algorithm focuses on the iteration of one solution and has a strong local search capability due to its greedy strategy. It has the advantages that it is a simple framework, has a small number of parameters, and is easy to encode and replicate. Considering the multi-factory feature of DBFSP_SDST and the diversity of solutions from a global perspective, we make some modifications to the IGA, such as designing iterative processes I and II to increase the diversity of solutions and focusing on the cooperation between global search and local search. Thus, we propose a multi-factory collaborative iterated greedy algorithm, i.e., mIG to solve DBFSP_SDST.

3.1. Algorithm Description

Figure 3 shows the flow chart of mIG. It is well-known that an initialization solution with high quality can enhance the convergence of the algorithm. Thus, we first design an enhanced NEH heuristic, $Refresh\_NEH\_en$, to initialize the solution by using refresh accelerated calculation (see line 1 of Algorithm 1). Then, we adopt a multi-neighborhood structures search based on the variable neighborhood descent ($mVND$) method to improve the quality of the initialization solution described above (see line 2 of Algorithm 1). Considering the multiple factories characteristic of DBFSP_SDST and enhancing the diversity of solutions from a global perspective, we also design two iterative stages, called *iterative process* I and *iterative process* II, and each iterative process is adopted with a certain probability (see lines 4–8 of Algorithm 1). After performing the above search strategy, a simulated annealing acceptance criterion is adopted to enhance the diversity of solutions. If the performance of the current new solution is not better than the original one, the original one is still retained using the following criterion, $r \leq \exp\{-(C_{\max}(\pi^{current}) - C_{\max}(\pi^{origin}))/T\}$, $T = \lambda T, \lambda \in (0,1), r \in (0,1)$. Furthermore, the proposed refresh accelerated calculation for inserting job method is adopted throughout the algorithm.

3.2. Solution Representation

Regarding the solution encoding of DBFSP_SDST, a solution is represented by adopting a discrete integer encoding. That is, a solution π can be expressed, $\{\pi_1, \pi_2, \cdots, \pi_f, \cdots, \pi_F\}$, with each π_f consisting of $\{\pi_f^1, \pi_f^2, \cdots, \pi_f^j, \cdots \pi_f^{\eta_f}\}$, in which π_f refers to the job sequence of factory f, and η_f refers to the number of jobs in factory f. The specific example can be found in Section 2, in which a solution can be expressed as $\pi = \{\pi_1, \pi_2\}$, where $\pi_1 = \{1, 4\}$, $\pi_2 = \{5, 3, 2\}$, $\eta_1 = 2$, and $\eta_2 = 3$. This means that factory 1 processes jobs 1 and 4 in the order $1 \to 4$. Similarly, factory 2 processes jobs 2, 3, and 5 in the order $5 \to 3 \to 2$.

Algorithm 1: The proposed mIG

Input: ρ is the probability value.
01: $\pi = Refresh\_NEH\_en$
02: $\pi^{temp} = mVND(\pi)$
03: **while** (the current CPU time <terminate time) **do**
04:    **if** $rand(0,1) > \rho$
05:        $\pi = iterative\ process\ I(\pi^{temp})$
06:    **else**
07:        $\pi = iterative\ process\ II(\pi^{temp})$
08:    **end if**
09:    $\pi^{best} = AcceptanceCriterion(\pi)$
10: **end while**
Output: BestSolution

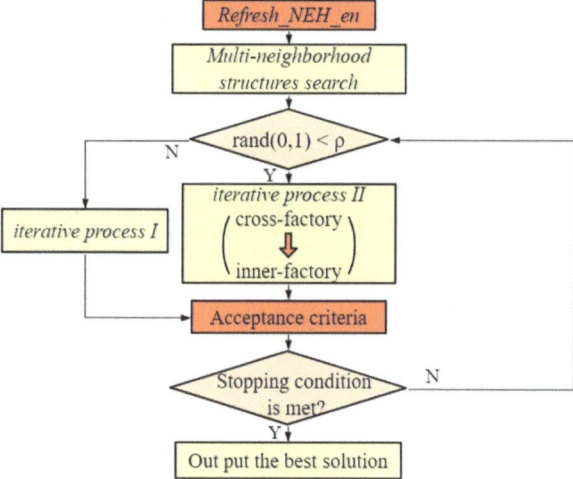

Figure 3. Flow chart of the mIG algorithm.

3.3. Initialization Solution

As mentioned above, an initialization sequence is closely related to the convergence nature of the algorithm. Thus, initialization operations are performed by using the heuristic method. According to the distributed characteristic of DBFSP_SDST, two issues need to be addressed. One is the assignment of jobs into factories, and the other is the arrangement of a reasonable scheduling sequence for each factory. NEH2_en presented by [11] has shown superior performance when optimizing a distributed flowshop scheduling problem and can solve the above two issues. However, NEH2_en has high time complexity due to the objective function needing to be reevaluated when jobs are put into all possible positions of all factories. Considering the problem characteristics and rapid evaluation method of the insertion job designed in Section 2.3, we propose a rapid initialization strategy *Refresh_NEH_en* by using refresh accelerated calculation.

Algorithm 2 shows the procedure of *Refresh_NEH_en* in detail. First, the total processing time P_j is calculated for every job on all machines (see line 1), and a scheduling sequence τ is obtained according to the descending of P_j (see line 2). Second, we take each job from the sequence τ and put it into each factory one by one (see lines 3–5), which ensures uniform allocation. The remaining jobs are removed one after another and put into all positions in all factories; finally the best position is selected (see lines 6–12). After finishing the insertion operator, we remove a job at position $pos_{f*} - 1$ or $pos_{f*} + 1$ from

π_{f*}, attempt it at all positions in π_{f*}, and select the position with minimal makespan (see lines 13–16).

Algorithm 2: *Refresh_NEH_en*

Input: an initial solution $\pi = \phi$.
01: $P_j = \sum_{m=1}^{M} p_{j,m}, j = 1, 2, \cdots, J$
02: $\tau = \{\tau^1, \tau^2, \cdots, \tau^J\}$ (Sort jobs according to decreasing P_j)
03: **for** $j = 1$ **to** F **do** %% uniformly allocate the jobs to the factories
04:     Take job τ^j from the set of jobs and assign it in π_j
05: **end for**
06: **for** $j = F + 1$ **to** J **do**
07:     **for** $f = 1$ **to** F **do**
08:         Insert τ^j in all positions in π_f and calculate the corresponding makespan by using refresh accelerated calculation
09:         $C_f = \min_{pos_f=1}^{\eta_f+1} C_f^{pos_f}$ and $pos_f = \arg(\min_{pos_f=1}^{\eta_f+1} C_f^{pos_f})$
10:     **end for**
11:     $pos_{f*} = \arg(\min_{f=1}^{F} C_f)$ %%pos_{f*} is the best position of factory with minimal makespan
12:     Insert τ^j into position pos_{f*} of π_{f*}
13:     Randomly select a job j' from $pos_{f*} - 1$ or $pos_{f*} + 1$ of π_{f*}
14:     Measure job j' in all positions using refresh accelerated calculation
15:     Insert job j' in the position with minimum makespan
16: **end for**
Output: the initial solution π

3.4. Multi-Neighborhood Structures Search

According to the distributed characteristic of DBFSP_SDST, a variable neighborhood descent based on the multiple neighborhood structures search ($mVND$) method is adopted to further disturb the current solution. Multiple parallel isomorphic factories exist in DBFSP_SDST; we consider using cross-factory and inner-factory neighborhood search to explore the global solution. In addition, a critical factory that is the one with maximum makespan decides the final makespan value of DBFSP_SDST. In view of this, two neighborhood structures search operators based on a critical factory and non-critical factory, i.e., *Critical_cross_swap*$1(\pi)$ and *Critical_inner_insert*$(\pi_{f_{critical}})$, are designed.

Critical_cross_swap$1(\pi)$ accomplishes the interaction between the critical factory and secondary factory, called a cross-factory interaction, where the secondary factory is the one with the second highest makespan. The details are as follows. First, a critical factory is found (if there are more than one critical factory, one will be chosen randomly) according to the current solution π. Second, a job is chosen from the critical factory. Third, another job is selected from the secondary factory. Next, the above two selected jobs are swapped and evaluated. If the objective value of the critical factory is reduced, the current solution will be updated.

Critical_inner_insert$(\pi_{f_{critical}})$ accomplishes the interaction within the critical factory, called inner-factory interaction. First, select a random job in the critical factory. Second, try the selected job in all positions of $\pi_{f_{critical}}$, and select the best position.

Algorithm 3 gives the pseudocode of the *multi-neighborhood structures search* algorithm.

3.5. Two Iterative Processes

As mentioned above, IGA is an efficient meta-heuristic algorithm with a simple framework. Because its structure is easy to reproduce, many good strategies can be ported to its framework to further improve the performance of IGA. In addition, considering the multiple factories characteristic of DBFSP_SDST and enhancing the diversity of solutions from a global perspective, two iterative processes are designed, called *iterative process* I and *iterative process* II, and each iterative process is adopted by a certain probability.

Algorithm 3: $mVND(\pi)$

Input: π is the initial solution.
01: Find a critical factory $f_{critical}$ and secondary factory $f_{secondary}$ and record their scheduling sequences $\pi_{f_{critical}}$ and $\pi_{f_{secondary}}$, respectively.
02: $p_{max} = 2$ and $p = 1$
03: **do** {
04:     **if** $p = 1$
05:         $\pi^{temp} = Critical\_cross\_swap1(\pi)$
06:     **else**
07:         $\pi^{temp} = Critical\_inner\_insert(\pi_{f_{critical}})$
08:     **end if**
09:     **if** C_{max} is improved
10:         $\pi = \pi^{temp}$
11:         $p = 1$
12:     **else**
13:         $p = p + 1$
14:     **end if**
15: } **while**($p \leq p_{max}$)
16: **end while**
Output: π

The *iterative process* I (see Algorithm 4) adopts $vDestruction\_Reconstruction(\pi)$ (see Algorithm 5) and $Critical\_cross\_swap1(\pi)$ (see Section 3.4) operators to disturb the current solution. The traditional destruction and reconstruction operators [11] are improved according to the distributed characteristics, abbreviated as $vDestruction\_Reconstruction(\pi)$. The details are as follows. First, initialize a parameter, d, using the random function $randbetween(2,6)$ and use it to generate an integer between 2 and 6. Second, a sequence π_R with d jobs is obtained, in which $d/2$ jobs are extracted from the critical factory, and the rest are randomly selected from the non-critical factories (see lines 2–9). At the same time, the above d jobs are sequentially removed from the original sequence. Third, adopt the jump reconstruction operator [39] to insert d jobs in all possible positions and finally select the best position (see lines 13–21). It should be noted that (1) the difference between jump reconstruction and the traditional reconstruction is that the former adopts a jumpy insertion when the insertion cannot improve the quality of the solution, which can accelerate insertion speed and reduce the time complexity; (2) a refresh accelerated calculation is adopted when performing the above insertion operator and calculation function value. The proposed $vDestruction\_Reconstruction(\pi)$ can further explore the deep neighborhood of the solution, increasing the diversity of solutions to prevent falling into the local optimum. Algorithm 5 displays the procedure of $vDestruction\_Reconstruction(\pi)$ in detail.

The *iterative process* II (see Algorithm 6) accomplishes the interaction of cross-factory and inner-factory. Since the completion time of the critical factory directly affects the optimal solution of the whole scheduling, it is necessary to appropriately schedule the critical factory. Combined with the distributed characteristic of DBFSP_SDST, the cross-factory and inner-factory strategies are designed, respectively. In this way, the development and exploration of the proposed algorithm can be balanced by the cooperation of the two strategies.

Multiple search strategies can improve the diversity of solutions. Therefore, in the cross-factory strategy, four disturbing operators are designed, i.e., $vDestruction\_Reconstruction(\pi)$, $Critical\_cross\_swap1(\pi)$, $Critical\_min\_swap(\pi)$, and $Critical\_cross\_swap2(\pi)$, to improve the opportunity of obtaining potential solutions. To further increase the search efficiency of mIG, the above four strategies will be adaptively selected (see Algorithm 6). In the inner-factory strategy, an operator $Critical\_inner\_swap(\pi_{f_{critical}})$ is proposed to optimize the sequence within the factory.

Algorithm 4: *iterative process* I

Input: π is the current primary solution; J is the total number of jobs in π.
01: Find a critical factory $f_{critical}$ and secondary factory $f_{secondary}$ and record their scheduling sequence $\pi_{f_{critical}}$ and $\pi_{f_{secondary}}$, respectively.
02: $\pi = vDestruction\_Reconstruction(\pi)$ %% Algorithm 5
03: **for** $cnt = 1$ **to** $J/2$ **do**
04:     $\pi^{temp} = Critical\_cross\_swap1(\pi)$ %% subSection 3.4
05:     **if** C_{max} is improved
06:         $\pi = \pi^{temp}$
07:     **end if**
08: **end for**
Output: π

Algorithm 5: $vDestruction\_Reconstruction(\pi)$

Input: π is the current primary solution; d is the number of removed jobs from π, $\pi_R=\varnothing$
01: Find a critical factory $f_{critical}$ and record its scheduling sequence $\pi_{f_{critical}}$
/* Destruction */
02: $d = randbetween(2,6)$
03: **for** $cnt = 1$ **to** $d/2$ **do**
04:     Select a random job j from $\pi_{f_{critical}}$
05:     $\pi_R \leftarrow j$ and $\pi_{f_{critical}} = \pi_{f_{critical}} \setminus j$
06: **end for**
07: **while** $|\pi_R| < d$ **do** %%$|\pi_R|$ refers to the number of jobs in π_R
08:     Randomly select a job j from $\pi_f (\pi_f \neq \pi_{f_{critical}})$ %%π_f is the sequence of factory f
09:     $\pi_R \leftarrow j$ and $\pi_f = \pi_f \setminus j$
10: **end while**
/* Reconstruction based on jumpy insertion and refresh accelerated calculation */
11: **for** $j = 1$ **to** d **do**
12:     **for** $f = 1$ **to** F **do**
13:         $pos = 0$ and $K = 1$
14:         **while** $pos \leq |\pi_f|$ **do**
15:             Measure job j at position pos of π_f^{temp} using refresh accelerated calculation
16:             **if** C_{max} is improved
17:                 Insert job j at pos of π_f^{temp}, and $K = 1$
18:             **else**
19:                 $K = K + 1$
20:             **end if**
21:             $pos = pos + K$
22:         **end while**
23:     **end for**
24: **end for**
Output: π

Except for $Critical\_cross\_swap1(\pi)$ and $vDestruction\_Reconstruction(\pi)$, which are stated in Sections 3.4 and 3.5, respectively, $Critical\_cross\_swap2(\pi)$, $Critical\_min\_swap(\pi)$, and $Critical\_inner\_swap(\pi_{f_{critical}})$ are as follows.

$Critical\_min\_swap(\pi)$ is the interaction between the two factories with maximal and minimal makespan. First, select two jobs from each of the two factories mentioned above. Second, the above two selected jobs are swapped and evaluated. If the objective value of the critical factory is reduced, the current solution will be updated.

$Critical\_cross\_swap2(\pi)$ performs the $Critical\_cross\_swap1(\pi)$ operation twice to explore the space more deeply and facilitate the improvement of the quality of the solution.

$Critical\_inner\_swap(S_s)$: Select two jobs at random from the sequence of critical factory. Next, swap the two selected jobs. This will get a new solution and apply this swap when a sequence of smaller makespan solutions is produced. If the objective value of the critical factory is reduced, the current solution will be updated.

In the self-adaptive strategy, two lists are defined, i.e., *List* and *BestList*. *List* contains sixty search strategies that are randomly selected from the above four strategies. *BestList* is initialized to empty. Each value of parameter R represents one of the four strategies, $R \in (1, 2, 3, 4)$. During the iteration, if the solution is improved, the corresponding strategy is saved to the *BestList*. Last, by using the strategies in the *BestList* to update *List* by parameter ω, ω determines how many strategies in *BestList* are available to update *List* (see lines 17–22). The details of *iterative process* II, including the self-adaptive strategy, are described in Algorithm 6.

Algorithm 6: *iterative process* II

Input: the current solution π, counter c, cnt, i
01: Find a critical factory $f_{critical}$ and secondary factory $f_{secondary}$ and a factory with minimal makespan f_{min}. Record their scheduling sequence $\pi_{f_{critical}}$, $\pi_{f_{secondary}}$, and $\pi_{f_{min}}$, respectively.
/* cross-factory */
02: **for** $c = 1$ **to** $|List|$ **do** %% $|List|$ is the length of *List*
03:     $R = randbetween(1,4)$
04:     **switch** (R)
05:         **case 1:** $\pi^{temp} = vDestruction\_Reconstruction(\pi)$ %% Section 3.5
06:             break;
07:         **case 2:** $\pi^{temp} = Critical\_min\_swap(\pi)$
08:             break;
09:         **case 3:** $\pi^{temp} = Critical\_cross\_swap1(\pi)$ %% Section 3.4
10:             break;
11:         **case 4:** $\pi^{temp} = Critical\_cross\_swap2(\pi)$
12:             break;
13:     **if** C_{max} is improved
14:         $\pi = \pi^{temp}$
15:         Record the R value in *BestList*
16: **end for**
17: **for** $i = 1$ **to** $\min\{\omega \times |List|, |BestList|\}$
18:     $List[i] = BestList[i]$
19: **end for**
20: **for** $i = \min\{\omega \times |List|, |BestList|\} + 1$ **to** $|List|$ **do**
21:     $List[i] = randbetween(1,4)$
22: **end for**
/* inner-factory */
23: **for** $cnt = 1$ **to** $J/2$ **do**
24:     $\pi^{temp} = Critical\_inner\_swap(\pi_{f_{critical}})$
25:     **if** C_{max} is improved
26:         $\pi = \pi^{temp}$
27:     **end if**
28: **end for**
Output: π

3.6. The Computational Complexity of mIG

In mIG, we suppose that there are n jobs, f factories, and m machines. Each factory contains $\frac{n}{f}$ jobs. The computational complexity of the mIG algorithm includes initialization, multi-neighborhood structures search, *iterative process* I, and *iterative process* II. First, the time complexity of *Refresh_NEH_en* is $O\left(mn + n\log_2 n + f + (n-f)\left(mn + 2\frac{n}{f} + m\frac{n}{f}\right)\right) \approx O(n^2)$. Second, the time complexity of the multi-neighborhood structures search is calculated as $O\left(\frac{n}{f} + \frac{n}{f} \times \frac{n}{f} \times m\right) \approx O(n^2)$. In addition, assume that the number of iterations of *iterative process* I and *iterative process* II are k_1 and k_2, respectively. For *iterative process* I, the complexity is $O\left(k_1 \times \frac{n}{2} \times m \times \frac{n}{J} \times 2\right) \approx O(n^2)$. For *iterative process* II, the complexity is $O\left(k_2 \times \frac{n}{2} \times m \times \frac{n}{J}\right) \approx O(n^2)$. In summary, the complexity of the whole mIG is $O(n^2)$.

4. Numerical Experiment and Analysis

This section gives the experimental design and analysis to demonstrate the effectiveness of mIG. The experiments are run on a PC with Intel(R) Core (TM) i7 CPU @ 2.90 GHz processor and 8 GB of RAM. For the proposed MILP model, the Gurobi 9.1.2 solver is adopted. For all the compared algorithms, C++ in the Visual Studio 2019 environment is used for coding and runs on the Release x64 platform. In the algorithm test, to ensure fairness, the maximum CPU elapsed time is adopted as the stopping criterion. In addition, it is considered that the algorithm has practical significance only when it can solve the problem in an acceptable time. Therefore, the termination condition is set as $TimeLimit = 5 \times J \times M$ milliseconds in this article. J and M indicate the total number of jobs and machines in the test instance, respectively. Each instance is run 5 times independently.

4.1. Test Data and Performance Metric

The experimental data used in this article can be referred to in [15]. This article test 270 instances with $F \times M \times J \times Factor$, where $F(F \in \{2, 3, 4, 5, 6, 7\})$ is the number of factories, $M(M \in \{5, 8, 10\})$ is the number of machines, $J(J \in \{100, 200, 300, 400, 500\})$ is the number of jobs, and *Factor* (*Factor* $\in \{25, 50, 100\}$) is the influence factor value that is used to generate different instances for the same scale size problem. From the above analysis, $6 \times 3 \times 5 \times 3 = 270$ combinations are obtained. Processing times for each job are evenly distributed within $[1, 99)$. The setup times of each job relative to the other jobs are calculated by the equation $(1 + rand()\%99) \times Factor/100$, where $rand()$ used to generate a random integer.

We adopt the relative percentage increase (RPI) as an evaluation indicator. RPI estimates the difference between the makespan obtained by an algorithm and the optimal makespan found so far. The equation to calculate the RPI is shown below:

$$RPI = \frac{M_i - M_{best}}{M_{best}} \times 100\% \quad (21)$$

where M_{best} is the minimal makespan found by all compared algorithms of 5 independent running for a test instance. M_i refers to the average makespan obtained by the ith algorithm of 5 independent running for a test instance. i belongs to ES [40], DABC [18], IGR [15], EA [14], and DDE [24]. Because there are 3 different instances for each scale instance, the average PRI is calculated for 3 different instances, called ARPI. Obviously, the smaller the RPI or ARPI, the better result the algorithm obtained.

4.2. Correctness Verification of MILP

The correctness of the presented MILP model is verified by using 8 small-scale instances. The model is written in Python on the Gurobi solver. In the exact solver, the maximum termination criterion is set to 3600 s [41,42]. The termination criterion of mIG is set to $TimeLimit = 5 \times J \times M$. Set each instance to run 5 times independently to reduce the randomness of mIG. Table 3 lists the respective makespan and running time of MILP and mIG. Among them, the makespan represents the best value found in the termination time. In addition, F_J_M denotes the numbers of factories, jobs, and machines, respectively.

Table 3. Result for the MILP model.

F_J_M	MILP		mIG	
	Makespan	Time (s)	Makespan	Time (s)
2_2_2	115	0.00	115	0.02
2_5_2	135	0.02	135	0.05
2_8_2	198	0.14	198	0.08
2_10_2	214	2.43	214	0.10
2_12_2	243	23.04	243	0.12
2_20_2	424	3600	424	0.20
2_35_2	763	3600	**742**	0.35
2_40_2	879	3600	**844**	0.40

Best values are indicated in bold.

Table 3 shows that the optimal solution can be found by MILP and takes less time when the instance size is small, i.e., 2_2_2, 2_5_2, 2_8_2, 2_10_2, and 2_12_2 instances. Within the termination time, the values of the makespan obtained by Gurobi are good for 6 (6/8) instances, suggesting that the MILP is correct and can find optimal solutions in small-scale instances. As the scale of the instances continues to grow, i.e., 2_35_2 and 2_40_2 instances, MILP cannot generate a good solution even if the run time is extended to 3600 s. However, mIG can obtain the best solution in a shorter time for all instances. Thus, mIG has better capacity to solve large-scale and complicated instances of DBFSP SDST than MILP.

4.3. Parameter Calibration

In the proposed mIG, two key parameters should be calibrated. One is the threshold value of two iterative processes, ρ, and the other is the proportion of $|BestList|$ to $|List|$, ω. To obtain a more intuitive sensitivity of the two parameters, the Taguchi method of design of experiment (DOE) is used to determine the best combination of parameter values. For each parameter, the four levels illustrated in Table 4 are considered, and 16 ($4 \times 4 = 16$) parameter combinations are listed in Table 5. To fairly investigate the sensitivity of these two parameters, three different instances are randomly selected (F_J_M), i.e., 2_100_5, 4_300_5, 7_500_10. For each instance, 16 combinations are run independently five times and obtain the average RPI values (see Table 5). Factor-level trends for each parameter are shown in Figure 4. Table 6 indicates the level of significance of the two parameters. The largest influence on the algorithm is exerted by the parameter ρ, followed by ω.

Table 4. Parameter level factor.

Parameters	Parameter Level			
	1	2	3	4
ρ	0	0.1	0.2	0.3
ω	0.6	0.7	0.8	0.9

From Tables 4–6 and Figure 4, the parameter ρ has the greatest influence on the experimental results. It directly affects the global and local search balance of the two iterative processes. As can be seen in Figure 4, when $\rho = 0$, *iterative process* I is invoked completely; *iterative process* II is not involved. At this time, the value of ARPI (1.282) is higher, suggesting that the IGA with only the *iterative process* I strategy easily falls into a local optimum. However, when $\rho = 0.1$, the average RPI (1.221) is better than that of $\rho = 0.2$ and $\rho = 0.3$. This can further illustrate the validity of our proposed *iterative process* II to increase the diversity of solutions and avoid local optima.

For the parameter ω, it determines how many strategies in *BestList* are available to update *List*. If the value is too small, it suggests that few good search strategies in *BestList* are used to update *List*, which may influence the convergence of the algorithm.

On the contrary, if the value is too large, the diversity of strategies in *List* may be reduced. Thus, the performance of mIG is tested under the values of ω being 0.6, 0.7, 0.8, and 0.9, respectively. Based on the experimental results of Table 5 and Figure 4, the value of ω is set 0.7.

Table 5. Orthogonal array and ARPI value.

Experiment Number	Parameters		Response (ARPI)
	ρ	ω	
1	0	0.6	1.27
2	0	0.7	1.33
3	0	0.8	1.23
4	0	0.9	1.30
5	0.1	0.6	1.39
6	0.1	0.7	1.08
7	0.1	0.8	1.15
8	0.1	0.9	1.26
9	0.2	0.6	1.27
10	0.2	0.7	1.34
11	0.2	0.8	1.39
12	0.2	0.9	1.34
13	0.3	0.6	1.30
14	0.3	0.7	1.25
15	0.3	0.8	1.28
16	0.3	0.9	1.31

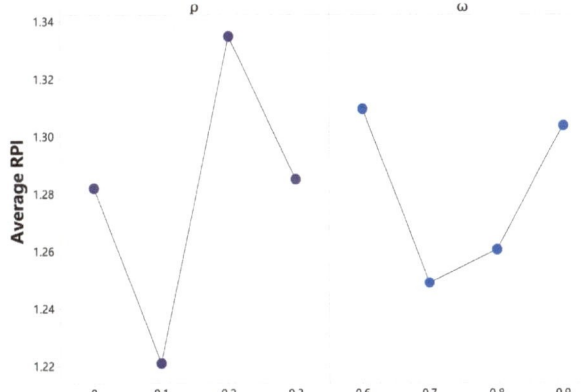

Figure 4. The trend of the parameter level.

Table 6. The average RPI response values.

Level	ρ	ω
1	1.282	1.310
2	1.221	1.249
3	1.335	1.260
4	1.285	1.304
Delta	**0.114**	0.061
Rank	1	2

Best values are indicated in bold.

4.4. Evaluation of the Proposed Problem-Specific mVND Operator

In this section, the proposed $mVND$ strategy is investigated to demonstrate its contribution. mIG_NV refers to the mIG without $mVND$. All instances were tested in the same experimental environment, and each instance was repeatedly run 5 times, with $TimeLimit = 5 \times J \times M$ milliseconds as the same termination time. ANOVA will be used to evaluate the RPI values of all instances as experimental results. From the results shown in Figure 5, the value of RPI yielded by mIG with $mVND$ is lower than that of mIG_NV. This suggests that the proposed multi-neighborhood structures search based on variable neighborhood descent can increase the diversity of mIG and provide more opportunities to generate potential solutions. In addition, the reason why $mVND$ has good performance is due t the designed neighborhood search strategies for cross-factory and inner-factory, which provide advantages for exploring the global solution.

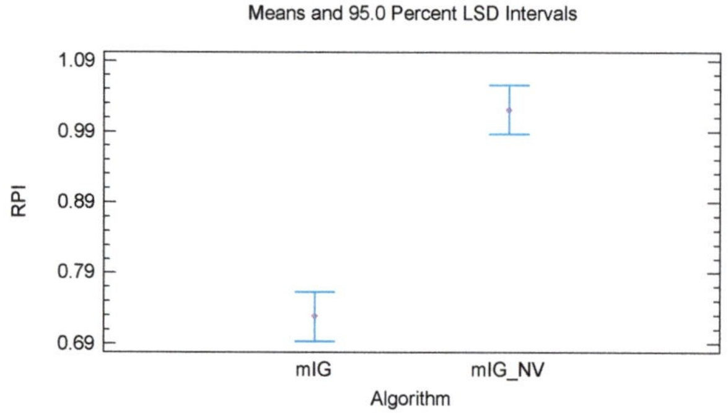

Figure 5. Confidence interval for mIG and mIG_NV.

4.5. Evaluation of mIG with Other Efficient Algorithms

This section compares the mIG algorithm with five intelligent optimization algorithms for solving DFSP, i.e., ES [40] and DDE [24], which are used to solving DBFSP, DABC [18], IGR [15], and EA [14], which are used to solving DPFSP. For fairness of comparison, all algorithms are carefully implemented according to the characteristics of the problem under the same termination conditions. The termination condition of all algorithms is set as $TimeLimit = 5 \times J \times M$ milliseconds. The mIG without refresh accelerated calculation, called mIG0, is also compared. In Table 7, J_M represents the scale with J jobs and M machines. In addition, we calculated the percentage values using equation $(P_{Comparing} - P_{mIG})/P_{Cmparing} \times 100\%$, where $P_{Comparing}$ and P_{mIG} refer to the values of Avg or ARPI obtained by the comparing algorithm and mIG, respectively. The calculated percentages represent how much better mIG is than other algorithms, and the data are marked in bold. For Avg, in different size instances of $F = 2$, the percentages of mIG superior to EA, DDE, DABC, IGR, ES, and mIG0 are 1.11%, 1.64%, 4.25%, 2.04%, and 1.10%, respectively. Similarly, for $F = 3, 4, 5, 6, 7$, the percentages are better than the six comparing algorithms. For ARPI, the percentages of mIG superior to the comparison algorithms, EA, DDE, DABC, IGR, ES, and mIG0 are 66.67%, 76.47%, 86.37%, 80.56%, 70.98%, and 50.88%, respectively. It is obviously the case that when $F = 3, 4, 5, 6, 7$, the percentages of mIG are still better than other algorithms.

Table 7. Average makespan and RPI values of ES, DABC, IGR, EA, DDE, mIG0, and mIG.

Factory	J_M	Time (s)	EA Avg	EA ARPI	DDE Avg	DDE ARPI	DABC Avg	DABC ARPI	IGR Avg	IGR ARPI	ES Avg	ES ARPI	mIG0 Avg	mIG0 ARPI	mIG Avg	mIG ARPI
F = 2	100_5	2.5	4464	1.80	4506	2.63	4478	2.05	4572	4.20	4537	3.44	4497	2.44	4416	0.62
	100_8	4	5030	2.01	5116	3.78	5060	2.62	5138	4.20	5113	3.68	5079	2.90	4976	0.90
	100_10	5	5170	1.45	5241	2.93	5184	1.77	5268	3.44	5255	3.12	5211	2.26	5139	0.83
	200_5	5	8775	1.83	8839	2.57	8833	2.54	8907	3.34	8797	2.12	8710	1.13	8688	0.75
	200_8	8	9726	1.34	9844	2.54	9799	2.11	9891	3.05	9761	1.69	9701	1.05	9647	0.47
	200_10	10	10,057	1.06	10,134	1.85	10,099	1.50	10,193	2.44	10,113	1.59	10,070	1.14	10,003	0.45
	300_5	7.5	13,106	1.99	13,182	2.59	13,388	4.14	13,221	2.87	13,054	1.59	12,939	0.66	12,920	0.50
	300_8	12	14,373	1.57	14,388	1.68	14,595	3.09	14,453	2.15	14,352	1.40	14,267	0.81	14,245	0.61
	300_10	15	14,929	1.80	15,005	2.36	15,154	3.28	15,070	2.79	14,905	1.58	14,781	0.77	14,771	0.68
	400_5	10	17,195	1.60	17,300	2.15	18,135	6.95	17,371	2.58	17,251	1.84	17,073	0.81	17,041	0.61
	400_8	16	18,864	1.77	18,935	2.15	19,483	5.03	18,989	2.45	18,766	1.20	18,665	0.67	18,608	0.35
	400_10	20	19,771	1.68	19,868	2.15	20,300	4.30	19,953	2.57	19,697	1.26	19,602	0.74	19,525	0.35
	500_5	12.5	21,294	2.12	21,374	2.52	23,006	10.13	21,435	2.82	21,293	2.09	20,995	0.66	20,921	0.28
	500_8	20	23,561	1.73	23,608	1.96	24,675	6.50	23,662	2.19	23,439	1.18	23,291	0.53	23,270	0.44
	500_10	25	24,559	1.42	24,660	1.84	25,590	5.61	24,733	2.12	24,505	1.14	24,349	0.52	24,348	0.51
	Mean	-	14,058	1.68	14,133	2.38	14,518	4.11	14,190	2.88	14,056	1.93	13,949	1.14	13,901	0.56
	Percentage	-	1.11%	66.67%	1.64%	76.47%	4.25%	86.37%	2.04%	80.56%	1.10%	70.98%	0.03%	50.88%	-	-
F = 3	100_5	2.5	3072	3.24	3122	4.85	3060	2.82	3146	5.69	3117	4.68	3074	3.23	3001	0.88
	100_8	4	3425	2.19	3464	3.38	3419	2.08	3488	4.08	3464	3.40	3425	2.16	3364	0.37
	100_10	5	3630	2.54	3650	3.14	3619	2.26	3675	3.83	3675	3.81	3628	2.43	3562	0.63
	200_5	5	5852	2.21	5874	2.65	5854	2.18	5925	3.50	5875	2.55	5828	1.72	5766	0.60
	200_8	8	6539	2.44	6615	3.62	6523	2.14	6633	3.91	6548	2.58	6506	1.85	6428	0.59
	200_10	10	6883	1.91	6968	3.18	6879	1.83	6991	3.51	6927	2.52	6881	1.84	6793	0.49
	300_5	7.5	8793	2.19	8850	2.87	8876	3.04	8875	3.14	8778	1.95	8731	1.40	8671	0.66
	300_8	12	9734	1.66	9759	1.97	9776	2.07	9793	2.27	9697	1.26	9658	0.84	9625	0.45
	300_10	15	10,070	1.54	10,122	2.04	10,102	1.83	10,157	2.39	10,065	1.44	10,026	1.04	9971	0.47
	400_5	10	11,705	1.93	11,749	2.34	11,941	3.84	11,807	2.84	11,671	1.56	11,596	0.92	11,529	0.30
	400_8	16	12,812	1.91	12,832	2.07	12,985	3.25	12,884	2.47	12,761	1.46	12,700	1.00	12,642	0.51
	400_10	20	13,263	1.69	13,313	2.12	13,408	2.78	13,353	2.40	13,242	1.50	13,180	1.03	13,104	0.40
	500_5	12.5	14,443	2.11	14,467	2.27	14,983	5.81	14,518	2.62	14,353	1.48	14,284	1.00	14,231	0.53
	500_8	20	15,879	2.13	15,898	2.31	16,271	4.54	15,953	2.64	15,795	1.53	15,725	1.05	15,649	0.53
	500_10	25	16,482	1.52	16,541	1.94	16,818	3.49	16,588	2.21	16,442	1.17	16,391	0.89	16,304	0.31
	Mean	-	9505	2.08	9548	2.72	9634	2.93	9586	3.17	9494	2.19	9442	1.49	9376	0.51
	Percentage	-	1.36%	75.48%	1.80%	81.25%	2.68%	82.59%	2.19%	83.91%	1.24%	76.71%	0.70%	65.77%	-	-

Table 7. Cont.

Factory	J_M	Time (s)	EA Avg	EA ARPI	DDE Avg	DDE ARPI	DABC Avg	DABC ARPI	Algorithms IGR Avg	IGR ARPI	ES Avg	ES ARPI	mIG0 Avg	mIG0 ARPI	mIG Avg	mIG ARPI
F = 4	100_5	2.5	2353	3.38	2387	4.98	2325	2.14	2397	5.38	2387	4.84	2337	2.67	2301	1.09
	100_8	4	2674	3.46	2702	4.57	2653	2.61	2696	4.32	2703	4.56	2648	2.47	2607	0.87
	100_10	5	2824	3.04	2851	4.11	2809	2.50	2860	4.35	2850	4.01	2797	2.05	2758	0.66
	200_5	5	4473	2.62	4473	2.60	4454	2.32	4514	3.52	4486	2.87	4462	2.26	4389	0.57
	200_8	8	5040	2.51	5092	3.51	5030	2.26	5093	3.55	5054	2.76	5021	2.08	4953	0.66
	200_10	10	5253	1.86	5290	2.52	5251	1.87	5332	3.34	5280	2.42	5244	1.73	5183	0.53
	300_5	7.5	6691	2.58	6713	2.91	6697	2.61	6732	3.17	6687	2.47	6651	1.90	6574	0.64
	300_8	12	7373	1.62	7407	2.16	7391	1.77	7429	2.44	7378	1.65	7356	1.28	7299	0.44
	300_10	15	7703	1.69	7752	2.35	7710	1.78	7773	2.62	7727	1.98	7690	1.49	7615	0.45
	400_5	10	8755	2.13	8769	2.29	8835	2.98	8794	2.57	8707	1.57	8672	1.12	8609	0.33
	400_8	16	9681	2.08	9720	2.49	9730	2.56	9760	2.90	9642	1.62	9635	1.52	9556	0.65
	400_10	20	10,162	1.84	10,201	2.24	10,210	2.27	10,227	2.51	10,142	1.58	10,133	1.52	10,030	0.44
	500_5	12.5	10,797	2.01	10,835	2.42	11,025	4.04	10,866	2.69	10,756	1.58	10,715	1.14	10,629	0.30
	500_8	20	11,995	1.47	12,041	1.85	12,178	2.91	12,076	2.14	11,974	1.19	11,957	1.09	11,867	0.26
	500_10	25	12,477	1.59	12,489	1.71	12,598	2.55	12,527	2.01	12,427	1.16	12,404	0.95	12,339	0.40
	Mean	-	7217	2.26	7248	2.85	7260	2.48	7272	3.17	7213	2.42	7182	1.68	7114	0.55
	Percentage	-	1.43%	75.66%	1.85%	80.70%	2.01%	77.82%	2.17%	82.65%	1.37%	77.27%	0.95%	67.26%		-
F = 5	100_5	2.5	1928	4.61	1945	5.50	1902	3.13	1946	5.61	1934	4.95	1894	2.71	1862	1.00
	100_8	4	2182	3.77	2189	4.10	2152	2.35	2200	4.62	2198	4.52	2150	2.22	2125	1.07
	100_10	5	2329	3.45	2357	4.67	2305	2.28	2359	4.73	2356	4.64	2303	2.24	2270	0.80
	200_5	5	3650	3.09	3656	3.30	3630	2.50	3675	3.79	3646	2.99	3617	2.05	3568	0.69
	200_8	8	4050	2.76	4070	3.33	4024	2.11	4073	3.35	4057	2.96	4026	2.14	3960	0.49
	200_10	10	4289	2.48	4313	3.08	4263	1.87	4329	3.42	4311	2.98	4272	2.09	4207	0.46
	300_5	7.5	5297	2.32	5302	2.43	5309	2.49	5323	2.81	5304	2.39	5269	1.70	5207	0.45
	300_8	12	5949	2.68	5966	3.00	5913	2.06	5987	3.33	5938	2.47	5907	1.90	5826	0.45
	300_10	15	6239	2.12	6293	3.04	6229	1.90	6311	3.36	6244	2.19	6225	1.85	6132	0.29
	400_5	10	7030	5.97	7059	2.41	7080	2.67	7080	2.71	7007	1.67	6991	1.38	6928	0.41
	400_8	16	7807	2.06	7826	2.31	7816	2.17	7845	2.56	7778	1.68	7757	1.40	7687	0.42
	400_10	20	8153	1.57	8193	2.09	8188	1.97	8217	2.38	8141	1.37	8130	1.22	8056	0.26
	500_5	12.5	8781	2.27	8785	2.32	8895	3.54	8814	2.63	8738	1.79	8689	1.21	8636	0.48
	500_8	20	9669	1.72	9714	2.27	9743	2.42	9735	2.48	9652	1.48	9643	1.38	9555	0.41
	500_10	25	10,139	1.91	10,183	2.37	10,156	2.06	10,198	2.53	10,110	1.61	10,084	1.36	10,008	0.48
	Mean	-	5833	2.85	5857	3.08	5840	2.37	5873	3.35	5828	2.65	5797	1.79	5735	0.54
	Percentage	-	1.68%	81.05%	2.08%	82.47%	1.80%	54.43%	2.35%	83.88%	1.60%	79.62%	1.07%	69.83%		-

Table 7. Cont.

Factory	J_M	Time (s)	EA		DDE		DABC		Algorithms IGR		ES		mIG0		mIG	
			Avg	ARPI	Avg	ARPI	Avg	ARPI	Avg	ARPI	Avg	ARPI	Avg	ARPI	Avg	ARPI
F = 6	100_5	2.5	1632	5.14	1637	5.41	1587	2.26	1636	5.42	1632	5.11	1593	2.64	1564	0.75
	100_8	4	1851	3.84	1851	3.87	1811	1.61	1858	4.21	1861	4.38	1818	2.01	1795	0.75
	100_10	5	2036	4.32	2053	5.22	1997	2.34	2047	4.90	2048	4.93	2005	2.75	1970	1.01
	200_5	5	3223	3.23	3081	3.46	3049	2.32	3091	3.84	3072	3.23	3046	2.21	2998	0.62
	200_8	8	3434	3.60	3456	4.24	3401	2.58	3477	4.87	3447	3.97	3403	2.55	3352	1.06
	200_10	10	3638	2.92	3659	3.58	3598	1.79	3670	3.89	3650	3.29	3609	2.10	3553	0.51
	300_5	7.5	4458	2.95	4473	3.28	4446	2.62	4489	3.65	4442	2.56	4427	2.18	4363	0.63
	300_8	12	5033	2.44	5051	2.89	5025	2.27	5063	3.11	5033	2.43	5012	1.94	4937	0.45
	300_10	15	5242	2.03	5267	2.46	5233	1.83	5290	2.92	5248	2.12	5228	1.69	5166	0.52
	400_5	10	5908	2.52	5928	2.89	5929	2.76	5939	3.10	5892	2.19	5855	1.57	5811	0.70
	400_8	16	6600	2.19	6615	2.42	6575	1.78	6636	2.74	6580	1.84	6567	1.65	6498	0.49
	400_10	20	6917	2.21	6945	2.68	6915	2.18	6953	2.80	6904	2.00	6873	1.55	6809	0.56
	500_5	12.5	7300	2.19	7302	2.21	7393	3.36	7326	2.53	7291	2.01	7260	1.53	7198	0.59
	500_8	20	8144	1.94	8155	2.09	8184	2.37	8172	2.31	8125	1.68	8096	1.29	8040	0.50
	500_10	25	8487	2.05	8519	2.48	8502	2.19	8526	2.55	8444	1.51	8421	1.25	8353	0.37
	Mean	-	4927	2.90	4933	3.28	4910	2.28	4945	3.52	4911	2.88	4881	1.93	4827	0.63
	Percentage	-	2.02%	78.28%	2.15%	80.79%	1.69%	72.37%	2.39%	82.10%	1.71%	78.13%	1.10%	67.36%	-	-
F = 7	100_5	2.5	1406	4.28	1409	4.44	1381	2.39	1413	4.80	1418	5.17	1375	1.98	1359	0.83
	100_8	4	1630	4.50	1642	5.28	1591	2.03	1636	4.91	1631	4.63	1594	2.19	1572	0.82
	100_10	5	1781	3.89	1795	4.69	1743	1.71	1785	4.10	1790	4.43	1746	1.90	1728	0.89
	200_5	5	2670	3.50	2672	3.65	2640	2.26	2685	4.08	2655	3.02	2639	2.29	2601	0.81
	200_8	8	3001	3.29	3012	3.72	2972	2.27	3020	3.99	3015	3.76	2972	2.24	2924	0.64
	200_10	10	3201	2.93	3212	3.33	3153	1.42	3208	3.17	3206	3.08	3168	1.84	3126	0.54
	300_5	7.5	3868	2.64	3880	2.94	3861	2.43	3899	3.45	3877	2.88	3842	1.94	3789	0.50
	300_8	12	4329	2.78	4340	3.02	4315	2.35	4352	3.31	4315	2.40	4294	1.89	4232	0.41
	300_10	15	4573	2.43	4592	2.93	4552	1.93	4603	3.13	4559	2.15	4540	1.67	4483	0.38
	400_5	10	5120	2.65	5131	2.88	5135	2.82	5136	2.99	5091	2.05	5072	1.64	5024	0.59
	400_8	16	5725	2.43	5745	2.80	5716	2.19	5753	2.94	5706	2.07	5684	1.67	5615	0.36
	400_10	20	5970	2.24	5982	2.44	5963	2.10	5990	2.57	5959	2.05	5930	1.53	5872	0.50
	500_5	12.5	6323	2.31	6359	2.83	6362	2.83	6368	3.00	6285	1.69	6273	1.46	6213	0.39
	500_8	20	6986	1.88	7005	2.17	7009	2.15	7029	2.49	6965	1.53	6951	1.31	6888	0.34
	500_10	25	7369	1.90	7411	2.53	7382	2.07	7418	2.61	7344	1.53	7322	1.23	7264	0.37
	Mean	-	4263	2.91	4279	3.31	4252	2.20	4286	3.44	4254	2.83	4227	1.79	4179	0.56
	Percentage	-	1.97%	80.76%	2.34%	83.08%	1.72%	74.55%	2.50%	83.72%	1.76%	80.21%	1.14%	68.72%	-	-

Best values are indicated in bold.

According to Table 7, (1) for most instances, the average makespan and RPI values obtained by mIG0 are smaller than those of EA, DDE, DABC, IGR, and ES, regardless of the number of factories being 2, 3, 4, 5, 6, and 7, respectively. The results demonstrate that the mIG0 is effective and has the ability to generate makespan. The advantages of mIG0 can be attributed to the fact that the proposed strategies, i.e., *Refresh_NEH_en*, *mVND*, and the two iterative processes, are designed based on the distributed multi-factories character of DBFSP. (2) For all the instances, the average makespan and RPI values obtained by mIG0 are better than those of mIG0, EA, DDE, DABC, IGR, and ES, regardless of the number of factories being 2, 3, 4, 5, 6, and 7, respectively. The results demonstrate that the mIG with refresh accelerated calculation has low time complexity and can have more opportunities to search potential solutions. Therefore, mIG shows superior performance compared with all the other algorithms. The main advantage of mIG relative to mIG0 can be attributed to the fact that the proposed refresh accelerated calculation based on job insertion can speed up the calculation of the objective and reduce the time complexity of the algorithm.

4.6. Evolutionary Curves and Interactions for the Compared Algorithms

This section further verifies the convergence of the algorithms by selecting two different scales, i.e., 100_6_10 and 400_7_10. The evolution curves of the mIG, ES, DABC, IGR, EA, and DDE algorithms are plotted as shown in Figure 6. The termination times for the two scales are $Timelimit = 10 \times J \times M$ and $Timelimit = 50 \times J \times M$, respectively. Different colors and symbols represent the six convergence curves obtained by six algorithms, respectively. The abscissa is the execution time of the algorithm (in milliseconds), and ordinate refers to the values of makespan.

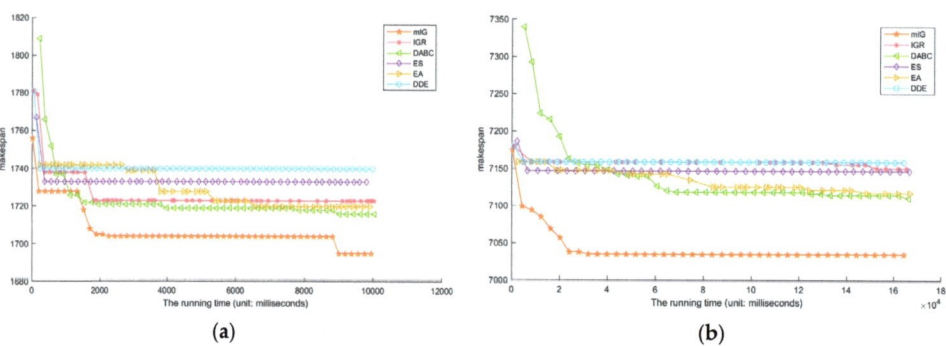

Figure 6. The evolutionary curves of compared algorithms. (**a**) 100_6_10. (**b**) 400_7_10.

From Figure 6a, we can observe that ES and DDE have the fastest convergence speed, but their solutions tend toward convergence as time increases. The evolutionary process of DABC and EA lasts for a long time, and the final results obtained are mediocre. The convergence speed of IGR is slightly faster than EA, and its solution is only better than ES and DDE. Obviously, mIG has good convergence and is constantly converging as time increases, and it is superior to other algorithms. Similarly, for the large-scale instance, mIG still has the best convergence, as shown in Figure 6b. The reason why the convergence curve of mIG is lower than those of compared algorithms may be that the proposed strategies, i.e., *Refresh_NEH_en*, *mVND*, and two iterative processes, can generate excellent solutions and effectively improve the convergence.

Although the above experiments have shown the superiority and competitiveness of the proposed mIG, it is necessary to verify whether its superiority is statistically significant. In view of this, a multifactor ANOVA analysis is done and uses different algorithms and the numbers of factories, jobs, and machines as influencing factors, respectively. From Figure 7a, the overall RPI values of all the compared algorithms are significantly different, in which the proposed mIG algorithm remarkably outperforms the other algorithms, followed by mIG0, EA and ES, DABC, DDE, and IGR. Figure 7c,d shows that the values of RPI obtained by mIG are better than those of compared algorithms, and the mIG can remain stable when the numbers of factories, jobs, and machines increase. The ANOVA analysis plotted is illustrated in Figure 7 and shows the significant difference between mIG and other algorithms.

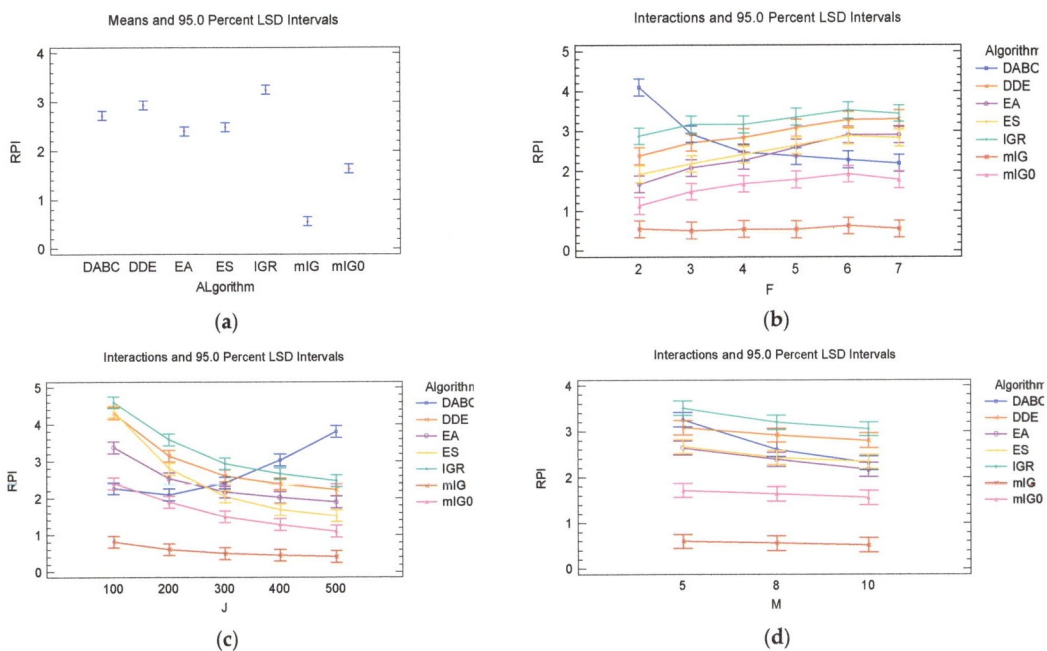

Figure 7. Interactions for ES, DABC, IGR, EA, DDE, mIG0, and mIG. (**a**) Means of all the compared algorithms. (**b**–**d**) are interactions of the numbers of factories, jobs, machines, and compared algorithms, respectively.

4.7. Friedman Tests

The Friedman test can verify whether multiple overall distributions are significantly different. Its original assumption is that all the algorithms involved in the comparison are not significantly different from each other. When a probability p-value is smaller than the given 0.05, the original assumption is rejected, and all algorithms are considered to be significantly different. Conversely, the original assumption cannot be rejected. It can be concluded that there are no significant differences between compared algorithms.

Table 8 gives the values of rank (Ranks), the number of test instances (CN), mean of RPI, standard deviation (Std. Deviation), minimum value (Min), and maximum value (Max) of makespan, respectively. The p-value obtained by the Friedman test is equal to 0.000, and its confidence level $\alpha = 0.050$. The values of Ranks, Mean, Std. Deviation, Min, and Max obtained by mIG are 1.04, 0.578, 0.2708, 0.11, and 1.53, and they are the smallest among all the compared algorithms. The proposed mIG performs very well in solving the DBFSP_SDST problem in general.

Table 8. Friedman test results (confidence level $\alpha = 0.050$).

Algorithms	Ranks	CN	Mean	Std. Deviation	Min	Max
EA	3.96	270	2.934	1.1850	0.49	6.39
DDE	5.36	270	3.469	1.3126	0.74	7.38
DABC	4.49	270	3.254	1.2517	1.13	11.29
IGR	6.49	270	3.789	1.2246	1.18	7.21
ES	4.24	270	3.014	1.3478	0.61	6.93
mIG0	2.41	270	2.160	0.8912	0.28	4.93
mIG	**1.04**	270	**0.578**	**0.2708**	**0.11**	**1.53**
p-value	0.000					

Best values are indicated in bold.

5. Conclusions and Future Research

There is very little literature about DBFSP_SDST. A MILP model is first constructed for DBFSP_SDST, and this paper uses the Gurobi solver to confirm its accuracy. Then, an efficient mIG algorithm is designed to optimize the above formulated model. For the proposed mIG algorithm, this article has done the following modifications.

1. A refresh acceleration calculation is proposed to reduce the complexity of the algorithm from $O(mn^2)$ to $O(mn)$.
2. A rapid evaluation mechanism, *Refresh_NEH_en*, is designed to reduce the computational complexity of the initialization process.
3. Iterative process I and II strategies are designed, and each iterative process is adopted by a certain probability to enhance the diversity of solutions from a global perspective.
4. According to characteristics of the distributed pattern, cross-factory and inner-factory strategies are presented to allocate the appropriate number and sequence of jobs for each factory, which balance the exploration and exploitation of the proposed mIG algorithm.
5. The proposed mIG algorithm obtains best solutions for a total of 270 instances when comparing to five state-of-the-art algorithms. The average makespan and RPI values of mIG are 1.93% and 78.35% better than the five comparison algorithms on average, respectively. The comprehensive results prove that the proposed mIG contains dual advantages of high quality and efficient solutions, which are more suitable for solving the DBFSP_SDST.

For future research, many issues of SDST-DBFSP need to be addressed urgently. First, multiple objectives should be considered, i.e., makespan, energy consumption, total flowtime, tardiness time [43] and earliness time, and so on. Second, from a practical production perspective, many uncertain factors should be considered, such as machine breakdowns, uncertain processing time, wrong operations, changes in due date, and so on. Last but not least, problem-specific operators or strategies should be designed according to the constraints and characteristics of problems.

Author Contributions: C.Z.: Conceptualization, Methodology, Data curation, Software, Validation, Writing—original draft. Y.H.: Conceptualization, Methodology, Software, Validation, Writing—original draft. Y.W.: Conceptualization, Methodology, Supervision, Writing—original draft. J.L.: Conceptualization, Methodology, Visualization, Investigation. K.G.: Conceptualization, Methodology, Writing—review and editing. All authors have read and agreed to the published version of the manuscript.

Funding: This research was funded by the National Natural Science Foundation of China, grant numbers 61973203, 62106073, 62173216, and 62173356. We are grateful for Guangyue Young Scholar Innovation Team of Liaocheng University under grant number LCUGYTD2022-03.

Data Availability Statement: The data that support the findings of this study are available from the corresponding author upon reasonable request.

Conflicts of Interest: The authors declare no conflict of interest.

References

1. Wang, L.; Shen, W. *Process Planning and Scheduling for Distributed Manufacturing (Springer Series in Advanced Manufacturing)*; Springer: Berlin/Heidelberg, Germany, 2007.
2. Koen, P.A. *The PDMA Handbook of New Product Development*; Wiley: Hoboken, NJ, USA, 2005.
3. Naderi, B.; Ruiz, R. The Distributed Permutation Flowshop Scheduling Problem. *Comput. Oper. Res.* **2010**, *37*, 754–768. [CrossRef]
4. Liu, H.; Gao, L. A Discrete Electromagnetism-Like Mechanism Algorithm for Solving Distributed Permutation Flowshop Scheduling Problem. In Proceedings of the 2010 International Conference on Manufacturing Automation, Hong Kong, China, 13–15 December 2010; pp. 156–163.
5. Gao, J.; Chen, R.; Deng, W.; Liu, Y. Solving Multi-Factory Flowshop Problems with a Novel Variable Neighbourhood Descent Algorithm. *J. Comput. Inf. Syst.* **2012**, *8*, 2025–2032.
6. Gao, J.; Chen, R.; Deng, W. An Efficient Tabu Search Algorithm for the Distributed Permutation Flowshop Scheduling Problem. *Int. J. Prod. Res.* **2012**, *51*, 641–651. [CrossRef]
7. Wang, S.; Wang, L.; Liu, M.; Xu, Y. An Effective Estimation of Distribution Algorithm for Solving the Distributed Permutation Flow-Shop Scheduling Problem. *Int. J. Prod. Econ.* **2013**, *145*, 387–396. [CrossRef]
8. Naderi, B.; Ruiz, R. A Scatter Search Algorithm for the Distributed Permutation Flowshop Scheduling Problem. *Eur. J. Oper. Res.* **2014**, *239*, 323–334. [CrossRef]
9. Fernandez-Viagas, V.; Framinan, J.M. A Bounded-Search Iterated Greedy Algorithm for the Distributed Permutation Flowshop Scheduling Problem. *Int. J. Prod. Res.* **2015**, *53*, 1111–1123. [CrossRef]
10. Komaki, M.; Malakooti, B. General Variable Neighborhood Search Algorithm to Minimize Makespan of the Distributed No-Wait Flow Shop Scheduling Problem. *Prod. Eng. Res. Devel.* **2017**, *11*, 315–329. [CrossRef]
11. Ruiz, R.; Pan, Q.-K.; Naderi, B. Iterated Greedy Methods for the Distributed Permutation Flowshop Scheduling Problem. *Omega* **2019**, *83*, 213–222. [CrossRef]
12. Pan, Q.-K.; Gao, L.; Wang, L. An Effective Cooperative Co-Evolutionary Algorithm for Distributed Flowshop Group Scheduling Problems. *IEEE Trans. Cybern.* **2022**, *52*, 5999–6012. [CrossRef]
13. Li, W.; Chen, X.; Li, J.; Sang, H.; Han, Y.; Du, S. An Improved Iterated Greedy Algorithm for Distributed Robotic Flowshop Scheduling Withorderconstraints. *Comput. Ind. Eng.* **2022**, *164*, 107907. [CrossRef]
14. Fernandez-Viagas, V.; Perez-Gonzalez, P.; Framinan, J.M. The Distributed Permutation Flow Shop to Minimise the Total Flowtime. *Comput. Ind. Eng.* **2018**, *118*, 464–477. [CrossRef]
15. Huang, J.-P.; Pan, Q.-K.; Gao, L. An Effective Iterated Greedy Method for the Distributed Permutation Flowshop Scheduling Problem with Sequence-Dependent Setup Times. *Swarm Evol. Comput.* **2020**, *59*, 100742. [CrossRef]
16. Han, X.; Han, Y.; Chen, Q.; Li, J.; Sang, H.; Liu, Y.; Pan, Q.; Nojima, Y. Distributed Flow Shop Scheduling with Sequence-Dependent Setup Times Using an Improved Iterated Greedy Algorithm. *Complex Syst. Model. Simul.* **2021**, *1*, 198–217. [CrossRef]
17. Li, Y.; Li, X.; Gao, L.; Zhang, B.; Pan, Q.-K.; Tasgetiren, M.F.; Meng, L. A Discrete Artificial Bee Colony Algorithm for Distributed Hybrid Flowshop Scheduling Problem with Sequence-Dependent Setup Times. *Int. J. Prod. Res.* **2021**, *59*, 3880–3899. [CrossRef]
18. Huang, J.-P.; Pan, Q.-K.; Miao, Z.-H.; Gao, L. Effective Constructive Heuristics and Discrete Bee Colony Optimization for Distributed Flowshop with Setup Times. *Eng. Appl. Artif. Intell.* **2021**, *97*, 104016. [CrossRef]
19. Karabulut, K.; Öztop, H.; Kizilay, D.; Tasgetiren, M.F.; Kandiller, L. An Evolution Strategy Approach for the Distributed Permutation Flowshop Scheduling Problem with Sequence-Dependent Setup Times. *Comput. Oper. Res.* **2022**, *142*, 105733. [CrossRef]
20. Song, H.-B.; Lin, J. A Genetic Programming Hyper-Heuristic for the Distributed Assembly Permutation Flow-Shop Scheduling Problem with Sequence Dependent Setup Times. *Swarm Evol. Comput.* **2021**, *60*, 100807. [CrossRef]
21. Companys, R.; Ribas, I. Efficient Constructive Procedures for the Distributed Blocking Flow Shop Scheduling Problem. In Proceedings of the 2015 International Conference on Industrial Engineering and Systems Management (IESM), Seville, Spain, 21–23 October 2015; pp. 92–98.
22. Zhang, G.; Liu, B.; Wang, L.; Yu, D.; Xing, K. Distributed Co-Evolutionary Memetic Algorithm for Distributed Hybrid Differentiation Flowshop Scheduling Problem. *IEEE Trans. Evol. Comput.* **2022**, *26*, 1043–1057. [CrossRef]
23. Ying, K.-C.; Lin, S.-W. Minimizing Makespan in Distributed Blocking Flowshops Using Hybrid Iterated Greedy Algorithms. *IEEE Access* **2017**, *5*, 15694–15705. [CrossRef]
24. Zhang, G.; Xing, K.; Cao, F. Discrete Differential Evolution Algorithm for Distributed Blocking Flowshop Scheduling with Makespan Criterion. *Eng. Appl. Artif. Intell.* **2018**, *76*, 96–107. [CrossRef]
25. Shao, Z.; Pi, D.; Shao, W. Hybrid Enhanced Discrete Fruit Fly Optimization Algorithm for Scheduling Blocking Flow-Shop in Distributed Environment. *Expert Syst. Appl.* **2020**, *145*, 113147. [CrossRef]
26. Zhao, F.; Zhao, L.; Wang, L.; Song, H. An Ensemble Discrete Differential Evolution for the Distributed Blocking Flowshop Scheduling with Minimizing Makespan Criterion. *Expert Syst. Appl.* **2020**, *160*, 113678. [CrossRef]
27. Han, X.; Han, Y.; Zhang, B.; Qin, H.; Li, J.; Liu, Y.; Gong, D. An Effective Iterative Greedy Algorithm for Distributed Blocking Flowshop Scheduling Problem with Balanced Energy Costs Criterion. *Appl. Soft Comput.* **2022**, *129*, 109502. [CrossRef]

28. Ruiz, R.; Stützle, T. A Simple and Effective Iterated Greedy Algorithm for the Permutation Flowshop Scheduling Problem. *Eur. J. Oper. Res.* **2007**, *177*, 2033–2049. [CrossRef]
29. Lin, S.-W.; Ying, K.-C.; Huang, C.-Y. Minimising Makespan in Distributed Permutation Flowshops Using a Modified Iterated Greedy Algorithm. *Int. J. Prod. Res.* **2013**, *51*, 5029–5038. [CrossRef]
30. Pan, Q.-K.; Ruiz, R. An Effective Iterated Greedy Algorithm for the Mixed No-Idle Permutation Flowshop Scheduling Problem. *Omega* **2014**, *44*, 41–50. [CrossRef]
31. Ying, K.-C.; Lin, S.-W.; Cheng, C.-Y.; He, C.-D. Iterated Reference Greedy Algorithm for Solving Distributed No-Idle Permutation Flowshop Scheduling Problems. *Comput. Ind. Eng.* **2017**, *110*, 413–423. [CrossRef]
32. Huang, Y.-Y.; Pan, Q.-K.; Huang, J.-P.; Suganthan, P.; Gao, L. An Improved Iterated Greedy Algorithm for the Distributed Assembly Permutation Flowshop Scheduling Problem. *Comput. Ind. Eng.* **2021**, *152*, 107021. [CrossRef]
33. Mao, J.; Pan, Q.; Miao, Z.; Gao, L. An Effective Multi-Start Iterated Greedy Algorithm to Minimize Makespan for the Distributed Permutation Flowshop Scheduling Problem with Preventive Maintenance. *Expert Syst. Appl.* **2021**, *169*, 114495. [CrossRef]
34. Ribas, I.; Companys, R.; Tort-Martorell, X. An Iterated Greedy Algorithm for Solving the Total Tardiness Parallel Blocking Flow Shop Scheduling Problem. *Expert Syst. Appl.* **2019**, *121*, 347–361. [CrossRef]
35. Qin, H.; Han, Y.; Chen, Q.; Li, J.; Sang, H. A Double Level Mutation Iterated Greedy Algorithm for Blocking Hybrid Flow Shop Scheduling. *Control Decis.* **2022**, *37*, 2323–2332. [CrossRef]
36. Chen, S.; Pan, Q.-K.; Gao, L. Production Scheduling for Blocking Flowshop in Distributed Environment Using Effective Heuristics and Iterated Greedy Algorithm. *Robot. Comput. Integr. Manuf.* **2021**, *71*, 102155. [CrossRef]
37. Öztop, H.; Fatih Tasgetiren, M.; Eliiyi, D.T.; Pan, Q.-K. Metaheuristic Algorithms for the Hybrid Flowshop Scheduling Problem. *Comput. Oper. Res.* **2019**, *111*, 177–196. [CrossRef]
38. Taillard, E. Some Efficient Heuristic Methods for the Flow Shop Sequencing Problem. *Eur. J. Oper. Res.* **1990**, *47*, 65–74. [CrossRef]
39. Missaoui, A.; Ruiz, R. A Parameter-Less Iterated Greedy Method for the Hybrid Flowshop Scheduling Problem with Setup Times and Due Date Windows. *Eur. J. Oper. Res.* **2022**, *303*, 99–113. [CrossRef]
40. Karabulut, K.; Kizilay, D.; Tasgetiren, M.F.; Gao, L.; Kandiller, L. An Evolution Strategy Approach for the Distributed Blocking Flowshop Scheduling Problem. *Comput. Ind. Eng.* **2022**, *163*, 107832. [CrossRef]
41. Meng, L.; Zhang, C.; Ren, Y.; Zhang, B.; Lv, C. Mixed-Integer Linear Programming and Constraint Programming Formulations for Solving Distributed Flexible Job Shop Scheduling Problem. *Comput. Ind. Eng.* **2020**, *142*, 106347. [CrossRef]
42. Meng, L.; Gao, K.; Ren, Y.; Zhang, B.; Sang, H.; Chaoyong, Z. Novel MILP and CP Models for Distributed Hybrid Flowshop Scheduling Problem with Sequence-Dependent Setup Times. *Swarm Evol. Comput.* **2022**, *71*, 101058. [CrossRef]
43. Zhao, F.; Di, S.; Wang, L. A Hyperheuristic With Q-Learning for the Multiobjective Energy-Efficient Distributed Blocking Flow Shop Scheduling Problem. *IEEE Trans. Cybern.* **2022**, 1–14. [CrossRef]

Disclaimer/Publisher's Note: The statements, opinions and data contained in all publications are solely those of the individual author(s) and contributor(s) and not of MDPI and/or the editor(s). MDPI and/or the editor(s) disclaim responsibility for any injury to people or property resulting from any ideas, methods, instructions or products referred to in the content.

Article

A Modified q-BFGS Algorithm for Unconstrained Optimization

Kin Keung Lai [1,*], Shashi Kant Mishra [2], Ravina Sharma [2], Manjari Sharma [2] and Bhagwat Ram [3]

1. International Business School, Shaanxi Normal University, Xi'an 710119, China
2. Department of Mathematics, Institute of Science, Banaras Hindu University, Varanasi 221005, India
3. Centre for Digital Transformation, Indian Institute of Management, Ahmedabad 380015, India
* Correspondence: mskklai@outlook.com

Abstract: This paper presents a modification of the q-BFGS method for nonlinear unconstrained optimization problems. For this modification, we use a simple symmetric positive definite matrix and propose a new q-quasi-Newton equation, which is close to the ordinary q-quasi-Newton equation in the limiting case. This method uses only first order q-derivatives to build an approximate q-Hessian over a number of iterations. The q-Armijo-Wolfe line search condition is used to calculate step length, which guarantees that the objective function value is decreasing. This modified q-BFGS method preserves the global convergence properties of the q-BFGS method, without the convexity assumption on the objective function. Numerical results on some test problems are presented, which show that an improvement has been achieved. Moreover, we depict the numerical results through the performance profiles.

Keywords: BFGS method; q-calculus; unconstrained optimization; global convergence

MSC: 65K10; 05A30; 90C26

1. Introduction

There are many methods for solving nonlinear unconstrained minimization problems [1–5], most of them are variants of the Newton and quasi-Newton methods. Newton's method uses the specification of the Hessian matrix, which is sometimes difficult to calculate, whereas the quasi-Newton method uses an approximation of Hessian. Over time, several attempts have been made to improve the effectiveness of quasi-Newton methods. The BFGS (Broyden–Fletcher–Goldfarb–Shanno) method is a quasi-Newton method for solving nonlinear unconstrained optimization problems, which is developed by Fletcher [6], Goldfarb [7], Shanno [8], and Broyden [9]. Since the 1970s, the BFGS method has become popular and is considered an effective quasi-Newton method. Some researchers have established that the BFGS method achieves global convergence under the assumption of convexity on the objective function. Mascarene has been shown with an example that the standard BFGS method fails with exact line search for non-convex functions [10]. Using inexact line search, some authors [11,12] established that the BFGS method achieves global convergence without the assumption of convexity on the objective function.

Quantum calculus (q-calculus) is a branch of mathematics and does not require limits to derive q-derivatives; therefore, it is also known as calculus without limits. In quantum calculus, we can obtain the q-derivative of a non-differentiable function by replacing the classical derivative with the q-difference operator, and if we take the limit $q \to 1$, then the q-derivative reduces to the classical derivative [13]. Since the 20th century, quantum calculus has been linking physics [14] and mathematics [15] that span from statistical mechanics [16] and quantum theory [17] to hyper-geometric functions and number theory [14]. Quantum analysis was first introduced in the 1740s when Euler wrote in Latin about the theory of partitions, also known as additive analytic number theory.

At the beginning of the 19th century, Jackson generalized the concepts of classical derivatives in the context of q-calculus, known as Jackson's derivative, or q-derivative operator, or q-difference operator or simply q-derivative [18]. He systematically developed quantum calculus based on pioneer work by Eular and Henie. His work introduced functions, mean value theorems [19], Taylor's formula and its remainder [20,21], fractional integrals [22], integral inequalities and generalizations of series in the context of q-calculus [23]. The first time Soterroni [24] introduced the q-gradient vector. To obtain this, instead of the classical first order partial derivative, the first order partial q-derivative obtained from the q-difference operator is used.

In unconstrained optimization first time, Soterroni [24] used the q-derivative to establish the q-variant of the steepest descent method. After that, he also introduced the q-gradient method for global optimization [25]. In recent years, some authors have given some numerical techniques in the context of q-calculus to solve nonlinear unconstrained optimization problems [26–28]. In these methods, instead of a general gradient, a q-gradient is used because it permits the descent direction to work in the broader set of directions to converse rapidly.

Moreover, optimization has a crucial role in the field of chemical science. In this field, optimization methods have been used to minimize the energy consumption process in plants, design optimum fluid flow systems, optimize product concentration and reaction time in systems, and optimize the separation process in plants [29–31]. Some authors [32,33] have shown that the BFGS method is systematically superior in obtaining stable molecular geometries by reducing the gradient norm in a monotonic fashion. In a similar way, the modified q-BFGS algorithm can be used to find stable molecular geometries for large molecules.

In this paper, we modify the q-BFGS method for nonlinear unconstrained optimization problems. For this modification, we propose a new q-quasi-Newton equation with the help of a positive definite matrix, and in the limiting case, our new q-quasi-Newton equation is close to the ordinary q-quasi-Newton equation. Instead of calculating the q-Hessian matrices, we approximate them using only the first order q-derivative of the function. We use an independent parameter $q \in (0,1)$ and quantum calculus based q-Armijo–Wolfe line search [34] to ensure that the objective function value is decreasing. The use of q-gradient in this line search is responsible for escaping the point from the local minimum to the global minimum at each iteration. The proposed method is globally convergent without the convexity assumption on the objective function. Then, numerical results on some test problems are presented to compare the new method with the existing approach. Moreover, we depict the numerical results through the performance profiles.

The organization of this paper is as follows: In Section 2, we recall essential preliminaries related to the q-calculus and the BFGS method. In the next section, we present a modified q-quasi-Newton equation, and using this, we give a modified q-BFGS algorithm and discuss its properties. In Section 4, we present the global convergence of the modified q-BFGS method. In the next section, we present numerical results. Finally, we give a conclusion in the last section.

2. Preliminaries

In this section, we reviewed some important definitions and other prerequisites from q-calculus and nonlinear unconstrained optimization.

Let $q \in (0,1)$, then, a q-complex number is denoted by $[b]_q$ and defined as follows [14]:

$$[b]_q = \frac{q^b - 1}{q - 1}, \quad b \in \mathbb{C}.$$

A q-natural number $[m]_q$ is defined as follows [13]:

$$[m]_q = 1 + q + \cdots + q^{m-1}, \quad m \in \mathbb{N}.$$

In q-calculus, the q-factorial [14] of a number $[m]_q$ is denoted by $[m]_q!$ and defined as follows:
$$[m]_q! = [1]_q[2]_q \ldots [m-1]_q[m]_q, \quad m \in \mathbb{N}$$
and
$$[0]_q! = 1.$$

The q-derivative ($q \neq 1$) [18] of a real-valued continuous function $f \colon \mathbb{R} \to \mathbb{R}$, provided that f is differentiable at 0, is denoted by $D_q f$ and defined as follows:
$$D_q f(x) = \begin{cases} \frac{f(x) - f(qx)}{(1-q)x}, & \text{if } x \neq 0 \\ f'(x), & \text{if } x = 0. \end{cases}$$

If provided that f is differentiable on $\mathbb{R}$ then in the limiting case ($q \to 1$), the q-derivative is equal to classical derivative.

Let $f \colon \mathbb{R}^n \to \mathbb{R}$ be a real continuous function, then for $x = (x_1, x_2, \ldots, x_n) \in \mathbb{R}^n$, consider an operator $\varepsilon_{q,i}$ on h as
$$(\varepsilon_{q,i} f)(x) = f(x_1, x_2, \ldots, qx_i, x_{i+1}, \ldots, x_n).$$

The partial q-derivative [22] of f at x with respect to x_i, denoted by $D_{q,x_i} f$ and defined as follows:
$$D_{q,x_i} f(x) = \begin{cases} \frac{f(x) - (\varepsilon_{q,i} f)(x)}{(1-q)x_i}, & \text{if } x_i \neq 0 \\ \frac{\partial f(x)}{\partial x_i}, & \text{if } x_i = 0. \end{cases}$$

In the same way, higher order partial q-derivatives are defined as follows:
$$D_q^0 = f(x),$$
$$D^m_{q, x_1^{k_1}, \ldots, x_i^{k_i}, \ldots, x_n^{k_n}} f(x) = \left(D_q, x_i \left(D^{m-1}_{q, x_1^{k_1} \ldots x_i^{k_i-1}, \ldots, x_n^{k_n}} f \right) \right)(x),$$
where $k_1 + k_2 + \cdots + k_n = m$ and $m = 1, 2, \ldots,$

Then, the q-gradient [24] of f is
$$(\nabla_q f(x)) = \left[D_{q,x_1} f(x), \ldots, D_{q,x_i} f(x), \ldots, D_{q,x_n} f(x) \right]^T.$$

To simplify the presentation, we use $A > 0$ (≥ 0) to denote any $n \times n$ symmetric and positive definite (semi-definite) matrix A, use $f \colon \mathbb{R}^n \to \mathbb{R}$ to denote a real-valued function, use $g_q(x)$ to denote the q-gradient of f at x, use $||x||$ to denote Euclidean norm of a vector $x \in \mathbb{R}^n$, use A^k to denotes the q-quasi-Newton update Hessian at x^k, throughout this paper.

Let $f \colon \mathbb{R}^n \to \mathbb{R}$ be continuously q-derivative then consider the following unconstrained optimization problem:
$$\min_{x \in \mathbb{R}^n} f(x). \tag{1}$$

The q-BFGS method [34] generates a sequence $\{x^k\}$ by the following iterative scheme:
$$x^{k+1} = x^k + \alpha^k d_q^k; \quad k \in \{0\} \cup \mathbb{N}, \tag{2}$$

where α^k and d_q^k are step length and q-BFGS descent direction, respectively.

The q-BFGS descent direction is obtained by solving the following linear equation:
$$g_q^k + A^k d_q^k = 0, \tag{3}$$

where A^k is the q-quasi-Newton update Hessian. The sequence A^k satisfies the following equation:
$$A^{k+1}\delta^k = \gamma^k,$$
where $\delta^k = x^{k+1} - x^k$ and $\gamma^k = g_q^{k+1} - g_q^k$. In the context of q-calculus, we refer to the Broyden–Fletcher–Goldfarb–Shanno (BFGS) update formula as the q-BFGS update formula. Thus, the Hessian A^k is updated by the following q-BFGS formula:

$$A^{k+1} = A^k - \frac{A^k \delta^k (\delta^k)^T A^k}{(\delta^k)^T A^k \delta^k} + \frac{\gamma^k (\gamma^k)^T}{(\delta^k)^T \gamma^k}, \quad (4)$$

3. Modified q-BFGS Algorithm

We modify the q-BFGS algorithm using the following function [35]:

$$f_k(x) = f(x) + \frac{1}{2}(x - x^k)^T B^k (x - x^k),$$

where B^k is a positive definite symmetric matrix. We obtain the following new q-quasi-Newton equation by using the function f_k to the q-quasi-Newton method in the kth iterate:

$$A^{k+1}\delta^k = \lambda^k, \quad (5)$$

where $\lambda^k = \gamma^k + B^k \delta^k$. If we take $k \to \infty$ and $\delta_k \to 0$, our new q-quasi-Newton equation is similar to the ordinary q-quasi-Newton equation. Using the above modification of the q-BFGS formula, we obtain the new one as follows:

$$A^{k+1} = A^k - \frac{A^k \delta^k (\delta^k)^T A^k}{(\delta^k)^T A^k \delta^k} + \frac{\lambda^k (\lambda^k)^T}{(\delta^k)^T \lambda^k}, \quad (6)$$

where $\lambda^k = \gamma^k + B^k \delta^k$.

To provide a better formula, the primary task of this research is to determine how to select a suitable B^k. We direct our attention to finding B^k as a simple structure that carries some second order information of objective function. In this part, we will discuss a new choice of f and assume it to be sufficiently smooth.

Using the following quadratic model for the objective function [36,37], we have

$$f(x) \simeq f(x^{k+1}) + (g_q^{k+1})^T (x - x^{k+1}) + \frac{1}{2}(x - x^{k+1})^T G^{k+1} (x - x^{k+1}), \quad (7)$$

where G^{k+1} denotes a Hessian matrix at point x^{k+1}.

Hence,

$$f(x^k) \simeq f(x^{k+1}) - (g_q^{k+1})^T \delta^k + \frac{1}{2}(\delta^k)^T G^{k+1} \delta^k. \quad (8)$$

Therefore,

$$\begin{aligned}(\delta^k)^T G^{k+1} \delta^k &\simeq 2(f^k - f^{k+1} + (g_q^{k+1})^T \delta^k), \\ &= 2(f^k - f^{k+1}) + (g_q^{k+1} + g_q^k)^T \delta^k + (\delta^k)^T \gamma^k,\end{aligned} \quad (9)$$

where f^k denotes the value of f at x^k.

By using (5), we have

$$(\delta^k)^T A^{k+1} \delta^k = (\delta^k)^T \lambda^k = (\delta^k)^T \gamma^k + (\delta^k)^T B^k \delta^k. \quad (10)$$

The combination of Equations (9) and (10) shows that the reasonable choice of B^k should satisfied the following new q-quasi-Newton equation:

$$(\delta^k)^T B^k \delta^k = \mu^k \quad (\mu^k = 2(f^k - f^{k+1}) + (g_q^{k+1} + g_q^k)^T \delta^k). \tag{11}$$

Theorem 1. *Assume that B^k satisfies (11) and A^k is generated by (6), then for any k,*

$$f(x^k) = f(x^{k+1}) + (g_q^{k+1})^T(x^k - x^{k+1}) + \frac{1}{2}(x^k - x^{k+1})^T A^{k+1}(x^k - x^{k+1}). \tag{12}$$

Proof. The conclusion follows immediately using Equations (10) and (11). □

The function f holds the Equation (12) without any convexity assumption on it and any formula derived from the original quasi-Newton equation fails to satisfy the Equation (12). From Equation (11), a choice of B^k can be defined as follows :

$$B^k \delta^k = \eta^k, \quad \left(\eta^k = \frac{\mu^k}{(\delta^k)^T v^k} v^k\right). \tag{13}$$

In above Equation (13), v^k is some vector such that $(\delta^k)^T v^k \neq 0$.

By the Equations (2) and (3), we know that if $\delta^k = 0$ then $g_q^k = 0$. Therefore, for all k we can always assume that $\|\delta^k\| \neq 0$; otherwise, at the kth iteration, the algorithm terminates. Hence, we can choose $v^k = \delta^k$. Taking $v^k = \delta^k$ in the Equation (10), we have a choice of B^k as follows:

$$B^k = \frac{\mu^k}{\|\delta^k\|^2} I, \tag{14}$$

where the norm is the Euclidean norm and $\mu^k = 2(f^k - f^{k+1}) + (g_q^{k+1} + g_q^k)^T \delta^k$.

Remark 1. *The structure of B^k is very simple, so we can construct and analyze it easily. We only need to consider the value of $B^k \delta^k$ to calculate the modified A^{k+1} from the modified quasi-Newton Equation (5). Thus, once v^k is fixed, different choices of B^k, which satisfied (13) gives the same A^{k+1}.*

For computing the step length following q-gradient based modified Armijo–Wolfe line search conditions [34] are used:

$$f(x^k + \alpha^k d_q^k) \leq f(x^k) + \sigma_1 \alpha^k (d_q^k)^T g_q^k, \tag{15}$$

and

$$\nabla_q f(x^k + \alpha^k d_q^k)^T d_q^k \geq \sigma_2 (d_q^k)^T g_q^k, \tag{16}$$

where $0 < \sigma_1 < \sigma_2 < 1$. Additionally, if $\alpha^k = 1$ satisfies (16), we take $\alpha^k = 1$. In the above line search, a sufficient reduction in the objective function and nonacceptance of short step length is ensured by (15) and (16), respectively.

A good property of Formula (6) is that A^{k+1} inherits the positive definiteness of A^k as long as $(\delta^k)^T \lambda^k > 0$; provided that f is convex and step length is computed by an above line search. However, when f is a non-convex function, then the above line search does not ensure the condition $(\delta^k)^T \lambda^k > 0$. Hence, in this case, A^{k+1} is not necessarily positive definite even if A^k is positive definite. Therefore, some extra caution updates should be introduced as follows:

Define the index set K as follows:

$$K = \left\{ k : \frac{(\delta^k)^T \lambda^k}{\|\delta^k\|^2} \geq \epsilon \|g_q^k\|^c \right\}, \tag{17}$$

where $\beta \in [\vartheta_1, \vartheta_2]$, with $0 < \vartheta_1 \leq \vartheta_2$ and ϵ are positive constants. We determine A^{k+1} by the following rule:

$$A^{k+1} = \begin{cases} A^k - \frac{A^k \delta^k (\delta^k)^T A^k}{(\delta^k)^T A^k \delta^k} + \frac{\lambda^k (\lambda^k)^T}{(\delta^k)^T \lambda^k} & \text{if } k \in K \\ A^k & \text{if } k \notin K. \end{cases} \tag{18}$$

Corollary 1. *Let B^k be chosen such Equation (13) holds and A^k is generated by (18), then $A^{k+1} > 0, \forall k \in \mathbb{N} \cup \{0\}$.*

Proof. Without loss of generality, let $\|g^k\| \neq 0, \forall k$. We use mathematical induction on k to prove this corollary. Since B^0 is chosen as a positive definite symmetric matrix, the result holds for $k = 0$. Let's assume that the result holds for $k = n$. We consider the case when $k = n + 1$. If $k \in K$, then from Equations (17) and (18), $(\delta^k)^T \lambda^k > 0$ holds. Hence, for $k = n + 1$, the result also holds. If $k \notin K$, then by our assumption, $A^{k+1} = A^k$ is also positive definite. This completes the proof. □

From the above modifications, we introduce the following Algorithm 1:

Algorithm 1 Modified q-BFGS algorithm

Require: Objective function $f : \mathbb{R}^n \to \mathbb{R}$, ϵ is tolerance for convergence. Select an initial point $x^0 \in \mathbb{R}^n$, fix $q \in (0, 1)$, and an initial positive definite symmetric matrix $A^o \in \mathbb{R}^{n \times m}$.

Ensure: With the corresponding objective value $f(x^*)$, the minimizer x^* is encountered.

1: Set $A^0 = I_n$.
2: **for** k = 0, 1, 2 . . . **do**
3:     **if** $\|g_q^k\| < \epsilon$ **then**
4:         Stop.
5:     **else**
6:         Solve the Equation (3) to find a q-descent direction d_q^k.
7:         Find a step length α^k satisfying Equations (15) and (16).
8:     **end if**
9:     Compute $x^{k+1} = x^k + \alpha^k d_q^k$ and using the following equation, calculate B^k:

$$B^k = \frac{\mu^k}{\|\delta^k\|^2} I,$$

where the norm is the Euclidean norm and

$$\mu^k = 2(f^k - f^{k+1}) + (g_q^{k+1} + g_q^k)^T \delta^k.$$

10:     Select two appropriate constants β, ϵ, then update A^{k+1} by (18).
11: **end for**

---

4. Analysis of the Convergence

Under the following two assumptions, the global convergence [11] of the modified q-BFGS algorithm is shown in this section.

Assumption 1. *The level set*
$$\Omega = \{x \in \mathbb{R}^n | f(x) \leq f(x^0)\}$$
is bounded.

Assumption 2. *The function f is continuously q-derivative on Ω, and there exist a constant (Lipschitz constant) $L > 0$, such that*
$$\|g_q(x_1) - g_q(x_2)\| \leq L\|x_1 - x_2\|, \ \forall \ x_1, x_2 \in \Omega. \tag{19}$$

Since $\{f^k\}$ is a decreasing sequence, it is clear that the sequence $\{x^k\}$ generated by the modified q-BFGS algorithm is contained in Ω.

To establish the global convergence of the modified q-BFGS algorithm in the context of q-calculus, first, we show the following lemma:

Lemma 1. *Let Assumptions 1 and 2 hold for f and with $q \in (0,1)$, $\{x^k\}$ be generated by Algorithm 1. If there exist positive constants a_1 and a_2 such that the following inequalities:*
$$\|A^k \delta^k\| \leq a_1 \|\delta^k\| \quad \text{and} \quad (\delta^k)^T A^k \delta^k \geq a_2 \|\delta^k\|^2, \tag{20}$$
holds for infinitely many k, then we have
$$\lim_{k \to \infty} \inf \|g_q(x^k)\| = 0 \tag{21}$$

Proof. Using Equations (2) and (3) in (20), we have
$$a_2 \|d_q^k\| \leq \|g_q^k\| \leq a_1 \|d_q^k\| \quad \text{and} \quad (d_q^k)^T A^k d_q^k \geq a_2 \|d_q^k\|^2. \tag{22}$$

We consider a new case using the q-Armijo type line search (15) with backtracking parameter $\rho \in (0,1)$. If $\alpha^k \neq 1$, then we have
$$\sigma_1 \rho^{-1} \alpha^k g_q(x^k)^T d_q^k < f(x^k + \rho^{-1} \alpha^k d_q^k) - f(x^k). \tag{23}$$

By the q-mean value theorem [19], there is a $\theta^k \in (0,1)$ such that
$$f(x^k + \rho^{-1} \alpha^k d_q^k) - f(x^k) = \rho^{-1} \alpha^k g_q(x^k + \theta^k \rho^{-1} \alpha^k d_q^k)^T d_q^k,$$
that is,
$$f(x^k + \rho^{-1} \alpha^k d_q^k) - f(x^k) = \rho^{-1} \alpha^k g_q(x^k)^T d_q^k + \rho^{-1} \alpha^k (g_q(x^k + \theta^k \rho^{-1} \alpha^k d_q^k) - g_q(x^k))^T d_q^k.$$

From Assumption 2, we obtain
$$f(x^k + \rho^{-1} \alpha^k d_q^k) - f(x^k) \leq \rho^{-1} \alpha^k g_q(x^k)^T d_q^k + L\rho^{-2}(\alpha^k)^2 \|d_q^k\|^2. \tag{24}$$

From (23) and (24), we obtain for any $k \in K$
$$\alpha^k \geq \frac{-(1-\sigma_1)\rho g_q^k(x^k)^T d_q^k}{L\|d_q^k\|^2}.$$

Since $-g_q(x^k) = A^k d_q^k$,
$$\alpha^k \geq \frac{(1-\sigma_1)\rho (d_q^k)^T A^k d_q^k}{L\|d_q^k\|^2}.$$

Using (22) in the above inequality, we obtain

$$\alpha^k \geq min\{1, (1-\sigma_1)a_2 L^{-1}\rho\} > 0. \tag{25}$$

We consider the case where line search (16) is used; then, from Assumption 2 and from the inequality (16), we obtain the following:

$$(\sigma_2 - 1)g_q(x^k)^T d_q^k \leq (g_q(x^k + \alpha^k d_q^k) - g_q(x^k))^T d_q^k \leq L\alpha^k \|d_q^k\|^2.$$

The above inequality implies that

$$\alpha^k \geq \frac{(\sigma_2 - 1)g_q(x^k)^T d_q^k}{L\|d_q^k\|^2}.$$

Since $-g_q^k = A^k d_q^k$,

$$\alpha^k \geq \frac{-(\sigma_2 - 1)(d_q^k)^T A^k d_q^k}{L\|d_q^k\|^2}.$$

Since $A^k d_q^k \geq a_2 \|d_q^k\|^2$,

$$\alpha^k \geq min\{1, (1-\sigma_2)a_2 L^{-1}\rho\} > 0. \tag{26}$$

The inequalities (25) and (26) together show that $\{\alpha_k\}_{k \in K}$ is bounded below away from zero whenever line search (16) and (15) are used. Moreover,

$$\sum_{k=0}^{\infty} [f(x^k) - f(x^{k+1})] = \lim_{i \to \infty} \sum_{k=1}^{i} [f(x^k) - f(x^{k+1})],$$
$$= f(x^1) - \lim_{i \to \infty} f(x^j).$$

That is,

$$\sum_{k=0}^{\infty} [f(x^k) - f(x^{k+1})] = f(x^1) - f(x^*).$$

This gives the following result

$$\sum_{k=1}^{\infty} [f(x^k) - f(x^{k+1})] < \infty.$$

The above inequality, together with (15) gives,

$$-\sum_{k=1}^{\infty} \alpha^k (g_q^k)^T d_q^k < \infty.$$

Since $g_q^k = -A^k d_q^k$,

$$\lim_{k \to \infty} (d_q^k)^T A^k d_q^k = -\lim_{k \to \infty} (g_q^k)^T d_q^k \to 0.$$

The above result, together with (22), implies (21). □

From the above Lemma 1, we can say that to establish the global convergence of Algorithm 1, it is sufficient to show that there are positive constants a_1 and a_2 such that the (20) holds for infinitely many k. To prove this, we need the following lemma [34]:

Lemma 2. *Let A^0 be a positive definite and symmetric matrix and A^k be updated by (18). Suppose that there exist positive constant $m < M$ such that, for each $k \geq 0$, λ^k and δ^k satisfy*

$$\frac{(\delta^k)^T \lambda^k}{\|\delta^k\|^2} \geq m \text{ and } \frac{\|\lambda^k\|^2}{(\delta)^T \lambda^k} \leq M. \tag{27}$$

Then, there exist constants $a_1, a_2 > 0$ such that for any positive integer t, (20) holds for at least $\lceil \frac{t}{2} \rceil$ values of $k \in \{1, 2, \ldots, t\}$.

By using Lemma 2 and Lemma 1, we can prove the following global convergence theorem for Algorithm 1.

Theorem 2. *Let f satisfy Assumption 1 and Assumption 2, and $\{x^k\}$ be generated by modified q-BFGS Algorithm 1, then the Equation (21) is satisfied.*

Proof. By using Lemma 1, it is sufficient to show that there are infinitely many k which satisfies (20).

If the set K is finite, then after a finite number of iterations, A^k remains constant. Since matrix, A^k is positive definite and symmetric for each k, and it is clear that there are positive constants a_1 and a_2 such that Equation (20) holds for all sufficiently large k.

Now, consider the case when K is an infinite set. We go forward by contradiction and assume that (21) is not true. Then, there exists a positive constant α such that $\|g_q^k\| > \alpha$, $\forall k$.

Then, from (17)

$$(\delta^k)^T \lambda^k \geq \epsilon \alpha^\beta \|\delta^k\|^2, \, \forall k \in K$$

$$\Rightarrow \frac{1}{(\delta^k)^T \lambda^k} \leq \frac{1}{\epsilon \alpha^\beta \|\delta^k\|^2}, \, \forall k \in K,$$

$$\Rightarrow \frac{\|\lambda^k\|^2}{(\delta^k)^T \lambda^k} \leq \frac{\|\lambda^k\|^2}{\epsilon \alpha^\beta \|\delta^k\|^2}, \, \forall k \in K.$$

From (19), we know that $\|\lambda^k\|^2 \leq L^2 \|\delta^k\|^2$. Thus, combining it with the above inequality, we obtain

$$\frac{\|\lambda^k\|^2}{(\delta^k)^T \lambda^k} \leq \frac{L^2}{\epsilon \alpha^\beta}, \, \forall k \in K.$$

Let $\frac{L^2}{\epsilon \alpha^\beta} = M$, then

$$\frac{\|\lambda^k\|^2}{(\delta^k)^T \lambda^k} \leq M, \, \forall k \in K.$$

Applying Lemma 2 to the matrix subsequence $\{A^k\}_{k \in K}$, we conclude that there exist constants $a_1, a_2 > 0$ such that the Equation (20) holds for infinitely many k. The proof is then complete. □

The above Theorem 2 shows that the modified q-BFGS algorithm is globally convergent even if convexity is not assumed for f [34].

5. Numerical Results

This section presents the comparison of numerical results obtained with the modified q-BFGS algorithm 1, the q-BFGS algorithm [34], and the BFGS Algorithm [38] for solving a collection of unconstrained optimization problems taken from [39]. For each test problem, we chose an initial matrix as a unit matrix, i.e., $A^0 = I$. Our numerical results are performed on Python3.7 (Google colab). Throughout this section 'NI', 'NF', and 'NG' indicate the total number of iterations, the total number of function evaluations, and the total number of gradient evaluations, respectively. For each test problem, the parameters are common to modified q-BFGS, q-BFGS, and BFGS algorithms. We set $q = 0.9999999$, $\sigma_1 = 0.0001$, and $\sigma_2 = 0.9$, and used the condition $\|g_q^k\| \leq 10^{-6}$ as the stopping criteria. Moreover, we set the parameter $\beta = 3$, when $\|g_q^k\| \leq 10^{-6}$ otherwise we take $\beta = 0.01$. In general, we take $q \to 1$ and $q \neq 1$. When $q \neq 1$, then the q-gradient can make any angle with the classical gradient and the search direction can point in any direction.

We have used performance profiles for evaluating and comparing the performance of algorithms on a given set of test problems through graphs. Dolan and More [40], presented an appropriate technique to demonstrate the performance profiles, which is a statistical process. We use this as an evaluation tool to show the performance of the algorithm. We are interested in using the number of the iteration, function evaluations, and q-gradient evaluations as the performance measure. The performance ratio is presented as

$$\rho_{p,s} = \frac{r_{(p,s)}}{min\{r_{(p,s)} : 1 \leq r \leq n_s\}}, \qquad (28)$$

Here, $r_{(p,s)}$ refers to the number of the iteration, function evaluations, and q-gradient evaluations, respectively, required to solve problem p by solver s and n_s refers to the number of problems in the model test. The cumulative distribution function is expressed as

$$p_s(\tau) = \frac{1}{n_p}\text{size}\{p \in \rho_{p,s} \leq \tau\}$$

where $p_s(\tau)$ is the probability that a performance ratio $\rho_{p,s}$ is within a factor of τ of the best possible ratio. That is, for a subset of the methods being analyzed, we plot the fraction $p_s(\tau)$ of problems for which any given method is within a factor (τ) of the best. Now we take the following examples to show the computational results:

Example 1. *Consider the non-convex Rosenbrock function $f : \mathbb{R}^2 \to \mathbb{R}$ such that*

$$f(x_1, x_2) = 100(x_2 - x_1^2)^2 + (x_1 - 1)^2.$$

Following Figure 1 represents the surface plot of the Rosenbrock function:

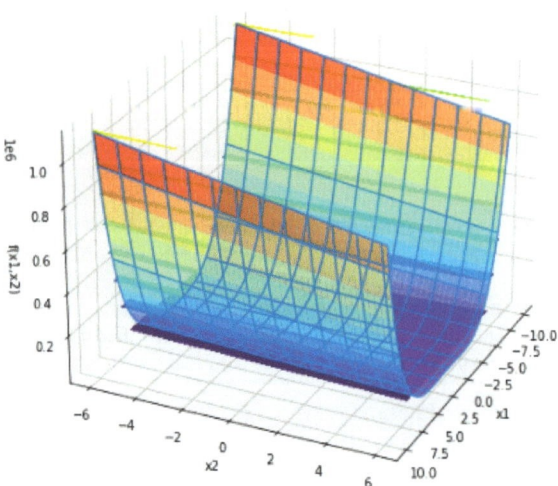

Figure 1. Surface plot of Rosenbrock function.

The Rosenbrock function was introduced by Rosenbrock in 1960. We tested modified q-BFGS, q-BFGS, and BFGS algorithms for 10 different initial points. Numerical results for the Rosenbrock function are given in the following Table 1:

Table 1. Comparison of numerical results of Modified q-BFGS, q-BFGS, and BFGS algorithms for the Rosenbrock function.

S.No.	x^0	Modified q-BFGS NI/NF/NG	q-BFGS NI/NF/NG	BFGS NI/NF/NG
1	$(-1.5, -1)^T$	25/95/47	47/198/66	49/213/71
2	$(0,0)^T$	22/77/35	21/78/26	20/75/25
3	$(-4,4)^T$	27/125/73	63/82/246	63/255/85
4	$(-3,0)^T$	28/118/64	55/210/70	58/210/70
5	$(10,0)^T$	54/197/91	40/150/50	85/372/120
6	$(7,-7)^T$	52/184/82	75/294/98	76/414/134
7	$(4,5)^T$	48/174/80	51/201/67	51/198/66
8	$(-2,-2)^T$	26/112/62	55/201/67	57/342/110
9	$(1,1.2)^T$	9/38/22	13/57/19	12/93/27
10	$(0,4)^T$	27/113/61	25/96/32	26/114/38

The Rosenbrock function converges to $x^* = (1,1)^T$ with value $f(x^*) = 0$, for the above starting points x^0. Figures 2–4 show the Dolan and More performance profiles of modified q-BFGS, q-BFGS, and BFGS algorithms for the Rosenbrock function, respectively.

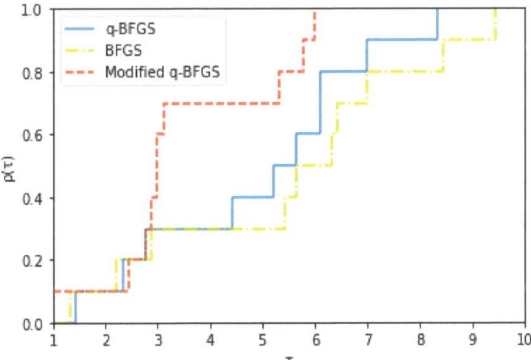

Figure 2. Performance profile based on number of iterations.

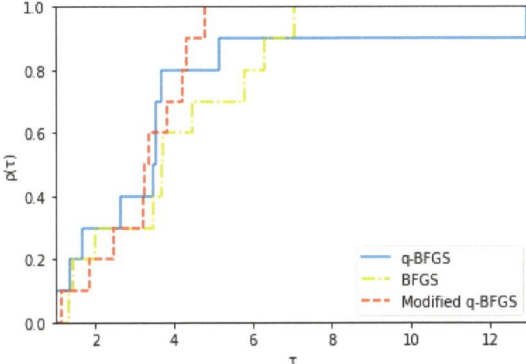

Figure 3. Performance profile based on number of gradient evaluations.

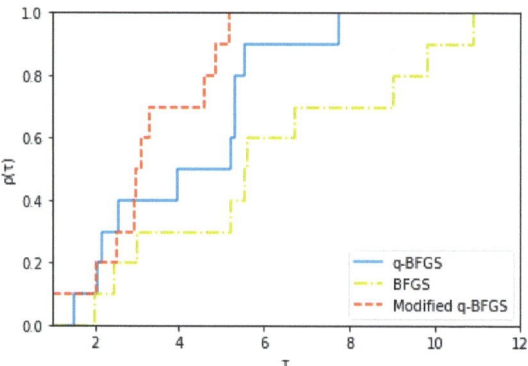

Figure 4. Performance profile based on number of function evaluations.

The global minima and plotting points of the Rosenbrock function using the modified q-BFGS algorithm can also be observed in Figure 5.

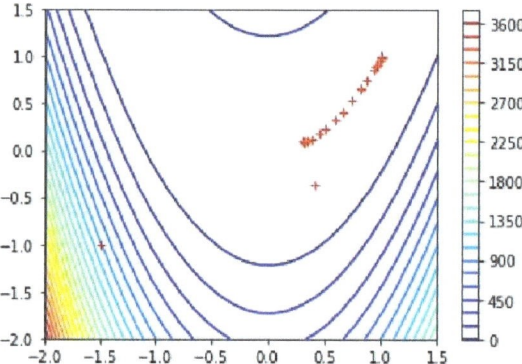

Figure 5. Global minima of the Rosenbrock function using modified q-BFGS algorithm.

For the starting point $x^0 = (-1.5, -1)$, the Rosenbrock function converges to

$$x^* = [0.999999996685342, 0.999999997414745]^T,$$

with

$$f(x^*) = 1.64642951315324e^{-15} \text{ and } \nabla_q f(x^*) = [-1.66435354e^{-06}, 7.98812111e^{-07}]^T,$$

in 25 iterations.

The global minima and plotting points of the Rosenbrock function using the q-BFGS algorithm can also be observed in Figure 6.

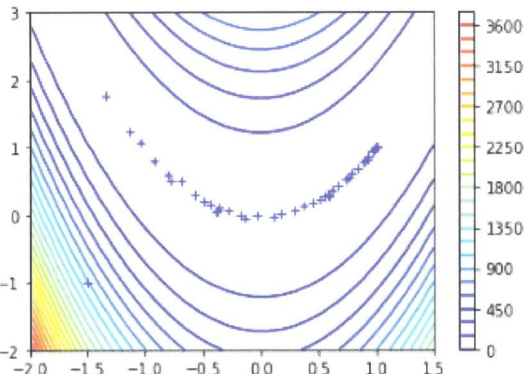

Figure 6. Global minima of the Rosenbrock function using q-BFGS algorithm [34].

For the starting point $x^0 = (-1.5, -1)$, the Rosenbrock function converges to

$x^* = [1.0000000, 1.00000001]^T$,

with

$f(x^*) = 1.541354346404984e^{-16}$ and $\nabla_q f(x^*) = [4.42018890e^{-07}, -2.47425057e^{-07}]^T$.

in 47 iterations.

The global minima and plotting points of the Rosenbrock function using the BFGS algorithm can also be observed in Figure 7.

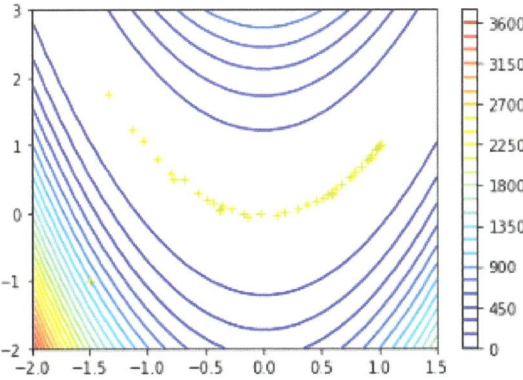

Figure 7. Global minima of the Rosenbrock function using BFGS algorithm.

For the starting point $x^0 = (-1.5, -1)$, the Rosenbrock function converges to

$x^* = [0.99999552, 0.99999103]^T$,

with

$f(x^*) = 2.0060569721431806e^{-11}$ and $\nabla_q f(x^*) = [7.91549092e^{-07}, -3.95920563e^{-07}]^T$,

in 49 iterations.

Example 2. *We consider*

$$f(x) = \begin{cases} x^2 - 2 & \text{if } x < 2 \\ x^2 + 2 & \text{if } x \geq 2, \end{cases}$$

which is non-differentiable at $x = 2$. For initial point $x^0 = 9$, using our modified q-BFGS algorithm we reach minima at $x^* = 0$ in 4 iterations, 10 function evaluations, and 5 gradient evaluations.

Example 3. *Consider the non-convex Rastrigin function f such that*

$$f(x) = 10d + \sum_{i=1}^{d}[x_i^2 - 10cos(2\pi x_i)]$$

Following Figure 8 represents the surface plot of the Rastrigin function:

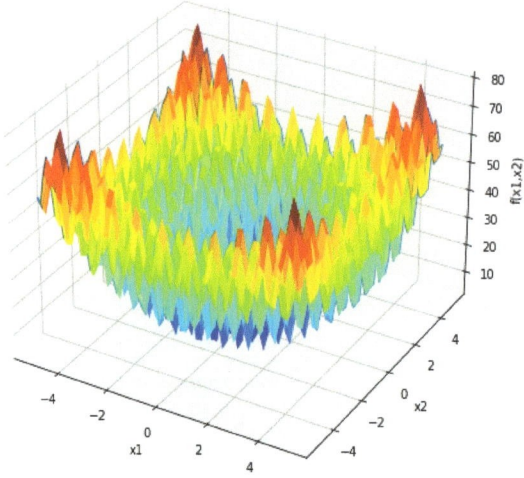

Figure 8. Surface plot of the Rastrigin function.

The Rastrigin function f has a global minimum at

$$x^* = (0, 0, \ldots, 0),$$

with value

$$f(x^*) = 0.$$

We tested modified q-BFGS, q-BFGS, and, BFGS algorithms for initial point $x^0 = (0.2, 0.2)$.
The global minima and plotting points of the Rastrigin function using the modified q-BFGS algorithm can be observed in Figure 9.

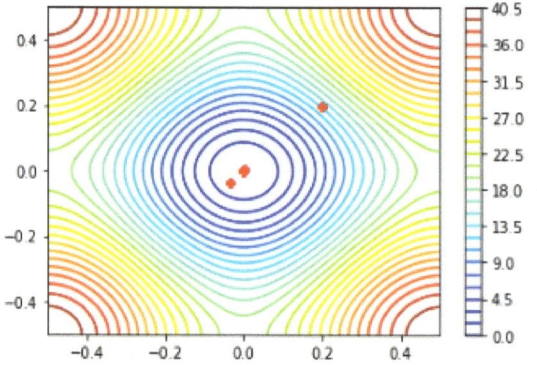

Figure 9. Global minima of the Rastrigin function using the modified q-BFGS algorithm.

The numerical results for the Rastrigin function, using the modified q-BFGS algorithm are as follows:

For the starting point $x^0 = (0.2, 0.2)$, the Rastrigin function converges to

$$x^* = [-6.83810097023008e^{-6}, -6.83810097023008e^{-6}]^T,$$

with

$$f(x^*) = 1.85534789132191e^{-9} \text{ and } \nabla_q f(x^*) = [-1.3676e^{-6}, -1.3676e^{-6}]^T.$$

NI/NF/NG = 4/18/6.

The global minima and plotting points of the Rastrigin function using the q-BFGS algorithm can be observed in Figure 10.

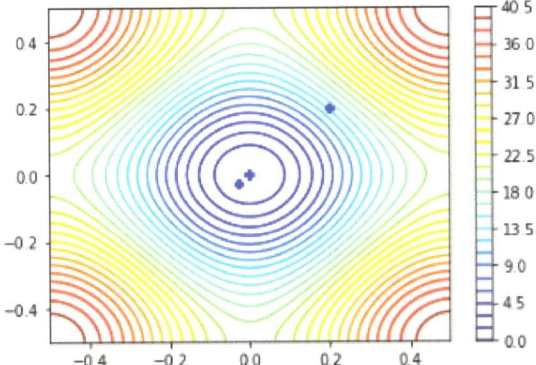

Figure 10. Global minima of the Rastrigin function using q-BFGS algorithm.

The numerical results for the Rastrigin function, using the q-BFGS algorithm are as follows:
For the starting point $x^0 = (0.2, 0.2)$, The Rastrigin function converges to

$$x^* = [-1.18906228e^{-06}, -2.65293229e^{-07}]^T,$$

with

$$f(x^*) = 2.944648969105401e^{-10} \text{ and } \nabla_q f(x^*) = [0., 0.]^T.$$

NI/NF/NG = 5/24/8.

The global minima and plotting points of the Rastrigin function using the BFGS algorithm can be observed in Figure 11.

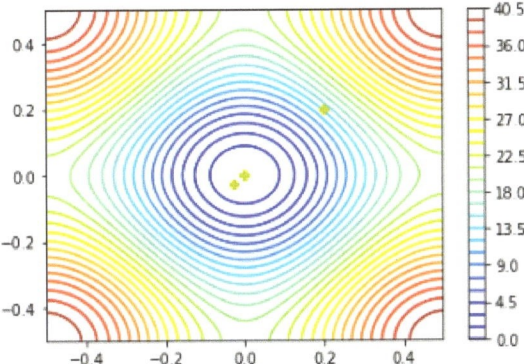

Figure 11. Global minima of the Rastrigin function using BFGS algorithm.

The numerical results for the Rastrigin function using the BFGS algorithm are as follows: For the starting point $x^0 = (0.2, 0.2)$, the Rastrigin function converges to

$$x^* = (-7.14289963e^{-09}, -7.37267609e^{-09})^T,$$

with

$$f(x^*) = 2.1316282072803006e^{-14} \text{ and } \nabla f(x^*) = (1.1920929e^{-07}, 0.0000000e^{00})^T.$$

NI/NF/NG = 7/36/12.

From the above numerical results, we conclude that using the modified q-BFGS algorithm, we can reach the critical point by taking the least number of iterations.

Example 4. Consider the SIX-HUMP CAMEL function $f: \mathbb{R}^2 \to \mathbb{R}$ such that

$$f(x) = \left(4 - 2.1x_1^2 + \frac{x_1^4}{3}\right)x_1^2 + x_1 x_2 + (-4 + 4x_2^2)x_2^2$$

The Figure 12 on the left shows the SIX-HUMP CAMEL function on its recommended input domain and on the right shows only a portion of this domain for easier view of the function's key characteristics. The function f has six local minima, two of which are global.

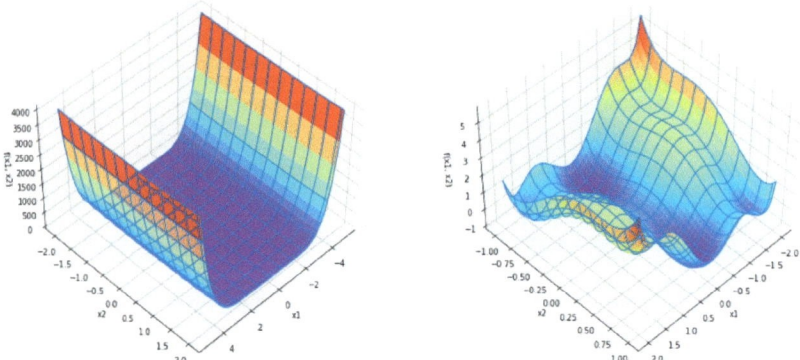

Figure 12. Surface plot of the SIX-HUMP CAMEL function.

Input Domain: The function is usually evaluated on the rectangle $x_1 \in [-3, 3]$, $x_2 \in [-2, 2]$. This function has a global minimum at

$$x^* = (0.0898, -0.7126) \text{ and } (-0.0898, 0.7126),$$

with value

$$f(x^*) = -1.0316.$$

For the starting point $x^0 = (1, 1)$, with the modified q-BFGS algorithm f converges to x^* in eight iterations whereas with q-BFGS and BFGS it takes 13 iterations. Tables 2–4 give numerical results and Figures 13–15 represents the global minima and sequence of iterative points generated with modified q-BFGS, q-BFGS and BFGS algorithms, respectively.

Table 2. Numerical results for Modified q-BFGS algorithm.

S.N.	x	$f(x)$	$\nabla_q f(x)$
1	$(1,1)^T$	3.23333333333333	$(2.59999999, 8.9999998)^T$
2	$(0.675, -0.12499997)^T$	1.27218227259399	$(2.97185835, 1.64374981)^T$
3	$(-0.06796459, -0.53593743)^T$	-0.764057148938559	$(-1.0770199, 1.75654714)^T$
4	$(-0.0353348602, -0.8064736058)^T$	-0.876032180235736	$(-1.08878201, -1.97602868)^T$
5	$(0.117691114989, -0.69297924267)^T$	-1.02498975962408	$(0.23490147, 0.33700269)^T$
6	$(0.087916835437, -0.709453427634)^T$	-1.03153652682667	$(-0.01181639, 0.05018343)^T$
7	$(0.089782273326, -0.71271422021)^T$	-1.03162840874522	$(-0.00052364, -0.00100674)^T$
8	$(0.089842117966, -0.71265601378)^T$	-1.03162845348855	$(1.20226364 \times 10^{-6}, 6.54303983 \times 10^{-6})^T$

Here, we obtain $x^* = (0.089842117966, -0.71265601378)^T$

$f(x^*) = -1.03162845348988$ and $\nabla_q f(x^*) = (-6.20473783 \times 10^{-09}, 0.00000000 \times 10^{+00})^T$

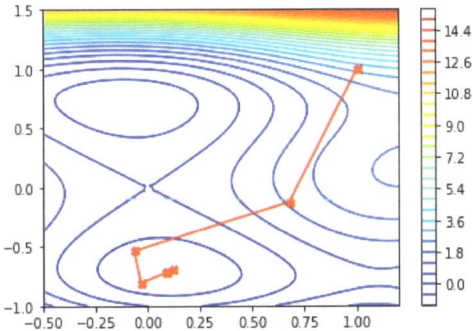

Figure 13. Global minima of SIX-HUMP CAMEL function using modified q-BFGS algorithm.

Table 3. Numerical results for q-BFGS algorithm [34].

S.N.	x	$f(x)$	$\nabla_q f(x)$
1	$(1,1)^T$	3.23333333333333	$(2.59999999, 8.9999998)^T$
2	$(0.71968495, 0.02967868)^T$	1.57257718494530	$(3.04212661, 0.4826738)^T$
3	$(-0.36642555, -0.07524058)^T$	0.505072874807150	$(-2.60658417, 0.22868392)^T$
4	$(0.13008033, -0.06568514)^T$	0.0413558838831559	$(0.95654292, 0.65102699)^T$
5	$(0.00245036, -0.12816569)^T$	-0.0649165012454617	$(-0.10856293, 0.99409097)^T$
6	$(-0.11507302, -0.35694646)^T$	-0.351034437749229	$(-1.26477125, 2.01283747)^T$
7	$(-0.23737914, -0.62081297)^T$	-0.581320173229039	$(-2.40899478, 0.90085665)^T$
8	$(-0.08148802, -0.6924283)^T$	-0.915418626192531	$(-1.33979439, 0.14610549)^T$
9	$(0.11917819, -0.6987523)^T$	-1.02633316281778	$(0.24050227, 0.25049034)^T$
10	$(0.0912121, -0.72252832)^T$	-1.03082558867975	$(0.00080671, -0.16366308)^T$
11	$(0.087625, -0.71111103)^T$	-1.03159319420704	$(-0.01575222, 0.02301181)^T$
12	$(0.09005303, -0.71260578)^T$	-1.03162824822151	$(0.00169591, 0.00104015)^T$
13	$(0.08983369, -0.71266332)^T$	-1.03162845277086	$(-7.18180083 \times 10^{-5}, -1.21481195 \times 10^{-4})^T$

Here, we obtain $x^* = (0.08983369, -0.71266332)^T$,

$f(x^*) = -1.0316284534898477$ and $\nabla_q f(x^*) = (-0.00000000 \times 10^{+00}, 9.65876859 \times 10^{-07})^T$.

Using this q-BFGS algorithm, we can reach the critical point by taking 13 iterations.

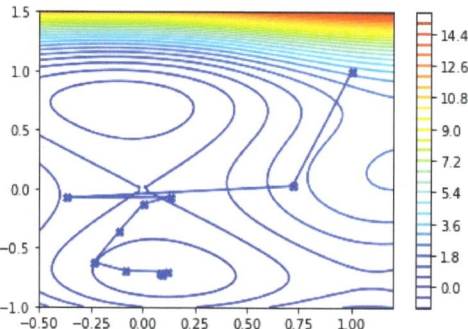

Figure 14. Global minima of SIX-HUMP CAMEL function using q-BFGS algorithm.

Table 4. Numerical results for BFGS algorithm.

S.N.	x	$f(x)$	$\nabla_q f(x)$
1	$(1,1)^T$	3.23333333333333	$(2.59999999, 8.9999998)^T$
2	$(0.71968497, 0.02967869)^T$	1.5725772653791203	$(3.04212611, 0.48267368)^T$
3	$(0.13008034, -0.06568512)^T$	0.041355907444434827	$(0.95654306, 0.65102689)^T$
4	$(0.00245035, -0.12816566)^T$	-0.06491646830150141	$(-0.10856298, 0.99409077)^T$
5	$(-0.11507301, -0.35694647)^T$	-0.35103445558228663	$(-1.26477118, 2.01283762)^T$
6	$(-0.23737911, -0.62081301)^T$	-0.5813202779118049	$(-2.40899456, 0.90085617)^T$
7	$(-0.08148803, -0.6924282)^T$	-0.9154186025665918	$(-1.33979439, 0.1461069)^T$
8	$(0.11917811, -0.69875236)^T$	-1.0263331977999757	$(0.24050162, 0.25048941)^T$
9	$(0.09121207, -0.72252828)^T$	-1.0308255945761227	$(0.00080669, -0.16366242)^T$
10	$(0.08762501, -0.71111104)^T$	-1.031593194593363	$(-0.01575207, 0.02301181)^T$
11	$(0.09005304, -0.71260578)^T$	-1.031628248214576	$(0.00169598, 0.00104006)^T$
12	$(0.08983368, -0.7126633)^T$	-1.0316284527721356	$(0.000016959, 0.000104006)^T$
13	$(0.08984197, 0.71265633)^T$	-1.0316284534898297	$(-7.19424520 \times 10^{-5}, -1.21236354 \times 10^{-4})^T$

Here, we obtain $x^* = (0.08984197, -0.71265633)^T$,

$f(x^*) = -1.0316284534898448$ and $\nabla f(x^*) = (-2.68220901 \times 10^{-07}, 9.98377800 \times 10^{-07})^T$.

Using this BFGS algorithm, we can reach the critical point by taking 13 iterations.

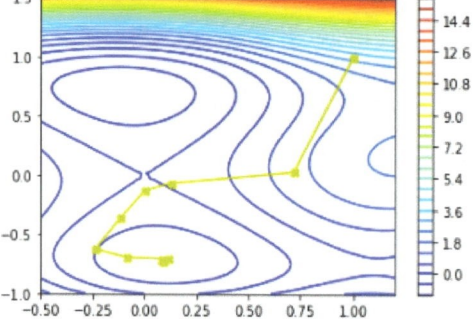

Figure 15. Global minima of SIX-HUMP CAMEL function using BFGS algorithm.

We conclude that using the modified q-BFGS algorithm, we can reach the critical point by taking the least number of iterations. From the performance results and plotting points for the multimodal functions it could be seen that the q-descent direction has a mechanism to escape from many local minima and move towards the global minimum.

Now, we compare the performance of numerical algorithms for large dimensional Rosenbrock and Wood function. Numerical results for these functions are given in Tables 5 and 6.

Numerical results for the large dimensional Rosenbrock function for $x^0 = (0, 0, \ldots, 0)$

$$f(x) = \sum_{i=1}^{d-1} [100(x_{i+1} - x_i^2)^2 + (x_i - 1)^2]$$

Table 5. Comparison of numerical results of Modified q-BFGS, q-BFGS, and BFGS algorithm for the large dimensional Rosenbrock function.

S.No.	Dimension	Modified q-BFGS NI/NF/NG	q-BFGS NI/NF/NG	BFGS NI/NF/NG
1	10	58/889/132	63/972/81	61/1365/123
2	50	242/15,432/300	253/17,316/324	253/17,199/337
3	100	466/63,088/604	486/64,056/636	479/64,741/641
4	200	904/209,912/1175	978/248,056/1228	956/253,674/1262

Numerical results for large dimensional WOOD function [39] for $x^0 = (0, 0, \ldots, 0)$

Table 6. Comparison of numerical results of Modified q-BFGS, q-BFGS, and BFGS algorithm for Large Dimensional Wood function.

S.No.	Dimension	Modified q-BFGS NI/NF/NG	q-BFGS NI/NF/NG	BFGS NI/NF/NG
1	20	85/1976/98	91/2872/130	103/2478/118
2	80	162/19,745/198	193/21,250/259	209/22,366/276
3	100	197/19,965/255	240/30,714/301	254/29,290/290
4	200	296/75,686/397	370/93,538/463	378/93,678/466

We have taken 20 test problems to show the proposed method's efficiency and numerical results. We take tolerance $\epsilon = 10^{-6}$, $\sigma_1 = 0.0001$, and $\sigma_2 = 0.9$. Our numerical results are shown in Tables 7–9 with the problem number(S.N.), problem name, Dimension (DIM), starting point, the total number of iterations (NI), the total number of function evaluations (NF), the total number of gradient evaluations (NG), respectively.

Table 7. Numerical results for Modified q-BFGS algorithm.

S.N.	Problems	x^0	DIM	NI	NF	NG	x^*
1	ROSENBROCK	$(-1.5, -1)^T$	2	25	95	47	$(1.0000, 1.0000)^T$
2	FROTH	$(0.5, -2)^T$	2	9	37	20	$(11.4128, -0.8968)^T$
3	BADSCP	$(0, 1)^T$	2	174	618	272	$(1.0981 \times 10^{-5}, 9.1062)^T$
4	BADSCB	$(1, 1)^T$	2	11	100	80	$(1000000.0000, 1.9999 \times 10^{-6})^T$
5	BEALE	$(3, 1)^T$	2	12	44	21	$(3.0000, 0.5000)^T$
6	JENSAM	$(1, 0.4)^T$	2	15	57	20	$(0.56094, 0.56094)^T$
7	WOOD	$(-3, -1, -3, -1)^T$	4	42	205	52	$(1.0000, 1.0000, 1.0000, 1.0000)^T$
8	POWELL SINGULAR	$(3, -1, 0, 1)^T$	4	23	91	46	$(-0.0011, 0.0001, 0.0009, 0.0009)^T$
9	RASTRIGIN	$(0.2, 0.2)^T$	2	4	18	6	$(-6.8381 \times 10^{-5}, -6.8381 \times 10^{-5})^T$
10	GOLDSTEIN PRICE	$(0.5, 0.5)^T$	2	12	106	84	$(5.4911 \times 10^{-5}, -1.0000)^T$
11	THREE-HUMP CAMEL	$(-2.5, 0)^T$	2	5	19	10	$(8.3463 \times 10^{-8}, 1.9707 \times 10^{-7})^T$
12	COLVILLE	$(0, 0, 0, 0)^T$	4	27	109	56	$(1.0000, 1.0000, 1.0000, 1.0000)^T$
13	BOOTH	$(2, 2)^T$	2	2	11	8	$(1.0000, 3.0000)^T$
14	SINE VALLEY	$(3\pi/2, -1)^T$	2	35	115	46	$(-1.4495 \times 10^{-11}, -1.6686 \times 10^{-11})^T$
15	BRANIN	$(9.3, 3)^T$	2	5	18	9	$(9.4248, 2.4750)^T$
16	SIX HUMP CAMEL	$(1, 1)^T$	2	8	32	17	$(0.0898, -0.7126)^T$
17	HIMMELBLAU	$(1, 1)^T$	2	9	37	20	$(3.0000, 2.0000)^T$
18	SHEKEL	$(0, 0, 0, 0)^T$	4	14	105	35	$(4.0007, 4.0005, 3.9997, 3.9995)^T$
19	HARTMAN 3D	$(0, 0.5, 0.4)^T$	3	10	100	21	$(0.1146, 0.5556, 0.8525)^T$
20	GRIEWANK	$(2, -1.2)^T$	2	8	25	9	$(-6.9305 \times 10^{-5}, -5.0749 \times 10^{-5})^T$

Table 8. Numerical results for q-BFGS algorithm.

S.N.	Problems	x^0	DIM	NI	NF	NG	x^*
1	ROSENBROCK	$(-1.5, -1)^T$	2	47	198	66	$(1.0000, 1.0000^T$
2	FROTH	$(0.5, -2)^T$	2	9	30	10	$(11.4127, -0.8968)^T$
3	BADSCP	$(0, 1)^T$	2	158	609	203	$(1.0981 \times 10^{-5}, 9.1061)^T$
4	BADSCB	$(1, 1)^T$	2	-	-	-	-
5	BEALE	$(3, 1)^T$	2	13	48	16	$(3.0000, 0.5000)^T$
6	JENSAM	$(1, 0.4)^T$	2	17	66	22	$(0.56095, 0.56095)^T$
7	WOOD	$(-3, -1, -3, -1)^T$	4	87	309	103	$(1.0000, 1.0000, 1.0000, 1.0000)^T$
8	POWELL SINGULAR	$(3, -1, 0, 1)^T$	4	37	126	42	$(2.3008 \times 10^{-4}, -2.3007 \times 10^{-5}, 9.0539 \times 10^{-4}, 9.0545 \times 10^{-4})^T$
9	RASTRIGIN	$(0.2, 0.2)^T$	2	5	24	8	$(-1.1890 \times 10^{-6}, -2.6529 \times 10^{-7})^T$
10	GOLDSTEIN PRICE	$(0.5, 0.5)^T$	2	-	-	-	-
11	THREE-HUMP CAMEL	$(-2.5, 0)^T$	2	8	36	12	$(-1.7475, 0.8738)^T$
12	COLVILLE	$(0, 0, 0, 0)^T$	4	26	102	34	$(1.0000, 1.0000, 1.0000, 1.0000)^T$
13	BOOTH	$(2, 2)^T$	2	3	15	5	$(1.0000, 3.0000)^T$
14	SINE VALLEY	$(3\pi/2, -1)^T$	2	37	132	44	$(4.0788 \times 10^{-10}, 4.262 \times 10^{-10})^T$
15	BRANIN	$(9.3, 3)^T$	2	6	24	8	$(9.4248, 2.4750)^T$
16	SIX HUMP CAMEL	$(1, 1)^T$	2	13	54	18	$(0.0898, -0.7126)^T$
17	HIMMELBLAU	$(1, 1)^T$	2	8	39	13	$(3.0000, 2.0000)^T$
18	SHEKEL	$(0, 0, 0, 0)^T$	4	14	105	35	$(4.0007, 4.0006, 3.9997, 3.9995)^T$
19	HARTMAN 3D	$(0, 0.5, 0.4)^T$	3	11	63	21	$(0.1088, 0.5556, 0.8526)^T$
20	GRIEWANK	$(2, -1.2)^T$	2	8	27	9	$(8.4001 \times 10^{-5}, 3.1323 \times 10^{-4})^T$

Table 9. Numerical results for BFGS algorithm.

S.N.	Problems	x^0	DIM	NI	NF	NG	x^*
1	ROSENBROCK	$(-1.5, -1)^T$	2	49	213	71	$(1.0000, 1.0000)^T$
2	FROTH	$(0.5, -2)^T$	2	9	30	10	$(11.4128, -0.8968)^T$
3	BADSCP	$(0, 1)^T$	2	-	-	-	-
4	BADSCB	$(1, 1)^T$	2	-	-	-	-
5	BEALE	$(3, 1)^T$	2	13	48	16	$(3.0000, 0.5000)^T$
6	JENSAM	$(1, 0.4)^T$	2	17	66	22	$(0.56095, 0.56095)^T$
7	WOOD	$(-3, -1, -3, -1)^T$	4	89	525	105	$(1.0000, 1.0000, 1.0000, 1.0000)^T$
8	POWELL SINGULAR	$(3, -1, 0, 1)^T$	4	41	230	46	$(7.759 \times 10^{-4}, -7.7607 \times 10^{-5}, -7.5812 \times 10^{-4}, -7.581 \times 10^{-4})^T$
9	RASTRIGIN	$(0.2, 0.2)^T$	2	7	36	12	$(-7.1429 \times 10^{-9}, -7.3727 \times 10^{-7})^T$
10	GOLDSTEIN PRICE	$(0.5, 0.5)^T$	2	17	75	25	$(-9.9828 \times 10^{-9}, -1.0000)^T$
11	THREE-HUMP CAMEL	$(-2.5, 0)^T$	2	8	36	12	$(-1.7475, 0.8738)^T$
12	COLVILLE	$(0, 0, 0, 0)^T$	4	31	190	38	$(1.0000, 1.0000, 1.0000, 1.0000)^T$
13	BOOTH	$(2, 2)^T$	2	3	15	5	$(1.0000, 3.0000)^T$
14	SINE VALLEY	$(3\pi/2, -1)^T$	2	37	141	47	$(-5.9619 \times 10^{-6}, -5.9674 \times 10^{-6})^T$
15	BRANIN	$(9.3, 3)^T$	2	6	24	8	$(9.4248, 2.4750)^T$
16	SIX HUMP CAMEL	$(1, 1)^T$	2	13	54	18	$(0.0898, -0.7126)^T$
17	HIMMELBLAU	$(1, 1)^T$	2	8	39	13	$(3.0000, 2.0000)^T$
18	SHEKEL	$(0, 0, 0, 0)^T$	4	12	160	32	$(4.0007, 4.0006, 3.9997, 3.9995)^T$
19	HARTMAN 3D	$(0, 0.5, 0.4)^T$	3	14	80	20	$(0.1146, 0.5556, 0.8525)^T$
20	GRIEWANK	$(2, -1.2)^T$	2	10	33	11	$(6.872 \times 10^{-8}, -7.2441 \times 10^{-4})^T$

Tables 5–9 show that the modified q-BFGS algorithm solves about 86% of the test problems with the least number of iterations, 82% of the test problems with the least number of function evaluations, and 52% of the test problems with the least number of gradient evaluations. Therefore, with Figures 16–18 we conclude that the modified q-BFGS performs better than other algorithms and improves the performance in fewer iterations, function evaluations, and gradient evaluations.

In Figures 17 and 18 the graph of q-BFGS and BFGS method does not converge to 1 as the methods fail to minimize two problems for each as given in Tables 8 and 9.

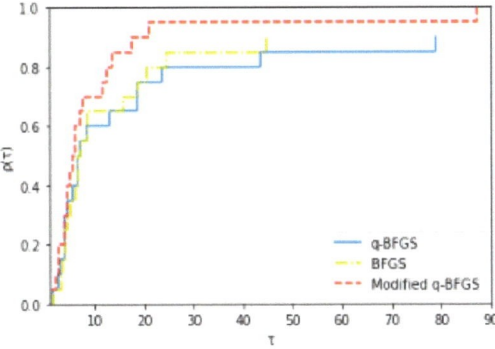

Figure 16. Performance Profile based on number of iterations.

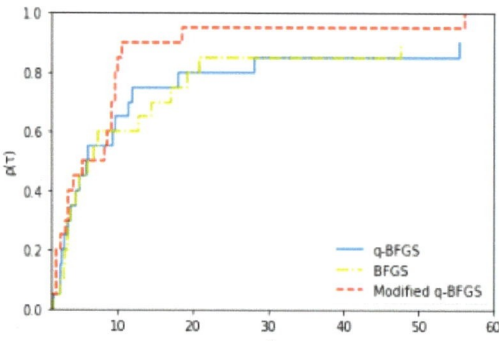

Figure 17. Performance Profile based on number of function evaluations.

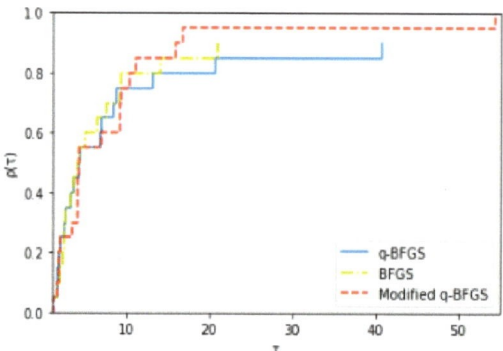

Figure 18. Performance Profile based on number of gradient evaluations.

6. Conclusions and Future Directions

We have given a new q-quasi-Newton equation and proposed a modified q-BFGS method for unconstrained minimization based on this new q-quasi-Newton equation. The method converges globally with a q-gradient-based Armijo–Wolfe line search. The q-gradient allows the search direction to be taken from a diverse set of directions and takes large steps to converge. From the performance results and plotting points for the multimodal functions, it could be seen that the q-descent direction and q-gradient-based line search have a mechanism to escape from many local minima and move towards the global minimum. The first order q-differentiability of the function is sufficient to prove the global convergence of the proposed method. The convergence and numerical results show that the algorithm given in this paper is very successful. However, many other q-quasi-Newton methods still need to be studied using the q-derivative.

Author Contributions: Formal analysis, K.K.L., S.K.M., R.S., M.S. and B.R.; funding acquisition, K.K.L.; investigation, S.K.M.; methodology, S.K.M., R.S., M.S. and B.R.; supervision, S.K.M.; validation, R.S.; writing—original draft, R.S.; writing—review and editing, K.K.L., R.S., M.S. and B.R. All authors have read and agreed to the published version of the manuscript.

Funding: The Second author is financially supported by Research Grant for Faculty (IoE Scheme) under Dev. Scheme No. 6031 and the third author is financially supported by the BHU-UGC Non-NET fellowship /R/Dev./ix-Sch.(BHU Res.Sch.)/2022-23/46476. The fifth author is financially supported by the Centre for Digital Transformation, Indian Institute of Management, Ahmedabad.

Institutional Review Board Statement: Not applicable.

Informed Consent Statement: Not applicable.

Data Availability Statement: No data were used to support this study.

Acknowledgments: The authors are indebted to the anonymous reviewers for their valuable comments and remarks that helped to improve the presentation and quality of the manuscript.

Conflicts of Interest: The authors declare no conflict of interest.

References

1. Mishra, S.K.; Ram, B. Conjugate gradient methods. In *Introduction to Unconstrained Optimization with R*; Springer Nature: Singapore, 2019; pp. 211–244.
2. Fletcher, R. *Practical Methods of Optimization*; John Wiley & Sons: Chichester, NY, USA, 2013.
3. Gill, P.; Murray, W.; Wright, M. *Practical Optimization*; Academic Press: Cambridge, MA, USA, 1981.
4. Mishra, S.K.; Ram, B. Newton's method. In *Introduction to Unconstrained Optimization with R*; Springer Nature: Singapore, 2019; pp. 175–209.
5. Mishra, S.K.; Ram, B. Quasi-Newton methods. In *Introduction to Unconstrained Optimization with R*; Springer Nature: Singapore, 2019; pp. 245–289.
6. Fletcher, R. A new approach to variable metric algorithms. *Comput. J.* **1970**, *13*, 317–322. [CrossRef]
7. Goldfarb, D. A family of variable-metric methods derived by variational means. *Math. Comput.* **1970**, *24*, 23–26. [CrossRef]
8. Shanno, D.F. Conditioning of quasi-Newton methods for function minimization. *Math. Comput.* **1970**, *24*, 647–656. [CrossRef]
9. Broyden, C.G. The convergence of a class of double-rank minimization algorithms: 2. The new algorithm. *IMA J. Appl. Math.* **1970**, *6*, 222–231. [CrossRef]
10. Mascarenhas, W.F. The BFGS method with exact line searches fails for non-convex objective functions. *Math. Program.* **2004**, *99*, 49. [CrossRef]
11. Li, D.H.; Fukushima, M. On the global convergence of the BFGS method for nonconvex unconstrained optimization problems. *SIAM J. Optim.* **2001**, *11*, 1054–1064. [CrossRef]
12. Li, D.; Fukushima, M. A globally and superlinearly convergent gauss–Newton-based BFGS method for symmetric nonlinear equations. *SIAM J. Numer. Anal.* **1999**, *37*, 152–172. [CrossRef]
13. Kac, V.G.; Cheung, P. *Quantum Calculus*; Springer: Berlin, Germany, 2002; Volume 113.
14. Ernst, T. *A Comprehensive Treatment of q-Calculus*; Springer: Basel, Switzerland, 2012.
15. Cieśliński, J.L. Improved q-exponential and q-trigonometric functions. *Appl. Math. Lett.* **2011**, *24*, 2110–2114. [CrossRef]
16. Borges, E.P. A possible deformed algebra and calculus inspired in nonextensive thermostatistics. *Phys. A Stat. Mech. Its Appl.* **2004**, *340*, 95–101. [CrossRef]
17. Tariboon, J.; Ntouyas, S.K. Quantum calculus on finite intervals and applications to impulsive difference equations. *Adv. Differ. Equations* **2013**, *2013*, 282. [CrossRef]
18. Jackson, F.H. XI.—On q-functions and a certain difference operator. *Earth Environ. Sci. Trans. R. Soc. Edinb.* **1909**, *46*, 253–281. [CrossRef]
19. Rajković, P.; Stanković, M.; Marinković, D, S. Mean value theorems in g-calculus. *Mat. Vesn.* **2002**, *54*, 171–178.
20. Ismail, M.E.; Stanton, D. Applications of q-Taylor theorems. *J. Comput. Appl. Math.* **2003**, *153*, 259–272. [CrossRef]
21. Jing, S.C.; Fan, H.Y. q-Taylor's Formula with Its q-Remainder1. *Commun. Theor. Phys.* **1995**, *23*, 117. [CrossRef]
22. Rajković, P.M.; Marinković, S.D.; Stanković, M.S. Fractional integrals and derivatives in q-calculus. *Appl. Anal. Disc. Math.* **2007**, *1*, 311–323.
23. Jackson, D.O.; Fukuda, T.; Dunn, O.; Majors, E. On q-definite integrals. *Q. J. Pure Appl. Math.* **1910**, *41*, 193–203.
24. Soterroni, A.C.; Galski, R.L.; Ramos, F.M. The q-gradient vector for unconstrained continuous optimization problems. In *Operations Research Proceedings 2010*; Springer: Heidelberg, Germany, 2011; pp. 365–370.
25. Gouvêa, É.J.; Regis, R.G.; Soterroni, A.C.; Scarabello, M.C.; Ramos, F.M. Global optimization using q-gradients. *Eur. J. Oper. Res.* **2016**, *251*, 727–738. [CrossRef]
26. Lai, K.K.; Mishra, S.K.; Ram, B. On q-quasi-Newton's method for unconstrained multiobjective optimization problems. *Mathematics* **2020**, *8*, 616. [CrossRef]
27. Mishra, S.K.; Samei, M.E.; Chakraborty, S.K.; Ram, B. On q-variant of Dai–Yuan conjugate gradient algorithm for unconstrained optimization problems. *Nonlinear Dyn.* **2021**, *104*, 2471–2496. [CrossRef]
28. Lai, K.K.; Mishra, S.K.; Ram, B. A q-conjugate gradient algorithm for unconstrained optimization problems. *Pac. J. Optim* **2021**, *17*, 57–76.
29. Van Voorhis, T.; Head-Gordon, M. A geometric approach to direct minimization. *Mol. Phys.* **2002**, *100*, 1713–1721. [CrossRef]
30. [yop] Dominic, S.; Shardt, Y.; Ding, S. Economic performance indicator based optimization for the air separation unit compressor trains. *IFAC-PapersOnLine* **2015**, *48*, 858–863. [CrossRef]
31. Dutta, S. *Optimization in Chemical Engineering*; Cambridge University Press: Cambridge, UK, 2016.
32. Head, J.D.; Zerner, M.C. A Broyden—Fletcher—Goldfarb—Shanno optimization procedure for molecular geometries. *Chem. Phys. Lett.* **1985**, *122*, 264–270. [CrossRef]
33. Ahuja, K.; Green, W.H.; Li, Y.P. Learning to optimize molecular geometries using reinforcement learning. *J. Chem. Theory Comput.* **2021**, *17*, 818–825. [CrossRef]

34. Mishra, S.K.; Panda, G.; Chakraborty, S.K.; Samei, M.E.; Ram, B. On q-BFGS algorithm for unconstrained optimization problems. *Adv. Differ. Equ.* **2020**, *2020*, 638. [CrossRef]
35. Wei, Z.; Li, G.; Qi, L. New quasi-Newton methods for unconstrained optimization problems. *Appl. Math. Comput.* **2006**, *175*, 1156–1188. [CrossRef]
36. Yuan, Y. A modified BFGS algorithm for unconstrained optimization. *IMA J. Numer. Anal.* **1991**, *11*, 325–332. [CrossRef]
37. Deng, N.; Li, Z. Some global convergence properties of a conic-variable metric algorithm for minimization with inexact line searches. *Optim. Methods Softw.* **1995**, *5*, 105–122. [CrossRef]
38. Li, D.H.; Fukushima, M. A modified BFGS method and its global convergence in nonconvex minimization. *J. Comput. Appl. Math.* **2001**, *129*, 15–35. [CrossRef]
39. Moré, J.J.; Garbow, B.S.; Hillstrom, K.E. Testing unconstrained optimization software. *ACM Trans. Math. Softw. (TOMS)* **1981**, *7*, 17–41. [CrossRef]
40. Dolan, E.D.; Moré, J.J. Benchmarking optimization software with performance profiles. *Math. Program.* **2002**, *91*, 201–213. [CrossRef]

Disclaimer/Publisher's Note: The statements, opinions and data contained in all publications are solely those of the individual author(s) and contributor(s) and not of MDPI and/or the editor(s). MDPI and/or the editor(s) disclaim responsibility for any injury to people or property resulting from any ideas, methods, instructions or products referred to in the content.

Article

Optimizing Retaining Walls through Reinforcement Learning Approaches and Metaheuristic Techniques

José Lemus-Romani [1], Diego Ossandón [2], Rocío Sepúlveda [2], Nicolás Carrasco-Astudillo [1], Victor Yepes [3] and José García [2,*]

1. Pontificia Universidad Católica de Chile, Facultad de Ingeniería, Escuela de Construcción Civil, Santiago 7820436, Chile; jose.lemus@uc.cl (J.L.-R.)
2. Pontificia Universidad Católica de Valparaíso, Facultad de Ingeniería, Escuela de Ingeniería de Construcción y Transporte, Valparaíso 2362807, Chile
3. Universitat Politècnica de València, Institute of Concrete Science and Technology (ICITECH), 46022 València, Spain
* Correspondence: jose.garcia@pucv.cl

Abstract: The structural design of civil works is closely tied to empirical knowledge and the design professional's experience. Based on this, adequate designs are generated in terms of strength, operability, and durability. However, such designs can be optimized to reduce conditions associated with the structure's design and execution, such as costs, CO_2 emissions, and related earthworks. In this study, a new discretization technique based on reinforcement learning and transfer functions is developed. The application of metaheuristic techniques to the retaining wall problem is examined, defining two objective functions: cost and CO_2 emissions. An extensive comparison is made with various metaheuristics and brute force methods, where the results show that the S-shaped transfer functions consistently yield more robust outcomes.

Keywords: metaheuristics; concrete retaining walls

MSC: 90C27

Citation: Lemus-Romani, J.; Ossandón, D.; Sepúlveda, R.; Carrasco-Astudillo, N.; Yepes, V.; García, J. Optimizing Retaining Walls through Reinforcement Learning Approaches and Metaheuristic Techniques. *Mathematics* 2023, 11, 2104. https://doi.org/10.3390/math11092104

Academic Editor: Frank Werner

Received: 17 March 2023
Revised: 21 April 2023
Accepted: 23 April 2023
Published: 28 April 2023

Copyright: © 2023 by the authors. Licensee MDPI, Basel, Switzerland. This article is an open access article distributed under the terms and conditions of the Creative Commons Attribution (CC BY) license (https://creativecommons.org/licenses/by/4.0/).

1. Introduction

Today's society is experiencing a period of rapid growth and technological advancement that has accelerated exponentially over the years. This progression compels various industries to modernize, adapting to the evolving needs of consumers and the available resources and technologies. In this context, the construction industry has made significant strides in its design methods, gradually incorporating innovative techniques that pave the way for interdisciplinary approaches. These advancements ensure that civil work designs are optimized in terms of cost, material usage, associated carbon emissions, and other critical parameters [1].

In the realm of sustainable design, it is important to recognize that the construction industry is responsible for 33% of the energy produced globally and 30% of the total greenhouse gas emissions worldwide [2]. This significant environmental impact stems from the considerable carbon dioxide emissions associated with various elements in civil works [3]. These include the materials and machinery utilized throughout a project's life cycle from construction and maintenance to eventual demolition [4]. As a result, the need for more sustainable practices and a reduced ecological footprint in the construction industry has become increasingly evident.

Given the pressing climate emergency, numerous processes and industries have been compelled to adopt sustainable measures or update existing practices. Developing sustainable building approaches can help mitigate the environmental impacts caused by human activity [5]. This global environmental situation has urged the construction sector to adopt and implement strategies to reduce or mitigate its ecological impact. Regarding carbon emissions, several studies have sought to minimize this parameter in various structures. For instance, ref. [6] employs a Finite Element Model (FEM) and a multi-objective genetic algorithm in the BIM modeling process to reduce a building's carbon emissions. Similarly, ref. [3] presents a comprehensive calculation of emissions involved in the life cycle of road construction, from material extraction to the end of its useful life, emphasizing the importance of earthworks and machinery efficiency. The study also highlights the relevance of material selection in optimizing emissions.

In [7], the researchers economically optimized footings using the MINLP (Mixed-Integer Non-Linear Programming) method. This study achieved a significant reduction of up to 63% in the total cost of the analyzed foundations. Additionally, various examples in the literature demonstrate the application of artificial intelligence algorithms within the construction industry. These include the use of computer vision for detecting cracks and defects in buildings [8], pavements [9], and bridges [10], as well as object detection on construction sites [11] and masonry segmentation [12].

In the domain of retaining walls, similar research efforts have been undertaken. For instance, ref. [13] presents a hybrid metaheuristic optimization method called h-BOASOS that minimizes the weight and cost of cantilever retaining walls. This approach combines the butterfly optimization algorithm (BOA) and symbiosis organism search (SOS) algorithm, outperforming other algorithms in benchmark tests, real-world engineering design problems, and cantilever retaining wall problems of various heights. In [14], the authors propose a hybrid k-means cuckoo search algorithm, merging the cuckoo search metaheuristic for continuous space optimization with the unsupervised k-means learning technique for discretizing solutions. The algorithm employs a random operator to assess the k-means operator's contribution and is benchmarked against a harmony search variant. The results reveal that incorporating the k-means operator significantly improves the solution quality, and the hybrid algorithm surpasses the harmony search approach. Finally, ref. [15] applies the shuffled shepherd optimization algorithm (SSOA) to optimize reinforced concrete cantilever retaining wall structures under static and seismic loading conditions. The optimization seeks to minimize the cost while adhering to stability and strength constraints based on ACI 318-05 requirements. Comparing SSOA results with other meta-heuristics highlights the algorithm's accuracy and convergence rate efficiency.

The numerous studies mentioned above highlight the ongoing efforts to optimize the design of various civil engineering elements and emphasize the importance of interdisciplinary collaboration in updating the industry. This article outlines the development process for optimizing retaining walls. Firstly, it explains the structural calculations and considerations required for designing the retaining wall. The second section discusses optimization techniques, their functionality, and their application to the problem.

Following this, the associated calculation model is parameterized to comply with the design standards, identifying crucial design aspects that can serve as variables in the optimization process. Subsequently, objective functions for each aspect are defined: one equation determines the economic cost, while another calculates carbon dioxide emissions, both applied to the retaining wall model.

Finally, a new algorithm that solves discrete problems using metaheuristics that naturally operate in continuous search spaces is proposed. Specifically, metaheuristic techniques such as the Sine Cosine Algorithm (SCA), Whale Optimization Algorithm (WOA), and Gray Wolf Optimization (GWO) are employed and integrated with SARSA and QL reinforcement learning techniques to address the discrete retaining wall problem and assess their performance and computational times. Statistical tests are used to compare the significance of the results obtained.

Extensive experiments were conducted to compare the implemented techniques, yielding notably robust and favorable results for static methods using S-shaped transfer functions. These results were obtained from 31 independent runs and their significance was validated through the Wilcoxon–Mann–Whitney [16] statistical test. The remainder of the paper is organized as follows: Section 2 outlines the retaining wall problem's modeling, while Section 3 introduces the optimization techniques. Section 4 presents the experimental findings, and Section 5 concludes the paper with discussions and final observations.

2. Concrete Retaining Walls

The present section lists the most critical design parameters considered. However, before delving into them, it is necessary to know the initial condition of the problem under consideration. At this point, it should be noted that the model considers the design of a cantilever-type wall with a structural backfill that has known resistance parameters and no overload. Furthermore, in geometrical terms, the model analyzes one linear wall meter as the problem's initial condition. Finally, the selection of the number and diameter of bars that meet the design requirements will be determined using the same. Having said that, the main calculation bases are detailed below.

Calculation of applicants: The design proposes that the structural fill exerts two types of thrust on the wall. The first type corresponds to the thrust of the soil under static conditions, while the second type corresponds to the thrust generated by the soil under pseudo-static (seismic) conditions [17]. These concepts are represented by Equations (1) and (2).

$$qe = c \cdot \gamma \cdot hz \cdot b \tag{1}$$

where:
qe = Static thrust exerted by the fill [T/m]
γ = Existing soil density [T/m^3].
z = Height of the wall [m].
c = Static thrust coefficient.
b = Wall width, corresponding to 1 [m].

$$qs = cs \cdot \gamma \cdot hz \cdot b \tag{2}$$

where:
qs = Seismic thrust exerted by the backfill [T/m].
γ = Existing soil density [T/m^3].
hz = Height of wall [m].
cs = Seismic thrust coefficient.
b = Wall width, corresponding to 1 [m].

Calculation of the requesting moment at point A: The design outlines the calculation of forces at point A, defined as the most unfavorable point on the wall in terms of stress caused by the soil thrust. This condition is represented through Equation (3) and Figure 1.

$$MsA = M_{active} + M_{seismic} \tag{3}$$

where:
MsA = Moment calculated at point A [T · m].
M_{active} = Static moment generated by the ground at point A [T · m].
$M_{seismic}$ = Seismic moment generated by the ground at point A [T · m].

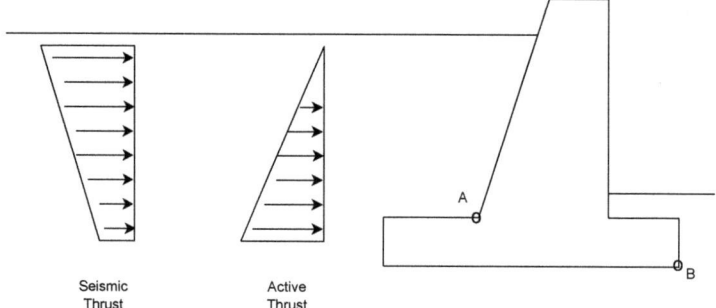

Figure 1. Stress distribution and location of point A in the retaining wall.

Quantification of the design requesting forces: Once the applied moment has been determined, the moment generated by the wall's self-weight at point A must be calculated. Finally, the applied moment is defined as the sum of the previously computed moments, which are then added to obtain the design moment and axial load, as illustrated in Equations (4)–(7).

$$M_{pp} = d1 \cdot N1 + d2 \cdot N2 \tag{4}$$

where:
M_{pp} = Moment generated by the self-weight at point A [T · m].
$d1$ = Distance from the centroid of the **prismatic** section of the wall to point A [m].
$N1$ = Eigenweight of the **prismatic** section of the wall [T].
$d2$ = Distance from the centroid of the **triangular** section of the wall to point A [m].
$N2$ = Eigenweight of the **triangular** section of the wall [T].

$$MA = MsA + M_{pp} \tag{5}$$

where:
MA = Total moment at point A [T · m].
MsA = Moment calculated at point A [T · m].
M_{pp} = Moment generated by self-weight at point A [T · m].

$$M_{eu} = MA \cdot \gamma f \tag{6}$$

where:
M_{eu} = Design moment [T · m].
MA = Total moment at point A [T · m].
γf = Moment majorization factor.

$$N_u = N_t \cdot \gamma f \tag{7}$$

where:
Nu = Design axial load [T].
Nt = Own weight of the wall [T].
γf = Moment magnification factor.

Steel amount for stirrups: For the calculation of the reinforcement required in the wall stirrups, the dimensionless method is applied, defined through Equations (8)–(11).

$$\mu = \frac{M_{eu}}{\phi \cdot \beta \cdot f'c \cdot b \cdot d} \tag{8}$$

where:
μ = Dimensionless calculation factor.
M_{eu} = Design moment [T · m].

ϕ = Reduction factor for flexocompression equal to 0.83.
β = Reduction of the characteristic strength of concrete equal to 0.85.
$f'c$ = Characteristic resistance of concrete to compression [T/m^2].
b = Width of the wall, corresponding to 1 [m].
d = Width of the base of the wall without covering [m].

$$\nu = \frac{N_u}{\phi \cdot \beta \cdot f'c \cdot b \cdot d} \tag{9}$$

where:
ν = Dimensionless shear factor in the structure.
N_u = Design axial load [T].
ϕ = Reduction factor for flexocompression equal to 0.83.
β = Reduction of the characteristic strength of concrete equal to 0.85.
$f'c$ = Characteristic resistance of concrete to compression [T/m^2].
b = Width of the wall, corresponding to 1 [m].
d = Width of the base of the wall without covering [m].

$$w = 1 - \sqrt{1 - 2 \cdot \mu} - \nu \tag{10}$$

where:
w = Calculation ratio for the steel area.
μ = Calculation dimensionless factor.
ν = Dimensionless shear factor in the structure.

$$A = \frac{w \cdot \beta \cdot f'c \cdot b \cdot d}{f_y} \tag{11}$$

where:
A = Required steel area [cm^2].
w = Calculation ratio for steel area.
β = Reduction of the characteristic strength of the concrete equal to 0.85.
$f'c$ = Characteristic resistance of concrete to compression [T * m^2].
b = Width of the wall, corresponding to 1 [m].
d = Width of the base of the wall without covering [m].
f_y = Steel creep [T/cm^2].

Verification of overturning resistance: For the overturning resistance verification, two central moments must be determined. The first one corresponds to the resistant moment exerted by the wall's self-weight, the foundation, and the soil on the bottom (Figure 2 and Equation (12)) up to the outermost point of the wall (the lower end of the foundation), defined as point B. Similarly, the moment generated by the active and seismic thrusts up to that point must be determined (Equation (13)). With this information, it is possible to calculate the overturning safety factor using Equations (14) and (15).

$$Mr = Ns \cdot x1 + Nm \cdot x2 + N1 \cdot x3 + Nf \cdot x4 \tag{12}$$

where:
M_r = Overturning resisting moment [T $\cdot$ m].
Ns = Self-weight of soil on bottom [T].
$x1$ = Distance from the centroid of Ns to point B [m].
Nm = Dead weight of the wall wedge and the soil above it [T].
$x2$ = Distance from the centroid of Nm to point B [m].
$N1$ = Self weight of the prismatic section of the wall [T].
$x3$ = Distance from the centroid of N1 to point B [m].
Nf = Self weight of the wall foundation [T].

$x4$ = Distance from the centroid of Nf to point B [m].

$$MsB = M_{active}B + M_{seismic}B \tag{13}$$

where:
MSB = Moment calculated at point B [T · m].
$M_{active}B$ = Static moment generated by the soil at point B [T · m].
$M_{seismic}B$ = Seismic moment generated by the soil at point B [T · m].

$$FSSV = \frac{Mr}{MsB} \tag{14}$$

where:
$FSSV$ = Overturning seismic safety factor.
Mr = Moment resisting overturning [T · m].
MsB = Moment calculated at point B [T · m].

$$FSEV = \frac{Mr}{M_{active}B} \tag{15}$$

where:
$FSEV$ = Rollover static safety factor. Mr = Moment resisting overturning [T · m]. MsB = Moment calculated at point B [T · m].

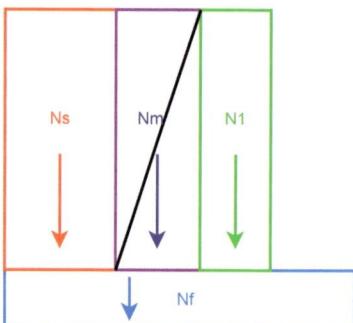

Figure 2. Resisting forces acting on the retaining wall.

Slip resistance verification: The procedure for the slip resistance verification follows the same principle as the rollover verification; that is, the applicant and resistant forces must be determined through Equations (16)–(19).

$$Fsol = (qe + qs) \cdot b \tag{16}$$

where:
$Fsol$ = Slip requesting force [T].
qe = Static thrust exerted by the filler [T/m].
qs = Seismic thrust exerted by the backfill [T/m].
b = Width of the wall, corresponding to 1 [m].

$$Fres = (Ns + Nm + N1 + Nf) \cdot \mu \tag{17}$$

where:
$Fres$ = Slip-resistant forces [T].
Ns = Self-weight of the soil on the bottom [T].
Nm = Self-weight of the wall wedge and the soil above it [T].
$N1$ = Self-weight of the prismatic section of the wall [T].

Nf = Self-weight of the wall foundation [T].
μ = Coefficient of friction between the foundation and the soil.

$$FSSD = \frac{Fres}{Fsol} \qquad (18)$$

where:
$FSSD$ = Seismic slip safety factor.
$Fres$ = Slip-resistant forces [T].
$Fsol$ = Slip-requesting force [T].

$$FSED = \frac{Fres}{qe} \qquad (19)$$

where:
$FSSD$ = Seismic slip safety factor.
$Fres$ = Slip-resistant forces [T].
qe = Static thrust exerted by the filler [T].

Verification of allowable stress: Within the verification section, it is necessary to check that the stresses transmitted to the soil (maximum and minimum) do not exceed the allowable stress given by the previous geotechnical study. The verification is carried out by means of Equation (20).

$$\sigma = \frac{Ns + Nm + N1 + Nf}{L \cdot b} \pm \frac{MsB - Ns \cdot x1 + Nm \cdot x2 + N1 \cdot x3}{\frac{b \cdot L^2}{6}} \qquad (20)$$

where:
σ = Stress transmitted to the foundation soil [T/m^2].
Ns = Self-weight of the soil on the bottom [T].
$x1$ = Distance from the centroid of Ns to point B [m].
Nm = Self-weight of the wall wedge and the soil above it [T].
$x2$ = Distance from the centroid of Nm to point B [m].
$N1$ = Self-weight of the prismatic section of the wall [T].
$x3$ = Distance from the centroid of N1 to point B [m].
Nf = Self-weight of the wall foundation [T].
L = Total length of the foundation [m].
b = Width of the wall, corresponding to 1 [m].
MsB = Moment calculated at point B [T · m].

Verification of percentage of support: Since the stress transmitted to the soil may adopt negative values, it must be checked that the foundation does not tend to lift out of the soil. Once the percentage of support has been defined, it is checked that the stress generated by the weight of the system does not exceed the admissible soil stress, with Equations (21)–(24).

$$e = \frac{MsB - Ns \cdot x1 + Nm \cdot x2 + N1 \cdot x3}{Ns + Nm + N1 + Nf} \qquad (21)$$

where:
e = Eccentricity of forces [m].
Ns = Self-weight of the soil on the bottom [T].
$x1$ = Distance from the centroid of Ns to point B [m].
Nm = Self-weight of the wall wedge and the soil above it [T].
$x2$ = Distance from the centroid of Nm to point B [m].
$N1$ = Self-weight of the prismatic section of the wall [T].
$x3$ = Distance from the centroid of N1 to point B [m].

Nf = Self-weight of the wall foundation [T].
MsB = Moment calculated at point B [T · m].

$$g = 3 \cdot \left(\frac{L}{2} - e\right) \tag{22}$$

where:
g = Section of the foundation supported on the ground [m].
L = Total length of the foundation [m].
e = Eccentricity of forces [m].

$$\sigma effective = \frac{2 \cdot (Ns + Nm + N1 + Nf)}{b \cdot g} \tag{23}$$

where:
$\sigma_{effective}$ = Effective stress applied to the foundation soil.
Ns = Self-weight of the soil on the bottom [T].
Nm = Self-weight of the wall wedge and the soil above it [T].
$N1$ = Self-weight of the prismatic section of the wall [T].
Nf = Self-weight of the wall foundation [T].
b = Width of the wall, which corresponds to 1 [m].
g = Section of the foundation supported on the ground [m].

$$\% of support = \frac{g}{L} \tag{24}$$

where:
g = Section of the foundation supported on the ground [m].
L = Total length of the foundation [m].

Reinforcing reinforcement for foundation under structural backfill: The uplift effect generated by the negative tension in the soffit area can generate additional tensile stresses in the foundation, so a reinforcement must be sized in the footing located in the soffit area of the wall. For this purpose, the design moment is determined from the forces involved (Figure 3) and then the dimensionless method is applied (Equation (25)).

$$Mdesign = 1.4 \cdot (Msr + Mf - Msf) \tag{25}$$

where:
$Mdesign$ = Design moment of reinforcement reinforcement [T · m].
Msr = Moment generated by backfill soil measured at design point [T · m].
Mf = Moment generated by the foundation measured at the design point [T · m].
Msf = Moment generated by the foundation soil measured at design point [T · m].

Foundation armor: In addition to the reinforcement calculated above, a reinforcement for the foundation, both longitudinal and transverse, must be dimensioned. This is carried out by means of Equations (26) and (27).

$$Mdl = \left(\frac{Bdt - Bm}{2} \cdot b\right) \cdot \left(\frac{1.4 \cdot Pp}{L \cdot b}\right) \cdot \left(\frac{Bdt - Bm}{4}\right) \tag{26}$$

where:
Mdl = Design moment of longitudinal reinforcement [T · m].
Bdt = Maximum foundation flight [m].
Bm = Width of the wall base [m].
Pp = Self-weight of the wall [T].
L = Total length of foundation [m].
b = width of the wall, corresponding to 1 [m].

$$Mdt = \frac{1.4 \cdot Pp \cdot b^2}{2 \cdot 1[m]} \qquad (27)$$

where:
Mdt = Design moment of transverse reinforcement [T · m].
Pp = Self-weight of the wall [T].
b = Width of the wall, which corresponds to 1 [m].

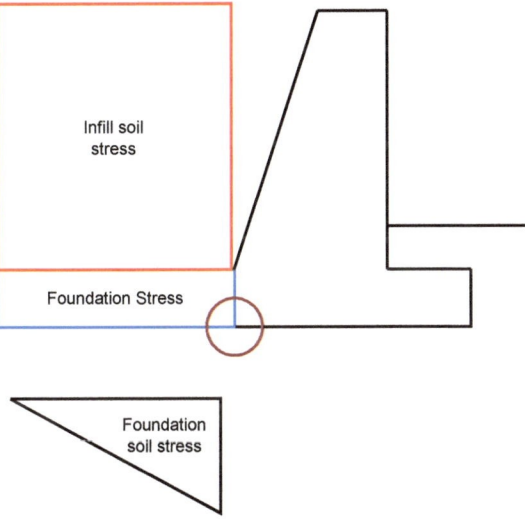

Figure 3. Stresses involved in structural reinforcement design.

Calculation of the steel area for the foundation: In the case of the reinforcement for the foundation, both longitudinal and transverse, the amount of steel required is determined with Equations (28) and (29).

$$T = \frac{Md}{0.9 \cdot d'} \qquad (28)$$

where:
T = Design stress [T].
Md = Corresponding design moment (Mdl or Mdt) [T · m].
d' = Effective shoe height (height without cover) [m].

$$As = \frac{T}{0.9 \cdot Fy} \qquad (29)$$

where:
As = Required steel area [cm^2].
T = Design stress generated by the design moment [T].
Fy = Yield stress of steel [T/cm^2].

Minimum armor: The amount of steel calculated above must be verified with respect to the corresponding minimum amount of steel, calculated through Equation (30).

$$emin = 0.0018 \cdot Ag \qquad (30)$$

where:
$emin$ = Minimum amount of steel required [cm^2].
Ag = Longitudinal or cross-sectional area of the footing, as appropriate [cm^2].

Verification of concrete shear strength: Check if the designed concrete section has the required minimum shear strength through the Equations (31) and (32).

$$Vu = \left(\frac{Bdt - Bm}{2} - d\right) \cdot b \cdot \frac{1.4 \cdot Pp}{L \cdot b} \tag{31}$$

where:
Vu = Design cut request [T].
Bdt = Maximum foundation flight [m].
Bm = Width of wall base [m].
d = Thickness of the uncoated shoe [m].
Pp = Self-weight of the wall [T].
L = Total length of foundation [m].
b = Width of the wall, corresponding to 1 [m].

$$Vc = 0.53 \cdot \lambda \cdot \sqrt{f'c} \cdot b \cdot d \tag{32}$$

where:
Vc = Shear strength of concrete section [T].
λ = Concrete modification factor. For normal concrete, $\lambda = 1$.
$f'c$ = Characteristic compressive strength of concrete [T/m^2].
b = Width of the wall, which corresponds to 1 [m].
d = Thickness of the uncoated shoe [m].

2.1. Restrictions

The design problem must respond to specific constraints to be considered correct. These limitations, known as constraints, will be fundamental in determining whether the solution proposed in the optimization process is (or is not) valid. The following are the constraints identified.

*µ*lim: According to the initial conditions for the application of the dimensionless sizing method used to determine the amount of steel required, the relationship of Equation (33).

$$\mu = \mu lim \tag{33}$$

where:
μ = Dimensionless factor, calculated in Equation (8).
μlim = Calculation limit dimensionless factor, equal to 0.3047 for the case of analysis.

Slip safety factor: As with the overturning safety factor, a minimum value of slip safety factor must be met to avoid the occurrence of this type of failure. That said, the restriction is set forth in Equations (34) and (35).

$$FSED \geq 1.5 \tag{34}$$

where:
$FSED$ = Static slip safety factor, calculated by Equation (19).

$$FSSD \geq 1.1 \tag{35}$$

where:
$FSSD$ = Seismic slip safety factor, calculated by Equation (18).

Rollover safety factor: The design must meet minimum safety criteria [18], including the overturning safety factor, which avoids abrupt failures due to overturning when loads not foreseen in the initial design are applied. Under this criterion, the conditions are defined in Equations (36) and (37).

$$FSEV \geq 1.5 \tag{36}$$

where:
$FSEV$ = Static rollover safety factor, calculated in Equation (15).

$$FSSV \geq 1.15 \cdot FSSD \tag{37}$$

where:
$FSSV$ = Seismic overturning factor of safety, calculated in Equation (14).
$FSSD$ = Seismic safety factor to slip, calculated in Equation (19).

Allowable stress: As a minimum requirement, the stresses produced by the interaction between the foundation and the supporting soil must be lower than the allowable bearing capacity provided by the geotechnical study accompanying any civil works design. The condition defining this restriction was previously established (Equations (20) and (23)).

Percentage of foundation support: Due to the eccentricity of the load system, there is a possibility that the stress distribution at the base of the foundation will generate a negative stress zone. In simple terms, this implies that the foundation would tend to uplift. To ensure that the stresses are properly distributed over the supporting soil, the percentage of the supported section (Equation (24)) must comply with the constraint outlined in Equation (38).

$$A \geq 80\% \tag{38}$$

where:
A = Percentage of foundation supported [%].

Shear strength: From the verification performed above (Equations (31) and (32)), the condition of Equation (39) must be fulfilled:

$$\Phi \cdot Vc \geq Vu \tag{39}$$

where:
Φ = Shear strength reduction factor of concrete, 0.75.
Vc = Shear strength of concrete section [T].
Vu = Foundation shear request [T].

2.2. Target Function

The objective functions representative of the parameters under study turn out to be linear, and are presented below.

$$CMt = CM1 \cdot PM1 + CM2 \cdot PM2 \tag{40}$$

where:
CMt = Total cost of retaining wall [CLP].
$CM1$ = Cost of one cubic meter of concrete [CLP/m^3].
$PM1$ = Total volume of concrete used [m^3].
$CM2$ = Cost of one kilogram of steel [CLP/kg].
$PM2$ = Total kilograms of steel used [kg].

$$EMt = EM1 \cdot PM1 + EM2 \cdot PM2 \tag{41}$$

where:
EMt = Total carbon dioxide emissions [T].
$EM1$ = Tons of carbon emitted per cubic meter of concrete [T/m^3].
$PM1$ = Total volume of concrete used [m^3].
$EM2$ = Tons of carbon emitted per kilogram of steel [T/kg].
$PM2$ = Total kilograms of steel used [kg].

$$CEMt = (CM1 \cdot PM1 + CM2 \cdot PM2) + EM1 \cdot PM1 + EM2 \cdot PM2 \tag{42}$$

where:
$CEMt$ = Total between the sum of cost and emissions.

3. Techniques to Be Used

In general, design problems involve numerous variables to consider, which may also be of different natures. The combination of multiple options results in a vast number of potential solutions that are impossible to cover manually or iteratively. The need arising from this type of analysis can be addressed through various currently available optimization techniques [19].

Before delving into the optimization techniques applied to the analysis problems relevant to this paper, it is essential to understand what the optimization methods entail. Generally, optimization methods consist of a set of rules and techniques applied to a problem to find the solution that best fits the objective pursued by the process. Optimization methods are divided into two main groups: the first group comprises techniques classified as exact, according to their characteristics [19], which can analyze the entire existing search space and find the best solution for the problem. On the other hand, there are cases where the search space is too large to be explored within a reasonable time frame [19]. In these situations, it is necessary to apply incomplete techniques that focus on analyzing local maxima identified within the function under study.

Another classification method applied to optimization problems focuses on the nature of the decision variables present. Thus, there are continuous optimization problems, meaning their variables represent continuous real spaces. On the other hand, combinatorial optimization problems have variables with integer values or sets of integers. Naturally, a third type of problem involves a mix of both variable types. In these cases, the problem's character is called mixed optimization.

Metaheuristics are iterative processes designed to be applied to any problem type (unlike heuristics, whose configuration is associated with a specific problem type) and, therefore, guide a subordinate heuristic to find an efficient solution in terms of approximation to the global optimum of the problem and the time required to find the proposed solution [20]. Likewise, metaheuristics are subdivided into two groups, depending on the type of solution they provide, and can be based on a single solution or a population of solutions. The above description is graphically represented in Figure 4.

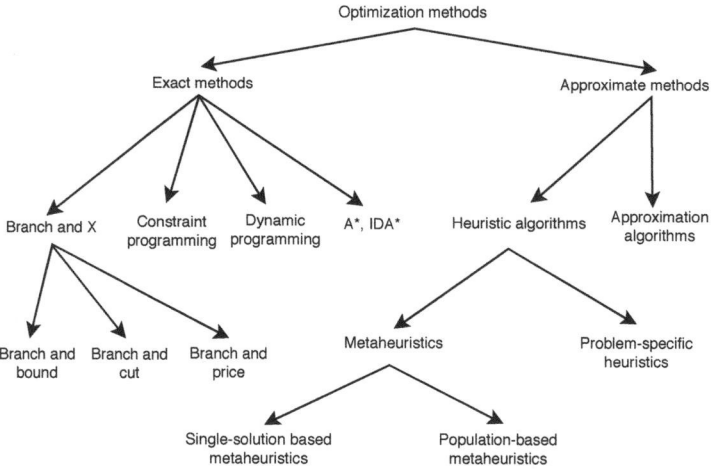

Figure 4. Optimization methods [21].

Regardless of the operation adopted for a metaheuristic, there are general parameters they must follow. First, the problem set must include an objective function, which represents the aspect of the problem to be optimized. For the purposes of this research, the objective functions to be designed will aim to quantify the costs and carbon dioxide emissions associated with the adopted design.

Once the objective function is defined, two concepts common to any function must be defined: the domain and its constraints. The domain of the objective function directly responds to the values that can be adopted by the variables considered in the problem, which are defined through the constraints. These constraints are conditions (formulated as functions) that limit the problem. All possible solutions that result from the intersection between the constraints of the problem make up the search space that will be considered in the optimization process.

Population-based metaheuristic techniques utilize a structured approach consisting of three "for" loops of iterations, solutions or individuals, and decision dimensions. Under this structure, perturbations to each dimension of the solutions during each iteration are performed through the method indicated in line 5 of Algorithm 1, where Δ refers to the characteristic perturbation or movement operators of each technique. As previously mentioned, in this paper, the metaheuristic techniques that have been implemented and discretized to adapt to the presented problem are: the Whale Optimization Algorithm (WOA) [22], the Sine Cosine Algorithm (SCA) [23], and the Grey Wolf Optimizer (GWO) [24]. The general scheme of each population-based metaheuristic is represented in Algorithm 1.

Algorithm 1 General scheme of metaheuristics.

1: Initialize a random swarm
2: **for** $iteration\ (t)$ **do**
3:     **for** $solution\ (i)$ **do**
4:         **for** $dimension\ (d)$ **do**
5:             $X_{i,d}^{t+1} = X_{i,d}^{t} + \Delta$
6:         end for
7:     end for
8: end for

---

4. Proposal: Discretization Schemes Selector

The resolution of complex and frequent combinatorial problems in industry is a priority for both academia and industries. A smart scheme selector for discretization is proposed, which integrates existing methods to balance exploration and exploitation, avoiding local optimizations. The balance between exploration and exploitation is a key factor in the performance of a metaheuristic. The method uses an intelligent operator to determine the appropriate discretization scheme at each iteration, to achieve the best quality results.

This proposal is based on the Binarization Schemes Selector (BSS), which has been proposed and utilized in [25–28], where a smart selector at a higher level selects from a set of actions, in this case transfer functions, to better choose how to discretize our continuous variables obtained from the metaheuristic, in order to use them in the discrete domain of our problem.

In this work, Q-Learning (QL) [29] and SARSA [30] are implemented as the intelligent operator of the proposal, which selects the discretization technique to be used based on a reward system, with which it learns in a deterministic manner.

The reward in the RL algorithm is crucial for the good performance of these algorithms; thus, in the literature, there are several methods to calculate rewards. We have implemented the same rewards used in BSS [25,26], which have been proposed in [31,32], which are presented in Equations (43)–(47).

$$withPenalty1 = \begin{cases} +1 & \text{if there is a fitness improvement} \\ -1 & \text{otherwise} \end{cases}, \quad (43)$$

$$withOutPentalty1 = \begin{cases} +1 & \text{if there is a fitness improvement} \\ 0 & \text{otherwise} \end{cases}, \quad (44)$$

$$globalBest = \begin{cases} \dfrac{W}{BestFitness} & \text{if there is a fitness improvement} \\ 0 & \text{otherwise} \end{cases}, \quad (45)$$

$$rootAdaptation = \begin{cases} \sqrt{BestFitness} & \text{if there is a fitness improvement} \\ 0 & \text{otherwise} \end{cases}, \quad (46)$$

and

$$EscalatingMultiplicativeAdaptation = \begin{cases} W \cdot BestFitness & \text{if there is a fitness improvement} \\ 0 & \text{otherwise} \end{cases}, \quad (47)$$

The reward or punishment is judged by the outcome obtained by the performance of the action. Thus, it is important to define which comparison measures will be used to discriminate the outcome. In this work, the comparison measure is the fitness obtained in each iteration of the optimization process, and it is compared with the best fitness obtained. If the fitness improves, the action is rewarded, whereas if the fitness worsens, the action is punished. In this work, two states are defined, which refer to the phases of a metaheuristic: exploration and exploitation. These states were not chosen randomly because, as previously mentioned, the objective of this work is to improve the balance between exploration and exploitation of the metaheuristics to obtain better results. This process is represented in Figure 5.

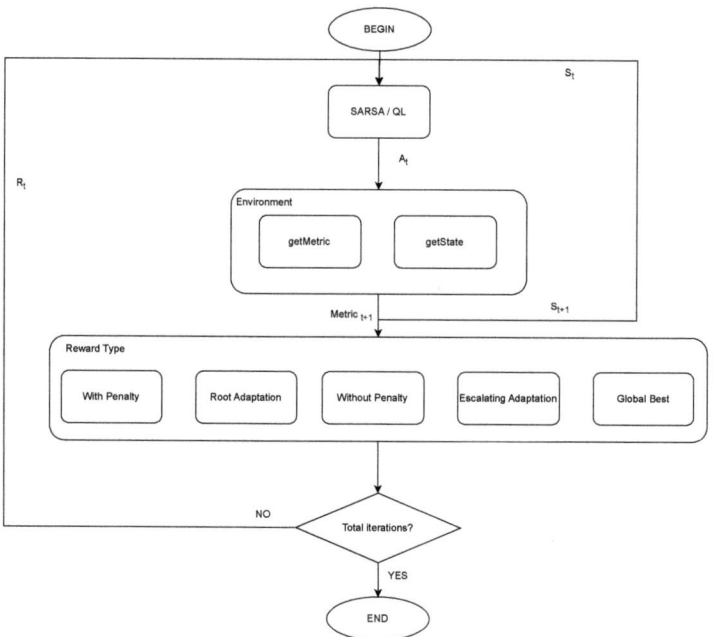

Figure 5. Q-Learning and SARSA scheme for different rewards.

In the literature, different authors [33,34] propose metrics that allow us to quantify the diversity of individuals in population algorithms, where the Dimensional Diversity by

Hussain stands out [35]. Let Div be the diversity of the population at a particular time, and to calculate Div, the following equation is used:

$$Div = \frac{1}{l \cdot n} \sum_{d=1}^{l} \sum_{i=1}^{n} |\bar{x}^d - x_i^d| \qquad (48)$$

where $\bar{x}^d$ denotes the average of individuals in dimension d, x_i^d is the value of the i-th individual in dimension d, n is the number of individuals in the population, and l is the size of the dimension of the individuals. One of the methods to estimate exploration and exploitation is proposed by Morales-Castañeda et al. [36], who, based on the quantification of the diversity of a population, proposed a method to estimate exploration and exploitation in terms of percentages. The percentages of exploration (XPL%) and exploitation (XPT%) are calculated as follows:

$$XPL\% = \frac{Div}{Div_{max}} \cdot 100 \qquad (49)$$

$$XPT\% = \frac{|Div - Div_{max}|}{Div_{max}} \cdot 100 \qquad (50)$$

where Div is the determination of the diversity state given by Equation (49) and Div_{max} denotes the maximum value of the diversity state found throughout the optimization problem. Equations (50) and (51) are generic, so it is possible to use any other metric that calculates the diversity of a population. Therefore, the transition of states will be determined through the following method (Figure 6).

$$next\ state = \begin{cases} Exploration & if\ XPL\% \geq XPT\% \\ Exploitation & if\ XPL\% < XPT\% \end{cases} \qquad (51)$$

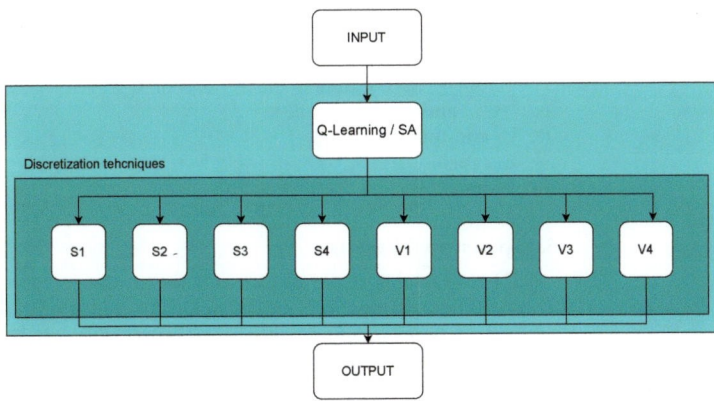

Figure 6. Discretization scheme selector with Q-Learning or SARSA as Smart Operator.

Discretization

There are various ways to transfer continuous values to binaries [37,38], but there is little documentation on discretization. In this proposal, discretization is generated through transfer functions commonly used in two-step binarization. The transfer functions achieve transferring a continuous value to a value in the range of [0, 1]. The discretization proposal is integrated under the general scheme of MH, as presented in Algorithm 2. This discretization function is broken down in Algorithm 3, where the input of the discretization function is the set of solutions, the user-defined parameter ***beta***, and the type of transfer function. In the algorithm, for each dimension (line 5), we check if the value of our position $X_{i,d}$ is greater than r_1, which corresponds to a random number between [0, 1] (line 6); if this is met and also the value of ***beta*** > r_2 another random number between [0, 1] (line 7), then we update our $X_{i,d}$ to the value of the best solution for that dimension (line 8), but if ***beta*** is not greater, then it is updated with a random value (line 10). Otherwise, if the value of $X_{i,d}$ is not greater than r_1, then the element is not updated. Finally (line 17), the discretized value of the solutions X is returned.

Algorithm 2 Discrete general scheme of metaheuristics.

1: Initialize a random swarm
2: **for** *iteration* (*t*) **do**
3:     **for** *solution* (*i*) **do**
4:         **for** *dimension* (*d*) **do**
5:             $X_{i,d}^{t+1} = X_{i,d}^{t} + \Delta$
6:         **end for**
7:     **end for**
8:     **Discretization (X)**
9: **end for**

Algorithm 3 Discretization algorithm.

1: **Function** Discretization(*X*, *beta*, *TF*)
2: Initialize r_1 and r_2 as randoms values between $[0,1]$.
3: *XProbability* ← appliedTransferFunction(*X*, *TF*)
4: **for** solution (*i*) **do**
5:     **for** dimension (*d*) **do**
6:         **if** $X_{i,d} > r_1$ **then**
7:             **if** *beta* > r_2 **then**
8:                 Update $X_{i,d}$ considering the best.
9:             **else**
10:                 Update $X_{i,d}$ with a random value allowed.
11:             **end if**
12:         **else**
13:             Do not update the element in $X_{i,d}$
14:         **end if**
15:     **end for**
16: **end for**
17: **return** *X*

---

5. Experimental Results

Three metaheuristics of different classes and complexities have been run for the experimental analysis: SCA, GWO, and WOA. These MH have been tested in 11 instances and run 31 times independently on an i9-10900k, with 32 Gb of RAM and in a Python 3.7 implementation. The extensive experimental comparison has also been carried out on different discretization schemes: on the one hand, on a static scheme using only one of the eight classical transfer functions (S-shaped and V-shaped); and together with the proposal explained in Section 4, using Q-Learning and SARSA as smart selector, each of them evaluating different rewards.

The representative design problem of a retaining wall involves several design variables. Given this situation, and depending on the time required for processing, a list of parameters considered as decision variables will be detailed. Subsequently, these points will take a variable value according to the evaluation to be performed, as determined in the iterative process of the optimization techniques. The following variables used are defined in Table 1.

In order to simplify the representation of results, the main results obtained will be presented, with access to all the results in the open repository https://github.com/joselemusr/DSS-Retaining-walls.

Table 1. Setting parameter.

Variables	Unit	Lower Limit	Upper Limit	Step Size	Possibilities
Concrete strength	Mpa	25	40	5	4
Steel tensil strength	Mpa	280	420	140	2
Width of crowning	m	0.15	0.95	0.01	81
Base width of the wall	m	0.3	1.5	0.01	121
Thickness of the footing	m	0.45	2.0	0.01	156
Density of the structural fill	T/m^3	1.6	2.0	0.1	5

Table 2 presents the nomenclature used to identify each variation of the algorithms, while Tables 3 and 4 present the results obtained by GWO using static schemes based on V-shaped and S-shaped, where this technique has presented the best performance in conjunction with static schemes, where in the first row we can see the version of the algorithm used, in the first column the name of the instance, where the terminations "-C" correspond to those whose objective function calculation is cost-based (Equation (40)), "-E" to those that correspond to CO_2 emissions (Equation (41)) and "-C+E" to the objective function that considers the sum of both (Equation (42)). The second column individualizes the best known value calculated by grid search, and then the three columns are repeated indicating the best value found by the version indicated in the column, the average value of the 31 independent runs and the Relative Percentile Destivation (RPD), which is calculated according to Equation (52). While in intermediate rows the average values for the set of instances using the same objective function are presented.

Table 2. Nomenclature of algorithms.

Name	Reward Types
V1	V-Shaped 1
V2	V-Shaped 2
V3	V-Shaped 3
V4	V-Shaped 4
S1	S-Shaped 1
S2	S-Shaped 2
S3	S-Shaped 3
S4	S-Shaped 4
SA1	With Penalty
SA2	Without Penalty
SA3	Global Best
SA4	Root Adaption
SA5	Scalating Adaption
QL1	With Penalty
QL2	Without Penalty
QL3	Global Best
QL4	Root Adaption
QL5	Scalating Adaption

Table 3. Comparison of the metaheuristics GWO S-shaped.

		S1			S2			S3			S4		
Inst.	Opt.	Best	Avg	RPD	Best	Avg	RPD	Best	Avg	RPD	Best	Avg	RPD
RW300-C	163,992.326	175,838.59	211,292.33	7.22	175,789.67	208,441.35	7.19	188,006.95	212,453.03	14.64	185,972.17	213,282.1	13.4
RW350-C	189,534.031	211,784.64	242,392.1	11.74	201,487.94	238,310.07	6.31	205,963.63	244,063.3	8.67	218,007.71	244,153.67	15.02
RW400-C	214,696.284	230,025.46	276,532.81	7.14	234,785.38	271,573.64	9.36	219,450.0	275,144.37	2.21	232,555.67	277,516.98	8.32
RW450-C	241,096.482	271,731.17	308,495.8	12.71	256,797.33	300,754.16	6.51	270,398.19	312,252.76	12.15	247,671.69	306,537.35	2.73
RW500-C	268,526.177	288,376.68	342,484.67	7.39	288,202.48	339,862.91	7.33	279,819.15	345,778.52	4.21	297,405.15	344,343.23	10.75
RW550-C	307,536.973	324,915.35	382,092.86	5.65	322,283.21	387,920.24	4.79	335,427.48	385,877.51	9.07	322,738.02	370,679.41	4.94
RW600-C	364,409.78	381,612.64	452,607.89	4.72	390,461.48	449,828.17	7.15	377,871.72	436,150.53	3.69	401,195.04	441,721.15	10.09
RW650-C	430,400.866	477,518.43	515,174.31	10.95	454,549.52	506,895.1	5.61	456,260.58	507,368.7	6.01	468,411.9	519,895.88	8.83
RW700-C	507,127.151	547,343.21	602,471.76	7.93	549,909.57	607,197.41	8.44	530,085.84	591,365.14	4.53	534,199.25	598,294.59	5.34
RW750-C	593,353.31	629,727.79	698,312.62	6.13	636,981.05	691,752.62	7.35	628,828.29	696,128.32	5.98	632,268.83	691,309.72	6.56
RW800-C	687,763.656	747,469.72	798,036.46	8.68	729,504.48	802,675.33	6.07	726,214.24	797,384.47	5.59	717,889.37	791,121.94	4.38

Table 3. Cont.

			S1			S2			S3			S4	
		389,667.61	439,081.24	8.21	385,522.92	436,837.36	6.92	383,484.19	436,724.24	6.98	387,119.55	436,259.64	8.21
RW300-E	612.204	641.96	753.69	4.86	656.77	763.8	7.28	631.33	763.38	3.12	639.91	766.05	4.53
RW350-E	708.081	756.27	882.66	6.81	808.12	909.04	14.13	778.03	891.86	9.88	762.6	871.11	7.7
RW400-E	802.088	849.79	990.06	5.95	883.34	1018.04	10.13	852.56	984.43	6.29	860.6	998.35	7.29
RW450-E	902.195	977.07	1121.36	8.3	1048.25	1147.36	16.19	912.78	1102.61	1.17	981.13	1099.76	8.75
RW500-E	1007.376	1036.58	1230.59	2.9	1103.16	1240.43	9.51	1085.86	1244.08	7.79	1103.02	1239.52	9.49
RW550-E	1122.621	1197.02	1363.12	6.63	1190.49	1374.09	6.05	1271.84	1369.23	13.29	1241.01	1383.01	10.55
RW600-E	1304.802	1389.11	1602.36	6.46	1391.43	1619.91	6.64	1376.69	1623.79	5.51	1483.51	1603.14	13.7
RW650-E	1545.005	1654.33	1854.43	7.08	1672.47	1837.53	8.25	1588.32	1833.09	2.8	1636.44	1824.26	5.92
RW700-E	1794.782	1955.23	2138.56	8.94	1885.35	2126.44	5.05	1918.4	2159.01	6.89	1846.2	2145.73	2.86
RW750-E	2099.338	2338.05	2516.84	11.37	2243.24	2479.23	6.85	2228.69	2466.35	6.16	2326.47	2522.93	10.82
RW800-E	2443.014	2491.57	2816.65	1.99	2616.19	2849.18	7.09	2697.48	2872.4	10.42	2565.34	2859.6	5.01
		1389.73	1570.03	6.48	1408.98	1578.64	8.83	1394.73	1573.66	6.67	1404.2	1573.95	7.87
RW300-C+E	164,604.53	185,539.96	214,019.57	12.72	179,481.45	208,019.2	9.04	179,206.6	213,775.7	8.87	172,436.99	210,863.58	4.76
RW350-C+E	190,242.112	199,602.67	244,365.08	4.92	203,491.26	246,884.7	6.96	219,538.11	246,767.27	15.4	202,238.98	248,453.56	6.31
RW400-C+E	215,498.372	232,137.79	280,602.84	7.72	230,658.08	273,676.46	7.03	247,064.05	274,698.16	14.65	241,930.5	283,040.63	12.27
RW450-C+E	241,998.678	272,140.43	312,344.84	12.46	266,323.07	309,147.94	10.05	282,508.4	307,997.32	16.74	259,877.32	306,812.62	7.39
RW500-C+E	269,533.553	300,055.55	342,565.29	11.32	295,864.13	335,482.28	9.77	297,761.9	345,023.04	10.47	282,150.29	344,841.59	4.68
RW550-C+E	308,696.291	341,354.54	392,273.06	10.58	340,443.21	390,449.89	10.28	328,562.36	386,558.52	6.44	337,135.95	389,219.89	9.21
RW600-C+E	365,784.894	382,089.49	445,844.69	4.46	390,360.72	451,336.16	6.72	392,607.8	451,473.09	7.33	396,949.96	447,302.6	8.52
RW650-C+E	432,031.377	459,594.11	514,964.67	6.38	466,505.36	517,304.52	7.98	479,176.62	532,639.0	10.91	464,753.64	516,490.98	7.57
RW700-C+E	508,928.933	532,789.38	590,952.6	4.69	550,408.06	609,037.86	8.15	528,020.86	602,847.0	3.75	513,662.21	609,215.53	0.93
RW750-C+E	595,461.955	644,986.79	710,876.08	8.32	622,985.91	695,917.34	4.62	619,227.4	683,463.27	3.99	622,615.54	700,706.2	4.56
RW800-C+E	690,374.634	722,411.98	789,371.57	4.64	730,441.36	789,492.83	5.8	727,830.26	795,986.71	5.43	744,199.77	794,967.2	7.8
		388,427.52	439,834.57	8.02	388,814.78	438,795.38	7.85	391,045.85	440,111.73	9.45	385,268.29	441,083.13	6.73

Table 4. Comparison of the metaheuristics GWO V-shaped.

		V1			V2			V3			V4		
Inst.	Opt.	Best	Avg	RPD	Best	Avg	RPD	Best	Avg	RPD	Best	Avg	RPD
RW300-C	163,992.326	182,558.0	250,774.4	11.32	180,561.07	244,698.22	10.1	180,277.56	255,746.94	9.93	197,594.94	255,313.99	20.49
RW350-C	189,534.031	235,483.99	289,786.83	24.24	236,058.47	296,464.92	24.55	214,982.26	283,628.58	13.43	214,535.82	294,068.78	13.19
RW400-C	214,696.284	256,441.43	311,691.32	19.44	243,710.67	318,303.28	13.51	267,778.96	332,668.32	24.72	239,710.27	328,589.26	11.65
RW450-C	241,096.482	269,111.65	373,108.99	11.62	294,022.51	359,189.16	21.95	280,855.89	388,628.93	16.49	292,597.93	379,517.3	21.36
RW500-C	268,526.177	327,984.08	410,488.65	22.14	299,902.86	411,098.33	11.31	291,171.59	403,594.99	8.43	332,901.71	411,212.61	23.97
RW550-C	307,536.973	371,451.6	459,106.72	20.78	341,735.03	427,316.78	11.12	351,092.89	453,093.61	14.16	349,801.0	448,319.8	13.78
RW600-C	364,409.78	432,595.44	508,425.9	18.71	404,496.27	500,401.85	11.0	415,212.59	501,977.08	13.94	412,811.66	531,849.77	13.28
RW650-C	430,400.866	451,496.13	581,702.33	4.9	454,861.21	596,746.32	5.68	462,874.92	588,805.31	7.55	454,683.35	564,397.16	5.64
RW700-C	507,127.151	566,328.17	680,987.16	11.67	546,341.0	663,127.9	7.73	566,174.43	688,008.95	11.64	538,815.13	664,311.96	6.25
RW750-C	593,353.31	674,866.42	772,500.43	13.74	671,254.82	810,994.06	13.13	677,228.39	778,620.07	14.14	664,697.49	760,457.32	12.02
RW800-C	687,763.656	753,558.36	854,181.21	9.57	757,749.41	907,114.91	10.18	743,863.99	864,887.58	8.16	797,794.43	899,780.3	16.0
		411,079.57	499,341.27	15.28	402,699.39	503,223.25	12.75	404,683.04	503,605.49	12.96	408,722.16	503,438.02	14.33
RW300-E	612.204	659.58	909.38	7.74	664.98	912.97	8.62	698.73	845.7	14.13	658.28	871.39	7.53
RW350-E	708.081	767.18	1061.7	8.35	752.24	1058.21	6.24	821.34	1064.88	16.0	757.65	1034.95	7.0
RW400-E	802.088	927.22	1199.83	15.6	893.96	1167.7	11.45	902.39	1143.52	12.51	887.53	1165.03	10.65
RW450-E	902.195	1003.83	1296.7	11.27	1045.85	1294.51	15.92	949.46	1284.35	5.24	1067.5	1329.86	18.32
RW500-E	1007.376	1170.35	1440.91	16.18	1141.76	1452.99	13.34	1140.6	1438.13	13.22	1123.48	1453.63	11.53
RW550-E	1122.621	1212.53	1613.66	8.01	1267.82	1546.48	12.93	1264.08	1575.83	12.6	1285.56	1626.73	14.51
RW600-E	1304.802	1517.0	1784.2	16.26	1346.81	1881.45	3.22	1416.88	1803.34	8.59	1476.89	1780.07	13.19
RW650-E	1545.005	1754.9	2118.18	13.59	1691.75	2142.13	9.5	1768.66	2130.36	14.48	1703.67	2032.29	10.27
RW700-E	1794.782	2078.11	2441.01	15.79	1935.22	2417.61	7.82	2046.04	2490.55	14.0	2012.62	2431.03	12.14
RW750-E	2099.338	2235.15	2817.56	6.47	2281.91	2719.19	8.7	2306.18	2753.93	9.85	2463.03	2741.43	17.32
RW800-E	2443.014	2763.26	3247.36	13.11	2791.38	3192.71	14.26	2730.05	3244.01	11.75	2627.68	3137.4	7.56
		1462.65	1811.86	12.03	1437.61	1798.72	10.18	1458.58	1797.69	12.03	1460.35	1782.16	11.82
RW300-C+E	164,604.53	189,414.91	256,656.74	15.07	212,808.88	258,560.11	29.28	197,941.42	265,472.25	20.25	191,681.13	255,487.66	16.45
RW350-C+E	190,242.112	226,684.74	289,406.05	19.16	205,267.83	292,174.09	7.9	227,189.95	296,419.26	19.42	215,111.35	298,268.07	13.07
RW400-C+E	215,498.372	249,648.6	320,535.05	15.85	256,337.8	332,853.23	18.95	247,634.93	309,550.68	14.91	251,690.95	325,641.74	16.79
RW450-C+E	241,998.678	266,795.28	368,021.74	10.25	263,973.35	371,100.48	9.08	275,476.78	359,906.58	13.83	292,449.06	365,729.58	20.85
RW500-C+E	269,533.553	319,208.41	396,647.42	18.43	316,227.72	422,102.42	17.32	305,604.13	412,775.82	13.38	300,555.16	397,084.1	11.51
RW550-C+E	308,696.291	345,813.94	434,424.21	12.02	338,561.16	439,581.9	9.67	346,528.45	436,983.83	12.26	375,283.31	460,338.62	21.57
RW600-C+E	365,784.894	391,172.58	511,973.28	6.94	407,135.87	521,235.07	11.3	397,012.72	487,463.91	8.54	389,349.99	513,184.4	6.44
RW650-C+E	432,031.377	500,484.16	576,125.09	15.84	473,065.76	587,658.71	9.5	459,287.25	592,636.18	6.31	511,205.87	587,279.57	18.33
RW700-C+E	508,928.933	570,302.85	685,760.21	12.06	563,174.88	684,648.85	10.66	538,618.15	687,472.3	5.83	568,892.82	693,412.7	11.78
RW750-C+E	595,461.955	676,216.3	773,236.37	13.56	635,506.85	770,898.72	6.73	651,205.08	782,023.88	9.36	638,043.63	775,221.47	7.15
RW800-C+E	690,374.634	766,429.86	887,074.98	11.02	743,847.17	866,593.73	7.75	775,324.71	907,251.95	12.3	740,457.9	903,472.02	7.25
		409,288.33	499,987.38	13.65	401,446.12	504,309.71	12.56	401,983.96	503,450.6	12.4	406,792.83	506,828.81	13.74

Tables 5–10 present the results obtained using the proposed dynamic techniques based on Q-Learning and SARSA.

$$\text{RPD} = \frac{100 \cdot (Best - Opt)}{Opt}. \tag{52}$$

Table 5. Comparison of the metaheuristics GWO-SARSA.

Inst.	Opt.	SA1 Best	SA1 Avg	SA1 RPD	SA2 Best	SA2 Avg	SA2 RPD	SA3 Best	SA3 Avg	SA3 RPD	SA4 Best	SA4 Avg	SA4 RPD	SA5 Best	SA5 Avg	SA5 RPD
RW300-C	163,992.326	175,196.07	240,291.06	6.83	190,461.88	240,768.21	16.14	192,583.95	256,177.38	17.43	196,839.18	255,401.78	20.03	216,562.33	264,100.1	32.06
RW350-C	189,534.031	203,087.74	281,263.13	7.15	212,870.8	280,268.45	12.31	210,817.52	285,790.58	11.23	210,340.34	278,309.36	10.98	204,914.73	284,691.97	8.12
RW400-C	214,696.284	258,788.8	333,047.04	20.54	242,036.31	310,250.08	12.73	263,222.46	332,463.94	22.6	245,698.67	318,591.49	14.44	235,369.05	331,751.44	9.63
RW450-C	241,096.482	246,740.28	360,069.11	2.34	286,128.55	369,184.84	18.68	267,031.65	354,429.31	10.76	290,538.95	370,155.53	20.51	278,411.61	368,804.08	15.48
RW500-C	268,526.177	311,349.28	395,127.49	15.95	333,135.41	420,370.16	24.06	321,064.4	405,607.81	19.57	323,016.44	401,123.74	20.29	313,862.48	404,380.5	16.88
RW550-C	307,536.973	336,252.03	445,129.77	9.34	346,365.66	440,180.83	12.63	355,482.59	434,091.04	15.59	361,102.91	463,967.68	17.42	389,536.95	473,340.33	26.66
RW600-C	364,409.78	401,095.99	499,661.3	10.07	405,588.71	515,558.07	11.3	441,602.08	530,358.24	21.18	422,909.9	510,678.08	16.05	404,582.25	512,612.77	11.02
RW650-C	430,400.866	458,804.21	582,967.98	6.6	488,836.68	592,609.35	13.58	492,186.98	576,837.93	14.36	454,978.62	581,907.37	5.71	485,257.62	608,371.4	12.75
RW700-C	507,127.151	575,813.19	684,980.88	13.54	554,050.72	685,077.06	9.25	574,657.66	692,581.64	13.32	567,477.69	676,364.38	11.9	544,574.66	684,794.22	7.38
RW750-C	593,353.31	651,806.07	775,414.42	9.85	611,414.67	786,125.19	3.04	645,845.55	760,061.05	8.85	628,166.6	791,136.95	5.87	650,375.1	782,284.09	9.61
RW800-C	687,763.656	764,159.62	885,664.16	11.11	719,035.64	875,590.27	4.55	710,899.7	870,215.39	3.36	744,944.09	882,911.76	8.31	752,379.95	909,523.9	9.4
		408,496.89	503,825.32	12.73	401,524.35	503,917.03	10.69	408,933.94	500,180.85	13.9	410,720.35	499,565.19	14.68	408,041.48	503,078.74	14.23
RW300-E	612.204	398,463.03	498,510.58	10.3	399,084.09	501,452.96	12.57	406,854.05	499,874.03	14.39	404,183.04	502,777.1	13.77	406,893.34	511,332.25	14.45
RW350-E	708.081	688.89	915.82	12.53	735.37	862.73	20.12	649.31	917.41	6.06	672.89	882.63	9.91	714.16	907.08	16.65
RW400-E	802.088	814.36	1040.69	15.01	790.0	997.42	11.57	846.06	1014.44	19.49	846.63	1067.25	19.57	797.17	1062.57	12.58
RW450-E	902.195	874.66	1189.78	9.05	951.48	1146.8	18.63	885.43	1153.58	10.39	874.08	1156.67	8.98	895.13	1100.51	11.6
RW500-E	1007.376	995.35	1310.04	10.33	958.01	1326.01	6.19	1090.58	1379.05	20.88	1072.61	1291.07	18.89	1004.47	1317.17	11.34
RW550-E	1122.621	1170.00	1458.72	16.15	1071.45	1412.96	6.36	1128.23	1429.47	12.0	1100.51	1352.45	9.25	1116.47	1400.13	10.83
RW600-E	1304.802	1217.65	1531.16	8.46	1206.12	1648.46	7.44	1286.32	1614.5	14.58	1236.62	1648.38	10.15	1248.95	1619.21	11.25
RW650-E	1545.005	1548.61	1869.69	18.69	1543.35	1890.14	18.28	1384.1	1854.52	6.08	1426.58	1812.32	9.33	1578.99	1838.44	21.01
RW700-E	1794.782	1751.98	2099.14	13.4	1754.98	2101.96	13.59	1797.42	2145.75	16.34	1669.69	2098.52	8.07	1765.0	2048.71	14.24
RW750-E	2099.338	2008.91	2415.51	11.93	1949.43	2409.81	8.62	1903.72	2439.5	6.07	2070.63	2538.31	15.37	2209.43	2428.17	23.1
RW800-E	2443.014	2334.47	2776.93	11.2	2319.57	2728.25	10.49	2350.17	2823.53	11.95	2274.59	2760.26	8.35	2426.48	2794.82	15.58
		2581.15	3093.66	5.65	2614.9	3183.37	7.04	2753.82	3185.19	12.72	2768.04	3206.42	13.3	2687.92	3195.96	10.02
RW300-C+E	164,604.53	1453.28	1791.01	12.04	1444.97	1791.63	11.67	1461.38	1814.27	12.41	1455.72	1801.3	11.92	1494.92	1792.07	14.38
RW350-C+E	190,242.112	197,103.77	254,652.15	19.74	164,604.53	251,794.23	0.0	200,235.29	243,330.92	21.65	192,397.52	244,942.0	16.88	198,983.16	263,415.37	20.89
RW400-C+E	215,498.372	205,742.77	295,777.2	8.15	229,743.06	285,923.85	20.76	221,939.8	292,721.98	16.66	215,602.98	295,647.97	13.33	235,526.35	295,891.04	23.8
RW450-C+E	241,998.678	247,338.81	324,435.82	14.78	223,604.65	335,216.13	3.76	233,300.25	316,385.12	8.26	274,532.12	321,902.05	27.39	261,487.63	331,584.94	21.34
RW500-C+E	269,533.553	256,669.92	372,503.2	6.06	263,918.15	378,251.78	9.06	284,180.87	381,454.14	17.43	270,973.96	360,798.33	11.97	277,313.67	369,895.78	14.59
RW550-C+E	308,696.291	287,771.69	398,587.27	6.77	318,733.92	402,187.03	18.25	304,260.04	396,166.19	12.88	329,154.77	406,779.27	22.12	303,022.33	401,482.1	12.42
RW600-C+E	365,784.894	348,667.99	447,725.75	12.95	331,104.97	456,668.02	7.26	340,195.47	450,174.08	10.2	348,179.54	442,063.23	12.79	355,412.73	449,238.6	15.13
RW650-C+E	432,031.377	439,355.55	504,231.19	20.11	420,512.59	501,087.63	14.96	438,608.77	499,684.3	19.91	412,736.13	503,312.77	12.84	381,018.45	512,924.1	4.16
RW700-C+E	508,928.933	494,343.87	593,056.91	14.42	478,256.47	592,585.29	10.7	484,001.98	599,800.75	12.03	481,665.55	581,066.43	11.49	462,419.8	577,629.07	7.03
RW750-C+E	595,461.955	573,299.69	673,059.0	12.65	567,096.46	682,061.35	11.43	587,805.05	674,570.95	15.5	565,677.47	673,489.21	11.15	578,495.41	681,417.61	13.67
RW800-C+E	690,374.634	664,560.38	793,803.33	11.6	685,914.43	782,065.86	15.19	653,984.87	765,896.12	9.83	641,280.95	786,801.82	7.69	680,615.86	787,048.52	14.3
		778,611.38	884,246.73	12.78	733,278.57	875,246.18	6.21	749,760.94	881,804.84	8.6	785,722.86	878,414.05	13.81	754,160.86	863,339.01	9.24

Table 6. Comparison of the metaheuristics WOA-SARSA.

Inst.	Opt.	SA1 Best	SA1 Avg	SA1 RPD	SA2 Best	SA2 Avg	SA2 RPD	SA3 Best	SA3 Avg	SA3 RPD	SA4 Best	SA4 Avg	SA4 RPD	SA5 Best	SA5 Avg	SA5 RPD
RW300-C	163,992.326	174,401.85	207,029.1	6.35	167,693.67	206,464.53	2.26	177,799.48	203,958.3	8.42	176,090.82	210,441.84	7.38	172,075.6	207,216.98	4.93
RW350-C	189,534.031	215,236.86	247,721.69	13.56	207,641.36	241,905.55	9.55	197,658.72	244,658.14	4.29	201,255.16	244,411.26	6.18	198,809.45	248,571.28	4.89
RW400-C	214,696.284	233,655.98	277,485.21	8.83	237,279.59	274,184.6	10.52	243,725.11	279,525.08	13.52	247,387.97	279,426.94	15.23	220,850.79	274,863.6	2.87
RW450-C	241,096.482	254,615.8	304,331.36	5.61	266,160.75	274,184.6	10.4	255,681.45	302,243.06	6.05	258,985.05	304,964.45	7.42	246,412.94	305,338.33	2.21
RW500-C	268,526.177	289,994.65	330,993.01	7.99	309,115.38	347,294.56	15.12	315,287.02	347,787.85	17.41	291,863.8	330,424.63	8.69	286,939.71	341,076.69	6.86
RW550-C	307,536.973	320,202.08	380,843.12	4.12	325,913.34	379,485.88	5.98	337,056.39	380,688.05	9.6	329,631.25	389,187.29	7.18	336,706.88	386,894.3	9.49
RW600-C	364,409.78	409,154.41	462,149.01	12.28	397,224.77	453,183.43	9.0	395,937.23	444,542.84	8.65	413,376.31	454,884.63	13.44	404,343.26	449,467.23	10.96
RW650-C	430,400.866	454,719.22	525,030.05	5.65	481,048.56	530,789.22	11.77	472,013.02	528,236.95	9.67	476,062.98	525,748.47	10.61	482,424.65	532,537.15	12.09
RW700-C	507,127.151	531,392.11	620,977.14	4.78	524,947.85	615,962.48	3.51	551,926.18	610,816.7	8.83	548,174.2	617,980.64	8.09	534,076.8	619,482.1	5.31
RW750-C	593,353.31	626,565.97	710,680.86	5.6	619,245.39	702,241.1	4.36	619,168.27	707,639.74	4.35	615,416.51	703,534.96	3.72	619,412.94	712,491.68	4.39
RW800-C	687,763.656	730,742.66	819,292.53	6.25	765,546.44	829,570.55	11.31	735,548.58	810,045.45	6.95	739,563.3	821,056.54	7.53	728,891.84	811,673.87	5.98
RW300-E	612.204	385,516.51	444,230.28	7.37	391,074.28	444,808.7	8.53	391,072.86	441,831.11	8.89	390,709.76	443,823.79	8.68	384,631.35	444,510.29	6.36
RW350-E	708.081	663.98	760.41	8.46	644.76	772.53	5.32	630.17	756.58	2.93	623.88	761.46	1.91	637.36	763.04	4.11
RW400-E	802.088	759.42	883.15	7.25	736.14	856.49	3.96	743.98	884.01	5.07	766.93	882.5	8.31	742.38	860.32	4.84
RW450-E	902.195	872.46	990.58	8.77	848.82	999.5	5.83	820.3	993.31	2.27	823.17	1008.7	2.63	867.04	988.42	8.1
RW500-E	1007.376	947.01	1098.09	4.97	951.08	1101.75	5.42	935.97	1099.21	3.74	995.66	1119.5	10.36	943.81	1097.13	4.61
RW550-E	1122.621	1043.18	1241.94	3.55	1080.83	1237.65	7.29	1072.62	1215.82	6.48	1119.17	1264.68	11.1	1059.68	1224.23	5.19
RW600-E	1304.802	1144.32	1384.74	1.93	1221.65	1368.57	8.82	1238.14	1367.13	10.29	1197.19	1390.5	6.64	1185.22	1392.82	5.58
RW650-E	1545.005	1419.08	1616.32	8.76	1373.27	1599.68	5.25	1391.69	1594.11	6.66	1394.72	1614.18	6.89	1406.36	1600.15	7.78
RW700-E	1794.782	1665.69	1887.99	7.81	1651.93	1861.29	6.92	1604.84	1874.46	3.87	1673.72	1884.58	8.33	1675.24	1904.6	8.43
RW750-E	2099.338	1962.45	2214.69	9.34	1982.95	2214.33	10.48	1954.1	2174.09	8.88	1902.16	2191.95	5.98	1945.27	2209.72	8.38
RW800-E	2443.014	2264.7	2571.84	7.88	2292.04	2575.99	9.18	2212.81	2539.55	5.41	2221.2	2521.84	5.8	2250.96	2552.38	7.22
		2663.93	2953.13	9.04	2722.65	2937.81	11.45	2823.38	3046.43	15.57	2605.43	2923.0	6.65	2629.9	2913.56	7.65
RW300-C+E	164,604.53	1400.57	1600.26	7.07	1409.65	1593.24	7.27	1402.55	1594.97	6.47	1393.02	1596.63	6.78	1394.84	1591.49	6.54
RW350-C+E	190,242.112	168,658.98	212,727.19	2.46	176,444.67	205,058.94	7.19	173,056.52	214,816.59	5.13	182,264.77	209,180.81	10.73	183,163.86	217,919.74	11.28
RW400-C+E	215,498.372	208,636.51	250,315.97	9.67	201,523.94	243,996.67	5.93	196,473.6	248,565.95	3.28	201,849.61	240,120.29	6.1	209,651.55	248,083.69	10.2
RW450-C+E	241,998.678	236,614.01	275,954.32	9.8	239,632.13	277,046.29	11.2	224,193.97	265,672.91	4.04	229,261.36	271,977.58	6.39	244,633.69	283,644.99	13.52
RW500-C+E	269,533.553	270,957.25	310,023.22	11.97	257,290.6	306,282.91	6.32	280,742.96	320,823.27	16.01	256,252.7	311,883.58	5.89	261,084.72	313,347.59	7.89
RW550-C+E	308,696.291	308,085.44	342,097.22	14.3	293,506.55	348,175.63	8.89	281,713.39	343,204.09	4.52	296,651.36	346,621.13	10.06	282,994.86	331,343.68	4.99
RW600-C+E	365,784.894	342,032.54	392,228.11	10.8	329,122.6	375,492.42	6.62	335,151.94	388,785.13	8.57	337,425.85	382,851.06	9.31	325,039.5	382,216.95	5.29
RW650-C+E	432,031.377	377,921.76	443,061.9	3.32	402,061.9	464,050.7	9.92	386,279.94	443,721.28	5.6	392,853.36	446,311.8	7.4	390,294.82	457,974.88	6.7
RW700-C+E	508,928.933	469,187.01	525,056.83	8.6	464,313.64	526,829.5	7.47	464,800.5	525,976.15	7.58	463,004.0	519,128.6	7.17	473,514.3	533,492.6	9.6
RW750-C+E	595,461.955	558,249.29	613,632.89	9.69	567,040.8	612,672.63	11.42	543,066.2	622,176.4	6.71	546,718.92	613,544.22	7.43	554,975.79	611,984.05	9.05
RW800-C+E	690,374.634	654,041.06	710,449.31	9.84	647,750.72	726,656.72	8.78	645,172.05	713,194.58	8.35	629,497.71	722,580.29	5.72	646,497.24	717,550.24	8.57
		746,445.96	821,317.48	8.12	758,672.75	821,534.7	9.89	728,552.96	812,729.46	5.53	738,894.47	821,098.05	7.03	740,506.94	826,309.19	7.26
		394,620.89	445,172.73	8.96	394,305.48	446,164.99	8.51	387,200.37	445,424.16	6.85	388,606.74	444,117.95	7.57	392,032.48	447,624.33	8.58

112

Table 7. Comparison of the metaheuristics SCA-SARSA.

Inst.	Opt.	SA1			SA2			SA3			SA4			SA5		
		Best	Avg	RPD	Best	Avg	RPD	Best	Avg	RPD	Best	Avg	RPD	Best	Avg	RPD
RW300-C	163,992.326	177,137.67	224,260.78	8.02	180,792.13	220,153.89	10.24	182,743.3	219,209.54	11.43	177,206.82	234,269.03	8.06	182,686.29	241,289.47	11.4
RW350-C	189,534.031	208,138.12	264,710.41	9.82	202,664.92	269,416.08	6.93	201,953.08	262,367.93	6.55	207,615.0	269,509.83	9.54	213,815.68	264,199.64	12.81
RW400-C	214,696.284	225,119.78	291,785.74	4.85	240,342.74	304,398.82	11.95	232,461.48	300,241.53	8.27	246,457.28	296,371.99	14.79	233,717.84	302,323.41	8.86
RW450-C	241,096.482	278,095.59	323,782.93	15.35	269,654.9	342,157.21	11.85	252,396.03	332,456.51	4.69	271,024.1	334,596.22	12.41	281,990.47	339,022.7	16.96
RW500-C	268,526.177	288,284.59	368,227.63	7.36	273,124.46	370,022.32	1.71	297,248.48	362,742.78	10.7	281,004.63	363,934.9	4.65	305,071.97	373,895.89	13.61
RW550-C	307,536.973	338,844.89	392,264.2	10.18	323,906.32	416,680.35	5.32	333,697.21	404,026.04	8.51	343,922.52	410,328.48	11.83	313,331.75	404,645.32	1.88
RW600-C	364,409.78	373,922.98	479,795.73	2.61	401,552.2	474,158.07	10.19	403,437.77	462,371.55	10.71	387,705.3	479,860.42	6.39	407,833.99	475,558.99	11.92
RW650-C	430,400.866	464,199.96	541,047.14	7.85	478,302.01	545,685.64	11.13	484,950.95	547,191.46	12.67	460,644.89	531,631.54	7.03	462,758.53	545,869.92	7.52
RW700-C	507,127.151	524,925.0	615,145.01	3.51	550,871.52	620,348.25	8.63	540,526.5	617,313.87	6.59	546,543.27	629,484.51	7.77	549,550.4	615,424.43	8.37
RW750-C	593,353.31	638,144.22	729,317.37	7.55	633,964.23	713,740.48	6.84	603,561.86	724,955.72	1.72	602,775.81	715,782.64	1.59	635,394.83	730,607.54	7.09
RW800-C	687,763.656	743,476.16	827,808.92	8.1	758,914.12	840,577.68	10.35	731,345.26	826,673.89	6.34	768,513.66	835,314.43	11.74	752,583.06	853,668.89	9.42
RW300-E	612.204	387,299.0	459,831.44	7.75	392,189.96	465,212.62	8.65	387,665.63	459,959.17	8.02	390,310.3	463,734.91	8.71	394,430.44	467,864.2	9.99
RW350-E	708.081	640.94	796.13	4.69	710.79	815.84	16.1	659.82	829.18	7.78	673.18	814.48	9.96	668.83	820.84	9.25
RW400-E	802.088	787.69	931.19	11.24	778.37	936.24	9.93	797.53	972.38	12.63	768.86	958.7	8.58	761.78	934.74	7.58
RW450-E	902.195	837.28	1044.97	4.39	854.25	1097.08	6.5	828.13	1082.06	3.25	877.33	1102.57	9.38	818.45	1038.65	2.04
RW500-E	1007.376	952.68	1167.46	5.6	926.25	1181.68	2.67	1003.99	1142.18	11.28	942.58	1204.58	4.48	922.21	1241.86	2.22
RW550-E	1122.621	1057.46	1333.02	4.97	1119.65	1287.35	11.15	1111.76	1273.86	10.36	1103.8	1330.23	9.57	1060.32	1300.37	5.26
RW600-E	1304.802	1171.26	1412.38	4.33	1241.98	1543.5	10.63	1194.15	1502.52	6.37	1204.02	1449.21	7.25	1256.45	1449.66	11.92
RW650-E	1545.005	1479.84	1705.17	13.41	1422.84	1709.0	9.05	1440.0	1693.05	10.36	1422.57	1742.77	9.03	1416.34	1665.51	8.55
RW700-E	1794.782	1673.44	1980.37	8.31	1657.88	1909.21	7.31	1712.47	2022.58	10.84	1760.84	1985.75	13.97	1710.21	1947.59	10.69
RW750-E	2099.338	2009.14	2256.78	11.94	1840.68	2215.83	2.56	1962.28	2304.68	9.33	1978.56	2249.0	10.24	2003.18	2266.59	11.61
RW800-E	2443.014	2277.72	2671.58	8.5	2323.97	2620.33	10.7	2300.57	2612.05	9.59	2300.95	2604.42	9.6	2236.35	2586.29	6.53
		2515.07	3020.55	2.95	2641.07	3107.25	8.11	2558.83	3070.21	4.74	2776.85	3050.21	13.66	2553.02	2943.3	4.5
RW300-C+E	164,604.53	1400.23	1665.42	7.3	1410.7	1674.85	8.61	1415.41	1682.25	8.78	1437.23	1681.08	9.61	1400.65	1654.13	7.29
RW350-C+E	190,242.112	191,743.67	226,511.74	16.49	181,596.71	230,891.6	10.32	180,976.64	234,010.52	9.95	195,423.7	231,432.35	18.72	175,920.48	237,062.88	6.87
RW400-C+E	215,498.372	222,804.94	273,797.72	17.12	218,336.27	258,386.31	14.77	211,417.37	257,122.1	11.13	205,444.15	267,836.18	7.99	214,776.6	255,807.43	12.9
RW450-C+E	241,998.678	240,584.89	297,668.72	11.64	244,314.74	295,141.6	13.37	243,681.08	297,702.5	13.08	244,374.07	304,452.39	13.4	235,532.13	292,965.37	9.3
RW500-C+E	269,533.553	260,571.64	319,689.99	7.67	275,969.78	351,627.98	14.04	270,337.65	324,947.75	11.71	266,661.81	329,405.83	10.19	282,489.65	333,755.77	16.73
RW550-C+E	308,696.291	294,207.44	362,719.28	9.15	292,405.83	382,757.22	8.49	308,064.16	368,159.31	14.3	287,093.28	354,839.89	6.51	304,824.33	385,826.92	13.09
RW600-C+E	365,784.894	338,155.87	407,161.79	9.54	332,058.08	397,247.0	7.57	347,456.95	403,418.66	12.56	345,919.22	409,010.58	12.06	350,825.92	411,122.26	13.65
RW650-C+E	432,031.377	394,037.68	474,484.14	7.72	392,325.69	466,762.67	7.26	396,665.15	473,394.71	8.44	371,338.58	464,602.41	1.52	395,092.17	466,928.06	8.01
RW700-C+E	508,928.933	465,552.5	537,368.9	7.76	463,945.52	559,430.69	7.39	450,055.53	540,802.93	4.17	489,920.9	544,086.45	13.4	453,510.51	536,280.48	4.97
RW750-C+E	595,461.955	539,416.34	611,180.39	5.99	539,475.72	656,532.65	6.0	550,291.12	637,226.63	8.13	547,315.59	648,959.9	7.54	528,800.69	625,629.17	3.9
RW800-C+E	690,374.634	631,156.69	725,192.7	5.99	658,561.1	716,445.05	10.6	664,568.92	723,674.37	11.61	646,749.89	734,467.67	8.61	618,807.48	722,541.13	3.92
		727,997.55	831,451.81	5.45	750,169.78	836,083.2	8.66	727,071.28	820,679.47	5.32	733,179.58	843,869.81	6.2	731,795.7	834,718.22	6.0
		391,475.38	460,657.02	9.5	395,378.11	468,300.54	9.86	395,507.8	461,921.72	10.04	393,947.34	466,633.04	9.65	390,215.97	463,876.15	9.03

113

Table 8. Comparison of the metaheuristics GWO-Q-Learning.

Inst.	Opt.	QL1 Best	QL1 Avg	QL1 RPD	QL2 Best	QL2 Avg	QL2 RPD	QL3 Best	QL3 Avg	QL3 RPD	QL4 Best	QL4 Avg	QL4 RPD	QL5 Best	QL5 Avg	QL5 RPD
RW300-C	163,992.326	197,892.79	257,638.59	20.67	206,934.24	250,757.28	26.19	203,568.86	259,082.85	24.13	172,736.65	246,105.69	5.33	177,495.95	249,255.49	8.23
RW350-C	189,534.031	217,737.04	283,106.81	14.88	220,049.1	297,439.17	16.1	204,505.07	278,060.04	7.9	235,434.81	284,381.8	24.22	220,907.56	282,927.24	16.55
RW400-C	214,696.284	223,424.83	322,090.81	4.07	232,013.55	314,385.08	8.07	244,249.75	335,600.85	13.77	261,056.46	331,349.56	21.59	239,791.93	328,211.09	11.69
RW450-C	241,096.482	262,957.21	360,952.11	9.07	272,207.68	360,699.95	12.9	299,063.03	385,244.17	24.04	284,841.37	350,877.47	18.14	306,208.81	362,661.94	27.01
RW500-C	268,526.177	329,483.68	405,237.1	22.7	303,501.72	412,561.15	13.03	325,572.9	397,863.76	21.24	287,946.31	397,195.24	7.23	325,128.92	404,403.3	21.08
RW550-C	307,536.973	344,772.37	457,779.42	12.11	358,873.14	451,495.97	16.69	359,432.96	447,394.56	16.87	350,131.68	445,150.53	13.85	358,348.11	458,279.49	16.52
RW600-C	364,409.78	396,926.79	506,912.79	8.92	396,683.7	522,148.78	8.86	391,759.26	504,070.17	7.51	424,489.24	518,622.63	16.49	425,651.66	513,125.41	16.81
RW650-C	430,400.866	519,592.66	588,642.14	20.72	493,303.76	596,264.8	14.61	475,749.49	583,199.11	10.54	480,635.17	579,539.01	11.67	456,432.52	574,790.37	6.05
RW700-C	507,127.151	548,096.45	668,941.43	8.08	558,827.52	667,943.89	10.19	577,373.47	692,838.03	13.85	568,190.05	671,328.82	12.04	562,920.67	689,582.48	11.0
RW750-C	593,353.31	695,346.84	794,320.97	17.19	637,025.4	773,971.02	7.36	649,041.8	777,650.2	9.39	653,562.37	770,229.26	10.15	655,015.04	776,344.95	10.39
RW800-C	687,763.656	746,206.77	908,642.62	8.5	741,355.73	870,059.87	7.79	754,644.88	890,950.53	9.72	755,281.03	897,244.36	9.82	779,030.16	884,149.4	13.27
RW300-E	612.204	407,494.31	504,933.16	13.36	401,888.69	501,611.54	12.89	407,723.77	504,723.12	14.45	406,755.01	499,274.94	13.68	409,721.03	502,157.38	14.42
RW350-E	708.081	651.3	910.98	6.39	723.88	878.64	18.24	747.7	954.87	22.13	665.48	919.97	8.7	638.55	876.09	4.3
RW400-E	802.088	826.31	1025.29	16.7	775.07	1079.81	9.46	788.2	1055.87	11.31	850.66	1043.48	20.14	792.36	1036.66	11.9
RW450-E	902.195	934.37	1173.44	16.49	929.92	1147.64	15.94	994.44	1202.56	23.98	936.8	1186.46	16.8	870.25	1218.5	8.5
RW500-E	1007.376	1066.1	1345.53	18.17	963.6	1318.08	6.81	970.66	1283.31	7.59	1055.42	1358.65	16.98	1007.98	1317.88	11.73
RW550-E	1122.621	1087.77	1482.4	7.98	1115.68	1494.89	10.75	1048.32	1422.36	4.06	1171.28	1420.02	16.27	1175.56	1443.05	16.7
RW600-E	1304.802	1327.25	1627.9	18.23	1176.47	1625.49	4.8	1202.67	1657.65	7.13	1351.81	1598.86	20.42	1194.37	1535.23	6.39
RW650-E	1545.005	1445.11	1812.71	10.75	1491.64	1852.81	14.32	1519.54	1833.87	16.46	1414.77	1843.88	8.43	1488.03	1850.23	14.04
RW700-E	1794.782	1653.79	2072.22	7.04	1810.77	2123.03	17.2	1655.41	2078.2	7.15	1768.8	2164.97	14.49	1707.91	2187.33	10.54
RW750-E	2099.338	1983.98	2408.77	10.54	1984.53	2458.17	10.57	2021.71	2394.12	12.64	1989.86	2449.14	10.87	2100.89	2411.72	17.06
RW800-E	2443.014	2449.23	2859.24	16.67	2175.81	2753.22	3.64	2375.99	2697.55	13.18	2338.62	2735.78	11.4	2495.79	2800.35	18.88
		2610.96	3175.52	6.87	2638.71	3241.34	8.01	2627.71	3143.76	7.56	2748.99	3135.94	12.52	2743.37	3198.12	12.29
RW300-C+E	164,604.53	1457.83	1808.55	12.35	1435.1	1815.74	10.89	1450.21	1793.1	12.11	1481.14	1805.2	14.27	1474.1	1806.83	12.03
RW350-C+E	190,242.112	185,796.05	243,809.71	12.87	202,162.53	243,757.6	22.82	183,278.96	260,952.12	11.35	183,137.41	255,109.24	11.26	183,496.26	250,417.07	11.48
RW400-C+E	215,498.372	212,734.69	274,328.31	11.82	199,602.67	289,577.45	4.92	209,225.59	282,636.96	9.98	226,184.6	285,846.74	18.89	211,233.18	301,547.46	11.03
RW450-C+E	241,998.678	255,409.44	328,338.0	18.52	259,207.31	332,639.78	20.28	266,267.21	326,303.42	23.56	246,328.62	321,452.6	14.31	228,861.37	317,274.1	6.2
RW500-C+E	269,533.553	293,601.11	378,530.34	21.32	290,544.7	361,951.9	20.06	267,252.84	351,208.7	10.44	283,005.24	359,741.31	16.94	271,356.09	368,247.58	12.13
RW550-C+E	308,696.291	326,651.82	399,949.35	21.19	348,778.15	424,617.96	29.4	317,728.91	394,358.37	17.88	305,303.79	393,611.82	13.27	294,511.1	396,863.42	9.27
RW600-C+E	365,784.894	355,227.94	436,084.62	15.07	367,449.96	454,832.35	19.03	343,368.19	455,531.22	11.23	347,258.97	440,703.81	12.49	357,505.5	457,301.15	15.81
RW650-C+E	432,031.377	393,744.02	503,790.36	7.64	401,591.38	496,164.09	9.79	448,987.03	529,621.12	22.75	386,989.19	505,689.04	5.8	419,763.84	535,334.0	14.76
RW700-C+E	508,928.933	510,668.26	600,033.77	18.2	483,963.46	586,909.4	12.02	488,789.99	574,895.06	13.14	473,926.61	579,769.97	7.73	488,983.79	578,679.85	13.18
RW750-C+E	595,461.955	585,704.28	689,313.24	15.09	545,300.46	679,389.03	7.15	572,869.47	668,470.81	12.56	548,274.64	680,069.01	7.73	552,305.67	678,685.23	8.52
RW800-C+E	690,374.634	619,243.47	758,516.92	3.99	633,591.06	776,961.42	6.4	646,726.63	772,444.18	8.61	672,807.9	792,451.82	12.99	660,934.61	785,924.37	11.0
		763,266.05	877,440.83	10.56	737,978.01	894,599.76	6.9	741,107.15	899,987.75	7.35	762,147.16	859,215.5	10.4	743,333.62	879,484.62	7.67
		409,277.01	499,103.22	14.21	406,379.06	503,763.7	14.43	407,782.0	501,491.79	13.53	403,214.92	497,605.53	12.16	401,116.82	504,523.53	11.0

114

Table 9. Comparison of the metaheuristics WOA-Q-Learning.

Inst.	Opt.	QL1 Best	QL1 Avg	QL1 RPD	QL2 Best	QL2 Avg	QL2 RPD	QL3 Best	QL3 Avg	QL3 RPD	QL4 Best	QL4 Avg	QL4 RPD	QL5 Best	QL5 Avg	QL5 RPD
RW300-C	163,992.326	179,177.48	209,734.64	9.26	173,509.5	203,596.77	5.8	170,706.86	207,633.81	4.09	185,312.43	213,852.83	13.0	163,992.33	205,627.47	0.0
RW350-C	189,534.031	205,752.81	241,320.7	8.56	203,569.89	238,574.78	7.41	211,172.74	242,262.91	11.42	213,805.06	246,293.15	12.81	209,309.7	246,491.78	10.43
RW400-C	214,696.284	227,324.11	276,268.73	5.88	227,531.0	283,235.62	5.98	223,522.86	275,191.01	4.11	245,809.55	273,823.44	14.49	225,086.49	278,784.69	4.84
RW450-C	241,096.482	264,259.18	302,763.29	9.61	264,773.19	317,063.15	9.82	261,357.87	307,262.55	8.4	258,086.05	302,749.37	7.05	250,145.73	299,479.43	3.75
RW500-C	268,526.177	304,701.79	343,712.18	13.47	298,170.23	344,511.81	11.04	298,629.9	344,978.57	11.21	273,665.15	344,935.49	1.91	287,240.58	339,252.49	6.97
RW550-C	307,536.973	332,096.06	375,328.34	7.99	323,977.91	378,769.29	5.35	315,787.31	376,502.94	2.68	340,849.45	390,008.5	10.83	325,698.68	383,431.79	5.91
RW600-C	364,409.78	372,143.69	440,450.72	2.12	398,219.72	448,192.85	9.28	392,734.46	457,851.82	7.77	378,012.35	449,357.08	3.73	396,509.26	447,343.62	8.81
RW650-C	430,400.866	458,835.67	523,675.6	6.61	457,330.96	530,599.28	6.26	462,444.22	537,511.2	7.45	465,973.89	521,804.69	8.27	455,764.04	519,138.09	5.89
RW700-C	507,127.151	530,806.81	608,609.13	4.67	540,729.04	619,650.83	6.63	533,396.7	624,480.25	5.18	542,663.49	608,858.11	7.01	566,906.53	625,117.17	11.79
RW750-C	593,353.31	669,062.95	721,546.44	12.76	540,694.98	710,998.3	7.98	621,468.68	713,327.48	4.74	630,088.45	710,117.84	6.19	644,004.67	720,258.11	8.54
RW800-C	687,763.656	731,559.18	821,138.33	6.37	741,347.04	811,804.51	7.79	741,720.21	833,808.12	7.85	739,752.64	823,544.81	7.56	736,943.23	823,397.66	7.15
RW300-E	612.204	388,701.79	442,231.65	7.94	388,168.5	444,272.47	7.58	384,812.89	447,346.42	6.81	388,547.14	444,122.3	8.44	387,418.29	444,392.94	6.73
RW350-E	708.081	681.66	770.1	11.35	651.95	747.04	6.49	651.75	753.42	6.46	626.13	766.51	2.27	665.47	763.41	8.7
RW400-E	802.088	755.94	886.8	6.76	777.37	877.05	9.79	771.3	897.6	8.93	743.82	876.41	5.05	761.48	881.68	7.54
RW450-E	902.195	892.45	998.25	11.27	824.23	999.57	2.76	870.41	985.51	8.52	835.8	1012.89	4.2	853.19	975.38	6.37
RW500-E	1007.376	956.45	1112.15	6.01	911.56	1099.19	1.04	941.79	1122.56	4.39	951.14	1113.93	5.43	961.24	1114.9	6.54
RW550-E	1122.621	1048.32	1270.49	4.06	1044.44	1238.39	3.68	1076.63	1233.77	6.87	1055.8	1247.12	4.81	1105.15	1245.1	9.71
RW600-E	1304.802	1230.99	1401.38	9.65	1227.75	1400.52	9.36	1210.35	1382.88	7.81	1170.27	1352.35	4.24	1189.31	1381.38	5.94
RW650-E	1545.005	1433.3	1584.19	9.85	1443.55	1584.51	10.63	1466.49	1649.07	12.39	1364.98	1576.17	4.61	1401.96	1632.68	7.45
RW700-E	1794.782	1651.73	1899.73	6.91	1674.59	1890.45	8.39	1681.7	1897.8	8.85	1714.19	1895.53	10.95	1665.06	1869.05	7.77
RW750-E	2099.338	1905.46	2178.49	6.17	1893.02	2183.6	5.47	1950.12	2182.28	8.65	1858.8	2161.97	3.57	1969.88	2171.85	9.76
RW800-E	2443.014	2249.11	2547.13	7.13	2236.64	2555.99	6.54	2294.51	2553.94	9.3	2301.72	2599.84	9.64	2310.63	2562.96	10.06
		2610.63	2945.13	6.86	2669.1	2954.83	9.25	2565.6	2948.68	5.02	2641.95	2973.11	8.14	2631.57	2958.9	7.72
RW300-C+E	164,604.53	1401.46	1599.44	7.82	1395.84	1593.74	6.67	1407.33	1600.66	7.93	1387.69	1597.8	5.72	1410.45	1596.12	7.96
RW350-C+E	190,242.112	192,163.04	217,195.43	16.74	180,503.12	208,418.99	9.66	175,837.81	210,338.41	6.82	184,342.08	211,341.16	11.99	180,867.27	208,979.87	9.88
RW400-C+E	215,498.372	205,706.7	244,438.78	8.13	198,685.25	235,924.1	4.44	212,783.52	245,577.84	11.85	204,786.43	246,370.21	7.65	212,304.11	243,465.48	11.6
RW450-C+E	241,998.678	233,881.15	278,527.63	8.53	232,257.03	272,418.78	7.78	240,999.43	282,502.8	11.83	235,011.55	273,551.43	9.05	239,611.42	279,434.38	11.19
RW500-C+E	269,533.553	269,162.46	309,912.24	11.22	251,926.58	313,113.95	4.1	262,562.55	310,494.65	8.5	250,607.99	313,224.14	3.56	266,679.25	316,270.77	10.2
RW550-C+E	308,696.291	290,900.58	345,075.04	7.93	293,399.22	341,136.74	8.85	284,434.62	329,608.51	5.53	281,154.2	334,725.13	4.31	290,972.35	346,654.16	7.95
RW600-C+E	365,784.894	324,837.6	378,041.39	5.23	333,413.4	388,181.0	8.01	342,165.68	386,204.37	10.84	339,325.66	390,623.98	9.92	345,612.72	386,947.89	11.96
RW650-C+E	432,031.377	392,542.47	448,391.81	7.32	408,737.83	446,852.2	11.74	390,921.15	450,464.34	6.87	400,027.15	447,415.89	9.36	397,653.18	445,113.56	8.71
RW700-C+E	508,928.933	453,990.37	521,024.94	5.08	462,994.09	520,041.75	7.17	451,717.44	521,551.42	4.56	447,965.11	523,135.28	3.69	458,944.13	533,686.33	6.23
RW750-C+E	595,461.955	541,769.0	628,241.11	6.45	537,410.91	622,687.44	5.6	551,167.05	626,569.19	8.3	543,383.44	613,361.01	6.77	563,812.97	614,530.51	10.78
RW800-C+E	690,374.634	667,404.79	716,299.26	12.08	630,451.77	718,923.87	5.88	638,116.46	702,900.44	7.16	621,906.63	717,452.25	4.44	635,051.81	706,863.81	6.65
		740,820.65	813,583.22	7.31	730,350.91	820,324.92	5.79	738,857.26	826,262.18	7.02	747,392.85	827,572.44	8.26	746,636.42	831,011.81	8.15
		392,107.16	445,520.99	8.73	387,284.56	444,365.79	7.18	389,960.27	444,770.38	8.12	386,900.28	445,342.99	7.18	394,376.88	446,632.6	9.39

Table 10. Comparison of the metaheuristics SCA-Q-Learning.

Inst.	Opt.	QL1 Best	QL1 Avg	QL1 RPD	QL2 Best	QL2 Avg	QL2 RPD	QL3 Best	QL3 Avg	QL3 RPD	QL4 Best	QL4 Avg	QL4 RPD	QL5 Best	QL5 Avg	QL5 RPD
RW300-C	163,992.326	188,225.91	248,806.82	14.78	195,606.76	236,316.91	19.28	184,526.82	223,465.47	12.52	183,603.67	229,561.85	11.96	177,677.74	230,346.92	8.35
RW350-C	189,534.031	217,879.52	257,241.39	14.96	216,835.07	256,504.85	14.4	205,495.03	261,925.48	8.42	211,586.52	266,579.83	11.64	215,455.42	277,412.0	13.68
RW400-C	214,696.284	235,792.62	279,424.7	9.83	230,798.16	295,828.39	7.5	235,671.72	287,764.41	9.77	242,036.31	291,843.42	12.73	239,067.96	295,594.1	11.35
RW450-C	241,096.482	266,759.5	328,945.35	10.64	271,344.08	349,763.96	12.55	250,013.86	331,926.05	3.7	269,800.8	336,849.14	11.91	259,670.35	322,917.8	7.7
RW500-C	268,526.177	281,939.86	372,031.88	5.0	302,788.88	355,070.33	12.76	294,629.87	362,128.18	9.72	301,693.73	368,002.89	12.35	290,550.45	362,554.5	8.2
RW550-C	307,536.973	349,715.87	418,383.02	13.72	329,285.89	394,564.02	7.07	325,982.9	400,606.42	6.0	335,261.5	401,572.64	9.02	326,635.26	412,105.97	6.21
RW600-C	364,409.78	393,011.66	468,298.77	7.85	404,226.59	471,480.97	10.93	407,253.36	466,503.2	11.76	418,274.55	482,988.21	14.78	426,792.95	490,546.86	17.12
RW650-C	430,400.866	468,004.2	537,036.27	8.74	483,925.17	559,743.39	12.44	480,992.54	543,497.99	11.75	455,179.93	543,497.21	5.76	466,139.62	521,064.32	8.3
RW700-C	507,127.151	558,644.81	644,791.06	10.16	558,153.57	629,733.8	10.06	543,519.45	617,948.04	7.18	526,938.59	619,240.21	3.91	548,814.34	630,356.1	8.22
RW750-C	593,353.31	642,805.71	736,044.64	8.33	610,013.64	710,919.85	2.81	632,854.68	716,246.25	6.66	627,942.79	710,817.92	5.83	627,750.72	737,856.51	5.8
RW800-C	687,763.656	733,356.26	837,946.92	6.63	738,021.36	836,901.23	7.31	762,410.42	834,888.46	10.85	723,901.08	810,431.78	5.25	745,269.57	838,912.62	8.36
RW300-E	612,204	632.53	466,268.26	10.06	394,636.29	463,347.97	10.65	393,031.88	458,809.09	8.94	390,565.41	460,125.92	9.56	393,074.94	465,424.34	9.39
RW350-E	708,081	775.24	787.52	3.32	627.73	850.08	2.54	662.77	824.1	8.26	685.78	810.94	12.02	690.43	829.65	12.78
RW400-E	802,088	881.25	966.1	9.48	729.99	916.66	3.09	771.07	935.3	8.9	758.6	935.43	7.13	779.8	942.15	10.13
RW450-E	902,195	955.88	1079.31	9.87	902.64	1064.21	12.54	858.14	1083.06	6.99	848.1	1088.94	5.74	880.95	1105.65	9.83
RW500-E	1007,376	1115.7	1163.21	5.95	981.23	1175.83	8.76	928.3	1220.16	2.89	1021.44	1176.07	13.22	1023.98	1192.25	13.5
RW550-E	1122,621	1224.69	1362.59	10.75	1133.5	1294.33	12.52	1066.27	1317.42	5.85	1114.7	1317.07	10.65	1071.88	1280.84	6.4
RW600-E	1304,802	1451.05	1492.48	9.09	1318.46	1495.19	17.44	1185.07	1505.19	5.56	1269.96	1512.38	13.12	1235.49	1520.3	10.05
RW650-E	1545,005	1643.72	1684.81	11.21	1440.04	1778.89	10.36	1409.39	1714.9	8.02	1461.23	1694.36	11.99	1477.48	1754.3	13.23
RW700-E	1794,782	1947.43	1958.12	6.39	1690.66	1941.53	9.43	1626.11	1969.11	5.25	1665.74	1963.95	7.81	1607.77	1972.57	4.06
RW750-E	2099,338	2316.53	2242.84	8.51	1960.46	2267.06	9.23	1929.02	2236.78	7.48	1895.92	2280.29	5.64	1878.92	2248.89	4.69
RW800-E	2443,014	2654.95	2580.85	10.35	2237.08	2591.88	6.56	2190.47	2579.14	4.34	2305.45	2623.37	9.82	2204.14	2579.3	4.99
			2964.9	8.68	2783.78	3032.84	13.95	2572.41	2965.77	5.3	2607.03	3060.59	6.71	2557.59	2981.4	4.69
RW300-C+E	164,604.53	1418.09	1662.07	8.51	1436.87	1673.5	9.67	1381.73	1668.27	6.26	1421.27	1678.49	9.44	1400.77	1673.39	8.58
RW350-C+E	190,242.112	178,117.75	218,093.56	8.21	174,480.66	218,954.42	6.0	178,552.1	228,386.25	8.47	175,423.38	227,357.91	6.57	177,436.63	217,508.53	7.8
RW400-C+E	215,498.372	211,036.84	265,385.47	10.93	202,716.35	254,733.66	6.56	225,144.99	278,282.7	18.35	208,876.32	263,848.8	9.79	208,058.71	255,324.14	9.37
RW450-C+E	241,998.678	233,635.68	300,872.86	8.42	252,481.47	302,436.59	17.16	232,996.34	305,644.45	8.12	246,074.32	313,417.21	14.19	232,666.38	302,175.97	7.97
RW500-C+E	269,533.553	252,589.42	342,970.47	4.38	273,417.79	334,499.99	12.98	269,754.56	340,325.28	11.47	270,090.54	328,724.7	11.61	255,095.97	333,278.29	5.41
RW550-C+E	308,696.291	312,593.43	361,128.9	15.98	300,549.66	372,079.4	11.51	282,690.22	379,290.8	4.88	285,100.9	368,225.15	5.78	301,263.97	370,004.36	11.77
RW600-C+E	365,784.894	321,599.14	401,669.81	4.18	335,613.38	414,082.42	8.72	346,142.33	410,142.05	12.13	344,482.35	413,813.22	11.59	353,362.3	410,923.12	14.47
RW650-C+E	432,031.377	380,615.59	472,031.82	4.05	413,513.62	483,327.05	13.05	406,735.23	478,947.71	11.2	413,275.63	491,019.25	12.98	400,832.43	475,439.54	9.58
RW700-C+E	508,928.933	462,077.04	537,604.78	6.95	460,609.49	541,804.88	6.61	466,736.14	542,475.14	8.03	465,974.21	528,475.14	7.86	463,620.51	552,228.91	7.31
RW750-C+E	595,461.955	546,000.95	637,165.32	7.28	549,446.46	616,198.15	7.96	541,173.79	640,621.23	6.34	559,246.37	639,752.38	9.89	561,079.68	636,865.36	10.25
RW800-C+E	690,374.634	642,054.47	728,172.58	7.82	647,973.23	714,062.88	8.82	663,569.76	732,790.77	11.44	627,776.99	729,641.43	5.43	674,321.71	745,833.69	13.24
		735,470.14	832,503.27	6.53	730,552.55	820,013.4	5.82	746,408.39	861,105.24	8.12	742,962.6	847,258.14	7.62	768,856.17	852,352.07	11.37
	388,708.22	463,418.08	7.7	394,668.61	461,108.44	9.56	396,354.9	472,546.51	9.87	394,480.33	468,320.88	9.39	399,690.41	468,357.63	9.87

116

In order to analyze the GWO technique, which was the best-performing technique, it is necessary to quantify the RPD obtained in ranges. These categorizations were established according to a minimum and maximum range, average and standard deviation (Table 11).

Table 11. RPD distribution in GWO.

	Lower Limit	Upper Limit	Mean	Standard Deviation
S	0.93	16.74	7.68	3.15
V	3.22	29.28	12.84	4.81
QL	3.64	29.4	13.21	5.43
SARSA	0	27.39	12.59	5.38

With the ranges already established, the distribution in GWO of the different techniques is represented in Table 12.

Table 12. RPD distribution in GWO.

	[0, 7.5[	[7.5, 15[	[15, 22.5[	[22.5, +
S1	19	14	0	0
S2	20	12	1	0
S3	19	12	2	0
S4	16	16	1	0
V1	3	16	13	1
V2	4	23	4	2
V3	3	25	4	1
V4	6	16	10	1
QL1	5	13	14	1
QL2	8	14	8	3
QL3	4	19	5	5
QL4	3	19	10	1
QL5	4	20	8	1
SA1	7	19	7	0
SA2	10	14	8	1
SA3	4	16	12	1
SA4	2	20	10	1
SA5	3	18	8	4

Table 13 presents the parameters utilized in this research, providing information about the set of instances used. The table comprises several data columns, organized as follows:

1. **Inst.** lists each of the studied walls in sequential order.
2. **Opt.** displays the optimal value for each respective instance.
3. **Best** indicates the best value achieved during the execution.
4. **Shape** identifies the top-performing algorithm that reached the best value.
5. **Fitness** denotes the fitness or efficiency value of the best algorithm.
6. The remaining columns represent the design parameters.

This tabular representation effectively communicates the key parameters and findings from our research, allowing readers to quickly grasp the results and assess the performance of various algorithms in the study.

Table 13. Design parameters of the best results for each version.

Inst.	Opt.	Best	Shape	Concrete	Steel	Crowning	Base	Footing
RW300-C	163,992.326	172,736.65	QL4	25	2.8	0.17	0.35	0.45
RW350-C	189,534.031	201,487.94	S2	25	2.8	0.16	0.37	0.45
RW400-C	214,696.284	219,450.	S3	25	2.8	0.17	0.31	0.45
RW450-C	241,096.482	246,740.28	SA1	25	2.8	0.17	0.31	0.45
RW500-C	268,526.177	279,819.15	S3	25	2.8	0.15	0.31	0.47
RW550-C	307,536.973	322,283.21	S2	25	2.8	0.16	0.3	0.5
RW600-C	364,409.78	377,871.72	S3	25	4.2	0.17	0.3	0.54
RW650-C	430,400.866	451,496.13	V1	30	2.8	0.15	0.32	0.57
RW700-C	507,127.151	530,085.84	S3	25	2.8	0.24	0.34	0.65
RW750-C	593,353.31	611,414.67	SA2	30	2.8	0.18	0.35	0.67
RW800-C	687,763.656	710,899.7	SA3	30	2.8	0.16	0.39	0.74
RW300-E	612.204	631.33	S3	25	4.2	0.18	0.3	0.45
RW350-E	708.081	752.24	V2	25	2.8	0.15	0.38	0.45
RW400-E	802.088	849.79	S1	30	4.2	0.2	0.32	0.45
RW450-E	902.195	912.78	S3	25	2.8	0.15	0.31	0.45
RW500-E	1007.376	1036.58	S1	25	2.8	0.15	0.32	0.46
RW550-E	1122.621	1176.47	QL2	30	2.8	0.2	0.31	0.46
RW600-E	1304.802	1346.81	V2	30	2.8	0.16	0.32	0.5
RW650-E	1545.005	1588.32	S3	30	2.8	0.15	0.35	0.55
RW700-E	1794.782	1846.2	S4	30	2.8	0.16	0.35	0.6
RW750-E	2099.338	2175.81	QL2	40	2.8	0.16	0.3	0.59
RW800-E	2443.014	2491.57	S1	30	2.8	0.19	0.36	0.72
RW300-C+E	164,604.53	164,604.53	SA2	25	2.8	0.15	0.3	0.45
RW350-C+E	190,242.112	199,602.67	S1	25	2.8	0.15	0.3	0.49
RW400-C+E	215,498.372	223,604.65	SA2	25	2.8	0.15	0.3	0.48
RW450-C+E	241,998.678	256,669.92	SA1	25	2.8	0.15	0.3	0.49
RW500-C+E	269,533.553	282,150.29	S4	25	2.8	0.15	0.3	0.48
RW550-C+E	308,696.291	328,562.36	S3	25	2.8	0.2	0.35	0.47
RW600-C+E	365,784.894	381,018.45	SA5	25	2.8	0.17	0.32	0.54
RW650-C+E	432,031.377	459,287.25	V3	25	4.2	0.17	0.35	0.61
RW700-C+E	508,928.933	513,662.21	S4	25	2.8	0.17	0.33	0.65
RW750-C+E	595,461.955	619,227.4	S3	30	2.8	0.16	0.38	0.67
RW800-C+E	690,374.634	722,411.98	S1	30	4.2	0.21	0.4	0.72

5.1. Distribution Analysis

The violin plots (Figures 7–9) presented in this section offer a clear and concise visualization of the results obtained from our investigation of the algorithms employed. A representative instance was selected to showcase the results using the best-performing metaheuristic: GWO. Upon examining the plots, it is evident that the violins corresponding to Algorithms S1–S4 exhibit lower data dispersion compared to the others, signifying a greater efficiency in minimizing the problem. Overall, the violin plots provide an effective and lucid representation of the findings from our study, which will assist researchers and subject matter experts in making informed decisions when selecting techniques for future research and practical applications. The plots are structured as follows: the Y-axis displays the fitness range, which refers to the data density at that level, while the X-axis represents all the evaluated algorithms.

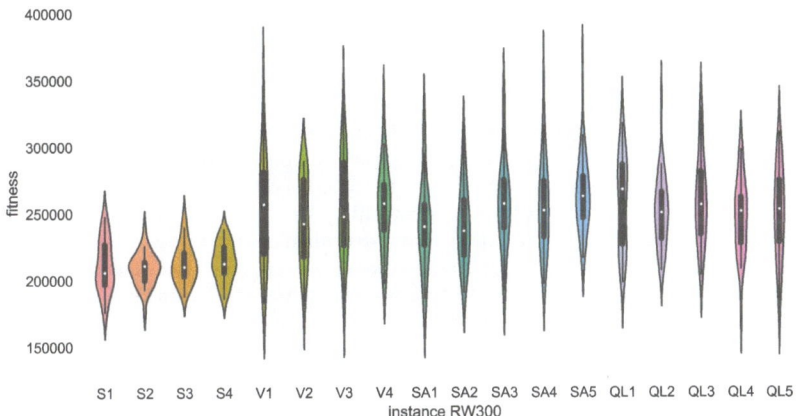

Figure 7. GWO Instance RW300—objective function cost.

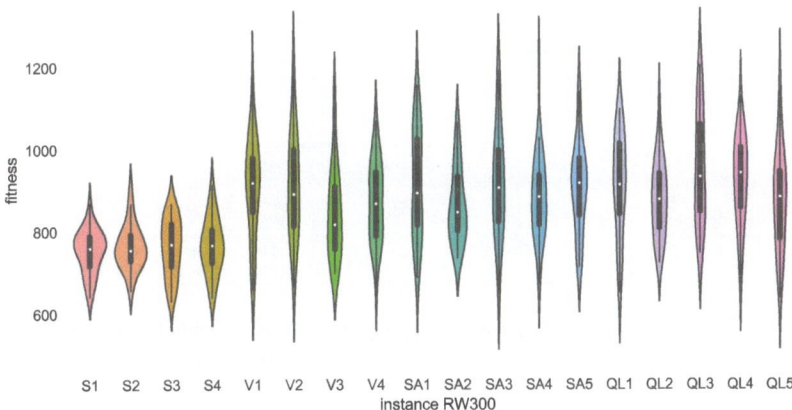

Figure 8. GWO Instance RW300—objective function CO_2 emissions.

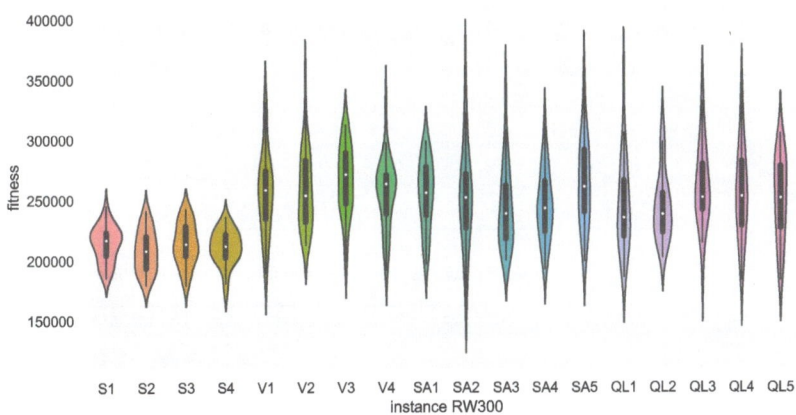

Figure 9. GWO Instance RW300—objective function cost + CO_2 emissions.

5.2. Statistical Test

The results displayed in Tables 14–16 concerning Algorithms S1–S4 in the Wilcoxon–Mann–Whitney statistical test corroborate earlier findings, suggesting that these algorithms excel in terms of minimization. Our statistical analysis reveals that the p-value of the test also supports these conclusions, as it is considerably lower than 0.05, signifying a statistically significant difference between the medians of algorithms S1–S4 and those of the remaining algorithms. In essence, the statistical test outcomes reinforce the violin plot findings, demonstrating that algorithms S1–S4 are indeed significantly superior.

The tables are structured as follows: the first row and column display the 18 algorithms under study and those to be compared. If the *p*-value is less than 0.05, the value is presented in bold and approximated to three decimal places. If the *p*-value exceeds 0.05, the value is replaced by ">0.05". When comparing identical algorithms, the symbol "-" is used to indicate that no comparison is made.

Table 14. Average *p*-value of GWO—objective function cost.

	S1	S2	S3	S4	V1	V2	V3	V4	SA1	SA2	SA3	SA4	SA5	QL1	QL2	QL3	QL4	QL5
S1	-	≥0.05	≥0.05	≥0.05	0.00	0.00	0.00	0.00	0.00	0.00	0.00	0.00	0.00	0.00	0.00	0.00	0.00	0.00
S2	≥0.05	-	≥0.05	≥0.05	0.00	0.00	0.00	0.00	0.00	0.00	0.00	0.00	0.00	0.00	0.00	0.00	0.00	0.00
S3	≥0.05	≥0.05	-	≥0.05	0.00	0.00	0.00	0.00	0.00	0.00	0.00	0.00	0.00	0.00	0.00	0.00	0.00	0.00
S4	≥0.05	≥0.05	≥0.05	-	0.00	0.00	0.00	0.00	0.00	0.00	0.00	0.00	0.00	0.00	0.00	0.00	0.00	0.00
V1	≥0.05	≥0.05	≥0.05	≥0.05	-	≥0.05	≥0.05	≥0.05	≥0.05	≥0.05	≥0.05	≥0.05	≥0.05	≥0.05	≥0.05	≥0.05	≥0.05	≥0.05
V2	≥0.05	≥0.05	≥0.05	≥0.05	≥0.05	-	≥0.05	≥0.05	≥0.05	≥0.05	≥0.05	≥0.05	≥0.05	≥0.05	≥0.05	≥0.05	≥0.05	≥0.05
V3	≥0.05	≥0.05	≥0.05	≥0.05	≥0.05	≥0.05	-	≥0.05	≥0.05	≥0.05	≥0.05	≥0.05	≥0.05	≥0.05	≥0.05	≥0.05	≥0.05	≥0.05
V4	≥0.05	≥0.05	≥0.05	≥0.05	≥0.05	≥0.05	≥0.05	-	≥0.05	≥0.05	≥0.05	≥0.05	≥0.05	≥0.05	≥0.05	≥0.05	≥0.05	≥0.05
SA1	≥0.05	≥0.05	≥0.05	≥0.05	≥0.05	≥0.05	≥0.05	≥0.05	-	≥0.05	≥0.05	≥0.05	≥0.05	≥0.05	≥0.05	≥0.05	≥0.05	≥0.05
SA2	≥0.05	≥0.05	≥0.05	≥0.05	≥0.05	≥0.05	≥0.05	≥0.05	≥0.05	-	≥0.05	≥0.05	≥0.05	≥0.05	≥0.05	≥0.05	≥0.05	≥0.05
SA3	≥0.05	≥0.05	≥0.05	≥0.05	≥0.05	≥0.05	≥0.05	≥0.05	≥0.05	≥0.05	-	≥0.05	≥0.05	≥0.05	≥0.05	≥0.05	≥0.05	≥0.05
SA4	≥0.05	≥0.05	≥0.05	≥0.05	≥0.05	≥0.05	≥0.05	≥0.05	≥0.05	≥0.05	≥0.05	-	≥0.05	≥0.05	≥0.05	≥0.05	≥0.05	≥0.05
SA5	≥0.05	≥0.05	≥0.05	≥0.05	≥0.05	≥0.05	≥0.05	≥0.05	≥0.05	≥0.05	≥0.05	≥0.05	-	≥0.05	≥0.05	≥0.05	≥0.05	≥0.05
QL1	≥0.05	≥0.05	≥0.05	≥0.05	≥0.05	≥0.05	≥0.05	≥0.05	≥0.05	≥0.05	≥0.05	≥0.05	≥0.05	-	≥0.05	≥0.05	≥0.05	≥0.05
QL2	≥0.05	≥0.05	≥0.05	≥0.05	≥0.05	≥0.05	≥0.05	≥0.05	≥0.05	≥0.05	≥0.05	≥0.05	≥0.05	≥0.05	-	≥0.05	≥0.05	≥0.05
QL3	≥0.05	≥0.05	≥0.05	≥0.05	≥0.05	≥0.05	≥0.05	≥0.05	≥0.05	≥0.05	≥0.05	≥0.05	≥0.05	≥0.05	≥0.05	-	≥0.05	≥0.05
QL4	≥0.05	≥0.05	≥0.05	≥0.05	≥0.05	≥0.05	≥0.05	≥0.05	≥0.05	≥0.05	≥0.05	≥0.05	≥0.05	≥0.05	≥0.05	≥0.05	-	≥0.05
QL5	≥0.05	≥0.05	≥0.05	≥0.05	≥0.05	≥0.05	≥0.05	≥0.05	≥0.05	≥0.05	≥0.05	≥0.05	≥0.05	≥0.05	≥0.05	≥0.05	≥0.05	-

Table 15. Average *p*-value of GWO—objective function CO_2 emissions.

	S1	S2	S3	S4	V1	V2	V3	V4	SA1	SA2	SA3	SA4	SA5	QL1	QL2	QL3	QL4	QL5
S1	-	≥0.05	≥0.05	≥0.05	0.00	0.00	0.00	0.00	0.00	0.00	0.00	0.00	0.00	0.00	0.00	0.00	0.00	0.00
S2	≥0.05	-	≥0.05	≥0.05	0.00	0.00	0.00	0.00	0.00	0.00	0.00	0.00	0.00	0.00	0.00	0.00	0.00	0.00
S3	≥0.05	≥0.05	-	≥0.05	0.00	0.00	0.00	0.00	0.00	0.00	0.00	0.00	0.00	0.00	0.00	0.00	0.00	0.00
S4	≥0.05	≥0.05	≥0.05	-	0.00	0.00	0.00	0.00	0.00	0.00	0.00	0.00	0.00	0.00	0.00	0.00	0.00	0.00
V1	≥0.05	≥0.05	≥0.05	≥0.05	-	≥0.05	≥0.05	≥0.05	≥0.05	≥0.05	≥0.05	≥0.05	≥0.05	≥0.05	≥0.05	≥0.05	≥0.05	≥0.05
V2	≥0.05	≥0.05	≥0.05	≥0.05	≥0.05	-	≥0.05	≥0.05	≥0.05	≥0.05	≥0.05	≥0.05	≥0.05	≥0.05	≥0.05	≥0.05	≥0.05	≥0.05
V3	≥0.05	≥0.05	≥0.05	≥0.05	≥0.05	≥0.05	-	≥0.05	≥0.05	≥0.05	≥0.05	≥0.05	≥0.05	≥0.05	≥0.05	≥0.05	≥0.05	≥0.05
V4	≥0.05	≥0.05	≥0.05	≥0.05	≥0.05	≥0.05	≥0.05	-	≥0.05	≥0.05	≥0.05	≥0.05	≥0.05	≥0.05	≥0.05	≥0.05	≥0.05	≥0.05
SA1	≥0.05	≥0.05	≥0.05	≥0.05	≥0.05	≥0.05	≥0.05	≥0.05	-	≥0.05	≥0.05	≥0.05	≥0.05	≥0.05	≥0.05	≥0.05	≥0.05	≥0.05
SA2	≥0.05	≥0.05	≥0.05	≥0.05	≥0.05	≥0.05	≥0.05	≥0.05	≥0.05	-	≥0.05	≥0.05	≥0.05	≥0.05	≥0.05	≥0.05	≥0.05	≥0.05
SA3	≥0.05	≥0.05	≥0.05	≥0.05	≥0.05	≥0.05	≥0.05	≥0.05	≥0.05	≥0.05	-	≥0.05	≥0.05	≥0.05	≥0.05	≥0.05	≥0.05	≥0.05
SA4	≥0.05	≥0.05	≥0.05	≥0.05	≥0.05	≥0.05	≥0.05	≥0.05	≥0.05	≥0.05	≥0.05	-	≥0.05	≥0.05	≥0.05	≥0.05	≥0.05	≥0.05
SA5	≥0.05	≥0.05	≥0.05	≥0.05	≥0.05	≥0.05	≥0.05	≥0.05	≥0.05	≥0.05	≥0.05	≥0.05	-	≥0.05	≥0.05	≥0.05	≥0.05	≥0.05
QL1	≥0.05	≥0.05	≥0.05	≥0.05	≥0.05	≥0.05	≥0.05	≥0.05	≥0.05	≥0.05	≥0.05	≥0.05	≥0.05	-	≥0.05	≥0.05	≥0.05	≥0.05
QL2	≥0.05	≥0.05	≥0.05	≥0.05	≥0.05	≥0.05	≥0.05	≥0.05	≥0.05	≥0.05	≥0.05	≥0.05	≥0.05	≥0.05	-	≥0.05	≥0.05	≥0.05
QL3	≥0.05	≥0.05	≥0.05	≥0.05	≥0.05	≥0.05	≥0.05	≥0.05	≥0.05	≥0.05	≥0.05	≥0.05	≥0.05	≥0.05	≥0.05	-	≥0.05	≥0.05
QL4	≥0.05	≥0.05	≥0.05	≥0.05	≥0.05	≥0.05	≥0.05	≥0.05	≥0.05	≥0.05	≥0.05	≥0.05	≥0.05	≥0.05	≥0.05	≥0.05	-	≥0.05
QL5	≥0.05	≥0.05	≥0.05	≥0.05	≥0.05	≥0.05	≥0.05	≥0.05	≥0.05	≥0.05	≥0.05	≥0.05	≥0.05	≥0.05	≥0.05	≥0.05	≥0.05	-

Table 16. Average *p*-value of GWO—objective function cost + CO_2 emissions.

	S1	S2	S3	S4	V1	V2	V3	V4	SA1	SA2	SA3	SA4	SA5	QL1	QL2	QL3	QL4	QL5
S1	-	≥0.05	≥0.05	≥0.05	0.00	0.00	0.00	0.00	0.00	0.00	0.00	0.00	0.00	0.00	0.00	0.00	0.00	0.00
S2	≥0.05	-	≥0.05	≥0.05	0.00	0.00	0.00	0.00	0.00	0.00	0.00	0.00	0.00	0.00	0.00	0.00	0.00	0.00
S3	≥0.05	≥0.05	-	≥0.05	0.00	0.00	0.00	0.00	0.00	0.00	0.00	0.00	0.00	0.00	0.00	0.00	0.00	0.00
S4	≥0.05	≥0.05	≥0.05	-	0.00	0.00	0.00	0.00	0.00	0.00	0.00	0.00	0.00	0.00	0.00	0.00	0.00	0.00
V1	≥0.05	≥0.05	≥0.05	≥0.05	-	≥0.05	≥0.05	≥0.05	≥0.05	≥0.05	≥0.05	≥0.05	≥0.05	≥0.05	≥0.05	≥0.05	≥0.05	≥0.05
V2	≥0.05	≥0.05	≥0.05	≥0.05	≥0.05	-	≥0.05	≥0.05	≥0.05	≥0.05	≥0.05	≥0.05	≥0.05	≥0.05	≥0.05	≥0.05	≥0.05	≥0.05
V3	≥0.05	≥0.05	≥0.05	≥0.05	≥0.05	≥0.05	-	≥0.05	≥0.05	≥0.05	≥0.05	≥0.05	≥0.05	≥0.05	≥0.05	≥0.05	≥0.05	≥0.05
V4	≥0.05	≥0.05	≥0.05	≥0.05	≥0.05	≥0.05	≥0.05	-	≥0.05	≥0.05	≥0.05	≥0.05	≥0.05	≥0.05	≥0.05	≥0.05	≥0.05	≥0.05
SA1	≥0.05	≥0.05	≥0.05	≥0.05	≥0.05	≥0.05	≥0.05	≥0.05	-	≥0.05	≥0.05	≥0.05	≥0.05	≥0.05	≥0.05	≥0.05	≥0.05	≥0.05

Table 16. Cont.

	S1	S2	S3	S4	V1	V2	V3	V4	SA1	SA2	SA3	SA4	SA5	QL1	QL2	QL3	QL4	QL5
SA2	≥0.05	≥0.05	≥0.05	≥0.05	≥0.05	≥0.05	≥0.05	≥0.05	≥0.05	-	≥0.05	≥0.05	≥0.05	≥0.05	≥0.05	≥0.05	≥0.05	≥0.05
SA3	≥0.05	≥0.05	≥0.05	≥0.05	≥0.05	≥0.05	≥0.05	≥0.05	≥0.05	≥0.05	-	≥0.05	≥0.05	≥0.05	≥0.05	≥0.05	≥0.05	≥0.05
SA4	≥0.05	≥0.05	≥0.05	≥0.05	≥0.05	≥0.05	≥0.05	≥0.05	≥0.05	≥0.05	≥0.05	-	≥0.05	≥0.05	≥0.05	≥0.05	≥0.05	≥0.05
SA5	≥0.05	≥0.05	≥0.05	≥0.05	≥0.05	≥0.05	≥0.05	≥0.05	≥0.05	≥0.05	≥0.05	≥0.05	-	≥0.05	≥0.05	≥0.05	≥0.05	≥0.05
QL1	≥0.05	≥0.05	≥0.05	≥0.05	≥0.05	≥0.05	≥0.05	≥0.05	≥0.05	≥0.05	≥0.05	≥0.05	≥0.05	-	≥0.05	≥0.05	≥0.05	≥0.05
QL2	≥0.05	≥0.05	≥0.05	≥0.05	≥0.05	≥0.05	≥0.05	≥0.05	≥0.05	≥0.05	≥0.05	≥0.05	≥0.05	≥0.05	-	≥0.05	≥0.05	≥0.05
QL3	≥0.05	≥0.05	≥0.05	≥0.05	≥0.05	≥0.05	≥0.05	≥0.05	≥0.05	≥0.05	≥0.05	≥0.05	≥0.05	≥0.05	≥0.05	-	≥0.05	≥0.05
QL4	≥0.05	≥0.05	≥0.05	≥0.05	≥0.05	≥0.05	≥0.05	≥0.05	≥0.05	≥0.05	≥0.05	≥0.05	≥0.05	≥0.05	≥0.05	≥0.05	-	≥0.05
QL5	≥0.05	≥0.05	≥0.05	≥0.05	≥0.05	≥0.05	≥0.05	≥0.05	≥0.05	≥0.05	≥0.05	≥0.05	≥0.05	≥0.05	≥0.05	≥0.05	≥0.05	-

6. Conclusions

This paper introduces a novel approach to optimizing retaining structural wall designs by implementing an innovative discretization method that utilizes reinforcement learning and transfer functions. Conventional structural design practices rely on empirical knowledge and experience, resulting in designs that prioritize strength, operability, and durability. However, these designs have room for improvement by minimizing their associated costs and CO_2 emissions.

Designs created using experience and empirical knowledge can produce feasible results that are often acceptable in cost and operability. However, these designs do not necessarily represent the optimal solution for a given scenario. Retaining wall design problems are considered combinatorial optimization challenges, which can quickly result in a combinatorial explosion due to the large number of variables and extensive discrete domains involved. Consequently, it is crucial to use incomplete techniques to solve these problems within a reasonable computational time frame. Metaheuristics have emerged as a prominent solution for addressing such challenges.

This work outlines the calculation procedure for determining the dimensions of a retaining wall, framing it as an optimization problem. Three metaheuristic techniques are implemented to evaluate their performance and use various transfer functions for the discretization process. Additionally, a novel discretization method, based on Q-Learning and SARSA, is employed to select the appropriate transfer function for each iteration during the discretization process.

The proposed model aims to minimize costs, CO_2 emissions, or a weighted combination of both, considering the design parameters detailed in Table 1 as problem variables, with the constraints being those inherent to the design of a retaining wall, as detailed in Section 2.1. Experimental results have been obtained using the Sine Cosine Algorithm (SCA), Whale Optimization Algorithm (WOA), and Gray Wolf Optimization (GWO) metaheuristics, with each run independently for 31 runs across 11 problem instances. After evaluating all the techniques across the three objective functions, the p-values obtained by the Wilcoxon–Mann–Whitney test for the GWO are presented, revealing the best results for the static versions using S-shaped transfer functions. GWO demonstrated significant differences in its results, indicating that it outperformed the other techniques for this specific problem. This does not imply that the other techniques are inadequate; rather, it suggests that the GWO S-shaped technique performs better for this particular problem.

The development of new optimization techniques, such as the one in this article, is crucial. It not only benefits the engineering profession, but also has considerable environmental and economic implications. By optimizing design processes and reducing costs and CO_2 emissions, the industry can contribute to a more sustainable future. One discussion point in this work is selecting transfer functions used in the discretization process. S-shaped functions provided the best results in terms of minimizing costs and CO_2 emissions, as demonstrated. However, other functions might offer better results for different problems or under various conditions, which the non-free lunch theorem also supports. Investigating how different transfer functions could affect results and determining an optimal function for a specific problem would be interesting.

Another discussion is the comparison of the results obtained with the different metaheuristic algorithms used in this work. While GWO with S-shaped transfer gave the best results, the other two algorithms also produced acceptable results. However, it could be argued that more metaheuristic algorithms should be compared to fully evaluate the effectiveness of this technique in retaining wall design optimization. In addition, it would be interesting to compare the results obtained with the approach proposed in this work with other retaining wall design optimization approaches, such as those based on other machine learning techniques.

Finally, the application of this approach to real-world design problems could be discussed. While the results are promising, it is possible that the implementation of this approach in real construction projects may be more complicated than the experimental results suggest. For example, there may be time and resource constraints that were not accounted for in this work that could affect the ability to use this approach in a real construction environment. Therefore, it could be argued that further research is needed to determine how this approach can be effectively implemented in real-world construction projects and how the practical challenges associated with its implementation can be addressed.

Future research should consider a broader range of assessment techniques, parameter variations, and other considerations. These distinctions could lead to results that are closer to reality. There also remains the challenge of extending these techniques to other construction problems, allowing specific processes to be designed more efficiently and accurately. Overall, the paper presents a promising approach to improving civil work designs, and the results suggest that further research in this field could lead to significant advances in the field.

Author Contributions: J.L.-R.: Writing—original draft, data curation, investigation, validation, software, visualization, formal analysis. D.O.: Investigation, methodology, project administration, resources, writing—original draft. R.S.: Investigation, methodology, project administration, resources, writing—original draft. N.C.-A.: Writing—original draft, visualization, formal analysis. V.Y.: Writing—review and editing. J.G.: Supervision, conceptualization, funding acquisition, investigation, methodology, writing—review and editing, project administration, resources, formal analysis. All authors have read and agreed to the published version of the manuscript.

Funding: Víctor Yepes is supported by Grant PID2020-117056RB-I00 funded by MCIN/AEI/10.13039/501100011033 and by "ERDF A way of making Europe". José Lemus-Romani is supported by National Agency for Research and Development (ANID)/Scholarship Program/DOCTORADO NACIONAL/2019-21191692.

Data Availability Statement: https://github.com/joselemusr/DSS-Retaining-walls.

Conflicts of Interest: The authors declare no conflict of interest.

Abbreviations

The following abbreviations are used in this manuscript:

Acronyms Part 1

MH	Metaheuristics
FEM	Finite Element Model
SCA	Sine-Cosine Algorithm
WOA	Whale Optimization Algorithm
GWO	Gray Wolf Optimization
MINLP	Mixed-Integer Non-Linear Programming
qe	Static thrust exerted by the fill [T/m]
γ	Existing soil density [T/m^3].
z	Height of the wall [m].
c	Static thrust coefficient.
b	Wall width, corresponding to 1 [m].
qs	Seismic thrust exerted by the backfill [T/m].

$gamma$	Existing soil density [T/m³].
hz	Height of wall [m].
cs	Seismic thrust coefficient.
MsA	Moment calculated at point A [T · m].
M_{active}	Static moment generated by the ground at point A [T · m].
$M_{seismic}$	Seismic moment generated by the ground at point A [T · m].
M_{pp}	Moment generated by the self-weight at point A [T · m].
$d1$	Distance from the centroid of the prismatic section of the wall to point A [m].
$N1$	Eigenweight of the prismatic section of the wall [T].
$d2$	Distance from the centroid of the triangular section of the wall to point A [m].
$N2$	Eigenweight of the triangular section of the wall [T].
MA	Total moment at point A [T · m].
MsA	Moment calculated at point A [T · m].
M_{pp}	Moment generated by self-weight at point A [T · m].
Meu	Design moment [T · m].
γf	Moment majorization factor.
Nu	Design axial load [T].
Nt	Own weight of the wall [T].
μ	Dimensionless calculation factor.
ϕ	Reduction factor for flexocompression equal to 0.83.
β	Reduction of the characteristic strength of concrete equal to 0.85.
$f'c$	Characteristic resistance of concrete to compression [T/m²].
b	Width of the wall, corresponding to 1 [m].
d	Width of the base of the wall without covering [m].
v	Dimensionless shear factor in the structure.
w	Calculation ratio for the steel area.
A	Dimensionless calculation factor.
fy	Width of the base of the wall without covering [m].
M_r	Overturning resisting moment [T · m].
Ns	Self-weight of soil on bottom [T].
$x1$	Distance from the centroid of Ns to point B [m].
Nm	Dead weight of the wall wedge and the soil above it [T].
$x2$	Distance from the centroid of Nm to point B [m].
$N1$	Self weight of the prismatic section of the wall [T].
$x3$	Distance from the centroid of N1 to point B [m].
Nf	Self weight of the wall foundation [T].
$x4$	Distance from the centroid of Nf to point B [m].
MSB	Moment resisting overturning [T].
$M_{active}B$	Self-weight of the soil on the bottom [T].
$M_{seismic}B$	Distance from the centroid of Ns to point B [m].
$FSSV$	Overturning seismic safety factor.
$FSEV$	Rollover static safety factor.
$Fsol$	Slip requesting force [T].
$Fres$	Slip resistant forces [T].
$FSSD$	Seismic slip safety factor.
L	Total length of foundation [m].
g	Section of the foundation supported on the ground [m].
e	Eccentricity of forces [m].
Acronyms Part 2	
$\sigma_{effective}$	Effective stress applied to the foundation soil.
$Mdesign$	Design moment of reinforcement reinforcement [T · m].
Mdl	Design moment of longitudinal reinforcement [T · m].
Bdt	Maximum foundation flight [m].
Bm	Width of wall base [m].
Pp	Self-weight of the wall [T].
Mdt	Design moment of transverse reinforcement [T · m].
T	Design stress [T].
Md	Corresponding design moment (Mdl or Mdt) [T · m].

d'	Effective shoe height (height without cover) [m].
As	Required steel area [cm^2].
Fy	Yield stress of steel [T/cm^2].
$emin$	Minimum amount of steel required [cm^2].
Ag	Longitudinal or cross-sectional area of the footing, as appropriate [cm^2].
Vu	Design cut request [T].
Vc	Shear strength of concrete section [T].
λ	Concrete modification factor. For normal concrete, $\lambda = 1$.
μlim	Calculation limit dimensionless factor, equal to 0.3047 for the case of analysis.
CMt	Total cost of retaining wall [CLP].
$CM1$	Cost of one cubic meter of concrete [CLP/m^3].
$PM1$	Total volume of concrete used [m^3].
$CM2$	Cost of one kilogram of steel [CLP/kg].
$PM2$	Total kilograms of steel used [kg].
EMt	Total carbon dioxide emissions [T].
$EM1$	Tons of carbon emitted per cubic meter of concrete [T/m^3].
$PM1$	Total volume of concrete used [m^3].
$EM2$	Tons of carbon emitted per kilogram of steel [T/kg].
$PM2$	Total kilograms of steel used [kg].
$CEMt$	Total between the sum of cost and emissions.
BSS	Binarization Schemes Selector
QL	Q-Learning
$\bar{x}^d$	Average of individuals in dimension d
x_i^d	Value of the i-th individual in dimension d
n	Number of individuals in the population
l	Size of the dimension of the individuals
Div	Determination of the diversity state
Div_{max}	Maximum value of the diversity state found
MH	Metahuristics
RPD	Relative Percentage Deviation

References

1. Mergos, P.E.; Mantoglou, F. Optimum design of reinforced concrete retaining walls with the flower pollination algorithm. *Struct. Multidiscip. Optim.* **2020**, *61*, 575–585. [CrossRef]
2. Choi, J.H. Strategy for reducing carbon dioxide emissions from maintenance and rehabilitation of highway pavement. *J. Clean. Prod.* **2019**, *209*, 88–100. [CrossRef]
3. Barandica, J.M.; Fernández-Sánchez, G.; Berzosa, Á.; Delgado, J.A.; Acosta, F.J. Applying life cycle thinking to reduce greenhouse gas emissions from road projects. *J. Clean. Prod.* **2013**, *57*, 79–91. [CrossRef]
4. Lee, K.H.; Kim, H.J.; Kwon, S.H.; Kim, M.J. The program development for environmental quality level and evaluation of carbon dioxide emission in construction works. *LHI J. Land Hous. Urban Aff.* **2012**, *3*, 399–406. [CrossRef]
5. Pons, J.J.; Penadés-Plà, V.; Yepes, V.; Martí, J.V. Life cycle assessment of earth-retaining walls: An environmental comparison. *J. Clean. Prod.* **2018**, *192*, 411–420. [CrossRef]
6. Eleftheriadis, S.; Duffour, P.; Greening, P.; James, J.; Stephenson, B.; Mumovic, D. Investigating relationships between cost and CO$_2$ emissions in reinforced concrete structures using a BIM-based design optimisation approach. *Energy Build.* **2018**, *166*, 330–346. [CrossRef]
7. Jelušič, P.; Žlender, B. Optimal design of pad footing based on MINLP optimization. *Soils Found.* **2018**, *58*, 277–289. [CrossRef]
8. Chen, J.; Cho, Y.K. CrackEmbed: Point feature embedding for crack segmentation from disaster site point clouds with anomaly detection. *Adv. Eng. Inform.* **2022**, *52*, 101550. [CrossRef]
9. Zhou, Q.; Qu, Z.; Wang, S.Y.; Bao, K.H. A Method of Potentially Promising Network for Crack Detection With Enhanced Convolution and Dynamic Feature Fusion. *IEEE Trans. Intell. Transp. Syst.* **2022**, *23*, 18736–18745. [CrossRef]
10. Wang, W.; Su, C. Automatic Classification of Reinforced Concrete Bridge Defects Using the Hybrid Network. *Arab. J. Sci. Eng.* **2022**, *47*, 5187–5195. [CrossRef]
11. Duan, R.; Deng, H.; Tian, M.; Deng, Y.; Lin, J. SODA: Site Object Detection dAtaset for Deep Learning in Construction. *arXiv* **2022**, arXiv:2202.09554.
12. Greeshma, A.; Edayadiyil, J.B. Automated progress monitoring of construction projects using Machine learning and image processing approach. *Mater. Today Proc.* **2022**, *65*, 554–563.
13. Sharma, S.; Saha, A.K.; Lohar, G. Optimization of weight and cost of cantilever retaining wall by a hybrid metaheuristic algorithm. *Eng. Comput.* **2022**, *38*, 2897–2923. [CrossRef]

14. García, J.; Yepes, V.; Martí, J.V. A hybrid k-means cuckoo search algorithm applied to the counterfort retaining walls problem. *Mathematics* **2020**, *8*, 555. [CrossRef]
15. Kaveh, A.; Biabani Hamedani, K.; Zaerreza, A. A set theoretical shuffled shepherd optimization algorithm for optimal design of cantilever retaining wall structures. *Eng. Comput.* **2021**, *37*, 3265–3282. [CrossRef]
16. Mann, H.B.; Whitney, D.R. On a test of whether one of two random variables is stochastically larger than the other. *Ann. Math. Stat.* **1947**, *18*, 50–60. [CrossRef]
17. Belarbi, A. *ACI 318-14. Building Code Requirements for Structural Concrete*; American Concrete Institute: Farmington Hills, MI, USA, 2014.
18. de Carreteras, M. *Manual de Carreteras*; Ministerio de Obras Publicas, Dirección de Vialidad: Santiago, Chile , 2015; Volume 3. Instrucciones y criterios de diseño.
19. Díaz López, E.; Martínez Prieto, A.; Gálvez Lio, D. Una implementación de la meta-heurística "Optimización en Mallas Variables" en la arquitectura CUDA. *Rev. Cuba. Cienc. Inform.* **2016**, *10*, 42–56.
20. Blum, C.; Roli, A. Metaheuristics in combinatorial optimization: Overview and conceptual comparison. *ACM Comput. Surv. (CSUR)* **2003**, *35*, 268–308. [CrossRef]
21. Talbi, E.G. *Metaheuristics: From Design to Implementation*; John Wiley & Sons: Hoboken, NJ, USA, 2009; Volume 74.
22. Mirjalili, S.; Lewis, A. The whale optimization algorithm. *Adv. Eng. Softw.* **2016**, *95*, 51–67. [CrossRef]
23. Mirjalili, S. SCA: A sine cosine algorithm for solving optimization problems. *Knowl.-Based Syst.* **2016**, *96*, 120–133. [CrossRef]
24. Mirjalili, S.; Mirjalili, S.M.; Lewis, A. Grey wolf optimizer. *Adv. Eng. Softw.* **2014**, *69*, 46–61. [CrossRef]
25. Crawford, B.; Soto, R.; Lemus-Romani, J.; Becerra-Rozas, M.; Lanza-Gutiérrez, J.M.; Caballé, N.; Castillo, M.; Tapia, D.; Cisternas-Caneo, F.; García, J.; et al. Q-learnheuristics: Towards data-driven balanced metaheuristics. *Mathematics* **2021**, *9*, 1839. [CrossRef]
26. Lemus-Romani, J.; Becerra-Rozas, M.; Crawford, B.; Soto, R.; Cisternas-Caneo, F.; Vega, E.; Castillo, M.; Tapia, D.; Astorga, G.; Palma, W.; et al. A novel learning-based binarization scheme selector for swarm algorithms solving combinatorial problems. *Mathematics* **2021**, *9*, 2887. [CrossRef]
27. Becerra-Rozas, M.; Lemus-Romani, J.; Cisternas-Caneo, F.; Crawford, B.; Soto, R.; García, J. Swarm-Inspired Computing to Solve Binary Optimization Problems: A Backward Q-Learning Binarization Scheme Selector. *Mathematics* **2022**, *10*, 4776. [CrossRef]
28. Becerra-Rozas, M.; Cisternas-Caneo, F.; Crawford, B.; Soto, R.; García, J.; Astorga, G.; Palma, W. Embedded Learning Approaches in the Whale Optimizer to Solve Coverage Combinatorial Problems. *Mathematics* **2022**, *10*, 4529. [CrossRef]
29. Watkins, C.J.; Dayan, P. Q-learning. *Mach. Learn.* **1992**, *8*, 279–292. [CrossRef]
30. Sutton, R.S.; Barto, A.G. *Reinforcement Learning: An Introduction*; MIT Press: Cambridge, MA, USA, 2018.
31. Xu, Y.; Pi, D. A reinforcement learning-based communication topology in particle swarm optimization. *Neural Comput. Appl.* **2019**, *32*, 10007–10032. [CrossRef]
32. Nareyek, A. Choosing search heuristics by non-stationary reinforcement learning. In *Metaheuristics: Computer Decision-Making*; Springer: Berlin/Heidelberg, Germany, 2003; pp. 523–544.
33. Salleh, M.N.M.; Hussain, K.; Cheng, S.; Shi, Y.; Muhammad, A.; Ullah, G.; Naseem, R. Exploration and exploitation measurement in swarm-based metaheuristic algorithms: An empirical analysis. In Proceedings of the International Conference on Soft Computing and Data Mining, Johor, Malaysia, 6–8 February 2018; Springer: Berlin/Heidelberg, Germany, 2018; pp. 24–32.
34. Cheng, S.; Shi, Y.; Qin, Q.; Zhang, Q.; Bai, R. Population Diversity Maintenance In Brain Storm Optimization Algorithm. *J. Artif. Intell. Soft Comput. Res.* **2014**, *4*, 83–97. [CrossRef]
35. Hussain, K.; Zhu, W.; Salleh, M.N.M. Long-term memory Harris' hawk optimization for high dimensional and optimal power flow problems. *IEEE Access* **2019**, *7*, 147596–147616. [CrossRef]
36. Morales-Castañeda, B.; Zaldivar, D.; Cuevas, E.; Fausto, F.; Rodríguez, A. A better balance in metaheuristic algorithms: Does it exist? *Swarm Evol. Comput.* **2020**, *54*, 100671. [CrossRef]
37. Crawford, B.; Soto, R.; Astorga, G.; García, J.; Castro, C.; Paredes, F. Putting continuous metaheuristics to work in binary search spaces. *Complexity* **2017**, *2017*, 8404231. [CrossRef]
38. Becerra-Rozas, M.; Lemus-Romani, J.; Cisternas-Caneo, F.; Crawford, B.; Soto, R.; Astorga, G.; Castro, C.; García, J. Continuous Metaheuristics for Binary Optimization Problems: An Updated Systematic Literature Review. *Mathematics* **2022**, *11*, 129. [CrossRef]

Disclaimer/Publisher's Note: The statements, opinions and data contained in all publications are solely those of the individual author(s) and contributor(s) and not of MDPI and/or the editor(s). MDPI and/or the editor(s) disclaim responsibility for any injury to people or property resulting from any ideas, methods, instructions or products referred to in the content.

Article

Weight Vector Definition for MOEA/D-Based Algorithms Using Augmented Covering Arrays for Many-Objective Optimization

Carlos Cobos [1,*], Cristian Ordoñez [2], Jose Torres-Jimenez [3], Hugo Ordoñez [1] and Martha Mendoza [1]

1. Information Technology Research Group (GTI), Universidad del Cauca, Popayán 190001, Colombia; hugoordonez@unicauca.edu.co (H.O.); mmendoza@unicauca.edu.co (M.M.)
2. Intelligent Management Systems, Fundación Universitaria de Popayán, Popayán 190001, Colombia; camilo.ordonez@docente.fup.edu.co
3. CINVESTAV Tamaulipas, Ciudad Victoria 87130, Mexico; jtj@cinvestav.mx
* Correspondence: ccobos@unicauca.edu.co; Tel.: +57-300-737-9062

Abstract: Many-objective optimization problems are today ever more common. The decomposition-based approach stands out among the evolutionary algorithms used for their solution, with MOEA/D and its variations playing significant roles. MOEA/D variations seek to improve weight vector definition, improve the dynamic adjustment of weight vectors during the evolution process, improve the evolutionary operators, use alternative decomposition methods, and hybridize with other metaheuristics, among others. Although an essential topic for the success of MOEA/D depends on how well the weight vectors are defined when decomposing the problem, not as much research has been performed on this topic as on the others. This paper proposes using a new mathematical object called augmented covering arrays (ACAs) that enable a better sampling of interactions of M objectives using the least number of weight vectors based on an interaction level (strength), defined a priori by the user. The proposed method obtains better results, measured in inverted generational distance, using small to medium populations (up to 850 solutions) of 30 to 100 objectives over DTLZ and WFG problems against the traditional weight vector definition used by MOEA/D-DE and results obtained by NSGA-III. Other MOEA/D variations can include the proposed approach and thus improve their results.

Keywords: optimization methods; many-objective optimization; decomposition; augmented covering arrays

MSC: 68T20; 90C59; 90C29

Citation: Cobos, C.; Ordoñez, C.; Torres-Jimenez, J.; Ordoñez, H.; Mendoza, M. Weight Vector Definition for MOEA/D-Based Algorithms Using Augmented Covering Arrays for Many-Objective Optimization. *Mathematics* **2024**, *12*, 1680. https://doi.org/10.3390/math12111680

Academic Editor: Frank Werner

Received: 28 March 2024
Revised: 22 April 2024
Accepted: 25 April 2024
Published: 28 May 2024

Copyright: © 2024 by the authors. Licensee MDPI, Basel, Switzerland. This article is an open access article distributed under the terms and conditions of the Creative Commons Attribution (CC BY) license (https://creativecommons.org/licenses/by/4.0/).

1. Introduction

The aim of evolutionary algorithms for multi-objective optimization, better known in the state of the art as multi-objective evolutionary algorithms (MOEAs) [1], is to find a set of solutions (rather than a single solution) to problems with two or three objectives, called multi-objective optimization problems (MOPs), where in many cases, these objectives conflict. In the last two decades, different algorithms have been proposed to address these problems, classifying the most successful proposals into three main approaches: dominance-based, indicator-based, and decomposition-based [2]. Prominent among these are NSGA-II [3], SPEA2 [4], IBEA [5], SME-EMOA [6], MSOPS [7], and MOEA/D [8]. These algorithms are commonly used to optimize systems with a low number of objectives (up to three), such as the planning of air routes [9], the design of aqueducts and sewers [10], and optimizing the routes and frequencies for bus rapid transit systems [11]. However, when dealing with many-objective optimization problems (MaOPs), i.e., four (4) or more objectives, traditional MOEAs are prone to fail or converge to local optima because, among other complications, many objectives make it difficult to define when one solution outperforms another as the space for representing the objectives becomes too large [12]. In recent years, several evolutionary algorithms (many-objective evolutionary algorithms, MaOEAs) have been proposed to optimize many objectives that seek to overcome the deficiencies of traditional MOEAs. These algorithms also have different approaches; among the most important are [12]:

Scalar-function-based (decomposition/aggregation): The first group seeks to solve the problem by decomposing it using multiple weighted objective functions, in which each objective has different weight values in each function. The second group, based on aggregation, uses functions to combine groups of objectives by working with a much smaller amount of these and solving them with traditional MOEAs. Within this approach, the MOEA/D algorithm [8] and its variations stand out, including for the improvement of evolution operators based on differential evolution, such as MOEA/D-DE [13], MOEA/D-HSE [14], and MOEA/D-oDE [15].

Reference-set-based: These algorithms guide the search process based on a list of solutions in a reference set. Notable here is the improved two-archive algorithm (TAA) [16] and, in particular, version 3 of the non-dominated sorting genetic algorithm NSGA-III [17].

Quality-indicator-based: These algorithms transform the problem of many objectives to a problem of optimizing a single objective that represents how good the solutions are compared to the rest of the population (indicator). The most widely recognized approaches are IBEA [18], I-SIBEA [19], artificial bee colony algorithm (E-MOABC) [20], and hypervolume adaptive grid algorithm (HAGA) [21].

Dimensional-reduction-based: These algorithms take the objectives of the original problem and reduce them in a low-dimension representation using, for example, principal component analysis (PCA), unsupervised feature selection, and greedy techniques. Prominent in this approach is PCA-NSGA-II [22].

Space-partitioning-based: These algorithms optimize subsets of the problem objectives in each iteration of the evolutionary process. The $\in$R-EMO [23] algorithm is a good example.

The decomposition-based approach has attracted much attention from researchers in the area. In particular, MOEA/D [8] has benefited from a number of improvements with the following principal aims: (1) to develop new methods for the defining and dynamic adjustment of weight vectors that decompose the problem into multiple single-objective problems; (2) to use new decomposition approaches; (3) to ensure the efficient allocation of computational resources; (4) to improve the search process by modifying the selection, crossover, mutation, and replacement operations of the algorithm; and (5) to hybridize with dominance-based approaches.

One of the least-researched limitations of MOEA/D focuses on defining the weight vectors that decompose the problem. In its original version, the algorithm seeks to conduct a uniformly random sampling of the weighting of the different objectives. However, this is not guaranteed to be the most appropriate approach, especially when the number of objectives grows [24]. This method does not work because the interrelationship between objectives is not adequately sampled. In addition, an exponential increase in the number of weight vectors is required to obtain adequate sampling when the number of targets grows [25].

Another option is based on the simplex method [21], in which the size of the population (the number of weight vectors) increases non-linearly with the increasing number of objectives, and the user cannot define the size of the population. In addition, making a uniform distribution of weight vectors does not ensure that the solutions sample the interaction between the objectives [22].

In this research [26], the use of augmented covering arrays (ACAs) is proposed for defining the weight vectors, considering that this new mathematical object guarantees the most significant coverage (a sampling with the highest coverage of interactions between several factors, in this case, optimization objectives) with the least possible effort. ACAs are a new type of covering array (CA), and they are formally presented for the first time later in Section 3.3. CAs, in general, have been used to support experimental design in fields such as agriculture, medicine, biology, and material design. Latterly, they are one of the most widely used tools for testing software and hardware. In all these fields, it is necessary to test combinations of different factors without conducting an exhaustive search of them due to restrictions of cost, time, and effort [27,28].

Experimental results show that the proposed method obtains better results on DTLZ and WFG problems using small and medium populations than MOEA/D-DE and NSGA-III. MOEA/D-DE-ACA (a new MOEA/D-DE version that uses ACAs) obtains better inverted generational distance results for 30 to 100 objectives supported in the Friedman non-parametric and Holm post hoc tests. Execution time was also significantly reduced, using only 40.7% or 8.9% of the time used by MOEA/D-DE and 4.8% or 7% of that of NSGA-III. The results showed no significant differences between MOEA/D-ACA and MOEA/D using large populations, except in 90 objectives in which MOEA/D-ACA performs better. In addition, MOEA/D-ACA further reduces execution times by using only 2.7% of the execution time of MOEA/D-DE and 6.2% of that used by NSGA-III. Given such results, the different variations of MOEA/D and decomposition-based algorithms might be expected to incorporate the proposed approach for defining the weight vectors, thereby improving the literature results.

The rest of this document is organized as follows: Section 2 presents previous work on defining weight vectors in MOEA/D. Section 3 presents orthogonal arrays (OA), covering arrays (CA), and augmented covering arrays (ACA) and a comparison between them for the definition of weight vectors. Section 4 details the process of defining weight vectors based on augmented covering arrays within the multi-objective evolutionary algorithm based on decomposition with differential evolution (MOEA/D-DE-ACA). Section 5 describes the experiments, starting with the characteristics of the problems used (DTLZ and WFG), the quality measure used for the comparison, and the results of the three defined experiments, which include the comparison with the multi-objective evolutionary algorithm based on decomposition with a differential evolution approach (MOEA/D-DE) and the non-dominated sorting genetic algorithm version 3 (NSGA-III) from 10 to 100 objectives, and the comparison against other proposals of the state of the art in constrained problems. Finally, Section 6 presents conclusions and recommends directions for future research.

2. Related Studies

MOEA/D is an algorithm that decomposes a multi-objective optimization problem into several single objective optimization subproblems. MOEA/D employs a method based on populations to optimize these subproblems concurrently and to find the Pareto front (PF) of the problem. The literature reports much theoretical and practical work using MOEA/D and variants [29]. Considering that the definition of weight vectors in MOEA/D significantly impacts the algorithm's results, previous works that have sought to improve this definition are presented below. Most recent work is focused more on the dynamic adjustment of weights during the evolutionary process than on the initialization process.

Many previous studies have looked how to generate uniform weight vectors, and they can be organized into three classical methods: (1) simplex-lattice design, first used by Scheffe in 1958 to obtain uniformly distributed weight vectors [30]; (2) simplex-centroid design, presented by Scheffe in 1963 [31]; and (3) axial design, put forward by Cornell in 1975 [32]. Using these concepts, the transformation method (uniform design) tries to find a set of aggregation weight vectors with an arbitrary amount, which is uniformly distributed in the objectives space [33,34]. The original MOEA/D version uses the simplex-lattice design method to generate the weight vectors, but this method has three main weaknesses. The first is that the resulting weight vector distribution is not very uniform for three or more objectives. The second is that the population size or the number of weight vectors increases non-linearly with the number of objectives, and the population size cannot be defined at will. The third weakness is that the uniform distribution of weight vectors does not guarantee that uniformly distributed Pareto optimal solutions are obtained [35].

In 2012 [36], a new version of MOEA/D with a uniform design called UMOEA/D was proposed and compared with MOEA/D and NSGA-II on some scalable test problems with three to five objectives, obtaining the best results. The authors claim that the number of weight vectors is restricted for the three classical methods, but the "practical" number of weight vectors is very flexible in most of the experiments. This paper has a significant number of citations in Scopus related to new proposals for the dynamic adjustment of weights during the evolutionary process, the study of the effect of weight vectors on the performance of decomposition-based algorithms, and several reviews of decomposition-based methods, among others. It is worth highlighting section about of "The Study of Generation Strategy of Weight Vector" of the "Survey of Decomposition Based Evolutionary Algorithms for Many-Objective Optimization Problems" published in 2022 by Xiaofang Guo [37], mentioning four systematic design methods of weight vector generation: simplex-lattice design used in MOEA/D, uniform design for experiments with mixtures (UDEM) used in UMOEA/D, a combination of the previous two used in MOEA/D-UMD, and a two-layer reference vector generation approach.

In 2014 [38], MOEA/D-UDM was proposed with uniform decomposition measurement to obtain uniform weight vectors in any amount and one modified Tchebycheff decomposition. However, this proposal deals with two difficulties in applying MOEA/D to solve MaOPs, namely: (1) the quantity of generated weight vectors is predetermined, and these vectors are primarily concentrated along the boundary of the objective space for MaOPs, and (2) in the Tchebycheff decomposition method employed by MOEA/D, the association between a subproblem's optimal solution and its weight vectors exhibits non-linearity.

Also, in 2014 [39], based on the geometric relationship between the weight vectors and the corresponding Tchebycheff-based optimal solutions, an initialization method of the weight vectors, called WS transformation, and an adaptive adjustment of the weight vectors in a new proposal called MOEA/D-AWA were proposed. WS transformation is redundant in two objectives. However, experimental studies on ten ZDT and DTLZ reference problems with three objectives demonstrated that MOEA/D obtains much better uniformly distributed Pareto optimal solutions. This work is also highly cited in Scopus for comparison against it, as a reference for an algorithm that initializes the weight vectors differently from the simplex-lattice design method, and for incorporating dynamic weight adjustment based on the same technique used for weight vector generation. A survey presented in 2020 cited this work and shows, in Sections III.B.1, III.B.4, and III.D, a list of weight vector generation methods for multi- and many-objective problems using the MOEA/D framework.

In 2015 [40], MOEA/D-UD was proposed. This work modified the initial definition of weights using a new method based on an experimental design called UD. It also proposed a dynamic adjustment of the weight vectors to remove them from crowding regions and add new ones into the sparse regions, previously distinguishing truly sparse regions from pseudo-sparse regions of the PF. MOEA/D-UD was compared with MOEA/D-DE, MOEA/D-AWA, and NSGA-II on nineteen test instances. The results show that MOEA/D-UD can obtain a well-converged and well-diversified set of solutions within an acceptable run time.

In 2017 [41], non-uniform weight vector distribution strategies were used to modify MOEA/D-DE to solve the unit commitment (UC) problem (a mixed-integer optimization problem) in an uncertain environment. The authors evaluated two methods; the first initially generates weight vectors using the simplex-lattice design method and then randomly removes weight vectors from the outer layers of the distribution to help the algorithm focus its search more toward the center of the Pareto front. Second, a sinusoidal function is selected to generate the weight vector distribution. The second proposal significantly outperforms the other variants and the traditional MOEA/D-DE method over the UC problem, providing a much better distribution of solutions.

Also, in 2017 [42], an evolutionary method for weight vector generation was presented. The algorithm initially creates a population of n weight vectors using a Latin hypercube design [43], then normalizes the population and evaluates the distance between all pairs of weight vectors to calculate the fitness value for each vector. Then, the evolutive process is executed until a stopping criterion is reached; in each evolution iteration, a new weight vector is created using a weight vector randomly selected from the population and a Gaussian perturbation; next, the Euclidian distances between the new vector and the rest of the weight vectors in the population are calculated, the fitness for the new vector is defined, and the new vector replaces the worst vector in the population if the new vector is better than the worst. The fitness function corresponds to the sum of the Euclidian distances to the closest neighbors in the population. Unlike the simplex-lattice design method, this method can create weight vectors without restricting the number of vectors. This paper has been cited by nine documents in Scopus, most related to applications in multi- and many objectives.

In 2018 [44], an alternative proposal was presented with two types of weight vector adjustments for many-objective optimization called MaOEA/D-2ADV. After performing the first evolution iteration, this proposal searches for the weight vectors with better solutions close to the optimal PF; if it finds a vector that does not satisfy certain qualifying conditions, it is eliminated and creates a new one as a replacement. It then uses the domain-based Pareto mechanism to detect the effectiveness of each vector. Finally, where a vector is in the wrong direction, the vector is adjusted to adapt better to the PF. This algorithm was compared with MOEA/D-AWA and RVEA using IGD in DTLZ problems of up to 10 objectives, concluding that MaOEA/D-2ADV is suitable for working on problems with a disconnected PF with 4 to 10 objectives.

The initialization of weight vectors using a self-organizing map (SOM) was put forward in a proposal called MOEA/D-SOM (2018) [45]. The normalized weight vectors are sent to SOM to create neighborhoods or groups of vectors. Those closest to the PF based on Euclidean distance are then selected. MOEA/D-SOM was evaluated in many-objective problems using 16 problems with and without constraints, including DTLZ, TOY, and MAOP. Their results were compared with those of MOEA/D-AWA, MOEA/DD, and M2M, among others, using IGD. Compared to the other algorithms, this proposal was observed to be superior, solving MaOPs with a degenerate PF [46].

Also, in 2018 [47], considering the fundamental role of weight vectors—ensuring good diversity and convergence of solutions in different problems, especially problems with a complex PF (discontinuous or with sharp peaks)—it was identified that the uniform distribution of the weight vectors in MOEA/D does not allow a set of solutions with good diversity to be obtained. The authors thus proposed the improved multi-objective evolutionary algorithm based on decomposition with adaptive weight adjustment, IMOEA/DA. This proposal first uses the uniform design method and crowding distance to generate a set of evenly distributed weight vectors. Then, according to the distances of the dominated solutions, it adapts the weight vectors to redistribute them in the subobjective spaces. The algorithm also uses a selection strategy to help each subobjective space to have at least one solution. This proposal was compared with state-of-the-art algorithms such as NSGA-II, MOEA/D, MOEA/D-AWA, EMOSA, RVEA, and KnEA on different test functions (DTLZ, WFG, UF, and ZDT) using three performance metrics, IGD, hypervolume (HV), and generational distance (GD). The Wilcoxon non-parametric test was used to analyze the results. With a 95% significance, it was determined that the proposal could find a set of solutions with greater diversity and convergence than the other compared algorithms.

The penalty-based boundary intersection (PBI) approach to defining weight vectors obtains better results in concave and convex problems than the uniform random definition of weights and the Tchebycheff method. However, its performance is degraded in problems with a complex PF because it defines fixed penalty values. As a result, in 2019 [48], an adaptive penalty scheme (AAP) was proposed to dynamically adjust each weight vector's penalty value during the algorithm's evolutionary process. This proposal, called MOEA/D-

AAP, was evaluated using six reference problems (F1 to F6) and compared with MOEA/D-DE and MOEA/D-STM, concluding that the proposed approach significantly improved the results measured in IGD.

Also, in 2019 [49], MOEA/HD was proposed, a method that uses a hierarchical decomposition strategy. The scalar subproblems are in different weight hierarchies, and the search direction of the solutions in the lower hierarchy subproblems is adjusted adaptively based on the results of the upper hierarchy. This proposal was evaluated and compared with four state-of-the-art proposals: MOEA/D-AWA, NSGA-III, MOEA/D-DRA, and NSGA-II in the problems DTLZ, WFG, and JY using IGD and HV and obtained the best results in all cases evaluated.

To date, there is no experimental comparison between the different proposals for the generation of weight vectors in MOEA/D, and all published proposals were evaluated using different problems and algorithms and using different numbers of objectives and solutions generated. Therefore, it cannot be established that one algorithm dominates another; it can only be defined that all proposals are better than the simplex-lattice design method used originally in MOEA/D. That is why carrying out a fair experimental comparison process for all proposals is an excellent future work.

3. Weight Vector Definition Using Combinatorial Designs

As previous studies reported, the definition of weight vectors in MOEA/D significantly impacts the algorithm's results, and this depends on how the weight vectors are sampled in the objective space. Therefore, in this work, we sought to explore alternative combinatorial designs to define weight vectors for MOEA/D-based algorithms to obtain better results over different kinds of many-objective problems. As a result, the alternative selected was augmented covering arrays (ACAs), but orthogonal arrays (OAs) and covering arrays (CAs) were also analyzed.

These three mathematical objects are represented as matrices and are characterized by four parameters: N, which is the number of rows, and in the algorithms based on MOEA/D, it corresponds to the size of the population (each row will allow defining the weight vector of one solution in the population); k, which is the number of columns and corresponds to the number of objectives of the problem that is being solved; v, representing the alphabet from which the values are defined for each cell of the matrix (values from 0 to v − 1); and t, representing the degree of interaction between the columns—this parameter forces the matrix to satisfy that for t columns, all the values of v^t occur exactly once in the OAs or at least once in the CAs and ACAs [50]. These objects are usually denoted as OA (N; t, k, v), CA (N; t, k, v), and ACA (N; t, k, v). Table 1 summarizes the variables used in this section of the document.

Table 1. Summary of variables in the combinatorial objects previously mentioned.

Variables	Description in OAs, CAs, and ACAs	Description in MOEA/D-ACA
N	Number of rows	Population size
k	Number of columns	Number of objectives of the problem
t	Degree of interaction between the columns	Degree of interaction between the problem objectives
v	Alphabet for each cell of the matrix	w = Weight values on weight vectors
-	-	α = Defines the level of granularity of the weights

To understand how each row of these three combinatorial designs can be used to define the weight vectors, we first designate M as a matrix of size N × k associated with any of the combinatorial designs (OA, CA, or ACA), and we have $M_{i,j}$, where $0 \leq i \leq N$, $0 \leq j \leq k-1$ represent the value in the i-th row of the j-th column. To derive the weight allocation of the j-th column using the i-th row, the calculation of $M_{i,j}/\alpha_i$ is made, where $\alpha_i = \sum_{c=0}^{k-1} M_{i,c}$ (the case of a row with all zeros is excluded). Considering k objectives ($k \geq 1$) and a value α that defines the level of granularity of the weights ($\alpha \geq 1$), the linear Diophantine equation with unit coefficients (LDEU) $a_0 + \ldots + a_{k-1} = \alpha$ allows sampling the weights of a row with a granularity $1/\alpha$ [36,45,51]. For example, Table 2 shows on its left side the first four rows of the ACA (42; 2; 10; 5) presented below in Table 3, and on the right side, the weight vectors defined row by row. It can be seen that in order to transform the ACA (OA or CA) from its integer domain to the real domain of the weight vectors, it is only required to perform a normalization process (the sum of the components of the weight vector is 1 as shown in the last column) dividing each row by the α value of each row (α_i). The value of α_i defines the granularity of the weights, i.e., the coarseness of the weights. For instance, if $\alpha_i = 10$, the granularity is in tenths, and if $\alpha_i = 100$, the granularity is in hundredths.

Table 2. First four rows of ACA (42; 2, 10, 5), on the left, and defined weight vectors on the right.

a_0	a_1	a_2	a_3	a_4	a_5	a_6	a_7	a_8	a_9	α		w_0	w_1	w_2	w_3	w_4	w_5	w_6	w_7	w_8	w_9	Σ
0	1	0	0	0	0	0	0	1	1	3	→	0	1/3	0	0	0	0	0	0	1/3	1/3	1
1	0	0	1	0	0	0	1	0	0	3	→	1/3	0	0	1/3	0	0	0	1/3	0	0	1
0	0	1	0	0	1	1	1	1	0	5	→	0	0	1/5	0	0	1/5	1/5	1/5	1/5	0	1
1	1	1	0	1	0	1	0	0	0	5	→	1/5	1/5	1/5	0	1/5	0	1/5	0	0	0	1

Table 3. OA (81; 2, 10, 9) with $a_0 + \ldots + a_9 = \alpha$.

	a_0	a_1	a_2	a_3	a_4	a_5	a_6	a_7	a_8	a_9	α		a_0	a_1	a_2	a_3	a_4	a_5	a_6	a_7	a_8	a_9	α
1	0	0	0	0	0	0	0	0	0	0	0	42	0	5	7	1	3	8	2	4	6	5	41
2	1	1	1	1	1	1	1	1	1	0	9	43	1	3	8	2	4	6	0	5	7	5	41
3	2	2	2	2	2	2	2	2	2	0	18	44	2	4	6	0	5	7	1	3	8	5	41
4	3	3	3	3	3	3	3	3	3	0	27	45	3	8	1	4	6	2	5	7	0	5	41
5	4	4	4	4	4	4	4	4	4	0	36	46	4	6	2	5	7	0	3	8	1	5	41
6	0	1	2	3	4	5	6	7	8	1	37	47	5	7	0	3	8	1	4	6	2	5	41
7	1	2	0	4	5	3	7	8	6	1	37	48	6	2	4	7	0	5	8	1	3	5	41
8	2	0	1	5	3	4	8	6	7	1	37	49	7	0	5	8	1	3	6	2	4	5	41
9	3	4	5	6	7	8	0	1	2	1	37	50	8	1	3	6	2	4	7	0	5	5	41
10	4	5	3	7	8	6	1	2	0	1	37	51	0	6	3	8	5	2	4	1	7	6	42
11	5	3	4	8	6	7	2	0	1	1	37	52	1	7	4	6	3	0	5	2	8	6	42
12	6	7	8	0	1	2	3	4	5	1	37	53	2	8	5	7	4	1	3	0	6	6	42
13	7	8	6	1	2	0	4	5	3	1	37	54	3	0	6	2	8	5	7	4	1	6	42
14	8	6	7	2	0	1	5	3	4	1	37	55	4	1	7	0	6	3	8	5	2	6	42
15	0	2	1	6	8	7	3	5	4	2	38	56	5	2	8	1	7	4	6	3	0	6	42
16	1	0	2	7	6	8	4	3	5	2	38	57	6	3	0	5	2	8	1	7	4	6	42
17	2	1	0	8	7	6	5	4	3	2	38	58	7	4	1	3	0	6	2	8	5	6	42
18	3	5	4	0	2	1	6	8	7	2	38	59	8	5	2	4	1	7	0	6	3	6	42
19	4	3	5	1	0	2	7	6	8	2	38	60	0	7	5	2	6	4	1	8	3	7	43
20	5	4	3	2	1	0	8	7	6	2	38	61	1	8	3	0	7	5	2	6	4	7	43
21	6	8	7	3	5	4	0	2	1	2	38	62	2	6	4	1	8	3	0	7	5	7	43
22	7	6	8	4	3	5	1	0	2	2	38	63	3	1	8	5	0	7	4	2	6	7	43
23	8	7	6	5	4	3	2	1	0	2	38	64	4	2	6	3	1	8	5	0	7	7	43

Table 3. Cont.

	a_0	a_1	a_2	a_3	a_4	a_5	a_6	a_7	a_8	a_9	α		a_0	a_1	a_2	a_3	a_4	a_5	a_6	a_7	a_8	a_9	α
24	0	3	6	4	7	1	8	2	5	3	39	65	5	0	7	4	2	6	3	1	8	7	43
25	1	4	7	5	8	2	6	0	3	3	39	66	6	4	2	8	3	1	7	5	0	7	43
26	2	5	8	3	6	0	7	1	4	3	39	67	7	5	0	6	4	2	8	3	1	7	43
27	3	6	0	7	1	4	2	5	8	3	39	68	8	3	1	7	5	0	6	4	2	7	43
28	4	7	1	8	2	5	0	3	6	3	39	69	0	8	4	5	1	6	7	3	2	8	44
29	5	8	2	6	0	3	1	4	7	3	39	70	1	6	5	3	2	7	8	4	0	8	44
30	6	0	3	1	4	7	5	8	2	3	39	71	2	7	3	4	0	8	6	5	1	8	44
31	7	1	4	2	5	8	3	6	0	3	39	72	3	2	7	8	4	0	1	6	5	8	44
32	8	2	5	0	3	6	4	7	1	3	39	73	4	0	8	6	5	1	2	7	3	8	44
33	0	4	8	7	2	3	5	6	1	4	40	74	5	1	6	7	3	2	0	8	4	8	44
34	1	5	6	8	0	4	3	7	2	4	40	75	6	5	1	2	7	3	4	0	8	8	44
35	2	3	7	6	1	5	4	8	0	4	40	76	7	3	2	0	8	4	5	1	6	8	44
36	3	7	2	1	5	6	8	0	4	4	40	77	8	4	0	1	6	5	3	2	7	8	44
37	4	8	0	2	3	7	6	1	5	4	40	78	5	5	5	5	5	5	5	5	5	0	45
38	5	6	1	0	4	8	7	2	3	4	40	79	6	6	6	6	6	6	6	6	6	0	54
39	6	1	5	4	8	0	2	3	7	4	40	80	7	7	7	7	7	7	7	7	7	0	63
40	7	2	3	5	6	1	0	4	8	4	40	81	8	8	8	8	8	8	8	8	8	0	72
41	8	0	4	3	7	2	1	5	6	4	40												

The number of solutions of the LDEU $a_0 + \ldots + a_{k-1} = \alpha$ is equal to $\binom{\alpha + k - 1}{k - 1}$, which is of exponential order, but since the exploration is also required for the possible values of α, an exhaustive search for granularities from 1 to α with k objectives would involve exploring $\sum_{i=1}^{\alpha} \binom{i + k - 1}{k - 1} = \binom{\alpha + k}{k} - 1$ weight vectors. For example, with $\alpha = 40$ and k = 10, the space to be explored is 10,272,278,169 possible weight vectors.

3.1. Orthogonal Arrays

A first way of sampling weight vector definition is to use orthogonal arrays of index unity (OAs). OAs are described by OA (N = v^t; t, k = v + 1, v). In an OA, each submatrix of size N × t contains as a row each t-tuple over the v symbols exactly once [52]. This constraint limits the existence of a solution for all combinations of k, v, and t [53]. The construction of OAs is an open topic for values of v that are not prime powers, but a general solution exists for OAs with values of v that are prime powers. Not having OAs for v values that are not prime powers represents a significant disadvantage when the number of columns (objectives of the problem) is large since the number of rows will always be N = v^t, where v is the prime power that satisfies v + 1 ≥ k. For example, for k = 100 objectives and t = 2, the OA that should be used is OA (N = 10,201; t = 2, k = 102, v = 101). This OA generates a huge population size that may be unfeasible to use in practice.

For a problem with 10 objectives (k = 10) and an interaction level of 2 (t = 2), the value of v that satisfies the constraint v + 1 ≥ k is v = 9 (OA alphabet). Therefore, to be able to define the weight vectors in the algorithm, it is necessary to have the OA (81; 2, 10, 9). This OA is constructed using the Bush algorithm [54] and is presented in Table 3. The columns are designated by $a_0, \ldots, a_9$ and their sum is the value of α. As each cell can take values from 0 to v − 1 = 9 − 1 = 8 and there are 10 columns (k), the possible values of α vary from

0 to k × (v − 1) = 10 × 8 = 80. The total sampling space is defined (as already described above) by $\binom{kv}{k} - 1$.

The weight vectors are obtained by dividing the columns a_0, ..., a_9 between the value α of each row. The sampling provided by this OA is concentrated in central values, 9 occurrences for α ∈ {37, 38, 39, 40, 41, 42, 43, 44}, 1 occurrence for α ∈ {0, 9, 18, 27, 36, 45, 54, 63, 72}, and the rest of the 65 α values are not sampled (80% (65/81) of unsampled α values).

From the above, it can be inferred, given the poor sampling obtained, that the use of OAs as a sampling mechanism of possible objective weight vectors does not represent a good alternative due to their sampling properties and because the size of the OA for more than 40 objectives and granularities of the order of 40 or more would demand a huge population size. A final problem that can occur with OAs is best understood by reviewing, for example, rows 80 and 81 of the OA presented in Table 3. These rows are {7, 7, 7, 7, 7, 7, 7, 7, 7, 0} and {8, 8, 8, 8, 8, 8, 8, 8, 8, 0} that, when divided by their corresponding α values, generate the same weight vector {0.11, 0.11, 0.11, 0.11, 0.11, 0.11, 0.11, 0.11, 0.11, 0}. This same situation occurs with other rows, for example, rows 2, 3, 4, and 5. These examples show that several lines sample the same weight vector, which is not desirable in algorithms based on MOEA/D.

3.2. Covering Arrays

A covering array CA (N; t, k, v) is a matrix with N rows and k columns, where each cell has one of v possible symbols such that every N × t submatrix contains as a row each t-tuple over the v symbols at least once [50]. The covering array number CAN (t, k, v) defines the minimum value of N such that a CA (N; t, k, v) exists. CAs have been used successfully in different areas, including experiment design and hardware and software testing [55].

CAs generally can be seen as a sampling mechanism in several contexts [56–60]. In this paper, we use CAs to sample solutions of multiple linear Diophantine equations with unit coefficients, where each row of the CA is used to construct a solution of an LDEU. Like OAs, each row in a CA is a possible solution of a corresponding LDEU. The LDEU associated with a row of a CA with k columns and alphabet v is: $a_0 + \ldots + a_{k-1} = \alpha$, where the value of α is obtained as the summation of the elements in a row of the CA. Its values are thus described by $\alpha \in \{0, \ldots, k*(v-1)\}$ (the zero value corresponds to a row with all cells of the row equal to zero, and $k*(v-1)$ corresponds to a row with all cell values equal to v − 1).

Given this, the total number of possible solutions of all the LDEUs potentially sampled in a CA grows exponentially according to the values of k (the number of columns in a CA that corresponds to the number of objectives in many-objective optimization) and the value of v (the alphabet v at the end determines the set of possible α values and transitively will define the granularity of weight assignment). Note that the cardinality of the space of weights is: $\binom{kv}{k} - 1$. Nevertheless, the number of solutions sampled by a CA is the number of rows. This number is bounded asymptotically by the expression that defines the covering array number (CAN). In [61–63] the CAN value corresponds to the Stein–Lovász–Johnson (SLJ) bound. Let t, k, and v be integers with ($k \geq t \geq 2$)($2(v \geq 2)$). Then, as $k \to \infty$ defined by $CAN(t,k,v) \leq \frac{\log\binom{k}{t} + t\log(v)}{\log(\frac{v^t}{v^t-1})}$. In this sense, the number of solutions sampled by the rows of a CA is much smaller than the number of possible solutions that correspond to all the LDEUs sampled. For instance, for k = 10, v = 5, and t = 2, a possible CA will have 36 rows and the total number of LDEUs will be $\binom{kv}{k} - 1 = \binom{50}{5} - 1 = 2,118,759$.

Table 4 shows the contents of CA (36; 2, 10, 5) and, in the 11th column (the last one), the value of α (summation of all the elements in each row of the CA). It is shown that $13 \leq \alpha \leq 30$, with 17 different values of α. The values of α that are not sampled are 24, so the proportion of non-sampled values is 58% (24/41) because the total number of classes of α is $1 + k(v - 1) = 41$. The proportion of non-sampled values is lower than OAs and has fewer constraints or problems when defining weight vectors in MOEA/D-based algorithms.

Table 4. CA (36; 2, 10, 5).

	a_0	a_1	a_2	a_3	a_4	a_5	a_6	a_7	a_8	a_9	α		a_0	a_1	a_2	a_3	a_4	a_5	a_6	a_7	a_8	a_9	α
1	4	0	0	2	0	4	1	0	0	2	13	19	3	0	2	1	2	3	2	1	3	4	21
2	1	0	1	3	2	2	0	3	0	2	14	20	1	0	2	2	4	2	3	4	2	1	21
3	2	1	1	0	0	2	3	1	2	3	15	21	3	4	4	1	3	4	0	1	0	1	21
4	0	0	4	2	1	0	4	1	1	3	16	22	2	3	2	3	0	4	2	2	0	3	21
5	3	3	4	0	2	2	1	0	1	0	16	23	1	1	4	2	0	3	0	2	4	4	21
6	1	4	2	1	0	0	1	4	3	0	16	24	1	2	3	4	1	2	2	0	4	3	22
7	0	2	3	3	0	3	1	2	1	1	16	25	3	1	3	4	4	0	3	2	0	2	22
8	2	2	0	3	3	0	0	0	2	4	16	26	2	0	3	4	3	4	1	1	4	0	22
9	0	2	2	1	2	1	3	0	4	2	17	27	1	4	0	0	3	4	3	3	1	4	23
10	2	1	0	4	1	1	4	0	3	1	17	28	4	4	0	3	1	2	1	2	2	4	23
11	0	1	0	4	2	4	2	2	2	0	17	29	2	4	4	2	2	1	2	4	1	2	24
12	2	2	2	0	1	3	4	3	0	0	17	30	0	3	3	2	3	2	2	3	3	3	24
13	1	3	0	1	1	3	3	1	2	2	17	31	4	1	2	4	3	3	0	4	1	3	25
14	1	0	1	0	3	1	4	2	3	2	17	32	4	2	4	3	4	1	3	1	3	0	25
15	2	1	1	1	4	1	1	3	1	3	18	33	0	4	1	4	4	3	2	0	4	4	26
16	0	3	3	0	4	1	0	4	0	4	19	34	4	4	3	1	2	2	4	2	2	3	27
17	4	3	1	0	2	0	2	3	4	1	20	35	3	3	4	4	0	1	4	3	2	4	28
18	3	2	1	2	1	4	0	4	3	0	20	36	3	1	0	3	4	4	4	4	4	3	30

3.3. Augmented Covering Arrays

An augmented covering array (ACA) is denoted by ACA (N; t, k, v), where the meaning of the parameters N, t, k, and v is the same as in OAs or CAs. An ACA is constructed progressively using an ACA with an alphabet lower than v and adding the necessary rows to satisfy the covering property. For instance, an ACA (M; t, k, 3) can be constructed by adding the necessary rows to an ACA (M; t, k, 2). Empirically we have found that it is desirable that the alphabets of a sequence of ACAs (one of these ACAs is described by $ACA_i(N_i; t, k, v_i), i = 0, 1, \ldots$) may follow the expression: $v_i = 2^i + 1$. The ACAs that will be used are then: ACA_0 (N_0; t, k, 2), ACA_1 (N_1; t, k, 3), ACA_2 (N_1; t, k, 5), ACA_3 (N_1; t, k, 9), ACA_4 (N_1; t, k, 17), ACA_5 (N_1; t, k, 33), ... ACA_i (N_i; t, k,2^i+1). This construction process generates an ACA with more rows than a CA with a similar configuration (values of t, k, and v). However, it adds an interweaving in the sampling important for defining weight vectors and extends the range of sampled alpha values.

Table 5 shows the ACA (42; 2; 10; 5) constructed using ACA (6; 2; 10; 2) and ACA (16; 2; 10; 3). Note that the α values are distributed in a range $3 \leq \alpha \leq 28$ with 15 different values of α. In this case, the values of α that are not sampled are 26, then the proportion of non-sampled values is 63% (26/41). This ACA has a range of α values between 3 and 28 while the CA in the previous section had a smaller α range, only between 13 and 30, even though it samples two additional α values.

Table 5. ACA (42; 2, 10, 5).

	a_0	a_1	a_2	a_3	a_4	a_5	a_6	a_7	a_8	a_9	α		a_0	a_1	a_2	a_3	a_4	a_5	a_6	a_7	a_8	a_9	α
1	0	1	0	0	0	0	0	0	1	1	3	22	4	0	1	4	4	0	3	4	1	1	22
2	1	0	0	1	0	0	0	1	0	0	3	23	1	0	4	4	1	2	0	3	4	3	22
3	0	0	1	0	0	1	1	1	1	0	5	24	1	3	4	2	4	3	1	0	0	4	22
4	1	1	1	0	1	0	1	0	0	0	5	25	2	3	4	1	3	0	4	3	1	1	22
5	0	1	0	1	1	1	1	1	0	1	7	26	3	4	2	1	1	3	3	0	4	1	22
6	1	0	1	1	1	1	0	0	1	1	7	27	4	2	2	4	3	4	1	0	0	3	23
7	0	2	1	2	1	1	2	2	0	1	12	28	2	4	3	1	4	4	0	1	1	3	23
8	0	0	2	0	2	2	0	2	2	2	12	29	2	2	3	3	0	0	1	4	4	4	23
9	2	1	0	2	0	2	1	2	0	2	12	30	4	4	3	0	2	3	3	3	2	0	24
10	1	2	2	1	0	1	2	0	2	2	13	31	4	3	0	3	2	1	3	2	3	3	24
11	2	0	2	1	1	2	2	1	1	1	13	32	1	4	3	2	3	2	3	4	0	2	24
12	2	2	0	0	2	1	2	1	2	1	13	33	2	2	4	4	0	3	3	1	3	2	24
13	1	1	2	1	2	0	2	2	2	0	13	34	4	3	2	1	1	2	0	4	3	4	24
14	1	0	1	2	1	2	1	1	2	2	13	35	0	3	3	4	3	4	2	2	3	0	24
15	2	2	2	2	2	2	1	0	0	0	13	36	3	2	2	3	4	2	4	3	0	2	25
16	2	2	1	2	2	0	0	2	1	2	14	37	4	3	1	2	0	4	4	1	4	2	25
17	3	0	1	3	3	3	0	1	1	4	19	38	3	3	4	0	2	4	4	4	2	0	26
18	3	4	1	2	0	0	1	3	3	3	20	39	0	4	4	3	4	3	2	2	4	0	26
19	1	0	3	3	1	4	4	0	3	1	20	40	3	4	0	4	3	1	4	2	2	4	27
20	0	1	0	0	4	3	4	4	3	3	22	41	4	1	4	3	4	1	2	3	2	3	27
21	0	1	0	0	3	4	3	3	4	4	22	42	3	1	3	4	2	1	2	4	4	4	28

3.4. Comparison between Orthogonal Arrays, Covering Arrays, and Augmented Covering Arrays for Weight Vector Definition

According to the information presented in the three previous subsections, it can be stated that the OAs are not a good alternative for sampling for the following reasons: (a) they cannot be constructed for all the desired combinations of v, k, and t; (b) they concentrate the sampling in the middle part of the possible values of $0 \leq \alpha \leq k(v-1)$; (c) the proportion of unsampled values is very high; (d) the size of an OA depends on v^t, where v is the smallest prime power satisfying $v + 1 \geq k$, and this value of N quickly exceeds the reasonable population size for an algorithm based on MOEA/D; and (e) in the process of transforming the domain from integer to real, several rows of the same OA can obtain the same weight vector, which is not desired in the context of defining the weight vectors.

CAs represent a better alternative to OAs for the following reasons: (a) they can be constructed for any combination of values of the parameters v, k, and t; (b) they perform a reasonably distributed sampling in the range of possible α values; (c) the proportions of unsampled α values are lower; and (d) the size of the CA grows logarithmically with the number of columns/objectives.

ACAs are an even better alternative since (a) like CAs they can be built for any combination of values k, v, and t; (b) the ranges of sampled α values are broader than in OAs and CAs; (c) the proportions of unsampled α values are lower than in OAs and similar to that of CAs; and (d) the size of the ACA grows similar to how a CA does, that is, logarithmically with the number of columns/objectives.

In summary, using OAs for weight vector definition is not recommended, and CAs and ACAs possess attractive characteristics. In light of this, we conducted an exploratory experiment using MOEA/D to compare CAs (MOEA/D-CAS) and ACAs (MOEA/D-ACAS) for defining weight vectors over the same problems (DTLZ and WFG test suites) and the experimental configuration is presented later in Section 5 with 10 to 100 objectives in intervals of 10, i.e., 10, 20, ..., 100, and CAs and ACs of strength 2 and alphabet 9. Inverted generational distance (IGD) results were tabulated, and the non-parametric Friedman test was applied to them, obtaining the results presented in Table 6. In this table, the ACAs obtain the first position (rank) in all compared objectives, and the test result is statistically significant (95%). With these preliminary results, it was decided to focus the experimentation on ACAs as the best option of the three combinatorial designs reviewed.

Table 6. Friedman rank for IGD results with strength ($t = 2$) and alphabet ($v = 9$).

Objectives (k)	MOEA/D-ACAS		MOEA/D-CAS		p-Value	Significative	ACAs Population Size (N)	CAs Population Size (N)	Population Size Δ
10	(1)	1.06	(2)	1.94	0.000465	True	136	81	55
20	(1)	1.25	(2)	1.75	0.045500	True	174	132	42
30	(1)	1.00	(2)	2.00	0.000063	True	197	148	49
40	(1)	1.13	(2)	1.88	0.002700	True	215	153	62
50	(1)	1.00	(2)	2.00	0.000063	True	232	153	79
60	(1)	1.06	(2)	1.94	0.000465	True	245	153	92
70	(1)	1.06	(2)	1.94	0.000465	True	256	153	103
80	(1)	1.06	(2)	1.94	0.000465	True	266	153	113
90	(1)	1.06	(2)	1.94	0.000465	True	277	153	124
100	(1)	1.06	(2)	1.94	0.000465	True	288	160	128

Although it is an expected fact (discussed in the previous section), it should be noted that in all the experiments (10 to 100 objectives), the population size with CAs is smaller than that of ACAs (a difference between 42 and 128 solutions), which puts the CAs at a disadvantage because they have fewer weight vectors to guide the approach to the Pareto front, even though the two algorithms carry out the same number of objective evaluations and therefore have a similar average run time.

Figure 1 below shows a visual comparison of weight vectors created by an orthogonal array, a covering array, and an augmented covering array with 3 objectives, strength 2, and an alphabet of 7. Analyzing these graphs is challenging, but the CA can be seen to sample the center of the objective space in more detail than the OA. The OA leaves some regions unsampled (near the vertices of the triangle), and the ACA uses more weight vectors (13 additional vectors) and samples more effectively a more considerable number of regions (borders, vertices, and center zone) of the objective space.

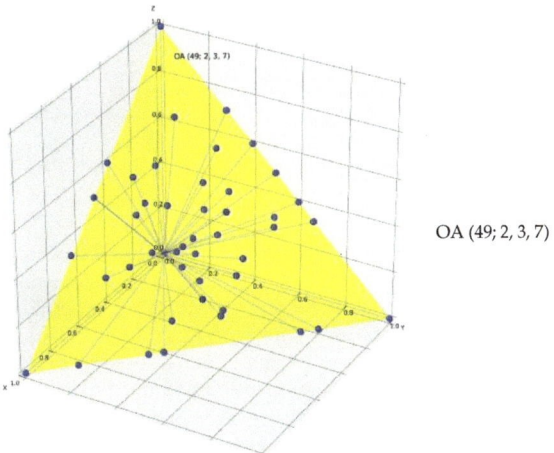

OA (49; 2, 3, 7)

Figure 1. *Cont.*

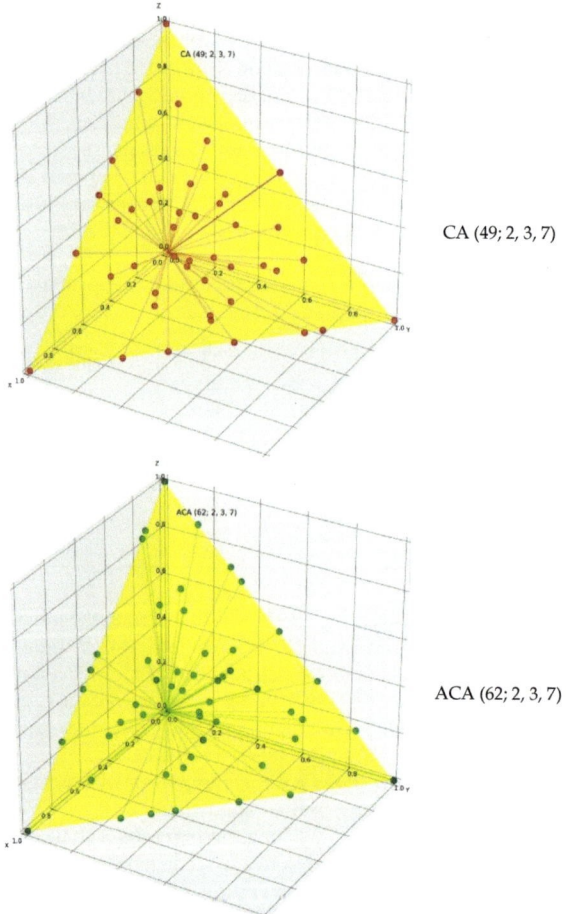

Figure 1. Visual comparison of an OA, CA, and ACA in 3D objectives with v = 7 and t = 2.

4. Weight Vector Definition Based on Augmented Covering Arrays

4.1. Main Hypothesis

The main hypothesis that we wish to test is that using an ACA with N rows, low strength values (t = {2, 3}), and low alphabet values (v = {9, 17}), the MOEA/D-DE algorithm obtains a better Pareto front than that obtained using the classical method of MOEA/D-DE (N uniformly distributed weight vectors).

4.2. The Proposed Algorithm

Algorithm 1 presents the multi-objective evolutionary algorithm proposal based on decomposition with differential evolution and augmented covering arrays (MOEA/D-DE-ACA). This proposal focuses on modifying (Step 1.1) the initialization of the random sampling of the weight vectors in MOEA/D-DE, incorporating an ACA to obtain a fixed size and better-distributed weight vector sample. The rest of the algorithm is equal to that originally proposed. The proposal maintains the genetic operators of the MOEA/D-DE algorithm [13]. The following explains in detail each component added in MOEA/D-DE-ACA and the problems solved by incorporating this method.

4.3. Fundamentals of the Proposal

The MOEA/D and MOEA/D-DE algorithms, in their initialization step, generate a random sampling as uniformly distributed as possible in the objective space for the definition of the weight vectors of the solutions in the population. This implies generating boundary weights (1, 0, 0, ..., 0), (0, 1, 0, ..., 0) ... (0, 0, 0, ..., 1) and then generating a large amount E (E >> N, where N corresponds to the population size) of candidate weight vectors. An iterative process is then conducted, selecting candidate weight vectors furthest from the previously selected list and including them until the N required weight vectors are completed, a task that is computationally costly when the value of E grows, with a complexity of $O(N \times E)$. This initialization method allows the user in these algorithms to maintain control over the growth in the number of weight vectors used for sampling the objective space through parameter N.

The quality of that sampling is affected by the exponential growth of weight vectors that must be considered in the objective search space, as explained in the previous section.

With the use of an ACA, the distribution of the weight vectors allows a better evaluation of the interaction between the objectives. In addition, the ACA's N value (number of rows) allows control of the size of the population. The ACA's N value is defined by the number of objectives, m, and its growth is controlled by the value of alphabet v and strength t. In addition, the ACAs were constructed previously and can be used as often as required, thereby reducing the execution time of the optimization algorithm for many purposes.

In Step 1.1 of Algorithm 1, each row of the ACA (N; t, k = m, v) is taken and converted from its integer domain to the real domain of the weight vectors. This conversion is conducted based on the alpha value, which automatically allows obtaining a normalized weight vector. This conversion is achieved by adding all values of the row and dividing each value (cell) of the row by that sum, a process repeated for the N rows of the ACA. In this way, N-normalized weight vectors are obtained.

Algorithm 1. MOEA/D-DE-ACA.

MOEA/D-DE-ACA
Input:
- Problem: Minimize $F(\vec{x}) = $ Minimize $\left(f_1(\vec{x}), f_2(\vec{x}), \ldots, f_m(\vec{x})\right)^T$, subject to $\vec{x} \in \Omega$ where Ω is the ***decision (variable or search) space***, $F: \Omega \to \mathbb{R}^m$ consists of m real-value objective functions, and $\mathbb{R}^m$ is called the ***objective space***. The attainable objective set is defined as the set $\{F(x) | \vec{x} \in \Omega\}$. If $\vec{x} \in \mathbb{R}^d$, all the objectives are continuous and described by $\{\vec{x} \in \mathbb{R}^d | h_j(\vec{x}) \le 0, j = 1, \ldots, m\}$ and, where h_j are continuous functions, the problem is called a continuous MOP.
- Nb: Number of weight vectors in the neighborhood of each weight vector.
- δ: Probability that parents' solutions are selected from the neighborhood.
- η_r: Maximum number of solutions replaced in each generation.
- ACA: Augmented Covering Array with N rows, strength t, m objectives (or k columns) and v alphabet. ACA (N; t, $k = m$, v).
- A stopping criterion.

Output:
- Approach to the Pareto set (PS): $\{\vec{x}_1, \ldots, \vec{x}_N\}$.
- Approach to the PF: $\{\vec{F}(\vec{x}_1), \ldots, \vec{F}(\vec{x}_N)\}$.

Step 1 Initialization

Algorithm 1. *Cont.*

Step 1.1 Define weight vectors using the ACA object. Define weight vectors $\vec{\lambda}_1, \ldots, \vec{\lambda}_N$ based on the normalization of the rows in the ACA and update the value of N if it was necessary to eliminate duplicate rows.

This means that a weight vector $\vec{\lambda}_i = ACA_i / \sum_{j=1}^m ACA_{i,j}$.

The set of weight vectors $\lambda = \bigcup_{i=1}^N \vec{\lambda}_i$ (not including duplicates).

Finally, $N = |\lambda|$.

Step 1.2 Compute the Euclidean distances between any two weight vectors and then work out the Nb closest weight vectors to each weight vector. In algorithmic terms:

For each $i = 1, \ldots, N$

Set $B(i) = \{i_1, \ldots, i_{Nb}\}$, as a list of weight vector indexes where $\vec{\lambda}_{i_1}, \ldots, \vec{\lambda}_{i_{Nb}}$ are the Nb closest weight vectors to $\vec{\lambda}_i$.

This means that $D = \begin{pmatrix} d(\vec{\lambda}_1, \vec{\lambda}_1) & d(\vec{\lambda}_1, \vec{\lambda}_2) & \ldots & d(\vec{\lambda}_1, \vec{\lambda}_N) \\ d(\vec{\lambda}_2, \vec{\lambda}_1) & d(\vec{\lambda}_2, \vec{\lambda}_2) & \ldots & d(\vec{\lambda}_2, \vec{\lambda}_N) \\ \vdots & \vdots & \ddots & \vdots \\ d(\vec{\lambda}_N, \vec{\lambda}_1) & d(\vec{\lambda}_N, \vec{\lambda}_2) & \ldots & d(\vec{\lambda}_N, \vec{\lambda}_N) \end{pmatrix}$

Where $d(\vec{\lambda}_i, \vec{\lambda}_j) = \sqrt{\sum_{k=1}^m (\lambda_{i,k} - \lambda_{j,k})^2}$.

$D_i = \{d_1, \ldots, d_j, \ldots, d_N\} = \{d(\vec{\lambda}_1, \vec{\lambda}_1), \ldots, d(\vec{\lambda}_1, \vec{\lambda}_j), \ldots, d(\vec{\lambda}_1, \vec{\lambda}_N)\}$.

$S\_D_i = sort(D_i)$, where $sort(D_i)$ sorts the elements in D_i in ascending order.

$B(i) = \{j \in S\_D_i \mid j \text{ is the index of } d_j \text{ and } d_j \text{ is one of the smallest } Nb \text{ in } S\_D_i\}$.

Step 1.3 Generate an initial population $p = (\vec{x}_1, \ldots, \vec{x}_N)$ randomly on Ω and for each $i = 1, \ldots, N$ calculate $F(\vec{x}_i)$. Also calculate and store for each $\vec{x}_i$ the individual objectives of $F(\vec{x}_i)$, i.e., $f_1(\vec{x}_i), f_2(\vec{x}_i), \ldots, f_m(\vec{x}_i)$.

This means that $P = \begin{pmatrix} x_{1,1} & x_{1,2} & \ldots & x_{1,d} \\ x_{2,1} & x_{2,2} & \ldots & x_{2,d} \\ \vdots & \vdots & \ddots & \vdots \\ x_{N,1} & x_{N,2} & \ldots & x_{N,d} \end{pmatrix}$

Where $\vec{x}_i = (x_{i,1}, \ldots, x_{i,j}, \ldots, x_{i,d})$ and each $x_{i,j}$ value is randomly generated in the range of the problem and d is the dimension of the decision (search) space.

$\begin{pmatrix} f_1(\vec{x}_1) & f_2(\vec{x}_1) & \ldots & f_m(\vec{x}_1) \\ f_1(\vec{x}_2) & f_2(\vec{x}_2) & \ldots & f_m(\vec{x}_2) \\ \vdots & \vdots & \ddots & \vdots \\ f_1(\vec{x}_N) & f_2(\vec{x}_N) & \ldots & f_m(\vec{x}_N) \end{pmatrix} = \begin{array}{c} \forall j \\ 1 \le j \le m \end{array} \begin{array}{c} \forall i \\ 1 \le i \le N \end{array}$ Compute $f_j(\vec{x}_i)$.

$\begin{pmatrix} F(\vec{x}_1) \\ F(\vec{x}_2) \\ \vdots \\ F(\vec{x}_N) \end{pmatrix} = \begin{array}{c} \forall i \\ 1 \le i \le N \end{array}$ Compute $F(\vec{x}_i)$, where $F(\vec{x}_i) = \sum_{j=1}^m \lambda_{i,j} * f_j(\vec{x}_i)$.

Step 1.4 Initialize $\vec{z} = (z_1, \ldots, z_m)^T$ where $z_j = \min_{1 \le i \le N} f_j(\vec{x}_i)$.

Step 2 Evolution

For $i = 1, \ldots, N$ do, i.e., $\begin{array}{c} \forall i \\ 1 \le i \le N \end{array}$

Step 2.1 Selection of Mating/Update Range: Uniformly generate a random number from $[0, 1]$. Then set $Q = \begin{cases} B(i) & \text{if } rand < \delta, \text{where } rand: [0,1] \to \mathbb{R}. \\ \bigcup_{i=1}^N i & \text{otherwise} \end{cases}$

Algorithm 1. *Cont.*

Step 2.2 Reproduction: Set $r_1 = i$ and randomly select two indexes r_2 and r_3 from P, generate a solution $\vec{y}$ from $\vec{x}_{r_1}$, $\vec{x}_{r_2}$, and $\vec{x}_{r_3}$ by a **DE** operator, and then perform a mutation operator on $\overline{y}$ with probability p_m to produce a new solution y. These operations can be summarized as:

$r_1 = i$.
$r_2 = g_1()$ where $g_1: [1, N] \setminus \{r_1\} \to \mathbb{N}$.
$r_3 = g_2()$ where $g_2: [1, N] \setminus \{r_1, r_2\} \to \mathbb{N}$.
$\vec{y} = DE\_operator(\vec{x}_{r_1}, \vec{x}_{r_2}, \vec{x}_{r_3})$ based on problem.
$\vec{y} = mutation(\vec{y}, p_m)$ based on problem.

Step 2.3 Repair: If an element of $\vec{y}$ is out of the boundary of Ω, its value is reset to be a randomly selected value inside the boundary. Calculate and store for each $\vec{y}$ its individual objectives, i.e., $f_1(\vec{y}), f_2(\vec{y}), \ldots, f_m(\vec{y})$. These two operations can be represented as:

$\vec{y} = repair(\vec{y}, p_m)$

$(f_1(\vec{y}), f_2(\vec{y}), \ldots, f_m(\vec{y})) = \underset{1 \leq j \leq m}{\forall_j}$ Compute $f_j(\vec{y})$.

Step 2.4 Update of $\vec{z}$: For each $j = 1, \ldots, m$, if $f_j(\vec{y}) < z_j$, then set $z_j = f_j(\vec{y})$. This step can be represented as:

$\vec{z} = (z_1, z_2, \ldots, z_3) \underset{1 \leq j \leq m}{\forall_j} z_j = \begin{cases} z_j & \text{if } z_j < f_j(\vec{y}) \\ f_j(\vec{y}) & \text{otherwise} \end{cases}$

Step 2.5 Update of Solutions.

Set $c = 0$.

While $Q \neq \phi$ do

a. If $c = \eta_r$ go to **Step 3**.
b. Randomly pick an index j from Q; i.e., $j = g_3()$ where $g_3: [1, N] \to \mathbb{N}$.
c. Compute $F(\vec{y})$, where $F(\vec{y}) = \sum_{k=1}^{m} \lambda_{i,k} * |f_k(\vec{y}) - z_k|$.
d. If $F(\vec{y}) \leq F(\vec{x}_j)$ then
   set $\vec{x}_j = \vec{y}$,
   $F(\vec{x}_j) = F(\vec{y})$.
   $c = c + 1$.
e. Remove j from Q; i.e., $Q = Q \setminus \{j\}$.

End while

Step 3 Stopping Criterion:

If the stopping criterion is satisfied, then
   Return $\{\vec{x}_1, \ldots, \vec{x}_N\}$ and $\{F(\vec{x}_1), \ldots, F(\vec{x}_N)\}$.
Otherwise go to **Step 2**.

Below is an example of this conversion based on row 26 highlighted in Table 5, corresponding to the following values: (3, 4, 2, 1, 1, 3, 3, 0, 4, 1). In this case, the sum of the values in the row is 22, corresponding to the value of α. The individual values are divided by the sum, and the following weight vector (0.14, 0.18, 0.09, 0.05, 0.05, 0.14, 0.14, 0.00, 0.18, 0.05) is obtained, which is also normalized as required by the rest of the algorithm.

When starting from an ACA with more columns than the objectives of the problem, the remaining columns are eliminated, and the result is still a valid ACA to which the normalization process can be applied. Meanwhile, when any two weight vectors are identical, the duplicates are eliminated, and the value of N is reduced to the number of unique weight vectors.

Below is an example of this situation. Where there are two rows of an ACA with 3 columns (objectives) and an alphabet of 9, it would be possible to have the following ACA vectors that are different in the discrete domain: (0, 2, 3) and (0, 4, 6). When calculating the α value of each, we would obtain 5 and 10, respectively. Then, when converting from integer domain to real domain, the result of these two vectors will be (0, 2/5, 3/5) and (0, 2/5, 3/5), which is why one must be removed from the list of weight vectors.

The source code and resources (ACAs) required to run the proposed method and experiments are available online at https://github.com/coboscarlos/MOEA_D_DE_ACA (accessed on 1 March 2024). The source code is based on MOEA Framework 2.12 or higher. The algorithm for constructing ACAs will be released after publication in an international journal; its explanation is not part of the purpose of this paper.

5. Experimentation

In this section, we first give the main characteristics of the many-objective problems used in evaluating and comparing the proposed algorithm (MOEA/D-DE-ACA) versus MOEA/D-DE and NSGA-III. The metric used to make the comparison in this case, inverted generational distance (IGD), is then described. Next, the experimental results are presented along with an analysis of three scenarios: (1) MOEA/D-DE-ACA with alphabet v = 9 and strength t = 2 (small population, from 136 to 288 solutions); (2) with alphabet v = 17 and strength t = 2 (medium population, from 416 to 838 solutions); and (3) alphabet v = 9 and strength t = 3 (large population, from 729 to 1457 solutions). These scenarios allow us to analyze the impact of variations in alphabet and strength. In the analysis of each scenario, the Friedman non-parametric and Holm post hoc tests are used to determine if the results have an appropriate level of statistical significance. All experiments were repeated 31 times to ensure that mean (or average) IGD values comply with the central limit theorem and genuinely represent the mean behavior of each algorithm. A comparison with another eight state-of-the-art algorithms is then made using the same problems (DTLZ and WFG) with 10–15 objectives. Finally, a comparison with another six state-of-the-art algorithms is made over constrained problems with 10–15 objectives.

5.1. Experimental Environment

5.1.1. The Many-Objective Problems Used for Evaluation and Comparison

Two test suites available in MOEA Framework 2.12 were used in this study, namely: Deb–Thiele–Laumanns–Zitzler (DTLZ) and Walking Fish Group (WFG) [64]. For each test problem, the number of objectives (m) varies from 10 to 100 in increments of 10, i.e., m ∈ {10, 20, 30, ..., 100}. All problems can be scaled to any number of objectives and decision variables. A summary of the main characteristics of these problems is presented in Table 7.

In the DTLZ test suite, DTLZ1 presents a linear and regular Pareto front (PF), making it relatively straightforward to solve. DTLZ3 and DTLZ7 exhibit numerous local PFs, adding complexity to the optimization task. DTLZ2 features a spherical PF, making it ideal for assessing the convergence of MOEAs to the global PF. DTLZ4 showcases a non-uniform distribution along the PF, providing a means to evaluate MOEAs' capacity to maintain a well-balanced distribution of solutions. A degenerate hypersurface characterizes DTLZ5's PF. DTLZ6 contains disjointed Pareto-optimal regions, making it suitable for evaluating MOEAs' ability to sustain subpopulations across disconnected segments of the objective space. The k1 parameter for these problems was set to 5 for the DTLZ1, DTLZ5, and DTLZ6 problems, 10 for the DTLZ2, DTLZ3, and DTLZ4 problems, and 20 for the DTLZ7 problem, in which the number of variables is D = m + k1 − 1.

Table 7. Properties of test problems using M objectives where M = {10, 20, 30, ..., 100}.

Problem	Shape of PF [65]	Multi-Modal [64]	Bias [64]	Disconnected [64,65]	Separable [64]	Deceptive [64,65]	Scaled [65]	No. of Variables (D = m + k1 − 1)	Generations
DTLZ1	Linear, Regular (Easy)	Yes [65]	No	No	Yes [66]	No		m + 4 (k1 = 5)	600
DTLZ2	Concave	No	No	No	Yes [66]	No		m + 9 (k1 = 10)	500
DTLZ3	Concave [67]	Yes [65]	No	No	Yes [66]	Yes		m + 9 (k1 = 10)	800
DTLZ4	Concave [67]	No	Yes	No	Yes [66]	No		m + 9 (k1 = 10)	500
DTLZ5	Concave, Degenerate, Irregular	No	No	Unknown	Unknown	No		m + 4 (k1 = 5)	500
DTLZ6	Concave, Degenerate, Irregular	No	Yes	Unknown	Unknown	No		m + 4 (k1 = 5)	500
DTLZ7	Mixed Sharp Tails	Yes	Yes [67]	Yes [65]	No	Yes	Yes	m + 19 (k1 = 20)	500
WFG1	Irregular, Convex, Mixed	No	Yes (polynomial, flat) [68]	No	Yes	No	Yes [69]	m + 9 (l = 10)	600
WFG2	Convex [68,69]	Yes (F1:M-1 no) [68]	No	Yes	No	No	Yes [69]	m + 9 (l = 10)	500
WFG3	Linear, Degenerate	No	No	No	No	No	Yes	m + 9 (l = 10)	500
WFG4	Concave, Regular	Yes (highly)	No	No	Yes [67]	No	Yes	m + 9 (l = 10)	500
WFG5	Concave, Regular	No	No	No	Yes	Yes	Yes	m + 9 (l = 10)	500
WFG6	Concave, Regular	No	No	No	No	No	Yes	m + 9 (l = 10)	500
WFG7	Concave, Regular	No	Yes (parameter dependent) [68]	No	Yes	No	Yes	m + 9 (l = 10)	500
WFG8	Concave, Regular	No	Yes (parameter dependent) [68]	No	No	No	Yes	m + 9 (l = 10)	500
WFG9	Concave, Regular	Yes (highly difficult)	Yes (parameter dependent) [68]	No	No	Yes	Yes	m + 9 (l = 10)	500

In the WFG test suite, the WFG1 problem is separable and uni-modal, like WFG7, but they have a different PF shape. The PF shapes on the WFG1, WFG2, and WFG3 problems are complicated, discontinuous, and partially degenerate. Five problems (WFG2, WFG3, WFG6, WFG8, and WFG9) are not separable. WFG7, WFG8, and WFG9 are connected and biased, WFG7 is not separable, and WFG9 presents a challenge due to its high modality. WFG4, like WFG9, also involves multi-modality but is not biased. The deceptiveness of WFG5 is more difficult than that of WFG9. The k1 parameter for these problems was set to k1 = m − 1, and the distance parameter l was set to l = 10, where D = k1 + l.

5.1.2. Comparison Metrics

Inverted generational distance is a metric designed to evaluate the quality of a set of solutions obtained in terms of convergence and diversity [70,71]. IGD is defined as follows [72]: $IGD(AP) = \frac{1}{|P^*|}\sum_{z^* \in P^*} dist(z^* \in AP)$ where AP is an approximation set to the Pareto front of the problem (solutions found by the algorithm); P^* is a set of reference points (non-dominated and evenly distributed) along the Pareto front; $dist(z^* \in AP)$ is from the Euclidean distance between z^* and its nearest neighbor in AP; and $|P^*|$ is the cardinality of P^*. With this definition, a lower IGD value indicates better algorithm performance, i.e., its solutions are closer to the PF.

IGD has two main advantages. The first is its computational efficiency. Secondly, it can measure convergence and diversity simultaneously whenever $|P^*|$ is large enough to cover the Pareto front easily. The number of reference points $|P^*|$ used in each experiment is shown further in the final column of Table 11. Values range from 3356 to 39,190.

In addition to the effectiveness measure (IGD) used to evaluate and compare the algorithms, their efficiency was also evaluated based on the computation time (execution time in seconds) required by each algorithm to run each experiment in a controlled environment (using the same hardware and software resources) [71].

5.1.3. Parameter Setting

Parameter settings for MOEA/D-DE and NSGA-III were adopted as recommended in the literature and summarized in Table 8, where pm and pc are the mutation and crossover probabilities, ηm and ηc are the distribution indexes of the crossover and mutation operators, respectively, CR is the crossover probability, F is the differential weight, δ is the probability of selecting parent solutions from the neighborhood, Nb is the neighborhood size of weight vectors, and nr is the maximum number of solutions replaced by each new solution.

Table 8. Parameter settings for the compared algorithms.

Algorithm	Parameter Settings
NSGA-III	pm = 1/n, pc = 1.0, ηm = 20, ηc = 30
MOEA/D-DE	pm = 1/n, ηm = 20, CR = 1, F = 0.5, δ = 0.9, Nb = 20, nr = 2
MOEA/D-DE-ACA	pm = 1/n, ηm = 20, CR = 1, F = 0.5, δ = 0.9, Nb = 20, nr = 2

The population size N was defined for all algorithms (MOEA/D-DE-ACA, MOEA/D-DE, and NSGA-III) based on the size of the selected ACA for the specific problem. The maximum number of function evaluations is the stopping criterion for all algorithms and results from multiplying the number of generations parameter (last column in Table 7) by the population size parameter.

5.2. Experiments with Strength t = 2 and Alphabet v = 9

Below, Tables 9 and 10 present the mean IGD results of the 31 repetitions for the three algorithms (MOEA/D-DE-ACA, MOEA/D-DE, and NSGA-III) using 10, 20, ..., up to 100 objectives in the seven DTLZ problems and nine WFG problems, respectively. Cells with bold text correspond to the best result in each experiment, and cells are highlighted with a gray background whenever the winner was MOEA/D-DE-ACA. Each cell shows the position (ranking) of the algorithm in parentheses and the mean IGD value achieved by the algorithm with the number of objectives established in the row on the problem defined in the column.

In Table 9, the following can be observed: (1) regardless of the number of objectives (10 to 100), MOEA/D-DE-ACA obtains better mean IGD values in problems DTLZ1, DTLZ2, and DTLZ3, which are linear (the first) and concave (the following two), do not have biases, do not have discontinuities, and are separable (the exception being with 40 objectives in DTLZ1 where it is surpassed by MOEA/D-DE in 0.0039); (2) in the DTLZ7 problem, MOEA/D-DE-ACA obtains the best IGD results from 10 to 70 objectives, which is a problem with a mixed, multi-modal Pareto front, disconnected, non-separable, and deceptive; (3) MOEA/D-DE-ACA obtains the best IGD for the DTLZ6 problem in 10 and from 50 up to 100 objectives and for the DTLZ5 problem from 70 to 100 objectives, problems that have a concave, degenerate, and irregular Pareto front, are not multi-modal, and are non-deceptive. In the remaining objectives (10 to 60 in DTLZ5 and 20 to 40 in DTLZ6), it occupies second place, being surpassed by MOEA/D-DE (between 0.00021 and 0.00099); (4) in problem DTLZ4, MOEA/D-DE-ACA only wins with 10 and 30 objectives. In the other objectives, it is only surpassed by MOEA/D-DE, and the differences are less than thirteen tenths. The DTLZ4 problem has similar characteristics to DTLZ2 but has bias; (5) the NSGA-III algorithm, in general, is last in all rankings, and the distances of the mean IGD values that it obtains from those obtained by the other two algorithms become greater as the number of objectives increases, which shows a critical weakness for the use of this algorithm with DTLZ problems with a high number of objectives and a small population size; and (6) MOEA/D-DE obtains first position in DTLZ6 between 20 and 40 objectives, in DTLZ5 between 10 and 60 objectives, and in DTLZ4 between 40 and 100 objectives, winning in DTLZ5 and DTLZ6 by narrow margins (thousandths) but in DTLZ4 by more.

Table 9. Mean IGD results in DTLZ problems using ACAs with strength 2 and alphabet 9.

Obj	Algorithm	DTLZ1	DTLZ2	DTLZ3	DTLZ4	DTLZ5	DTLZ6	DTLZ7
10	MOEA/D-DE-ACA	(1) **0.1457**	(1) **0.3194**	(1) **0.1888**	(1) **0.2919**	(2) 0.1505	(1) **0.1044**	(1) **0.6671**
	MOEA/D-DE	(2) 0.1513	(2) 0.3582	(2) 0.2033	(3) 0.3163	(1) **0.1481**	(2) 0.1046	(2) 0.7505
	NSGA-III	(3) 0.1696	(3) 0.3746	(3) 0.2989	(2) 0.3024	(3) 0.2172	(3) 0.5621	(3) 1.1480
20	MOEA/D-DE-ACA	(1) **0.1232**	(1) **0.4372**	(1) **0.1411**	(2) 0.3697	(2) 0.2045	(2) 0.1279	(1) **1.1480**
	MOEA/D-DE	(2) 0.1364	(3) 0.4820	(2) 0.1471	(3) 0.4221	(1) **0.2024**	(1) **0.1179**	(2) 1.5285
	NSGA-III	(3) 0.1612	(2) 0.4458	(3) 0.4070	(1) **0.3295**	(3) 0.2341	(3) 0.4297	(3) 1.7975
30	MOEA/D-DE-ACA	(1) **0.1245**	(1) **0.4905**	(1) **0.1647**	(1) **0.4614**	(2) 0.2010	(2) 0.1049	(1) **1.7280**
	MOEA/D-DE	(2) 0.1423	(2) 0.5359	(2) 0.1673	(2) 0.4825	(1) **0.1939**	(1) **0.0992**	(2) 2.0447
	NSGA-III	(3) 0.2119	(3) 0.6693	(3) 0.3213	(3) 0.4966	(3) 0.2951	(3) 0.4388	(3) 2.2949
40	MOEA/D-DE-ACA	(2) 0.1039	(1) **0.5235**	(1) **0.1571**	(2) 0.5359	(2) 0.1618	(2) 0.0912	(1) **2.2291**
	MOEA/D-DE	(1) **0.1000**	(2) 0.5718	(2) 0.1673	(1) **0.5092**	(1) **0.1590**	(1) **0.0906**	(2) 2.5549
	NSGA-III	(3) 0.1758	(3) 0.7721	(3) 0.3086	(3) 0.5871	(3) 0.2965	(3) 0.4688	(3) 2.6981
50	MOEA/D-DE-ACA	(1) **0.0663**	(1) **0.5547**	(1) **0.1250**	(2) 0.6354	(2) 0.1869	(1) **0.0887**	(1) **2.6861**
	MOEA/D-DE	(2) 0.0698	(2) 0.6165	(2) 0.1337	(1) **0.5506**	(1) **0.1846**	(2) 0.0903	(2) 2.9569
	NSGA-III	(3) 0.1169	(3) 0.8753	(3) 0.3301	(3) 0.6740	(3) 0.2929	(3) 0.4995	(3) 3.0068
60	MOEA/D-DE-ACA	(1) **0.0615**	(1) **0.5812**	(1) **0.1226**	(2) 0.6891	(2) 0.1816	(1) **0.0722**	(1) **3.0971**
	MOEA/D-DE	(2) 0.0746	(2) 0.6349	(2) 0.1298	(1) **0.5763**	(1) **0.1800**	(2) 0.0759	(2) 3.2730
	NSGA-III	(3) 0.1325	(3) 0.9522	(3) 0.4146	(3) 0.7245	(3) 0.2877	(3) 0.5283	(3) 3.3230
70	MOEA/D-DE-ACA	(1) **0.0835**	(1) **0.6065**	(1) **0.1230**	(2) 0.7266	(1) **0.1807**	(1) **0.0670**	(1) **3.4231**
	MOEA/D-DE	(2) 0.0926	(2) 0.6516	(2) 0.1285	(1) **0.6016**	(2) 0.1809	(2) 0.0716	(3) 3.6111
	NSGA-III	(3) 0.1425	(3) 0.9849	(3) 0.5539	(3) 0.7859	(3) 0.2934	(3) 0.6775	(2) 3.5931
80	MOEA/D-DE-ACA	(1) **0.0906**	(1) **0.6148**	(1) **0.1329**	(2) 0.7491	(1) **0.1861**	(1) **0.0626**	(2) 3.7727
	MOEA/D-DE	(2) 0.0947	(2) 0.6498	(2) 0.1458	(1) **0.6209**	(2) 0.1891	(2) 0.0725	(3) 3.9323
	NSGA-III	(3) 0.1614	(3) 0.9839	(3) 0.6074	(3) 0.8184	(3) 0.2952	(3) 1.1399	(1) **3.7696**
90	MOEA/D-DE-ACA	(1) **0.0914**	(1) **0.6224**	(1) **0.1444**	(2) 0.7710	(1) **0.1981**	(1) **0.0824**	(2) 4.1787
	MOEA/D-DE	(2) 0.1018	(2) 0.6635	(2) 0.1596	(1) **0.6381**	(2) 0.2027	(2) 0.0977	(3) 4.2406
	NSGA-III	(3) 0.1750	(3) 1.0005	(3) 0.7430	(3) 0.8398	(3) 0.3099	(3) 4.2159	(1) **4.0912**
100	MOEA/D-DE-ACA	(1) **0.1063**	(1) **0.6304**	(1) **0.1342**	(2) 0.7967	(1) **0.1719**	(1) **0.0824**	(3) 4.5781
	MOEA/D-DE	(2) 0.1160	(2) 0.6758	(2) 0.1454	(1) **0.6692**	(2) 0.1757	(2) 0.0977	(2) 4.5343
	NSGA-III	(3) 0.1994	(3) 1.0274	(3) 0.6672	(3) 0.8838	(3) 0.3037	(3) 4.2159	(1) **4.2818**

Table 10. Mean IGD results in WFG problems using ACAs with strength 2 and alphabet 9.

Obj	Algorithm	WFG1	WFG2	WFG3	WFG4	WFG5	WFG6	WFG7	WFG8	WFG9
10	MOEA/D-DE-ACA	(2) 0.1089	(1) **0.1059**	(1) **0.1792**	(3) 0.4017	(3) 0.3018	(3) 0.4681	(3) 0.3453	(3) 0.4983	(3) 0.3782
	MOEA/D-DE	(1) **0.0861**	(2) 0.1127	(3) 0.2074	(2) 0.3719	(2) 0.2834	(2) 0.4176	(2) 0.3440	(2) 0.4603	(2) 0.3460
	NSGA-III	(3) 0.1779	(3) 0.1676	(2) 0.1836	(1) **0.3441**	(1) **0.2755**	(1) **0.3651**	(1) **0.3213**	(1) **0.3808**	(1) **0.2964**
20	MOEA/D-DE-ACA	(2) 3.3927	(1) **0.1268**	(3) 0.2264	(3) 0.4800	(2) 0.3958	(3) 0.5574	(2) 0.4782	(2) 0.5703	(2) 0.4503
	MOEA/D-DE	(3) 4.2079	(2) 0.1507	(2) 0.2218	(2) 0.4764	(3) 0.4662	(2) 0.5858	(3) 0.5280	(3) 0.5747	(3) 0.4892
	NSGA-III	(1) **0.9033**	(3) 0.2007	(1) **0.2103**	(1) **0.3963**	(1) **0.3272**	(1) **0.3942**	(1) **0.3664**	(1) **0.4135**	(1) **0.3443**
30	MOEA/D-DE-ACA	(2) 4.1126	(1) **0.1564**	(3) 0.2377	(1) **0.5587**	(1) **0.4487**	(1) **0.6216**	(2) 0.5629	(1) **0.6175**	(2) 0.5107
	MOEA/D-DE	(3) 6.4187	(2) 0.1921	(2) 0.2302	(2) 0.6130	(2) 0.4825	(2) 0.6427	(3) 0.5859	(3) 0.6342	(3) 0.5352
	NSGA-III	(1) **1.0403**	(3) 0.2431	(1) **0.2135**	(3) 0.6403	(3) 0.5015	(3) 0.6354	(1) **0.5171**	(2) 0.6301	(1) **0.5049**
40	MOEA/D-DE-ACA	(2) 9.8444	(1) **0.1768**	(3) 0.2669	(1) **0.5783**	(1) **0.4802**	(1) **0.6320**	(1) **0.5886**	(1) **0.6111**	(1) **0.6022**
	MOEA/D-DE	(3) 11.751	(2) 0.2150	(2) 0.2587	(2) 0.6321	(2) 0.5115	(2) 0.6711	(3) 0.6386	(2) 0.6433	(2) 0.6168
	NSGA-III	(1) **2.0611**	(3) 0.2657	(1) **0.2259**	(3) 0.7516	(3) 0.5776	(3) 0.7555	(2) 0.6133	(3) 0.7156	(3) 0.7088
50	MOEA/D-DE-ACA	(3) 15.400	(1) **0.1896**	(2) 0.2748	(1) **0.6079**	(1) **0.4979**	(1) **0.6621**	(1) **0.6270**	(1) **0.6438**	(1) **0.6390**
	MOEA/D-DE	(2) 14.295	(2) 0.2214	(3) 0.2755	(2) 0.6790	(2) 0.5326	(2) 0.7115	(2) 0.6554	(2) 0.6972	(2) 0.6410
	NSGA-III	(1) **5.3195**	(3) 0.2760	(1) **0.2237**	(3) 0.8358	(3) 0.6319	(3) 0.8348	(3) 0.6837	(3) 0.8072	(3) 0.8069
60	MOEA/D-DE-ACA	(3) 9.6503	(2) 0.2472	(3) 0.3087	(1) **0.6349**	(1) **0.5237**	(1) **0.6884**	(1) **0.6406**	(1) **0.6806**	(2) 0.6610
	MOEA/D-DE	(2) 7.1777	(1) **0.2564**	(2) 0.2868	(2) 0.6899	(2) 0.5406	(2) 0.7334	(2) 0.6524	(2) 0.7288	(1) **0.6473**
	NSGA-III	(1) **4.1623**	(3) 0.3080	(1) **0.2416**	(3) 0.8932	(3) 0.6802	(3) 0.9006	(3) 0.6412	(3) 0.9166	(3) 0.8777
70	MOEA/D-DE-ACA	(3) 43.702	(2) 0.2905	(3) 0.3317	(1) **0.6496**	(1) **0.5407**	(1) **0.7016**	(1) **0.6643**	(1) **0.7013**	(2) 0.6953
	MOEA/D-DE	(2) 26.651	(1) **0.2819**	(2) 0.3141	(2) 0.7093	(2) 0.5579	(2) 0.7560	(2) 0.6888	(2) 0.7459	(1) **0.6577**
	NSGA-III	(1) **22.747**	(3) 0.3266	(1) **0.2290**	(3) 0.9360	(3) 0.6958	(3) 0.9388	(3) 0.6692	(3) 0.9770	(3) 0.9486
80	MOEA/D-DE-ACA	(3) 4.9379	(2) 0.3527	(3) 0.3534	(1) **0.6500**	(1) **0.5574**	(1) **0.7168**	(3) 0.6902	(1) **0.7118**	(2) 0.6722
	MOEA/D-DE	(2) 2.9548	(1) **0.2980**	(2) 0.3347	(2) 0.7014	(2) 0.5698	(2) 0.7562	(1) **0.6756**	(2) 0.7452	(1) **0.6742**
	NSGA-III	(1) **2.5396**	(3) 0.3512	(1) **0.2236**	(3) 0.9627	(3) 0.7295	(3) 0.9944	(2) 0.6833	(3) 1.0088	(3) 1.0464
90	MOEA/D-DE-ACA	(2) 3.0815	(2) 0.3612	(3) 0.3428	(1) **0.6653**	(1) **0.5692**	(1) **0.7177**	(2) 0.7226	(1) **0.7056**	(2) 0.7461
	MOEA/D-DE	(3) 3.3289	(1) **0.3103**	(2) 0.3205	(2) 0.7182	(2) 0.5837	(2) 0.7641	(1) **0.7002**	(2) 0.7415	(1) **0.6669**
	NSGA-III	(1) **2.0892**	(3) 0.3766	(1) **0.2394**	(3) 0.9852	(3) 0.7565	(3) 1.0150	(3) 0.7403	(3) 1.0465	(3) 1.0802
100	MOEA/D-DE-ACA	(2) 3.5191	(2) 0.3960	(3) 0.3538	(1) **0.6602**	(1) **0.5731**	(1) **0.7161**	(3) 0.7167	(1) **0.6930**	(2) 0.7771
	MOEA/D-DE	(3) 3.6717	(1) **0.3455**	(2) 0.3502	(2) 0.7234	(2) 0.5907	(2) 0.7739	(1) **0.7032**	(2) 0.7473	(1) **0.6738**
	NSGA-III	(1) **1.2328**	(3) 0.3807	(1) **0.2465**	(3) 1.0142	(3) 0.7612	(3) 1.0453	(2) 0.7032	(3) 1.0746	(3) 1.1486

Table 10 shows the following: (1) in problems WF4, WF5, WF6, and WF8, from 30 to 100 objectives, MOEA/D-DE-ACA obtains the best mean IGD values. These problems are characterized by having a concave and regular Pareto front, being scalable, and not being disconnected. Some are multi-modal, others not, and the same happens with having bias or not, being separable or not, or being deceptive or not; (2) in problem WF2 from 10 to 60 objectives, MOEA/D-DE-ACA obtains the best mean IGD values, followed by MOEA/D-DE with differences that increase little by little as the number of objectives increases. This problem is convex, multi-modal, disconnected, and scaled; (3) in problem WFG7 from 40 to 70 objectives, MOEA/D-DE-ACA obtains the best IGD values, followed by MOEA/D-DE with differences that decrease little by little as the number of objectives increases. This problem is similar to WFG8, where the algorithm is dominant from 30 to 100 objectives, but the fact that it is separable leads to it having better results in this problem; (4) the NSGA-III algorithm has the best values in a low number of objectives (10 and 20 in problems WFG4 to WFG9), but as the number of objectives grows the values tend to rise, that is, to deteriorate. Despite this, for problems WFG1 and WFG3, NSGA-III is dominant from 20 to 100 objectives with significant differences in mean IGD values, these problems are not multi-modal, and their Pareto fronts' shapes are not disconnected nor deceptive; and (5) MOED/D-DE obtains, in general, intermediate values of IGD in these problems and achieves dominance in problem WFG9 from 60 objectives with a concave and regular Pareto front. In this sense, the initialization of weights with an ACA allows MOEA/D-DE to improve its performance in WFG problems with irregular, discontinuous Pareto fronts that are scaled.

Since the previous analysis makes it difficult to determine precisely which algorithm is best and in what kind of problems, the mean behavior of the three algorithms in these problems was evaluated using the Friedman non-parametric and Holm post hoc tests. This test was performed with 2 degrees of freedom, and Holm results were evaluated with a significance level of 90% and 95%.

Table 11 shows in the first column the number of objectives (10 to 100) evaluated in the DTLZ and WFG problems, then the three algorithms with their ranking (1, 2, or 3) and the Friedman ranking and, finally, the p-value obtained in the test and whether the said value is significant (True or False). The result of the Holm post hoc test is then seen with a 3×3 matrix, where the first row and column refer to Algorithm A (MOEA/D-DE-ACA), the second row and column Algorithm B (MOEA/D-DE), and the third row and column Algorithm C (NSGA-III). The symbol • indicates that results obtained with the algorithm in the row are better than those obtained with the algorithm in the column, while the symbol ○ indicates that the algorithm in the column outperforms the algorithm in the row. The values above the diagonal have a significance level of 90%, while those below the diagonal have a significance of 95%. The table then shows the population size with which the three algorithms were executed, a value defined by the ACA used in MOEA/D-DE-ACA and that has the strength to grow logarithmically based on the number of objectives (population size = $6.5686 \times 10^1 \times \ln(objectives) - 2.1801 \times 10^1$ with $R^2 = 0.992$). The last column in this table shows the number of reference points used by the MOEA Framework for calculating IGD in the problems, according to the number of objectives, in this case, 3356 for 10 objectives and 7416 for 100 objectives. In Table 11, it can be seen that the MOEA/D-DE-ACA algorithm obtains number 1 ranking in all cases, but in 10 and 20 objectives, this ranking is not statistically significant (the p-value obtained is not less than 0.05), which is why the Holm post hoc test is not performed for these two experiments.

Based on the Holm test, between 30 and 60 objectives, MOEA/D-DE-ACA outperforms MOEA/D-DE and NSGA-III with a significance level of 95%. Between 70 and 100 objectives, a dominant relationship between MOEA/D-DE-ACA and MOEA/D-DE cannot be established, but these two algorithms outperform NSGA-III with 90% significance. This relationship can be defined with 95% significance with 70 and 90 objectives. With 90 objectives, MOEA/D-DE-ACA also outperforms MOEA/D-DE with 95% significance.

Table 11. Friedman rank and Holm post hoc for IGD results with strength 2 and alphabet 9.

Obj	MOEA/D-DE-ACA (A)		MOEA/D-DE (B)		NSGA-III (C)		p-Value	Sig	Holm	Population Size	Reference Points
10	(1)	1.88	(2)	2.00	(3)	2.13	0.77880	False	-	136	3356
20	(1)	1.81	(3)	2.38	(1)	1.81	0.18498	False	-	174	4830
30	(1)	1.44	(2)	2.19	(3)	2.38	0.01950	True	A: -,•,• / B: ○,-,- / C: ○,-,-	197	5414
40	(1)	1.44	(2)	1.88	(3)	2.69	0.00160	True	A: -,•,• / B: ○,-,• / C: ○,○,-	40	(1)
50	(1)	1.31	(2)	1.94	(3)	2.75	0.00025	True	A: -,•,• / B: ○,-,• / C: ○,○,-	232	6303
60	(1)	1.44	(2)	1.88	(3)	2.69	0.00160	True	A: -,•,• / B: ○,-,• / C: ○,○,-	245	6576
70	(1)	1.44	(2)	1.94	(3)	2.63	0.00339	True	A: -,-,• / B: -,-,• / C: ○,○,-	256	6390
80	(1)	1.69	(2)	1.81	(3)	2.50	0.04677	True	A: -,-,• / B: -,-,- / C: ○,-,-	266	6753
90	(1)	1.50	(2)	1.88	(3)	2.63	0.00525	True	A: -,•,• / B: ○,-,- / C: ○,○,-	277	7416
100	(1)	1.69	(2)	1.81	(3)	2.50	0.04677	True	A: -,-,• / B: -,-,• / C: ○,○,-	288	7416

Figure 2 shows the average execution time (AET) of the three algorithms for all DTLZ and WFG datasets with each number of objectives, from 10 to 100. The execution time of NSGA-III is much greater than that of the other two algorithms. The complexity growth is quadratic ($AET = 2.131 \times 10^2 \times objectives^2 - 1.0533 \times 10^4 \times objectives + 1.21769 \times 10^5$) with an $R^2 = 0.9966$. This figure shows that the processing executed by NSGA-III beyond the objective function evaluations is much greater than that performed by the other two algorithms since they all execute the same number of fitness function evaluations. The execution times of MOEA/D-DE ($AET = 8.3186 \times 10^0 \times objectives^2 + 2.459 \times 10^2 \times objectives - 2.8955 \times 10^3$) with an $R^2 = 0.9953$ and MOEA/D-DE-ACA ($AET = 3.6936 \times 10^0 \times objectives^2 + 6.3126 \times 10^1 \times objectives - 3.9744 \times 10^2$) with an $R^2 = 0.998$ also have a quadratic tendency where MOEA/D-DE-ACA has the shortest execution time. The difference obtained in time between the two versions of MOEA/D is explained in the time saved in Step 1.1 Initialization; the use of a previously manufactured ACA gives an advantage in time with the proposed approach.

Figure 3 shows a box plot graphic that visually summarizes the median and quartiles of the IGD values obtained by the three algorithms in the 16 problems (DTLZ and WFG) in the experiments with t = 2 and v = 9 from 10 to 100 objectives. It can be observed that in 12 problems (DTLZ1 to DTLZ3, DTLZ5 to DTLZ7, WFG2, and WFG4 to WFG8), i.e., in 75% of the 16 problems, MOEA/D-DE-ACA obtains better (lower) mean IGD values than the other two algorithms, followed by MOEA/D-DE.

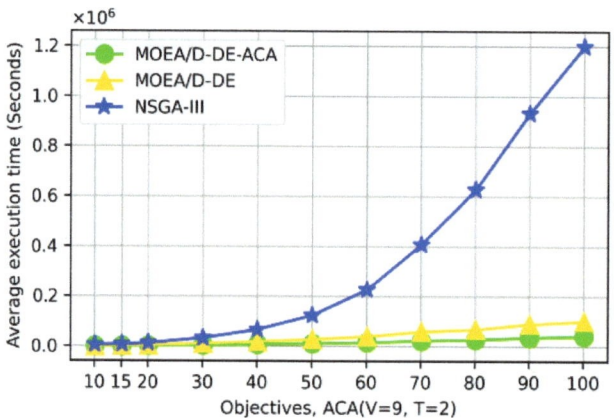

Figure 2. Average execution time in seconds for all algorithms in the experiments with strength 2 and alphabet 9.

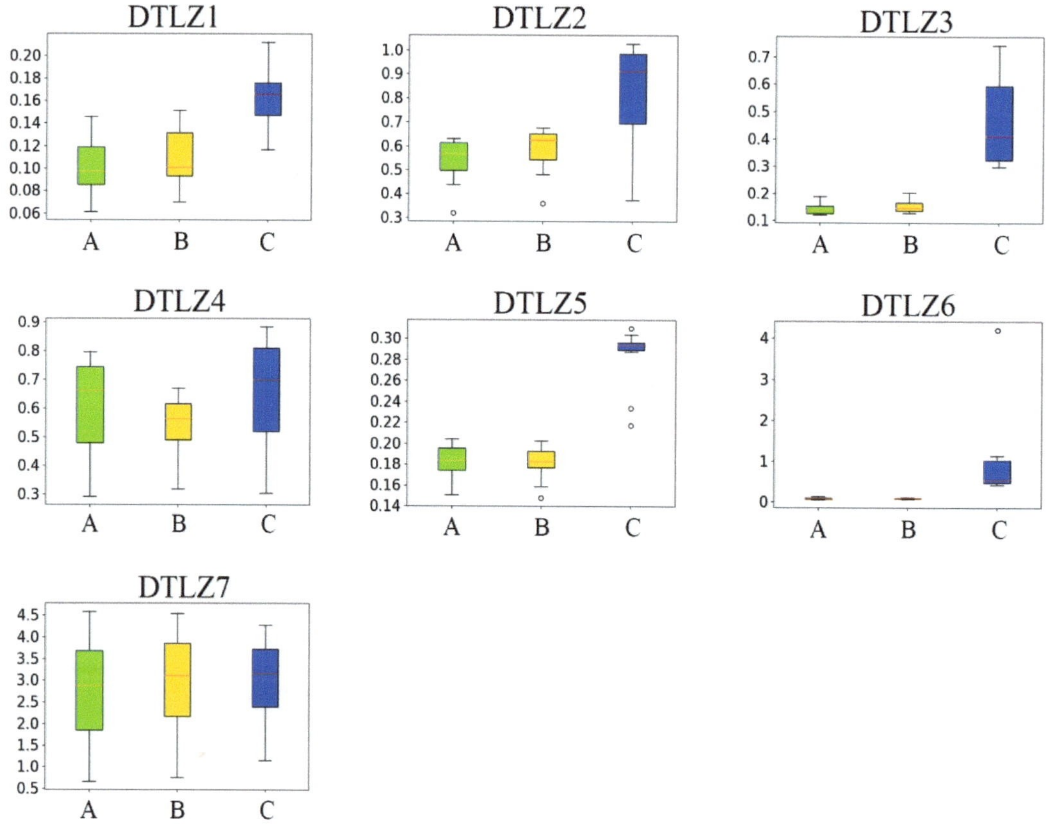

Figure 3. *Cont.*

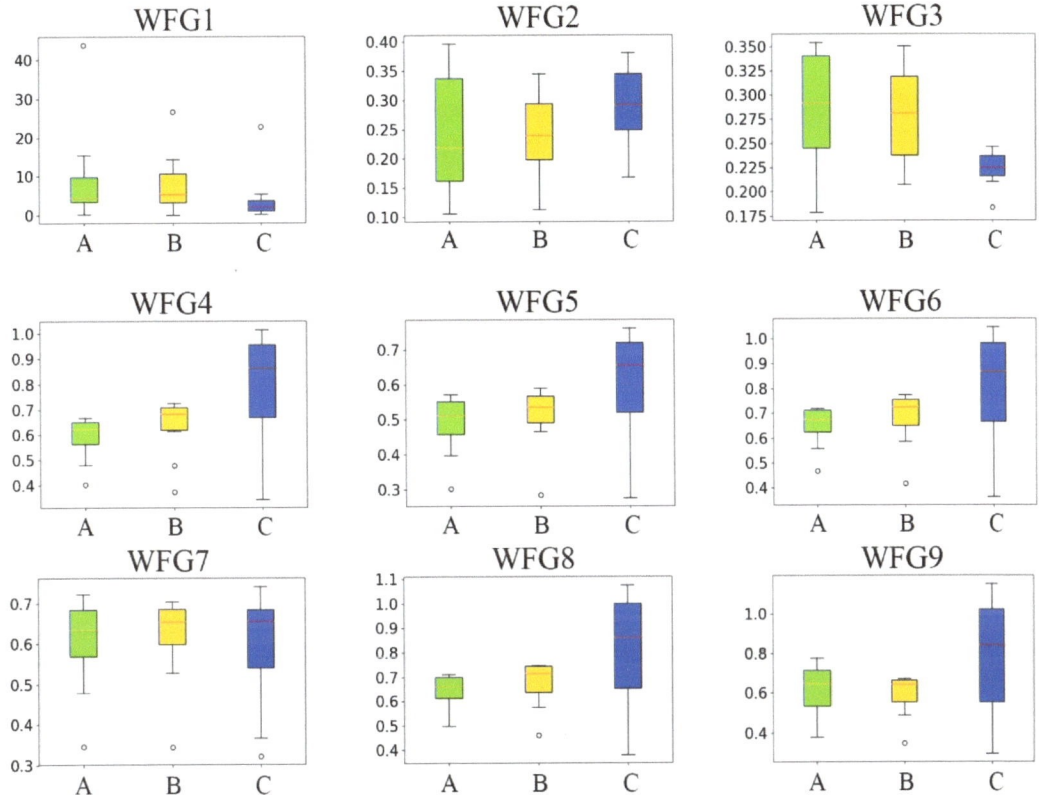

Figure 3. IGD values obtained for all algorithms in the evaluation of strength 2 and alphabet 9 from 10 to 100 objectives. A: MOEA/D-DE-ACA, B: MOEA/D-DE, and C: NSGA-III.

In DTLZ4 and WFG9, MOEA/D-DE-ACA is outperformed by MOEA/D-DE, and in WFG1 and WFG3, the best results are obtained by NSGA-III, leaving MOEA/D-DE-ACA in second place in the first problem and third place the other.

5.3. Experiments with Strength t = 2 and Alphabet v = 17

Concerning the previous experiment, in this one, the value of the alphabet increases from 9 to 17, which implies that the used ACAs have a larger number of rows, and a larger population is established. With 10 objectives, there is an increase from 136 rows in v = 9 to 416 with v = 17, which establishes a relation of 1 to 3.06, while with 100 objectives, the increase is from 288 with v = 9 to 838 with v = 17, which is a ratio of 1 to 2.91. In the intermediate relations for the other objectives, a maximum of 1 to 3.45 was obtained; this shows that doubling (approximately) the alphabet triples (approximately) the number of rows in the ACA and, therefore, the number of weight vectors in the population of MOEA/D-DE-ACA.

As in the previous section, a table with the results for the DTLZ problems was built; from this table, the following was observed: (1) MOEA/D-DE-ACA obtains better mean IGD values from 40 to 100 objectives in all DTLZ problems, with five exceptions in which it comes second (with a maximum difference of 0.0316) and in DTLZ4 where it is outperformed by the other two algorithms (maximum difference of 0.149); (2) in problems DTLZ3 and DTLZ7, MOEA/D-DE-ACA obtains the best IGD results from 20 objectives upward, the first of these problems being concave and the second mixed; both are multi-modal, one is disconnected and the other not, one is separable and the other not, and both are deceptive. MOEA/D-DE-ACA improves the performance in these two problems when the objective number grows to 60–70, and this is then maintained up to 100 objectives; (3) MOEA/D-DE-ACA in 10 to 30 objectives of problems DTLZ5 and DTLZ6 occupies second place, being outperformed by MOEA/D-DE (differences between 0.0005 and 0.0053; (4) the NSGA-III algorithm generally leads the rankings of the mean IGD values of 10 and 20 objectives of problems DTLZ1 to DTLZ4, but its values are later exceeded by those obtained by the MOEA/D-DE with increases in the number of objectives; this reveals a critical weakness for the use of this algorithm with DTLZ problems with a high number of objectives and a population size lower than 900; and (5) MOEA/D-DE in general—like in the previous experiment—obtains second place except in some cases, most of which are from 10 to 30 objectives.

In the results related to WDG problems, it could be observed that: (1) in problem WFG2 from 20 to 100 objectives, MOEA/D-DE-ACA obtains better mean IGD values, followed by MOEA/D-DE with differences that increase little by little as the number of objectives increases; (2) in problems WF4 and WF6 from 50 to 100 objectives, MOEA/D-DE-ACA obtains better mean IGD values, and these problems are characterized by having a concave Pareto front, being regular, not having bias, not being disconnected, not being deceptive, and being scaled, but the first is highly multi-modal and the second is not; (3) in problems WF5 and WF8 from 60 to 100 objectives, MOEA/D-DE-ACA obtains better mean IGD values, and these problems are characterized by having a concave Pareto front, being regular, not being multi-modal, and not being disconnected. The first one is separable and the second one is not, the first is deceptive but the second is not and is scaled; (4) in general, the NSGA-III algorithm occupies first place in the WFG problems from 10 to 40 objectives, except in WFG2, but, with more objectives, the mean IGD value for this algorithm becomes larger (it moves away from the ideal PF). Despite this, the WFG3 and WFG7 problems give the best results with up to 100 objectives and the best results are given in WFG1 with 20, 30, 40, 50, 90, and 100 objectives.

After evaluating the average behavior of the three algorithms in these problems, Friedman's non-parametric statistical test and the Holm post hoc test were also executed. In these tests, the NSGA-III algorithm ranks 1 in 10, 20, and 30 objectives, showing that it outperforms MOEA/D-DE and MOEA/D-DE-ACA in 10 and 20 objectives with a 95% significance level. In addition, with 10 objectives, MOEA/D-DE outperforms MOEA/D-DE-ACA with the same significance level. In 30 objectives, the Friedman ranking is not significant (the p-value obtained is not less than 0.05). As such, the Holm post hoc test is not performed. MOEA/D-DE-ACA ranks 1 from 40 to 100 objectives, but in 50 objectives, this ranking is not statistically significant. Based on the Holm test for 40 objectives, MOEA/D-DE-ACA outperforms MOEA/D-DE, with a 95% significance level. In 60, 70, 80, 90, and 100 objectives, MOEA/D-DE-ACA and MOEA/D-DE are seen to outperform NSGA-III with 95% significance. In 70 objectives, MOEA/D-DE-ACA outperforms MOEA/D-DE with 90% significance. The situation is similar in 80 objectives, except that the dominance of MOEA/D-DE-ACA over MOEA/D-DE is more remarkable, with a significance of 95%. Here, the population size can be defined as $1.8644 \times 10^2 \times \ln(objectives) - 0.3125 \times 10^0$ with $R^2 = 0.9596$.

On the other hand, the execution time of NSGA-III is much greater than that of the other two algorithms. In this case, $AET = 1.0635 \times 10^4 \times objectives^2 - 5.30145 \times 10^5 \times objectives + 9 \times 10^6$ with an $R^2 = 0.9333$; this shows that the processing executed by NSGA-III beyond the evaluations of the objective function is much greater than that of the other two algorithms. The execution time of MOEA/D-DE ($AET = 9.2652 \times 10^2 \times objectives^2 + 2.51005 \times 10^5 \times objectives - 1 \times 10^6$ with an $R^2 = 0.9099$) shows that when the population increases, the execution time increases, especially after 50 objectives where it even manages to be greater than that of the other two algorithms. This also shows that using a previously constructed ACA for executing MOEA/D-DE and avoiding this task in the initialization step significantly reduces processing time. For MOEA/D-DE-

ACA, the $AET = 7.5386 \times 10^2 \times objectives^2 - 5.6509 \times 10^4 \times objectives + 2 \times 10^6$ (with an $R^2 = 0.9093$) also has a quadratic tendency, so MOEA/D-DE-ACA is the one presenting the shortest execution time in all cases.

A box plot graphic (like Figure 3) was also used to visually summarizes the median and quartiles of the IGD values obtained by the three algorithms in the 16 problems (7 DTLZ and 9 WFG) during the experiment for t = 2 and v = 17 from 10 to 100 objectives. As a result, the following was observed: (1) in 11 of the problems (DTLZ1 to DTLZ3, DTLZ5 to DTLZ7, WFG2, WFG4 to WFG6, and WFG8 to WFG9), that correspond to 68.75% of the 16 problems, MOEA/D-DE-ACA obtains better median values and its quartiles are closer to the median (less dispersed) than the other algorithms; (2) in WFG3, WFG5, and WFG7 problems, NSGA-III obtains better results, followed by MOEA/D-DE-ACA and then by MOEA/D-DE, and in DTLZ4, NSGA-III obtains the best results this time followed by MOEA/D-DE-ACA; (3) in the WFG1 problem, MOEA/D-DE obtains the best results, followed by NSGA-III and MOEA/D-DE-ACA. Although the results are not the same as in the previous experiment, they are generally similar. Furthermore, suppose the results in the figures only included the values from 40 to 100 objectives, which is where the MOEA/D-DE-ACA algorithm obtains the best results. In that case, the proposed algorithm will be the best for all problems.

5.4. Experiments with Strength t = 3 and Alphabet v = 9

This experiment was performed only up to 90 objectives because the execution times of MOEA/D-DE and NSGA-III were too great for the execution of the 31 repetitions. The results of DTLZ problems show the following: (1) MOEA/D-DE-ACA obtains better mean IGD values in problems DTLZ1, DTLZ2, and DTLZ3 with 20 objectives with two exceptions in DTLZ1 and DTLZ2 and one exception for DTLZ3; (2) in the DTLZ7 problem, MOEA/D-DE-ACA obtains the best IGD results from 30 to 100 objectives, improving the results due to the increasing number of objectives for this problem, a problem with a complex Pareto front; (3) MOEA/D-DE obtains the best IGD for problem DTLZ6 from 10 objectives and, for problem DTLZ5 from 20 to 100 objectives, this algorithm produces the best solutions. As the number of objectives grows, its performance improves; (4) in problem DTLZ4, the two versions of MOEA/D are exceeded by NSGA-III in the different objectives, although the differences are minor; this problem has similar characteristics to DTLZ2 but has bias; and (5) the MOEA/D-DE-ACA MOEA/D-DE algorithms generally lead the rankings of mean IGD values from 20 to 100 objectives. The results on WFG problems shows the following: (1) in problem WFG2 from 30 to 90 objectives, MOEA/D-DE-ACA obtains better mean IGD values; (2) in problems WFG4, WFG6, and WFG8 from 80 to 90 objectives, MOEA/D-DE-ACA obtains better mean IGD values, followed by MOEA/D-DE with differences that increase; (3) in general, the MOEA/D-DE-ACA algorithm does not perform well with 50 objectives or fewer, since NSGA-III obtains the best results, and it only competes for second place with MOEA/D-DE. NSGA-III stands out in problems WFG3, WFG4, WFG5, WFG6, WFG7, WFG8, and WFG9; and (4) MOEA/D-DE-ACA leads the experiments in WFG problems with many objectives, 80 and 90 objectives precisely. Furthermore, the difference from NSGA-III is significant.

The Friedman non-parametric test and the Holm post hoc test shows that the MOEA/D-DE-ACA algorithm obtains the number 1 ranking in 70 and 90 objectives. In 20, 30, 40, 60, and 70 objectives, Friedman's ranking is not statistically significant (the *p*-value obtained is not less than 0.05), which again is why the Holm post hoc test is not performed for these experiments. Based on the Holm test for 10 objectives, the NSGA-III algorithm outperforms MOEA/D-DE-ACA and MOEA/D-DE with 95% significance. For 80 objectives, MOEA/D-DE and MOEA/D-DE-ACA outperform NSGA-III with a significance level of 90%. Finally, MOEA/D-DE-ACA and MOEA/D-DE are seen to outperform NSGA-III in 90 objectives with a level of significance of 95%.

On the other hand, the average execution time (AET) of NSGA-III decreases compared to the previous experiments. The growth is also quadratic ($AET = 1.342 \times 10^3 \times objectives^2 - 4.69 \times 10^3 \times objectives + 2.06500 \times 10^5$ with an $R^2 = 0.9795$). The processing executed by MOEA/D-DE is observed to be much greater than that of the other two algorithms ($AET = 9.012 \times 10^2 \times objectives^2 + 1.53215 \times 10^5 \times objectives - 6.39727 \times 10^5$ with an $R^2 = 0.9881$). The average execution time of MOEA/D-DE-ACA ($AET = 8.7379 \times 10^1 \times objectives^2 - 1.2631 \times 10^3 \times objetives + 4.8970 \times 10^4$ with an $R^2 = 0.8843$) continues to be quadratic and is the shortest execution time in this experiment, as in previous experiments. Considering that MOEA/D-DE and MOEA/D-DE-ACA differ only in the initialization step, it is evident that the increase in the number of weight vectors enormously increases the weight vector definition time.

After performing the three experiments, it was observed that the incorporation of ACAs, independently of the strength and alphabet in MOEA/D-DE, decreases the execution time since when using t = 2, v = 9, the proposal uses 40.7% of the time that MOEA/D-DE uses and only 4.8% of the time used by NSGA-III. Then with t = 2, v = 17, MOEA/D-DE-ACA uses only 8.9% of the time used by MOEA/D-DE and 7% of the time that NSGA-III uses. Finally, with t = 3, v = 9, it is observed that MOEA/D-DE-ACA uses only 2.7% of the execution time that MOEA/D-DE uses and only 6.2% of the time that NSGA-III uses.

Moreover, the random generation of weight vectors in MOEA/D-DE, when the population is large, causes the execution time to be so high that it exceeds the cost of NSGA-III in the experiments with small and medium populations, highlighting the importance of incorporating ACAs into this algorithm without diminishing the quality of the IGD results. The execution time of MOEA/D-DE-ACA ($AET = 8.7379 \times 10^1 \times objectives^2 - 1.2631 \times 10^3 \times objetives + 4.8970 \times 10^4$ with an $R^2 = 0.8843$) continues to be quadratic and is the shortest execution time in this experiment, as in previous experiments.

A box plot graphic of the IGD values obtained by the three algorithms in the 16 evaluated problems showed that MOEA/D-DE-ACA obtains better (lower) IGD values, and its mean is the lowest in 6 (37.5%) of the 16 evaluated problems (DTLZ1, DTLZ2, DTLZ6, DTLZ7, WFG1, and WFG2). Meanwhile, the performance of NSGA-III in all the problems improves compared to the previous experiments, where in 9 (56.3%) of the 16 evaluated problems, it slightly surpasses the results of MOEA/D-DE-ACA and MOEA/D-DE.

5.5. Data Analysis and Discussion

Seeking to identify the impact that the strength (t) and alphabet (v) of the ACA have on the performance of the MOEA/D-DE-ACA algorithm concerning the characteristics of the problems, a table was constructed in a minable view way with the data generated in the three experiments previously presented. The data were extracted from Table 7, where the characteristics of the problems were described, and Tables 9–11, which present the results of the experiments with small population sizes (t = 2 and v = 9)—similarly, the results of the experiments with medium populations (t = 2 and v = 17) and large populations (t = 3 and v = 9) were used. As a result, a minable view with 464 instances, 13 attributes, and 1 class variable (the ranking obtained by MOEA/D-DE-ACA in each experiment with each problem related to MOEA/D-DE and NSGA-III) was obtained. The class variable corresponds to Rank = 1 (207 instances where MOEA/D-DE-ACA ranked first) and Rank = 2 (257 instances where MOEA/D-DE-ACA occupied second or third place).

Using RapidMiner Studio Educational 10.3.001, a mining process implemented cross-validation with ten folds and a "decision tree" classifier using the Optimize Parameter operator, the following hyperparameters were defined: accuracy for criterion, seven for maximal depth, false for pruning, false for prepruning, and fifty-five for minimal leaf size. As a result, the operator generates the decision rules of Table 12 with 80% accuracy, 86% precision, and 77% recall. From this figure, the following general rules in favor of MOEA/D-DE-ACA can be summarized:

- If the problem is DTLZ1, DTLZ2, DTLZ3, DTLZ7, or WFG2, then MOEA/D-DE-ACA has a probability between 76% and 86% to be the best option.
- If the problem is DTLZ6, WFG4, WFG6, or WFG8 and strength = 2, then MOEA/D-DE-ACA has a probability between 65% and 70% to be the best option.
- If the problem is WFG5 and strength = 2 and alphabet = 9, then MOEA/D-DE-ACA has a probability of 80% of being the best option.

Also, from Table 12, the following conditions when MOEA/D-DE-ACA did not win (lost against MOEA/D or NSGA-III) can be summarized:

- If the problem is DTLZ4, DTLZ5, WFG1, WFG3, WFG7, or WFG9, with a probability between 72% and 97%.
- If the problem is DTLZ6, WFG4, WFG5, WFG6, or WFG8 and strength = 3, with a probability between 67% and 100%.
- If the problem is WFG5 and strength = 2 and alphabet = 17, with a probability of 60%.

These rules apply regardless of the number of objectives and population size, which is remarkably interesting. They only require the values of strength, alphabet, and problem. Unfortunately, the classifier could not find characteristics (shape, multi-modal, and deceptive, among others) of the problems without loss of generality, so more experiment data must be used in future work.

Table 12. Decision rules to define the rank of MOEA/D-DE-ACA.

Condition	Rank	Confidence	Rank = 1	Rank = 2
Problem = DTLZ3	1	86%	25	4
Problem = DTLZ7	1	79%	23	6
Problem = DTLZ1	1	76%	22	7
Problem = DTLZ2	1	76%	22	7
Problem = WFG2	1	76%	22	7
Problem = WFG4 and Strength $\leq$ 2.5	1	70%	14	6
Problem = WFG6 and Strength $\leq$ 2.5	1	70%	14	6
Problem = DTLZ6 and Strength $\leq$ 2.5	1	65%	13	7
Problem = WFG8 and Strength $\leq$ 2.5	1	65%	13	7
Problem = WFG5 and Strength $\leq$ 2.5 and Alphabet $\leq$ 13	1	80%	8	2
Problem = WFG3	2	97%	1	28
Problem = DTLZ4	2	93%	2	27
Problem = WFG1	2	93%	2	27
Problem = WFG9	2	90%	3	26
Problem = WFG7	2	86%	4	25
Problem = DTLZ5	2	72%	8	21
Problem = DTLZ6 and Strength > 2.5	2	100%	0	9
Problem = WFG5 and Strength > 2.5	2	100%	0	9
Problem = WFG6 and Strength > 2.5	2	78%	2	7
Problem = WFG8 and Strength > 2.5	2	78%	2	7
Problem = WFG4 and Strength > 2.5	2	67%	3	6
Problem = WFG5 and Strength $\leq$ 2.5 and Alphabet > 13	2	60%	4	6

To understand why MOEA/D-DE-ACA exceeds the results of MOEA/D-DE in small and medium populations, the angular distance between the different weight vectors sampled by each of the algorithms was calculated (value between 0 and 90 degrees, since the components of the weight vectors are positive, and these are always in the first quadrant of the multi-dimensional space). Figure 4 shows these angular distances organized in a frequency histogram observed every $2°$ for 30 and 60 objectives with the three population sizes (small, medium, and large).

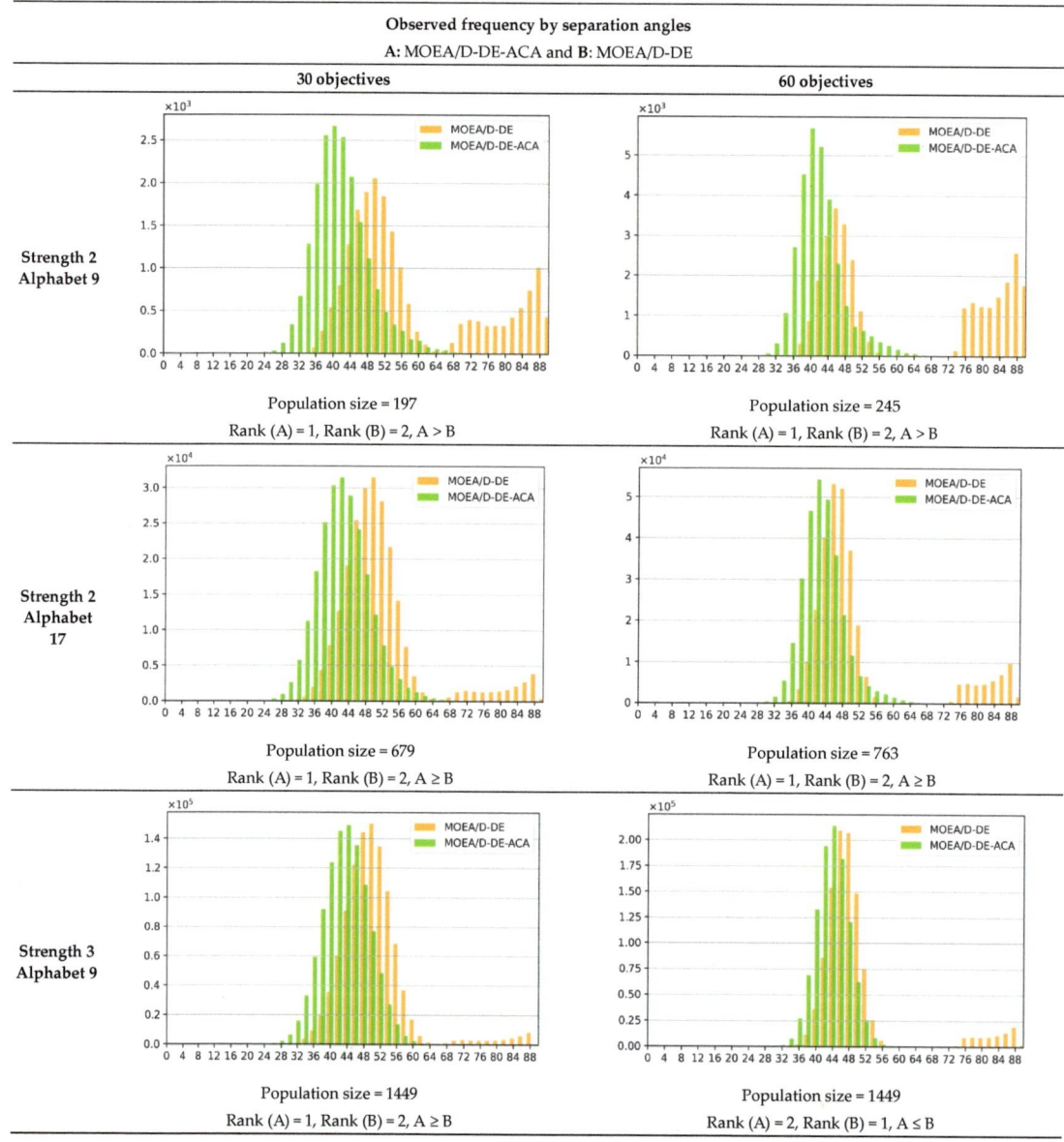

Figure 4. Histograms for comparison of separation angles with different numbers of objectives and population sizes.

On analyzing the first column of this figure (30 objectives), the histogram of the separation angles between the weight vectors obtained by MOEA/D-DE-ACA (light green color) has a symmetrical shape, a range that goes from 20° to 70°, and an average that varies between 42° and 43°; this means that, in the worst case, a weight vector has a neighboring vector at 20° and that two weight vectors that are as far from each other as possible are at 70°. In contrast, the histogram of the angles obtained by MOEA/D-DE (yellow-orange color) has an asymmetric shape towards the right side, a broader range from 30° to 90°, and an average between 52° and 59°. At first glance, the distribution of the weight vectors at the level of the angles of separation between each other is more uniform for MOEA/D-DE-ACA. In addition, the experimental results show that with 30 objectives, whether in small, medium, or large populations, MOEA/D-DE-ACA wins (in most cases) in the Friedman ranking over MOEA/D-DE, which in Figure 4 is expressed as Rank (A) = 1 and Rank (B) = 2. In this case, with a small population (t = 2, v = 9), MOEA/D-DE-ACA dominates with a 95% level of significance (A > B), but as the population grows, the domination relationship begins to fade (A $\geq$ B). Observing the histograms shows the reason. As more weight vectors can be generated, MOEA/D-DE begins to generate weight vectors with a distribution that is increasingly like the way MOEA/D-DE-ACA generates them from the beginning, but with a much higher computational cost. The tail on the right presented by MOEA/D-DE decreases from a smaller to a larger population but does not disappear; this tail refers to weight vectors found at the borders of the objective space—for example, with five objectives, it would include (1, 0, 0, 0, 0), (0, 1, 0, 0, 0), among many others.

The results of the second column (60 objectives) in Figure 4 follow the same pattern. MOEA/D-DE-ACA obtains a more symmetrical distribution that gives better results than MOEA/D-DE in small and medium populations, the domination vanishing from being significant in the small population to not being significant in the medium population and the ranking inverting in the large population since here the first in the ranking is MOEA/D-DE. These graphs show how MOEA/D-DE mimics MOEAD/D-DE-ACA in so far as it can create more weight vectors (larger population) except the right-hand tail is not removed at all; it also seems that it may be beneficial with a large number of objectives, as occurs with 60 objectives. The latter motivates future work in which rows that sample these extremes (border weight vectors) are included in the construction of ACAs.

Figure 5 shows, as an example, four graphs of parallel coordinates of the non-dominated solutions obtained after executing MOEA/D-DE and MOEA/D-DE-ACA (strength 2 and alphabet 9) for problems DTLZ6, DTLZ7, WFG1, and WFG2. The initialization of the two algorithms establishes the same initial (random) position in the search space for the solutions in the population. The only difference between the two populations is the weight vectors.

Although it is a challenge to analyze the results obtained with these graphs visually, in Figure 5, the solutions obtained by the two algorithms are substantially different concerning the values of their 30 objectives. In the case of DTLZ6, the results obtained by MOEA/D-DE (goldenrod color) measured in IGD are slightly better than those obtained by MOEA/D-DE-ACA (green color), which is visually represented with a higher density of goldenrod lines at the bottom of each of the objectives. The case of DTLZ7 is more difficult to interpret since, in several objectives, there is a concentration of better results for MOEA/D-DE, while others relate better results for MOEA/D-DE-ACA; this is evidenced by a remarkably similar value of IGD for the two algorithms. In WFG1 and WFG2, the IGD value for MOEA/D-DE-ACA is better than that of MOEA/D-DE. This fact can be seen in the graph of WFG1 from the more significant presence of green lines in the lower part of the graph, despite the peaks in several objectives. In the graph of WFG2, the green lines in the lower part cannot be visualized since they are hidden by the goldenrod lines (in the tool used to make these graphs, there is no option to manage transparencies).

Regarding execution time, it can be seen that even though all the algorithms perform the same number of objective evaluations and are executed on the same machine with the same conditions, in all experiments, MOEA/D-DE-ACA runs faster than MOEA/D-DE and NSGA-III because initializing weight vectors in MOEA/D-DE or reference sets in NSGA-III is a computationally expensive step, while that in MOEA/D-DE-ACA is summarized in reading a file with the ACA that will run the algorithm. This file with the ACA must be created using an ACA creation algorithm, usually a metaheuristic, which can be computationally expensive. Still, this work is performed only once, and then MOEA/D-DE-ACA can use it as many times as needed. This file can also be acquired from third parties, such as the repository of Professor José Torres-Jiménez at CINVESTAV Tamaulipas (Mexico).

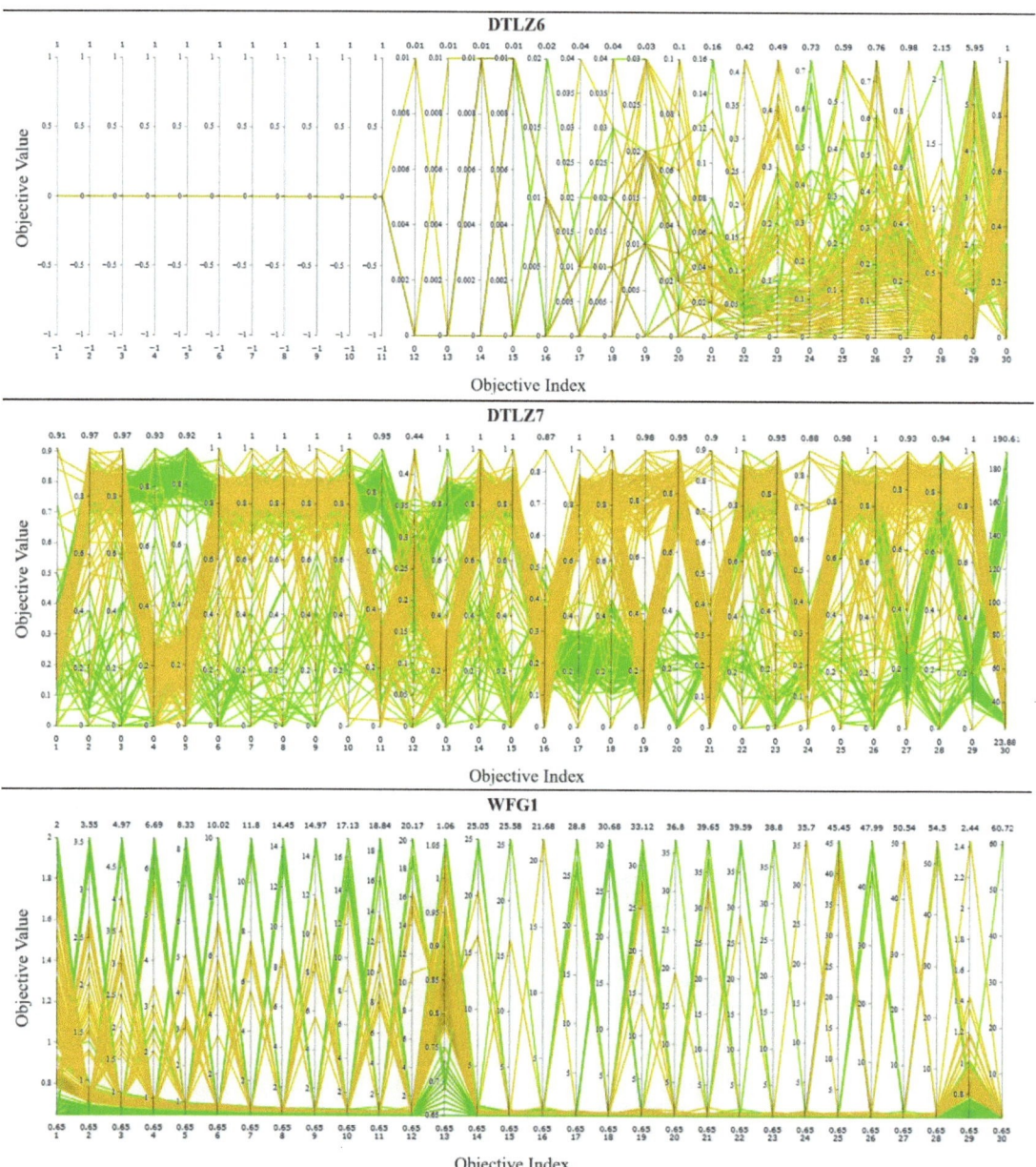

Figure 5. *Cont.*

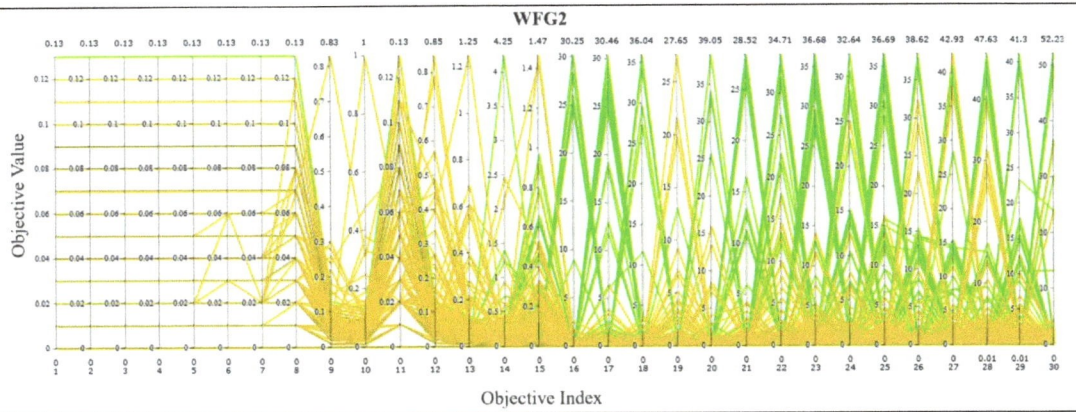

Figure 5. Non-dominated solutions for MOEA/D-DE (goldenrod color) and MOEA/D-DE-ACA (green color) for problems DTLZ6, DTLZ7, WFG1, and WFG2 with 30 objectives.

As mentioned as early as the Introduction section, in multiple or many-objective optimization algorithms based on the decomposition approach, such as MOEA/D, the proper initialization of the weight vectors is not the only way to improve the quality of the results. Still, suppose it uses a better initialization method and is combined with other strategies, such as the dynamic adjustment of the weight vectors during the evolutionary process. In that case, the results obtained may be better; this is future work that the research group hopes to conduct.

5.6. Comparison with Other State-of-the-Art Algorithms Using DTLZ and WFG Problems

The performance of the proposed algorithm was compared with the results of eight state-of-the-art MOEAs for solving MaOPs with 10 and 15 objectives [73]. The algorithms compared were NSGA-III [17], ANSGA-III [74], MOEA/D-PBI [8], EAG-MOEA/D [75], MOEA/DD [76], IBEA [5], SME-EMOA [6], and IDMOPSO [73].

To make a fair comparison, all algorithms' population sizes (popsize or N parameter), including the present proposal, were configured as similar values [73]. Table 13 summarizes the population size used for each algorithm. MOEA/D-DE-ACA was executed with an ACA (N = 277; t = 2, k = 10, v = 9) for 10 objectives and an ACA (N = 132; t = 2, k = 15, v = 9) for 15 objectives. Each algorithm is terminated after a prespecified number of fitness function evaluations (these values and other specific parameters for each algorithm are the same used in [73]). For WFG problems, each algorithm stops after 200,000 and 300,000 fitness evaluations for 10 and 15 objectives, respectively. For DTLZ1 problems, each algorithm stops after 2500 generations for 10 and 15 objectives. For DTLZ2, each algorithm stops after 750 and 1000 generations for 10 and 15 objective problems. For DTLZ4, each algorithm stops after 2000 and 3000 generations for 10 and 15 objective problems. For DTLZ5 to DTLZ7, each algorithm stops after 1000 and 1500 generations for 10 and 15 objective problems.

Table 13. Number of reference points/directions and corresponding population sizes used in algorithms.

Obj (M)	Ref. Points/Ref. Directions	NSGA-III and ANSGA-III Popsize (N)	Other Algorithms and IDMOPSO Popsize (N)	MOEA/D-DE-ACA Popsize (N)
10	275	276	275	277
15	135	136	135	132

Table 14 shows the IGD results for all algorithms on DTLZ and WFG problems with 10 objectives. The results obtained for MOEA/D-DE-ACA were the best for most of the problems regardless of the shape of the Pareto front or other characteristics of the problem. The last line of this table also shows the Friedman ranking obtained using a Friedman statistic (distributed according to chi-square with 8 degrees of freedom) of 55.73 and a p-value of 2.243×10^{-12} computed by the Iman and Davenport test. Friedman test results show MOEA/D-DE-ACA as the best option, MOEA/DD in second place, and IDMOPSO in third place. The Holm post hoc test shows that MOEA/D-DE-ACA results dominate all algorithms except for MOEA/DD and IDMOPSO, with a 95% significance level. MOEA/DD dominates MOEA/D-PBI and SMS-EMOA with the same significance level, and IDMOPSO only dominates MOEA/D-PBI.

Table 14. IGD results for all algorithms on DTLZ and WFG problems with 10 objectives.

PROBLEM	MOEA/D-DE-ACA	MOEA/DD	IDMOPSO	NSGA-III	ANSGA-III	EAG-MOEA/D	IBEA	SMS-EMOA	MOEA/D-PBI
DTLZ1	(1) 0.048	0.109	0.108	0.113	0.125	0.204	0.236	15.617	0.110
DTLZ2	(1) 0.134	0.422	0.430	0.474	0.540	0.674	0.428	0.498	0.423
DTLZ4	(1) 0.135	0.422	0.456	0.432	0.441	0.714	0.429	0.583	0.512
DTLZ5	(3) 0.094	0.133	(1) 0.016	0.615	0.692	0.094	0.098	0.117	(2) 0.020
DTLZ6	(3) 0.055	0.121	(1) 0.018	2.775	4.225	0.117	0.331	1.210	(2) 0.019
DTLZ7	(1) 0.730	2.336	1.224	1.116	1.122	1.112	0.959	4.763	3.037
WFG1	(1) 0.041	1.075	1.035	1.242	1.222	2.120	1.506	2.633	2.554
WFG2	(1) 0.042	5.730	5.926	5.898	5.726	1.987	14.887	5.776	16.681
WFG3	(1) 0.075	0.391	2.532	0.815	1.106	1.047	2.759	1.873	5.342
WFG4	(1) 0.152	4.469	5.361	4.719	4.545	4.776	6.289	5.794	9.084
WFG5	(1) 0.064	4.474	4.234	4.476	4.529	4.607	6.339	4.432	8.238
WFG6	(1) 0.193	4.621	4.674	5.691	4.726	6.014	6.439	6.883	9.294
WFG7	(1) 0.098	4.541	4.341	4.606	4.544	5.114	6.005	4.543	9.304
WFG8	(1) 0.212	4.575	5.084	5.369	4.993	6.526	5.618	5.895	8.444
WFG9	(1) 0.105	4.122	4.012	4.443	4.447	5.454	6.227	5.357	8.838
Fried. Rank	(1) 1.30	(2) 3.40	(3) 3.73	(4) 5.20	(5) 5.33	(6) 5.9	(7) 6.33	(8) 6.7333	(9) 7.07

Table 15 shows the IGD results with 15 objectives. The results obtained for MOEA/D-DE-ACA were the best for all problems except for DTLZ5 and DTLZ6, which is outdone only by IDMOPSO, as in 10 objectives. The Friedman ranking (obtained using a Friedman statistic of 57.99, distributed according to chi-square with 8 degrees of freedom, and a p-value computed by Iman and Davenport test of 3.407×10^{-13}) shows MOEA/D-DE-ACA as the best option, followed by MOEA/DD and IDMOPSO. The Holm post hoc test shows that MOEA/D-DE-ACA results dominate ANSGA-III, NSGA-III, MOEA/D-PBI, EAG-MOEA/D, IBEA, and SMS-EMOA algorithms with a 95% significance level. MOEA/DD and IDMOPSO dominate MOEA/D-PBI with the same significance level.

Results for 10 and 15 objectives in DTLZ and WFG problems show MOEA/D-DE-ACA as the best option using a population size of 277 and 132, respectively. The results on WFG problems are remarkable. Good results of MOEA/DD could be improved using ACAs for weight initialization instead of the Das and Dennis method [77]; this represents future work for our research group.

Table 15. IGD results for all algorithms on DTLZ and WFG problems with 15 objectives.

Problem	MOEA/D-DE-ACA	MOEA/DD	IDMOPSO	NSGA-III	ANSGA-III	EAG-MOEA/D	IBEA	SMS-EMOA	MOEA/D-PBI
DTLZ1	(1) 0.105	0.177	0.138	0.214	0.214	0.275	0.349	2.516	0.176
DTLZ2	(1) 0.178	0.621	0.604	0.759	0.750	0.940	0.615	0.930	0.622
DTLZ4	(1) 0.174	0.620	0.641	0.671	0.713	0.943	0.622	0.609	0.678
DTLZ5	(2) 0.099	0.161	(1) 0.027	0.483	0.449	0.113	0.276	0.193	0.096
DTLZ6	(2) 0.096	0.163	(1) 0.022	6.120	6.103	0.115	0.356	1.150	0.096
DTLZ7	(1) 1.139	3.385	2.063	6.167	5.980	2.344	5.016	11.140	2.720
WFG1	(1) 0.052	1.851	1.452	2.378	2.575	2.645	2.528	3.174	3.283
WFG2	(1) 0.101	16.348	13.507	13.550	13.407	3.349	26.045	19.176	27.325
WFG3	(1) 0.154	0.986	6.973	6.461	6.485	2.368	7.156	1.590	9.038
WFG4	(1) 0.206	9.269	10.412	9.418	9.443	9.313	13.759	18.744	15.158
WFG5	(1) 0.112	9.177	14.837	9.280	9.361	9.523	12.697	18.564	14.881
WFG6	(1) 0.272	9.138	10.421	11.299	11.116	14.374	13.034	15.941	15.849
WFG7	(1) 0.213	8.980	8.813	9.383	9.374	14.382	13.605	16.921	16.078
WFG8	(1) 0.390	8.796	8.715	10.581	10.709	14.721	11.341	16.174	14.421
WFG9	(1) 0.246	8.490	16.623	9.312	9.360	13.346	11.574	18.474	15.222
Fried. Rank	(1) 1.27	(2) 3.40	(3) 3.60	(4) 5.47	(5) 5.60	(6) 5.67	(7) 6.07	(9) 7.53	(8) 6.40

5.7. Comparison with Other State-of-the-Art Algorithms over Constrained Problems

The performance of the proposed algorithm was compared with the results of six state-of-the-art MOEAs for solving constrained many-objective optimization problems with 10 and 15 objectives [78]. The algorithms compared were: C-MOEA/DD [76], C-NSGA-III [17], C-RVEA [79], I-DBEA [80], C-TAEA [81], and C-AnEA [78]. To manage constraints, C-NSGA-III and I-DBEA adopted the feasibility-driven strategy. Conversely, C-MOEA/DD, C-TAEA, C-RVEA, and C-AnEA utilized infeasibility information. MOEA/D-DE-ACA also adopted the feasibility-driven approach, as Jain and Deb describe in [17].

Problems used for evaluation and comparison were the six available problems in the C-DTLZ test suite [17]. C-DTLZ is based on DTLZ but includes three types of constraints in the objective space, namely: (1) where the original PF is still optimal, but there is an infeasible barrier in approaching the PF; (2) where only the region located inside each of the M+1 hyperspheres with radius r is feasible; and (3) where the PF is composed of several constraint surfaces. The reference points for these problems were 275 and 135 for 10 and 15 objectives, respectively. The population size for the six compared algorithms was 276 and 136 for 10 and 15 objectives. As in the previous experiment, the population size for MOEA/D-DE-ACA was 277 and 132 for 10 and 15 objectives (see Table 13).

All algorithms were terminated after a prespecified number of fitness function evaluations (these values and other specific parameters for each algorithm are the same used in [78]). For C1-DTLZ1, each algorithm stops after 276,000 and 204,000 fitness evaluations (FEs) for 10 and 15 objectives, respectively. For C1-DTLZ3, each algorithm stops after 966,000 and 680,000 FEs for 10 and 15 objectives. For C2-DTLZ2, each algorithm stops after 207,000 and 136,000 FEs for 10 and 15 objectives. And for C2-DTLZ2*, C3-DTLZ1, and C3-DTLZ4, each algorithm stops after 828,000 and 544,000 FEs for 10 and 15 objectives.

Table 16 shows the IGD results for all algorithms on C-DTLZ problems with 10 and 15 objectives. The results for 10 objectives show that MOEA/D-DE-ACA was the best for most (five out of six) problems. The eighth line of this table also indicates the Friedman ranking obtained using a Friedman statistic (distributed according to chi-square with 6 degrees of freedom) of 26.78 and a p-value computed by the Iman and Davenport test of 1.042×10^{-7}. Friedman test results show MOEA/D-DE-ACA as the best option, followed by C-AnEA and C-RVEA. The Holm post hoc test only shows that MOEA/D-DE-ACA and C-AnEA results dominate I-DBEA with a 95% significance level. Still, using a 90% significance level, the Holm post hoc test shows that MOEA/D-DE-ACA also dominates C-NSGA-III and C-TAEA.

Table 16. IGD results for all algorithms on C-DTLZ problems with 10 and 15 objectives. C2-DTLZ2 * denotes C2-convex-DTLZ2.

Problem	Obj (M)	MOEA/D-DE-ACA	C-AnEA	C-RVEA	C-MOEA/DD	C-NSGA-III	C-TAEA	I-DBEA
C1-DTLZ1	10	(1) 0.075	0.114	0.116	0.117	0.118	0.130	0.498
C1-DTLZ3	10	(1) 0.211	0.420	14.139	13.277	14.221	0.581	14.848
C2-DTLZ2	10	(2) 0.203	0.265	0.268	0.266	0.299	(1) 0.181	1.272
C2-DTLZ2 *	10	(1) 0.033	0.132	0.135	0.145	0.107	0.304	0.520
C3-DTLZ1	10	(1) 0.071	0.230	0.235	0.235	0.235	0.272	0.659
C3-DTLZ4	10	(1) 0.107	0.562	0.568	0.569	0.578	0.590	0.746
Friedman Rank	10	(1) 1.17	(2) 2.33	(3) 3.83	(4) 4.33	(5) 4.67	(6) 4.67	(7) 7.00
C1-DTLZ1	15	(1) 0.125	0.181	0.188	0.187	0.200	0.198	0.570
C1-DTLZ3	15	(1) 0.165	0.594	14.206	14.211	18.786	0.862	14.914
C2-DTLZ2	15	(4) 0.430	(2) 0.250	(3) 0.355	0.576	0.651	(1) 0.192	1.415
C2-DTLZ2 *	15	(1) 0.087	0.291	0.162	0.174	0.187	0.336	0.790
C3-DTLZ1	15	(1) 0.148	0.366	0.381	0.383	0.461	0.503	1.237
C3-DTLZ4	15	(1) 0.150	0.808	0.771	0.773	1.302	0.768	1.354
Friedman Rank	15	(1) 1.50	(2) 3.00	(3) 3.17	(5) 4.00	(6) 5.67	(4) 3.83	(7) 6.83

Table 16 also shows the results for 15 objectives, like those for 10. MOEA/D-DE-ACA was the best for most (five out of six) problems. This table also shows, on the last line, the Friedman ranking for 15 objectives obtained using a Friedman statistic (distributed according to chi-square with 6 degrees of freedom) of 24.14 and a p-value computed by the Iman and Davenport test of 3.787×10^{-6}. Friedman test results reveal MOEA/D-DE-ACA as the best option, C-AnEA in second place, and C-RVEA in third place, equal to 10 objectives. The Holm post hoc test only shows that MOEA/D-DE-ACA and C-AnEA dominate I-DBEA, and MOEA/D-DE-ACA dominates C-NSGA-III with 95% significance. Still, using a 90% significance level, the Holm post hoc test shows that C-RVEA results dominate those of I-DBEA.

Of the three best algorithms (MOEA/D-DE-ACA, C-AnEA, and C-RVEA) for solving constrained problems in the C-DTLZ test suite with 10 and 15 objectives, only MOEA/D-DE-ACA adopts the feasibility-driven strategy, the others utilize infeasibility information.

6. Conclusions and Future Work

This work proposes the definition of weight vectors in MOEA/D-DE based on augmented covering arrays (ACAs) in a new version of the algorithm called MOEA/D-DE-ACA. This new version was compared with the original version of MOEA/D-DE and NSGA-III in seven DTLZ problems and nine WFG problems of 10 to 100 objectives using small (t = 2, v = 9), medium (t = 2, v = 17), and large (t = 3, v = 9) populations.

About the hypothesis initially raised in this research, it can be concluded that with a low value of strength (t = 2) and a low–medium value of alphabet (v = 9 or v = 17), meaning small populations with 136 to 288 solutions and medium ones with 416 to 838 solutions, the MOEA/D-DE-ACA algorithm obtains better IGD results than MOEA/D-DE between 30 and 100 objectives regardless of the characteristics of the problems and the shapes of their Pareto fronts; this implies that initialization of the weight vectors is more appropriate based on ACAs and that the execution time is significantly reduced to 40.7% and 8.9% of the time executed by MOEA/D-DE. When using a strength t = 3 (large population with 729 to 1457 solutions), the results are similar between MOEA/D-DE-ACA and MOEA/D-DE, i.e., there is no statistically significant difference between MOEA/D-DE-ACA and MOEA/D-DE, except in 90 objectives where MOEA/D-DE-ACA performs best, but the execution time with these populations is much reduced to 2.7% of the execution time of MOEA/D-DE.

In experiments with small and medium populations, two algorithms, MOEA/D-DE-ACA and MOEA/D-DE, outperform NSGA-III, but when there are 10 or 20 objectives and medium populations, results are better with NSGA-III. With a large population, NSGA-III obtains better results than the other two algorithms for 10 to 70 objectives, but those results are not statistically superior to those obtained by MOEA/D-DE-ACA and MOEA/D-DE. MOEA/D-DE-ACA, in all cases, executes faster than NSGA-III, using in small populations only 4.8% of the time used by NSGA-III, in medium populations only 7%, and in large populations, only 6.2%.

In future work, the research group expects to directly compare the proposed initialization scheme with other initialization schemes in other decomposition-based algorithms like MOEA/DD, MaOEA/D-2ADV, or MOEA/D-SOM. In addition, it is hoped to use the initialization scheme proposed in conjunction with a recent version of MOEA/D which adapts the direction of the weight vectors and improves the selection operators, define the key characteristics of the ACAs to improve the results in specific kinds of MaOPs, and, finally, design ACAs that include more border weight vectors and evaluate their impact in many-objective optimization problems.

Author Contributions: Methodology, C.C., C.O., J.T.-J., H.O. and M.M.; Software, C.C., C.O. and J.T.-J.; Supervision, C.C.; Writing—original draft, C.C. and C.O.; Writing—review and editing, C.C., C.O., J.T.-J., H.O. and M.M. All authors have read and agreed to the published version of the manuscript.

Funding: The Universidad del Cauca (Colombia) and the Fundación Universitaria de Popayán (Colombia) supported the work in this paper. The third author is grateful to CONAHCYT for the grant CF-2023-I-1014 "Construcción de un repositorio de Cluster Covering Arrays usando una metodología de tres etapas" that partially funded the research reported in this paper.

Data Availability Statement: The data presented in this study are available on request from the corresponding author.

Acknowledgments: The authors sincerely thank the Universidad del Cauca, the Fundación Universitaria de Popayán, and the CINVESTAV Tamaulipas (Mexico) for their invaluable support throughout this research.

Conflicts of Interest: The authors declare no conflict of interest.

References

1. Chand, S.; Wagner, M. Evolutionary Many-Objective Optimization: A Quick-Start Guide. *Surv. Oper. Res. Manag. Sci.* **2015**, *20*, 35–42. [CrossRef]
2. Jiang, S.; Yang, S. An Improved Multiobjective Optimization Evolutionary Algorithm Based on Decomposition for Complex Pareto Fronts. *IEEE Trans. Cybern.* **2016**, *46*, 421–437. [CrossRef] [PubMed]
3. Deb, K.; Pratap, A.; Agarwal, S.; Meyarivan, T.; Pratab, S.; Agarwal, S.; Meyarivan, T.; Pratap, A.; Agarwal, S.; Meyarivan, T. A Fast and Elitist Multiobjective Genetic Algorithm: NSGA-II. *IEEE Trans. Evol. Comput.* **2002**, *6*, 182–197. [CrossRef]
4. Zitzler, E.; Laumanns, M.; Thiele, L. *SPEA2: Improving the Strength Pareto Evolutionary Algorithm*; Technical Report; Gloriastrasse: Zurich, Switzerland, 2001.
5. Zitzler, E.; Künzli, S. Indicator-Based Selection in Multiobjective Search. *Lect. Notes Comput. Sci.* **2004**, *3242*, 832–842. [CrossRef] [PubMed]
6. Beume, N.; Naujoks, B.; Emmerich, M. SMS-EMOA: Multiobjective Selection Based on Dominated Hypervolume. *Eur. J. Oper. Res.* **2007**, *181*, 1653–1669. [CrossRef]
7. Hughes, E.J. Multiple Single Objective Pareto Sampling. In Proceedings of the 2003 Congress on Evolutionary Computation (CEC 2003), Canberra, Australia, 8–12 December 2003; Volume 4, pp. 2678–2684.
8. Zhang, Q.; Li, H. MOEA/D: A Multiobjective Evolutionary Algorithm Based on Decomposition. *IEEE Trans. Evol. Comput.* **2007**, *11*, 712–731. [CrossRef]
9. Hui, Y.; Xin, Y.; Min, S. Particle Swarm Optimization Route Planner Algorithm for Air Vehicle. In Proceedings of the ICCIA 2010–2010 International Conference on Computer and Information Application, Tianjin, China, 3–5 December 2010; pp. 319–322.
10. Li, Y.; Bai, X.; Wu, Z. The Determination of Optimal Design Plan of the Sha-He Aqueduct. In Proceedings of the ICIME 2010–2010 2nd IEEE International Conference on Information Management and Engineering, Chengdu, China, 16–18 April 2010; Volume 6, pp. 319–323.

11. Ruano, E.; Cobos, C.; Torres-Jimenez, J. Transit Network Frequencies-Setting Problem Solved Using a New Multi-Objective Global-Best Harmony Search Algorithm and Discrete Event Simulation. *Lect. Notes Comput. Sci.* **2017**, *10062*, 341–352. [CrossRef] [PubMed]
12. Li, B.; Li, J.; Tang, K.; Yao, X. Many-Objective Evolutionary Algorithms: A Survey. *ACM Comput. Surv.* **2015**, *48*, 1–35. [CrossRef]
13. Li, H.; Zhang, Q. Multiobjective Optimization Problems With Complicated Pareto Sets, MOEA/D and NSGA-II. *IEEE Trans. Evol. Comput.* **2009**, *13*, 284–302. [CrossRef]
14. Chen, Z.; Zhou, Y.; Zhao, X.; Xiang, Y.; Wang, J. A Historical Solutions Based Evolution Operator for Decomposition-Based Many-Objective Optimization. *Swarm Evol. Comput.* **2018**, *41*, 167–189. [CrossRef]
15. Zheng, W.; Tan, Y.; Fang, X.; Li, S. An Improved MOEA/D with Optimal DE Schemes for Many-Objective Optimization Problems. *Algorithms* **2017**, *10*, 86. [CrossRef]
16. Li, B.; Li, J.; Tang, K.; Yao, X. An Improved Two Archive Algorithm for Many-Objective Optimization. In Proceedings of the 2014 IEEE Congress on Evolutionary Computation (CEC'2014), Beijing, China, 6–11 July 2014; pp. 2869–2876.
17. Jain, H.; Deb, K. An Evolutionary Many-Objective Optimization Algorithm Using Reference-Point Based Nondominated Sorting Approach, Part II: Handling Constraints and Extending to an Adaptive Approach. *IEEE Trans. Evol. Comput.* **2014**, *18*, 602–622. [CrossRef]
18. Bhagavatula, S.S.; Sanjeevi, S.G.; Kumar, D.; Yadav, C.K. Multi-Objective Indicator Based Evolutionary Algorithm for Portfolio Optimization. In Proceedings of the Souvenir of the 2014 IEEE International Advance Computing Conference, IACC 2014, Gurgaon, India, 21–22 February 2014; pp. 1206–1210.
19. Chugh, T.; Sindhya, K.; Hakanen, J.; Miettinen, K. An Interactive Simple Indicator-Based Evolutionary Algorithm (I-SIBEA) for Multiobjective Optimization Problems. *Lect. Notes Comput. Sci.* **2015**, *9078*, 277–291. [CrossRef] [PubMed]
20. Luo, J.; Liu, Q.; Yang, Y.; Li, X.; Chen, M.; Cao, W. An Artificial Bee Colony Algorithm for Multi-Objective Optimisation. *Appl. Soft Comput.* **2017**, *50*, 235–251. [CrossRef]
21. Rostami, S.; Neri, F. A Fast Hypervolume Driven Selection Mechanism for Many-Objective Optimisation Problems. *Swarm Evol. Comput.* **2017**, *34*, 50–67. [CrossRef]
22. Xie, H.; Li, J.; Xue, H. A Survey of Dimensionality Reduction Techniques Based on Random Projection. *arXiv* **2017**, arXiv:1706.04371.
23. Aguirre, H.; Tanaka, K. Adaptive ε-Ranking on Mnk-Landscapes. In Proceedings of the 2009 IEEE Symposium on Computational Intelligence in Multi-Criteria Decision-Making, MCDM, Nashville, TN, USA, 30 March–2 April 2009; pp. 104–111.
24. Zou, J.; Ji, C.; Yang, S.; Zhang, Y.; Zheng, J.; Li, K. A Knee-Point-Based Evolutionary Algorithm Using Weighted Subpopulation for Many-Objective Optimization. *Swarm Evol. Comput.* **2019**, *47*, 33–43. [CrossRef]
25. Ishibuchi, H.; Akedo, N.; Nojima, Y. Relation between Neighborhood Size and MOEA/D Performance on Many-Objective Problems Content of This Presentation. *Evol. Multi-Criterion Optim.* **2013**, *7811*, 459–474.
26. Ordóñez-Quintero, C.-C. *Definición de Pesos En MOEA/D Usando Arreglos de Cubrimiento Para Resolver Problemas de Optimización de Muchos Objetivos*; Universidad del Cauca: Popayán, Colombia, 2019.
27. Torres-Jimenez, J.; Ramirez-Acuna, D.O.; Acevedo-Juárez, B.; Avila-George, H. New Upper Bounds for Sequence Covering Arrays Using a 3-Stage Approach. *Expert Syst. Appl.* **2022**, *207*, 118022. [CrossRef]
28. Torres-jimenez, J.; Rodriguez-cristerna, A. A Metaheuristic Post-Optimization of the NIST Repository of Covering Arrays. *CAAI Trans. Intell. Technol.* **2017**, *2*, 6–13. [CrossRef]
29. Xu, Q.; Xu, Z.; Ma, T. A Survey of Multiobjective Evolutionary Algorithms Based on Decomposition: Variants, Challenges and Future Directions. *IEEE Access* **2020**, *8*, 41588–41614. [CrossRef]
30. Scheffé, H. Experiments with Mixtures. *J. R. Stat. Soc. Ser. B* **1958**, *20*, 344–360. [CrossRef]
31. Scheffe, H. The Simplex-Centroid Design for Experiments with Mixtures. *J. R. Stat. Soc. Ser. B* **1963**, *25*, 235–263. [CrossRef]
32. Cornell, J.A. Some Comments on Designs for Cox's Mixture Polynomial. *Technometrics* **1975**, *17*, 25–35. [CrossRef]
33. Prescott, P. Nearly Uniform Designs for Mixture Experiments. *Commun. Stat. Theory Methods* **2008**, *37*, 2095–2115. [CrossRef]
34. Borkowski, J.J.; Piepel, G.F. Uniform Designs for Highly Constrained Mixture Experiments. *J. Qual. Technol.* **2009**, *41*, 35–47. [CrossRef]
35. Trivedi, A.; Srinivasan, D.; Sanyal, K.; Ghosh, A. A Survey of Multiobjective Evolutionary Algorithms Based on Decomposition. *IEEE Trans. Evol. Comput.* **2017**, *21*, 440–462. [CrossRef]
36. Tan, Y.Y.; Jiao, Y.C.; Li, H.; Wang, X.K. MOEA/D + Uniform Design: A New Version of MOEA/D for Optimization Problems with Many Objectives. *Comput. Oper. Res.* **2013**, *40*, 1648–1660. [CrossRef]
37. Guo, X. A Survey of Decomposition Based Evolutionary Algorithms for Many-Objective Optimization Problems. *IEEE Access* **2022**, *10*, 72825–72838. [CrossRef]
38. Ma, X.; Qi, Y.; Li, L.; Liu, F.; Jiao, L.; Wu, J. MOEA/D with Uniform Decomposition Measurement for Many-Objective Problems. *Soft Comput.* **2014**, *18*, 2541–2564. [CrossRef]
39. Qi, Y.; Ma, X.; Liu, F.; Jiao, L.; Sun, J.; Wu, J. MOEA/D with Adaptive Weight Adjustment. *Evol. Comput.* **2014**, *22*, 231–264. [CrossRef] [PubMed]
40. Zhang, Y.; Yang, R.; Zuo, J.; Jing, X. Enhancing MOEA/D with Uniform Population Initialization, Weight Vector Design and Adjustment Using Uniform Design. *J. Syst. Eng. Electron.* **2015**, *26*, 1010–1022. [CrossRef]

41. Trivedi, A.; Srinivasan, D.; Pal, K.; Reindl, T. A MOEA/D with Non-Uniform Weight Vector Distribution Strategy for Solving the Unit Commitment Problem in Uncertain Environment. In *Artificial Life and Computational Intelligence, Proceedings of the Australasian Conference on Artificial Life and Computational Intelligence, Geelong, Australia, 31 January–2 February 2017*; Wagner, M., Li, X., Hendtlass, T., Eds.; Lecture Notes in Computer Science; Springer International Publishing: Cham, Switzerland, 2017; Volume 10142, pp. 378–390.
42. Meneghini, I.R.; Guimarães, F.G. Evolutionary Method for Weight Vector Generation in Multi-Objective Evolutionary Algorithms Based on Decomposition and Aggregation. In Proceedings of the 2017 IEEE Congress on Evolutionary Computation (CEC), Donostia, Spain, 5–8 June 2017; pp. 1900–1907.
43. Tang, B. Orthogonal Array-Based Latin Hypercubes. *J. Am. Stat. Assoc.* **1993**, *88*, 1392–1397. [CrossRef]
44. Cai, X.; Mei, Z.; Fan, Z. A Decomposition-Based Many-Objective Evolutionary Algorithm with Two Types of Adjustments for Direction Vectors. *IEEE Trans. Cybern.* **2018**, *48*, 2335–2348. [CrossRef] [PubMed]
45. Gu, F.; Cheung, Y.M. Self-Organizing Map-Based Weight Design for Decomposition-Based Many-Objective Evolutionary Algorithm. *IEEE Trans. Evol. Comput.* **2018**, *22*, 211–225. [CrossRef]
46. Liu, H.L.; Gu, F.; Zhang, Q. Decomposition of a Multiobjective Optimization Problem into a Number of Simple Multiobjective Subproblems. *IEEE Trans. Evol. Comput.* **2014**, *18*, 450–455. [CrossRef]
47. Dai, C.; Lei, X. A Decomposition-Based Multiobjective Evolutionary Algorithm with Adaptive Weight Adjustment. *Complexity* **2018**, *2018*, 1753071. [CrossRef]
48. Qiao, J.; Zhou, H.; Yang, C.; Yang, S. A Decomposition-Based Multiobjective Evolutionary Algorithm with Angle-Based Adaptive Penalty. *Appl. Soft Comput.* **2019**, *74*, 190–205. [CrossRef]
49. Xu, H.; Zeng, W.; Zhang, D.; Zeng, X. MOEA/HD: A Multiobjective Evolutionary Algorithm Based on Hierarchical Decomposition. *IEEE Trans. Cybern.* **2019**, *49*, 517–526. [CrossRef] [PubMed]
50. Torres-Jimenez, J.; Izquierdo-Marquez, I.; Avila-George, H. Methods to Construct Uniform Covering Arrays. *IEEE Access* **2019**, *7*, 42774–42797. [CrossRef]
51. Sato, H. Inverted PBI in MOEA/D and Its Impact on the Search Performance on Multi and Many-Objective Optimization. In Proceedings of the GECCO 2014 Genetic and Evolutionary Computation Conference, ACM, New York, NY, USA, 12–16 July 2014; pp. 645–652.
52. Xu, M.; Tian, Z. A Flexible Image Cipher Based on Orthogonal Arrays. *Inf. Sci.* **2021**, *551*, 39–53. [CrossRef]
53. Hedayat, A.S.; Sloane, N.J.A.; Stufken, J. *Orthogonal Arrays: Theory and Applications*, 1st ed.; Springer: New York, NY, USA, 1999; ISBN 978-0-387-98766-8.
54. Bush, K.A. Orthogonal Arrays of Index Unity. *Ann. Math. Stat.* **1952**, *23*, 426–434. [CrossRef]
55. Muazu, A.A.; Hashim, A.S.; Sarlan, A.; Abdullahi, M. SCIPOG: Seeding and Constraint Support in IPOG Strategy for Combinatorial t-Way Testing to Generate Optimum Test Cases. *J. King Saud Univ. Comput. Inf. Sci.* **2023**, *35*, 185–201. [CrossRef]
56. Ordoñez, H.; Torres-jimenez, J.; Ordoñez, A.; Cobos, C. Clustering Business Process Models Based on Multimodal Search and Covering Arrays. *Lect. Notes Comput. Sci.* **2017**, *10062*, 317–328. [CrossRef] [PubMed]
57. Ruano-Daza, E.; Cobos, C.; Torres-Jimenez, J.; Mendoza, M.; Paz, A. A Multiobjective Bilevel Approach Based on Global-Best Harmony Search for Defining Optimal Routes and Frequencies for Bus Rapid Transit Systems. *Appl. Soft Comput.* **2018**, *67*, 567–583. [CrossRef]
58. Ordoñez, H.; Torres-Jimenez, J.; Cobos, C.; Ordoñez, A.; Herrera-Viedma, E.; Maldonado-Martinez, G. A Business Process Clustering Algorithm Using Incremental Covering Arrays to Explore Search Space and Balanced Bayesian Information Criterion to Evaluate Quality of Solutions. *PLoS ONE* **2019**, *14*, e0217686. [CrossRef]
59. Vivas, S.; Cobos, C.; Mendoza, M. Covering Arrays to Support the Process of Feature Selection in the Random Forest Classifier. *Lect. Notes Comput. Sci.* **2019**, *11331*, 64–76. [CrossRef] [PubMed]
60. Dorado, H.; Cobos, C.; Torres-Jimenez, J.; Burra, D.D.; Mendoza, M.; Jimenez, D. Wrapper for Building Classification Models Using Covering Arrays. *IEEE Access* **2019**, *7*, 148297–148312. [CrossRef]
61. Johnson, D.S. Approximation Algorithms for Combinatorial Problems. *J. Comput. Syst. Sci.* **1974**, *9*, 256–278. [CrossRef]
62. Lovász, L. On the Ratio of Optimal Integral and Fractional Covers. *Discret. Math.* **1975**, *13*, 383–390. [CrossRef]
63. Stein, S.K. Two Combinatorial Covering Theorems. *J. Comb. Theory Ser. A* **1974**, *16*, 391–397. [CrossRef]
64. Huband, S.; Hingston, P.; Barone, L.; While, L. A Review of Multiobjective Test Problems and a Scalable Test Problem Toolkit. *IEEE Trans. Evol. Comput.* **2006**, *10*, 477–506. [CrossRef]
65. Zhou, C.; Dai, G.; Zhang, C.; Li, X.; Ma, K. Entropy Based Evolutionary Algorithm with Adaptive Reference Points for Many-Objective Optimization Problems. *Inf. Sci.* **2018**, *465*, 232–247. [CrossRef]
66. Khan, B.; Hanoun, S.; Johnstone, M.; Lim, C.P.; Creighton, D.; Nahavandi, S. A Scalarization-Based Dominance Evolutionary Algorithm for Many-Objective Optimization. *Inf. Sci.* **2019**, *474*, 236–252. [CrossRef]
67. Zou, J.; Zhang, Y.; Yang, S.; Liu, Y.; Zheng, J. Adaptive Neighborhood Selection for Many-Objective Optimization Problems. *Appl. Soft Comput.* **2018**, *64*, 186–198. [CrossRef]
68. Lin, Q.; Zhu, Q.; Huang, P.; Chen, J.; Ming, Z.; Yu, J. A Novel Hybrid Multi-Objective Immune Algorithm with Adaptive Differential Evolution. *Comput. Oper. Res.* **2015**, *62*, 95–111. [CrossRef]
69. Sengupta, R.; Saha, S. Reference Point Based Archived Many Objective Simulated Annealing. *Inf. Sci.* **2018**, *467*, 725–749. [CrossRef]

70. Zitzler, E.; Thiele, L.; Laumanns, M.; Fonseca, C.M.; Da Fonseca, V.G. Performance Assessment of Multiobjective Optimizers: An Analysis and Review. *IEEE Trans. Evol. Comput.* **2003**, *7*, 117–132. [CrossRef]
71. Halim, A.H.; Ismail, I.; Das, S. Performance Assessment of the Metaheuristic Optimization Algorithms: An Exhaustive Review. *Artif. Intell. Rev.* **2020**, *54*, 2323–2409. [CrossRef]
72. Coello, C.A.C.; Lamont, G.B.; Van Veldhuizen, D.A. *Evolutionary Algorithms for Solving Multi-Objective Problems (Genetic and Evolutionary Computation)*; Springer: Berlin/Heidelberg, Germany, 2006; ISBN 0387332545.
73. Luo, J.; Huang, X.; Yang, Y.; Li, X.; Wang, Z.; Feng, J. A Many-Objective Particle Swarm Optimizer Based on Indicator and Direction Vectors for Many-Objective Optimization. *Inf. Sci.* **2020**, *514*, 166–202. [CrossRef]
74. Cheng, Q.; Du, B.; Zhang, L.; Liu, R. ANSGA-III: A Multiobjective Endmember Extraction Algorithm for Hyperspectral Images. *IEEE J. Sel. Top. Appl. Earth Obs. Remote Sens.* **2019**, *12*, 700–721. [CrossRef]
75. Cai, X.; Li, Y.; Fan, Z.; Zhang, Q. An External Archive Guided Multiobjective Evolutionary Algorithm Based on Decomposition for Combinatorial Optimization. *IEEE Trans. Evol. Comput.* **2015**, *19*, 508–523. [CrossRef]
76. Li, K.; Deb, K.; Zhang, Q.; Kwong, S. An Evolutionary Many-Objective Optimization Algorithm Based on Dominance and Decomposition. *IEEE Trans. Evol. Comput.* **2015**, *19*, 694–716. [CrossRef]
77. Das, I.; Dennis, J.E. Normal-Boundary Intersection: A New Method for Generating the Pareto Surface in Nonlinear Multicriteria Optimization Problems. *SIAM J. Optim.* **1998**, *8*, 631–657. [CrossRef]
78. Wang, C.; Xu, R. An Angle Based Evolutionary Algorithm with Infeasibility Information for Constrained Many-Objective Optimization. *Appl. Soft Comput.* **2020**, *86*, 105911. [CrossRef]
79. Cheng, R.; Jin, Y.; Olhofer, M.; Sendhoff, B. A Reference Vector Guided Evolutionary Algorithm for Many-Objective Optimization. *IEEE Trans. Evol. Comput.* **2016**, *20*, 773–791. [CrossRef]
80. Asafuddoula, M.; Ray, T.; Sarker, R. A Decomposition-Based Evolutionary Algorithm for Many Objective Optimization. *IEEE Trans. Evol. Comput.* **2015**, *19*, 445–460. [CrossRef]
81. Li, K.; Chen, R.; Fu, G.; Yao, X. Two-Archive Evolutionary Algorithm for Constrained Multiobjective Optimization. *IEEE Trans. Evol. Comput.* **2019**, *23*, 303–315. [CrossRef]

Disclaimer/Publisher's Note: The statements, opinions and data contained in all publications are solely those of the individual author(s) and contributor(s) and not of MDPI and/or the editor(s). MDPI and/or the editor(s) disclaim responsibility for any injury to people or property resulting from any ideas, methods, instructions or products referred to in the content.

Article

A New Hybrid Descent Algorithm for Large-Scale Nonconvex Optimization and Application to Some Image Restoration Problems

Shuai Wang [1], Xiaoliang Wang [2,*], Yuzhu Tian [3] and Liping Pang [1]

[1] School of Mathematical Sciences, Dalian University of Technology, Dalian 116024, China; gacktshuaishuai@163.com (S.W.); lppang@dlut.edu.cn (L.P.)
[2] Department of Mathematics and Science, School of Science, Zhejiang Sci-Tech University, Hangzhou 310018, China
[3] School of Mathematics, Liaoning Normal University, Dalian 116026, China; tianyuzhu@lnnu.edu.cn
* Correspondence: xliangwang@126.com

Abstract: Conjugate gradient methods are widely used and attractive for large-scale unconstrained smooth optimization problems, with simple computation, low memory requirements, and interesting theoretical information on the features of curvature. Based on the strongly convergent property of the Dai–Yuan method and attractive numerical performance of the Hestenes–Stiefel method, a new hybrid descent conjugate gradient method is proposed in this paper. The proposed method satisfies the sufficient descent property independent of the accuracy of the line search strategies. Under the standard conditions, the trust region property and the global convergence are established, respectively. Numerical results of 61 problems with 9 large-scale dimensions and 46 ill-conditioned matrix problems reveal that the proposed method is more effective, robust, and reliable than the other methods. Additionally, the hybrid method also demonstrates reliable results for some image restoration problems.

Keywords: hybrid conjugate gradient method; acceleration scheme; sufficient descent property; global convergence; ill-conditioned matrix; image restoration

MSC: 65K05; 90C26

Citation: Wang, S.; Wang, X.; Tian, Y.; Pang, L. A New Hybrid Descent Algorithm for Large-Scale Nonconvex Optimization and Application to Some Image Restoration Problems. *Mathematics* **2024**, *12*, 3088. https://doi.org/10.3390/math12193088

Academic Editors: Moudafi Abdellatif and Andrea Scozzari

Received: 18 August 2024
Revised: 25 September 2024
Accepted: 27 September 2024
Published: 2 October 2024

Copyright: © 2024 by the authors. Licensee MDPI, Basel, Switzerland. This article is an open access article distributed under the terms and conditions of the Creative Commons Attribution (CC BY) license (https://creativecommons.org/licenses/by/4.0/).

1. Introduction

In this paper, we consider the following unconstrained problem:

$$\min_{x \in \mathbb{R}^n} f(x), \tag{1}$$

where $f: \mathbb{R}^n \to \mathbb{R}$ is continuously differentiable, bound below, and its gradient is available. There are many effective methods for problem (1), such as Newton-type methods, quasi-Newton-type methods, spectral gradient methods, and conjugate gradient (CG for abbreviation) methods [1–11], etc. Meanwhile, there are also various free gradient optimization tools such as Nelder–Mead, generalized simulated annealing, and genetic algorithm [12–14], etc., for problem (1). In this part, we focus on CG methods and propose a new hybrid CG method for a large-scale problem (1). Actually, CG methods are one of the most effective methods for unconstrained problems, especially for large-scale cases, due to their low storage and globally convergent properties [3], in which the iterative point is usually generated by

$$x_{k+1} = x_k + \alpha_k d_k, \quad k = 0, 1, \ldots, \tag{2}$$

where x_k is the current iteration; the scalar $\alpha_k > 0$ is the step length, determined by some line search strategy; and d_k is the search direction, defined by

$$d_k = \begin{cases} -g_k, & \text{if } k = 0, \\ -g_k + \beta_k d_{k-1}, & \text{if } k \geq 1, \end{cases} \qquad (3)$$

where $g_k := g(x_k) = \nabla f(x_k)$ and β_k is called the conjugate parameter. A number of CG methods have been proposed by various modifications of the direction d_k and the parameter β_k; see [4–11,15–20], etc. Some CG methods have strong convergence properties, but their numerical performances may not be good in practice due to the jamming phenomenon [4]. These methods include Fletcher–Reeves (FR) [5], Dai–Yuan (DY) [6], and Fletcher (CD) [7], with the following conjugate parameters:

$$\beta_{k+1}^{FR} = \frac{\|g_{k+1}\|^2}{\|g_k\|^2}, \quad \beta_{k+1}^{DY} = \frac{\|g_{k+1}\|^2}{y_k^T d_k}, \quad \beta_{k+1}^{CD} = -\frac{\|g_{k+1}\|^2}{g_k^T d_k},$$

where $g_{k+1} = \nabla f(x_{k+1})$, $y_k = g_{k+1} - g_k$, and $\|\cdot\|$ stands for the Euclidean norm. On the other hand, some other CG methods may perform well in practice, but their convergence may be not guaranteed, especially for nonconvex functions. These methods include Hestenes–Stiefel (HS) [8], Polak–Ribière–Polyak (PRP) [9,10], and Liu–Storey (LS) [11], with the following conjugate parameters:

$$\beta_{k+1}^{HS} = \frac{g_{k+1}^T y_k}{y_k^T d_k}, \quad \beta_{k+1}^{PRP} = \frac{g_{k+1}^T y_k}{\|g_k\|^2}, \quad \beta_{k+1}^{LS} = -\frac{g_{k+1}^T y_k}{g_k^T d_k}.$$

In fact, these methods possess an automatically approximate restart feature which can avoid the jamming phenomenon, that is, when the step s_k is small, the factor y_k tends to zero, resulting in the conjugate parameter β_{k+1} becoming small and the new direction d_{k+1} approximating to the steepest descent direction $-g_{k+1}$.

To attain good computational performance and maintain the attractive feature of strong global convergence, many scholars have paid special attention to hybridizing these CG methods. Specifically, the authors in [21] proposed a hybrid PRP-FR CG method (H1 method in [22]) and the corresponding conjugate parameter was defined as $\beta_{k+1}^{H1} = \max\{0, \min\{\beta_{k+1}^{FR}, \beta_{k+1}^{PRP}\}\}$. Moreover, based on the above hybrid conjugate parameter, a new form was proposed in [23], where the parameter was defined by $\beta_{k+1} = \max\{-\beta_{k+1}^{FR}, \min\{\beta_{k+1}^{FR}, \beta_{k+1}^{PRP}\}\}$, and the global convergence property was established for the general function without the convexity assumption. In [24], a hybrid of the HS method and DY method was proposed in which the conjugate parameter was defined by $\beta_{k+1}^{H2} = \max\{0, \min\{\beta_{k+1}^{HS}, \beta_{k+1}^{DY}\}\}$. The numerical results indicated that the above hybrid method was more effective than the PRP algorithm. In the above hybrid CG methods, the search direction was in the form of (3). Moreover, the authors in [25] proposed a new hybrid three-term method in which the conjugate parameter is β_{k+1}^{H2} and the direction is $d_{k+1} = -g_{k+1} + (1 - \lambda_{k+1})\beta_{k+1}^{H2}d_k + \lambda_{k+1}\theta_{k+1}g_k$, where λ_{k+1} is the convex parameter. The above hybrid method demonstrates attractive numerical performance. Furthermore, in [22], the authors proposed two new hybrid methods based on the above conjugate parameters with different search directions. Concretely, the directions have the following common form:

$$d_{k+1} = -\left(1 + \beta_{k+1}\frac{g_{k+1}^T d_k}{\|g_{k+1}\|^2}\right)g_{k+1} + \beta_{k+1}d_k, \qquad (4)$$

where $\beta_{k+1} = \beta_{k+1}^{H1}$ or $\beta_{k+1} = \beta_{k+1}^{H2}$. A remarkable feature of the above directions is that the sufficient descent property is automatically satisfied, independent of the accuracy of the line search strategy.

Motivated by the above discussions, in this paper, we propose a new hybrid descent CG method for large-scale nonconvex problems. The proposed hybrid method automatically enjoys the sufficient descent property independent of the accuracy of the line search technique. Furthermore, the global convergence for the general functions without convexity is established under the standard conditions. Numerical results of 549 large-scale problems and 46 ill-conditioned matrix problems indicate the proposed method is attractive and promising. Finally, we also apply the proposed method to some image restoration problems, which also verifies its reliability and effectiveness.

The rest of the paper is organized as follows. In Section 2, we propose a descent hybrid CG method which is based on the MHS method and DY method. Moreover, the sufficient descent property is satisfied independent of the accuracy of the line search techniques. Global convergence is established for the general function in Section 3. Numerical results are given in Section 4 to indicate the effectiveness and reliability of the proposed algorithm. Finally, some conclusions are presented.

2. Motivation, Algorithm, and Sufficient Descent Property

As mentioned in the above section, the HS method is generally regarded as one of the most effective CG methods, but its global convergence for general nonlinear functions is still erratic. Additionally, the HS method does not guarantee the descent property during the iterative process, that is, the condition $g_k^T d_k < 0$ may not be satisfied for $\forall\, k \geq 1$. Therefore, many researchers have been devoted to designing some descent HS conjugate gradient methods [4,24,26–30], etc. Specifically, to obtain an intuitively modified conjugate parameter, the authors in [26] approximated the direction d_{k+1}^{THS} by the two-term direction (3), where d_{k+1}^{THS} was defined by (4) with $\beta_{k+1} = \beta_{k+1}^{HS}$. Concretely, the least squares problem $\min_\beta \| -g_{k+1} + \beta_{k+1} d_k - d_{k+1}^{THS} \|^2$ was solved. After some algebraic manipulations, the unique solution was

$$\beta_{k+1}^{MHS} = \frac{g_{k+1}^T y_k}{y_k^T d_k}\left(1 - \frac{(g_{k+1}^T d_k)^2}{\|g_{k+1}\|^2 \|d_k\|^2}\right) = \beta_{k+1}^{HS} \vartheta_k, \quad (5)$$

where

$$\vartheta_k = 1 - \frac{(g_{k+1}^T d_k)^2}{\|g_{k+1}\|^2 \|d_k\|^2}. \quad (6)$$

The above parameter and its modifications have some nice theoretical properties [26] and the method with (5) and (3) performs well. Meanwhile, it is clear that if the exact line search is adopted (i.e., $g_{k+1}^T d_k = 0$), it holds that $\beta_{k+1}^{MHS} = \beta_{k+1}^{HS} = \beta_{k+1}^{PRP}$.

To attain attractive computational performance and good theoretical properties, many researchers have proposed hybrid CG methods. Among these methods, hybridizations of the HS method and the DY method have shown promising numerical performance [31–34], etc. The HS method has a nice property of automatically satisfying the conjugate condition $d_{k+1}^T y_k = 0$ for $\forall\, k \geq 0$ independent of the accuracy of the line search strategies and the convexity of the objective function and performs well in practice. On the other hand, the DY method has remarkable convergence properties. These characteristics motivate us to propose new hybridizations of the HS method and the DY method which not only have attractive theoretical properties but also better numerical performance for large-scale nonconvex problems.

In the following, we focus on the conjugate parameter β_{k+1}^{MHS} and propose a new hybrid conjugate parameter of β_{k+1}^{DY} and β_{k+1}^{MHS}:

$$\beta_{k+1}^N = \max\left\{0, \min\left\{\beta_{k+1}^{DY}, \beta_{k+1}^{MHS}\right\}\right\}. \quad (7)$$

Now, based on the new hybrid conjugate parameter β_{k+1}^N and the modified descent direction (8), we propose our hybrid algorithm (NMHSDY) in detail.

It should be noted that the line search technique in Algorithm 1 is not fixed: It can be selected by the users. Next, we show that the search direction d_k generated by Algorithm 1 automatically has a sufficient descent property independent of any line search strategy.

Algorithm 1 New descent hybrid algorithm of MHS and DY methods (NMHSDY) for nonconvex functions.

Step 0. Input and Initialization. Select an initial point $x_0 \in \mathbb{R}^n$, parameter $\varepsilon \geq 0$ and compute $f_0 = f(x_0)$ and $g_0 = g(x_0)$. Set $d_0 = -g_0$ and $k = 0$;
Step 1. If $\|g_k\| \leq \varepsilon$, then stop;
Step 2. Compute step length α_k along direction d_k by some line search strategy;
Step 3. Let $x_{k+1} = x_k + \alpha_k d_k$;
Step 4. Compute the conjugate parameter β_{k+1}^N by (7) and the search direction d_{k+1} by

$$d_{k+1} = -\left(1 + \beta_{k+1}^N \frac{g_{k+1}^T d_k}{\|g_{k+1}\|^2}\right) g_{k+1} + \beta_{k+1}^N d_k, \tag{8}$$

Step 5. Set $k := k + 1$ and go to Step 2.

Theorem 1. *Let the search direction d_k be defined by (8) in Algorithm 1. Then, for any line search strategy, the sufficient descent property holds for nonconvex function $f(x)$, that is,*

$$g_k^T d_k = -\|g_k\|^2, \quad \forall k \geq 0. \tag{9}$$

Proof. By the definition of d_{k+1} in (8), we have

$$g_{k+1}^T d_{k+1} = -\|g_{k+1}\|^2 - \beta_{k+1} g_{k+1}^T d_k + \beta_{k+1} g_{k+1}^T d_k = -\|g_{k+1}\|^2.$$

Since $d_0 = -g_0$, then $d_0^T g_0 = -\|g_0\|^2$. All in all, (9) holds. This completes the proof. □

3. Convergence for General Nonlinear Functions

In this section, the global convergence of the NMHSDY method is presented. Before that, some common assumptions are listed.

Assumption 1. *The level set $\mathbb{L} = \{x \in \mathbb{R}^n : f(x) \leq f(x_0)\}$ is bounded, where x_0 is the initial point, i.e., there exists a positive constant $D > 0$ such that*

$$\|x\| \leq D, \quad \forall x \in \mathbb{L}. \tag{10}$$

Assumption 2. *In some neighborhood $\mathbb{N}$ of $\mathbb{L}$, the gradient $g(x) = \nabla f(x)$ is Lipschitz continuous, i.e., there exists a constant $L_1 > 0$ such that*

$$\|g(x) - g(y)\| \leq L_1 \|x - y\|, \quad \forall x, y \in \mathbb{N}. \tag{11}$$

Based on the above assumptions, we further obtain that there exists a constant $M > 0$ such that

$$\|g(x)\| \leq M, \quad \forall x \in \mathbb{L}. \tag{12}$$

In fact, it holds that $\|g(x)\| = \|g(x) - g(x_0) + g(x_0)\| \leq \|g(x) - g(x_0)\| + \|g(x_0)\| \leq L_1\|x - x_0\| + \|g(x_0)\| \leq 2L_1 D + \|g(x_0)\|$; hence, M can be $2L_1 E + \|g(x_0)\|$ or larger than that.

The line search strategy is another important element in iterative methods. In this part, we take the standard Wolfe line search strategy:

$$f(x_k + \alpha_k d_k) \leq f_k + \sigma_1 \alpha_k g_k^T d_k, \quad g(x_k + \alpha_k d_k)^T d_k \geq \sigma_2 g_k^T d_k, \tag{13}$$

where $0 < \sigma_1 < \sigma_2 < 1$. By property (9) and line search (13), it is satisfied that

$$f_{k+1} \leq f_k - \sigma_1 \alpha_k \|g_k\|^2 \leq f_k,$$

that is, the sequence $\{f_k\}$ is non-increasing and the sequence $\{x_k\}$ generated by Algorithm 1 is contained in the level set $\mathbb{L}$. Since f is continuously differentiable and the set $\mathbb{L}$ is bounded, then there exists a constant f^* such that

$$\lim_{k \to \infty} f(x_k) = f^*.$$

The Zoutendijk condition [35] plays an essential role in the global convergence of nonlinear CG methods. For completeness, we here state the lemma but omit its proof.

Lemma 1. *Suppose that Assumptions 1 and 2 hold. Consider any nonlinear CG method, in which α_k is obtained by the standard Wolfe line search (13) and d_k is a descent direction ($g_k^T d_k < 0$). Then, we have*

$$\sum_{k=1}^{\infty} \frac{(g_k^T d_k)^2}{\|d_k\|^2} < \infty. \tag{14}$$

Thereafter, the convergence property is presented in the following theorem for the general functions without convexity assumption.

Theorem 2. *Let Assumptions 1 and 2 hold and the sequence $\{x_k\}$ be generated by the NMHSDY algorithm. Set $l_{k+1} = \frac{\beta_{k+1}^N}{\beta_{k+1}^{DY}}$, and if $l_{k+1} \in [-\frac{1-\sigma_2}{1+\sigma_2}, 1 - \sigma_2]$ holds, then we have*

$$\liminf_{k \to \infty} \|g_k\| = 0. \tag{15}$$

Proof. We now prove (15) by contradiction and assume that there exists a constant $\mu > 0$ such that

$$\|g_k\| \geq \mu, \quad \forall k \geq 0. \tag{16}$$

Let γ_{k+1} be $1 + \beta_{k+1}^N \frac{g_{k+1}^T d_k}{\|g_{k+1}\|^2}$, then the direction (8) can be rewritten as

$$d_{k+1} = -\gamma_{k+1} g_{k+1} + \beta_{k+1}^N d_k.$$

After some algebraic manipulation, we have

$$\|d_{k+1}\|^2 = (\beta_{k+1}^N)^2 \|d_k\|^2 - 2\gamma_{k+1} g_{k+1}^T d_{k+1} - \gamma_{k+1}^2 \|g_{k+1}\|^2.$$

Dividing both sides of the above equality by $(g_{k+1}^T d_{k+1})^2$, from (9), we have

$$\begin{aligned}
\frac{\|d_{k+1}\|^2}{\|g_{k+1}\|^4} &= (\beta_{k+1}^N)^2 \frac{\|d_k\|^2}{\|g_{k+1}\|^4} + \frac{2\gamma_{k+1}}{\|g_{k+1}\|^2} - \frac{\gamma_{k+1}^2}{\|g_{k+1}\|^2} \\
&= (\beta_{k+1}^N)^2 \frac{\|d_k\|^2}{\|g_{k+1}\|^4} + \frac{1}{\|g_{k+1}\|^2} - \frac{(\gamma_{k+1} - 1)^2}{\|g_{k+1}\|^2}, \\
&= l_{k+1}^2 \frac{\|d_k\|^2}{(d_k^T y_k)^2} + \frac{1}{\|g_{k+1}\|^2} - \frac{(\gamma_{k+1} - 1)^2}{\|g_{k+1}\|^2}, \\
&\leq \frac{l_{k+1}^2}{(1 - \sigma_2)^2} \frac{\|d_k\|^2}{\|g_k\|^4} + \frac{1}{\|g_{k+1}\|^2} \leq \frac{\|d_k\|^2}{\|g_k\|^4} + \frac{1}{\|g_{k+1}\|^2},
\end{aligned} \tag{17}$$

where the first inequality holds by $d_k^T y_k \geq (\sigma_2 - 1)g_k^T d_k = (1 - \sigma_2)\|g_k\|^2$ and the last inequality holds by the bound for the scale l_{k+1}. By (17) and $\|d_0\|^2 = \|g_0\|^2$, it holds that

$$\frac{\|d_k\|^2}{\|g_k\|^4} \leq \sum_{i=0}^{k} \frac{1}{\|g_i\|^2}.$$

Then, by the above inequality and (16), it follows that

$$\frac{\|g_k\|^4}{\|d_k\|^2} \geq \frac{\mu^2}{k+1},$$

which indicates that

$$\sum_{k=1}^{\infty} \frac{\|g_k\|^4}{\|d_k\|^2} = \sum_{k=1}^{\infty} \frac{(g_k^T d_k)^2}{\|d_k\|^2} = \infty,$$

which contradicts the Zoutendijk condition (14). So, (15) holds. □

Remark 1. *In [24], the authors presented a class of hybrid conjugate parameters, one of which is $\beta_{k+1} = \max\{0, \min\{\beta_{k+1}^{DY}, \beta_{k+1}^{HS}\}\}$, with the corresponding interval for l_{k+1} being $[-(1-\sigma_2)/(1+\sigma_2), 1]$. It is reasonable that the interval in our paper is smaller since we take β_{k+1}^{MHS} instead of β_{k+1}^{HS} and $0 < \vartheta_k \leq 1$.*

In the following, we discuss the global convergence of Algorithm 1 for general non-linear functions in the case of $l_{k+1} \notin [-\frac{1-\sigma_2}{1+\sigma_2}, 1 - \sigma_2]$. Motivated by the modified secant conditions in [36,37], in this part, based on the Wolfe line search strategy (13), we consider the following settings:

$$\bar{y}_k = y_k + m s_k, \tag{18}$$

where $m > 0$ is a constant. With the above setting, the modified conjugate parameter becomes

$$\beta_{k+1}^{NN} = \max\left\{0, \min\left\{\beta_{k+1}^{NDY}, \beta_{k+1}^{NMHS}\right\}\right\}, \tag{19}$$

where β_{k+1}^{NDY} and β_{k+1}^{NMHS} are, respectively,

$$\beta_{k+1}^{NDY} = \frac{\|g_{k+1}\|^2}{\bar{y}_k^T s_k}, \quad \beta_{k+1}^{NMHS} = \frac{g_{k+1}^T \bar{y}_k}{\bar{y}_k^T s_k}\left(1 - \frac{(g_{k+1}^T s_k)^2}{\|g_{k+1}\|^2 \|s_k\|^2}\right).$$

Meanwhile, the corresponding direction turns to

$$d_{k+1}^N = -\left(1 + \beta_{k+1}^{NN} \frac{g_{k+1}^T s_k}{\|g_{k+1}\|^2}\right) g_{k+1} + \beta_{k+1}^{NN} s_k, \tag{20}$$

The following lemma indicates the property of the scalar $\bar{y}_k^T s_k$ and $\|\bar{y}_k\|$.

Lemma 2. *Let $\bar{y}_k$ be defined by (18); then, adopting the Wolfe line search strategy (13), we obtain*

$$\bar{y}_k^T s_k \geq m\|s_k\|^2, \tag{21}$$

and

$$\|\bar{y}_k\| \leq (L_1 + m)\|s_k\|. \tag{22}$$

Proof. By the Wolfe line search strategy (13), we have

$$y_k^T s_k = (g_{k+1} - g_k)^T s_k \geq (\sigma_2 - 1)g_k^T s_k \geq (1 - \sigma_2)\alpha_k \|g_k\|^2 \geq 0,$$

which indicates $y_k^T s_k \geq 0$. Therefore, it holds that

$$\bar{y}_k^T s_k = y_k^T s_k + m\|s_k\|^2 \geq m\|s_k\|^2.$$

Hence, (21) holds. Meanwhile, we also have

$$\|\bar{y}_k\| = \|y_k + m s_k\| \leq \|y_k\| + m\|s_k\| \leq (L_1 + m)\|s_k\|,$$

where the second inequality holds by Assumption 2. Hence, (22) holds. This completes the proof. □

In the following, we assume that Algorithm 1 never stops and there exists a constant $\mu > 0$ such that for all k, (16) holds.

Lemma 3. *Suppose that Assumptions 1 and 2 and (16) hold. The sequences $\{x_k\}$ and $\{d_k^N\}$ are generated by Algorithm 1 with the conjugate parameter β_k^{NN} and adopting the Wolfe line search technique (13). Then, there exists a positive constant Γ such that*

$$\|g_k\| \leq \|d_k^N\| \leq (1 + 2\Gamma)\|g_k\|. \tag{23}$$

Proof. Based on the Wolfe line search technique (13), it holds that

$$\bar{y}_k^T d_k^N = y_k^T d_k^N + m\alpha_k \|d_k^N\|^2 \geq y_k^T d_k^N = -(1-\sigma_2) g_k^T d_k^N = (1-\sigma_2)\|g_k\|^2, \tag{24}$$

where the first inequality holds by the non-negativity of α_k and the last inequality holds by the sufficient descent property (9). Meanwhile, by (9) and the Cauchy–Schwartz inequality, it holds that, for $\forall k \geq 0$,

$$\|g_k\| \|d_k^N\| \geq -g_k^T d_k^N = \|g_k\|^2,$$

which implies that from condition (16),

$$\|d_k^N\| \geq \|g_k\| \geq \mu, \quad \forall k \geq 0. \tag{25}$$

By the definition of β_{k+1}^{NN}, we obtain that

$$\begin{aligned}
|\beta_{k+1}^{NN}| &\leq \max\left\{\frac{\|g_{k+1}\|^2}{|\bar{y}_k^T s_k|}, \frac{|g_{k+1}^T \bar{y}_k|}{|\bar{y}_k^T s_k|}\right\} \leq \max\left\{\frac{\|g_{k+1}\|^2}{m\|s_k\|^2}, \frac{\|g_{k+1}\|\|\bar{y}_k\|}{m\|s_k\|^2}\right\} \\
&\leq \frac{\|g_{k+1}\|}{\|s_k\|} \max\left\{\frac{\|g_{k+1}\|}{m\|s_k\|}, \frac{L_1+m}{m}\right\} \leq \frac{\|g_{k+1}\|}{\|s_k\|} \max\left\{\frac{M}{m\bar{\alpha}\|d_k^N\|}, \frac{L_1+m}{m}\right\} \\
&\leq \frac{\|g_{k+1}\|}{\|s_k\|} \max\left\{\frac{M}{m\bar{\alpha}\|g_k\|}, \frac{L_1+m}{m}\right\} \\
&\leq \frac{\|g_{k+1}\|}{\|s_k\|} \max\left\{\frac{M}{m\bar{\alpha}\mu}, \frac{L_1+m}{m}\right\} := \Gamma \frac{\|g_{k+1}\|}{\|s_k\|},
\end{aligned}$$

where the second inequality holds by (21), the third inequality holds by (22), the fourth inequality holds by the condition $\alpha_k \geq \alpha > 0$ for all $k \geq 0$, the fifth inequality holds by (25), and the last inequality holds by the condition (16). Furthermore, we have

$$\left|\beta_{k+1}^{NN} \frac{g_{k+1}^T s_k}{\|g_{k+1}\|^2}\right| \leq |\beta_{k+1}^{NN}| \frac{\|g_{k+1}\|\|s_k\|}{\|g_{k+1}\|^2} \leq \Gamma \frac{\|g_{k+1}\|}{\|s_k\|} \frac{\|s_k\|}{\|g_{k+1}\|} = \Gamma.$$

By the definition of d_k^N in (20) and the above discussions, it holds that

$$\begin{aligned}
\|d_{k+1}^N\| &\leq \|g_{k+1}\| + \left|\beta_{k+1}^{NN}\frac{g_{k+1}^T s_k}{\|g_{k+1}\|^2}\right|\|g_{k+1}\| + |\beta_{k+1}^{NN}|\|s_k\| \\
&\leq \|g_{k+1}\| + \Gamma\|g_{k+1}\| + \Gamma\frac{\|g_{k+1}\|}{\|s_k\|}\|s_k\| \\
&= (1 + 2\Gamma)\|g_{k+1}\|.
\end{aligned}$$

With the help of (25), we conclude that

$$\|g_{k+1}\| \leq \|d_{k+1}^N\| \leq (1 + 2\Gamma)\|g_{k+1}\|.$$

Hence, (23) holds. This completes the proof. □

Theorem 3. *Suppose that Assumptions 1 and 2 hold. The sequences $\{x_k\}$ and $\{d_k^N\}$ are generated by Algorithm 1 with the conjugate parameter β_k^{NN} and the Wolfe line search technique (13) is adopted. Then, Algorithm 1 converges in the sense of (15).*

Proof. We prove the conclusion by contradiction and assume that there exists a positive constant μ such that (16) holds. Otherwise, Algorithm 1 converges in the sense of (15). From (9), we conclude that the new direction enjoys the sufficient descent property. Therefore, Lemma 1 holds, which implies that

$$+\infty = \sum_{k=1}^{+\infty}\frac{\mu^2}{(1+2\Gamma)^2} \leq \sum_{k=1}^{+\infty}\frac{\|g_k\|^2}{(1+2\Gamma)^2} = \sum_{k=1}^{+\infty}\frac{\|g_k\|^4}{(1+2\Gamma)^2\|g_k\|^2} \leq \sum_{k=1}^{+\infty}\frac{(g_k^T d_k^N)^2}{\|d_k^N\|^2} < +\infty,$$

where the first inequality holds by (16), the second inequality holds by (9) and (23), and the last inequality holds by Lemma 1. However, that is a contradiction and the assumption does not hold. So, the $\liminf_{k\to+\infty}\|g_k\| = 0$ holds. This completes the proof. □

4. Numerical Performance

In this section, we focus on the numerical performance of Algorithm 1 and compare it with several effective CG methods. In the experiment, we code these algorithms in Matlab 2016b and perform them on a PC computer, whose processor has AMD 2.10 GHz, RAM of 16.00 GB and the Windows 10 operating system.

4.1. Performance on Benchmark Problems

In this subsection, we check the performance of the NMHSDY method and compare it with two effective modified HS methods in [26,28] and the hybrid method in [24]. In [26], the authors proposed an effective modified HS method (MHSCG method for abbreviation) in which the conjugate parameter is

$$\beta_{k+1} = \max\{0, \bar{\beta}_{k+1}^{MHS}\}, \quad \bar{\beta}_{k+1}^{MHS} = \beta_{k+1}^{MHS} - \lambda\left(\frac{\|y_k\|\vartheta_k}{y_k^T d_k}\right)^2 g_{k+1}^T d_k,$$

where $\lambda > 1/4$ is a parameter. The direction in [26] is in the form of (3) and the corresponding method has attractive numerical performance. Dai and Kou in [28] introduced another effective class of CG schemes (DK+ method for abbreviation) depending on the parameter τ_k, where the corresponding conjugate parameter β_{k+1} is defined by

$$\beta_{k+1}^{DK}(\tau_k) = \beta_{k+1}^{HS} - \left(\tau_k + \frac{\|y_k\|^2}{y_k^T s_k} - \frac{y_k^T s_k}{\|s_k\|^2}\right)\frac{g_{k+1}^T s_k}{y_k^T d_k}, \quad s_k = x_{k+1} - x_k.$$

The direction in [28] is also in the form of (3). To establish global convergence for general nonlinear functions, a truncated strategy is used, that is,

$$\beta_{k+1}^{DK+}(\tau_k) = \max\left\{\beta_{k+1}^{DK}(\tau_k), \eta \frac{g_{k+1}^T d_k}{\|d_k\|^2}\right\},$$

where $\eta \in [0,1)$ is a parameter. The numerical results indicated the DK+ method has good and reliable numerical performance. Dai and Yuan, in [24], proposed an effective hybrid CG method (HSDY method for abbreviation) in which the conjugate parameter is

$$\beta_{k+1} = \max\{0, \min\{\beta_{k+1}^{DY}, \beta_{k+1}^{HS}\}\}.$$

The hybrid method also has global convergence and attractive numerical performance.

In the following, we focus on the numerical performance and the large-scale unconstrained problems in Table 1 (see [38] for details). In order to improve numerical performance, Andrei, in [39], proposed an accelerated strategy which modified the step in a multiplicative manner. In this part, we also utilize this strategy and regard Algorithm 1 with the accelerated strategy as Algorithm 1. To compare the conjugate parameters and the search directions fairly, here we adopt the Wolfe line search technique (13) for all methods.

Table 1. The test problems.

No.	Problem	No.	Problem
1	Extended Freudenstein and Roth Function	32	ARWHEAD (CUTE)
2	Extended Trigonometric Function	33	NONDIA (Shanno-78) (CUTE)
3	Extended Rosenbrock Function	34	DQDRTIC (CUTE)
4	Extended Beale Function	35	EG2 (CUTE)
5	Extended Penalty Function	36	DIXMAANA (CUTE)
6	Perturbed Quadratic Function	37	DIXMAANB (CUTE)
7	Raydan 1 Function	38	DIXMAANC (CUTE)
8	Raydan 2 Function	39	DIXMAANE (CUTE)
9	Diagonal 3 Function	40	Broyden Tridiagonal
10	Generalized Tridiagonal-1 Function	41	Almost Perturbed Quadratic
11	Extended Tridiagonal-1 Function	42	Tridiagonal Perturbed Quadratic
12	Extended Three Exponential Terms	43	EDENSCH Function (CUTE)
13	Generalized Tridiagonal-2	44	VARDIM Function (CUTE)
14	Diagonal 4 Function	45	LIARWHD (CUTE)
15	Diagonal 5 Function	46	DIAGONAL 6
16	Extended Himmelblau Function	47	DIXMAANF (CUTE)
17	Generalized PSC1 Function	48	DIXMAANG (CUTE)
18	Extended PSC1 Function	49	DIXMAANH (CUTE)
19	Extended Powell Function	50	DIXMAANI (CUTE)
20	Extended Cliff Function	51	DIXMAANJ (CUTE)
21	Quadratic Diagonal Perturbed Function	52	DIXMAANK (CUTE)
22	Extended Wood Function	53	DIXMAANL (CUTE)
23	Extended Hiebert Function	54	DIXMAAND (CUTE)
24	Quadratic Function QF1	55	ENGVAL1 (CUTE)
25	Extended Quadratic Penalty QP1 Function	56	COSINE (CUTE)
26	Extended Quadratic Penalty QP2 Function	57	Extended DENSCHNB (CUTE)
27	A Quadratic Function QF2 Function	58	Extended DENSCHNF (CUTE)
28	Extended EP1 Function	59	SINQUAD (CUTE)
29	Extended Tridiagonal-2 Function	60	Scaled Quadratic SQ1
30	BDQRTIC (CUTE)	61	Scaled Quadratic SQ2
31	TRIDIA (CUTE)		

In the experiment, for each problem we consider nine large-scale dimensions with 300, 600, 900, 3000, 6000, 9000, 30,000, 60,000 and 90,000 variables. The parameters used in the Wolfe line search are $\sigma_1 = 0.20$ and $\sigma_2 = 0.85$. The other parameters for the MHSCG method and the DK+ method are as default.

During the progress, the Himmeblau stopping rule is adopted: if $|f(x_k)| > \varepsilon_1$, let $stop1 = \frac{|f(x_k) - f(x_{k+1})|}{|f(x_k)|}$, otherwise, $stop1 = |f(x_k) - f(x_{k-1})|$. If the conditions $\|g_k\| \leq \varepsilon$ or $stop1 \leq \varepsilon_2$ are satisfied, then the progress is stopped, where the values of parameters ε, ε_1, and ε_2 are $\varepsilon = 10^{-6}$, and $\varepsilon_1 = \varepsilon_2 = 10^{-5}$. Meanwhile, we also stop the algorithm when the number of iterations is greater than 5000.

In order to present the performances of methods more intuitively, the tool in [40] is adopted to analyze the profiles of these methods. Robustness and efficiency rates are readable on the right and left vertical axes of the corresponding performance profiles, respectively. To present a detailed numerical comparison, two different scales have been considered for the τ-axis. One is $\tau \in [1, 1.5]$, which shows what happens for the values of τ near to 1. The other is used to present the trend for large values of τ. In Figures 1–3, we, respectively, show the performance of these methods relative to the number of iterations (NI), the number of function-gradient valuations (NFG; which is the sum of the number of function valuations and gradient valuations), and the CPU time consumed in seconds.

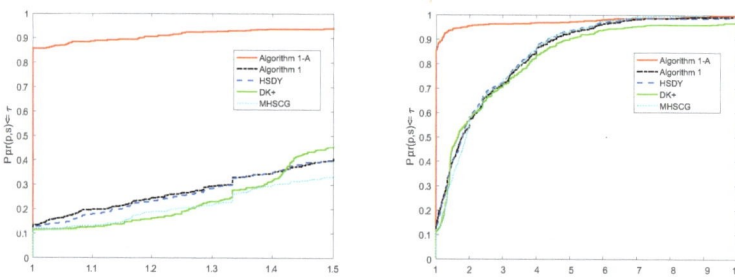

Figure 1. Performance profiles of the methods in the number of iterations case.

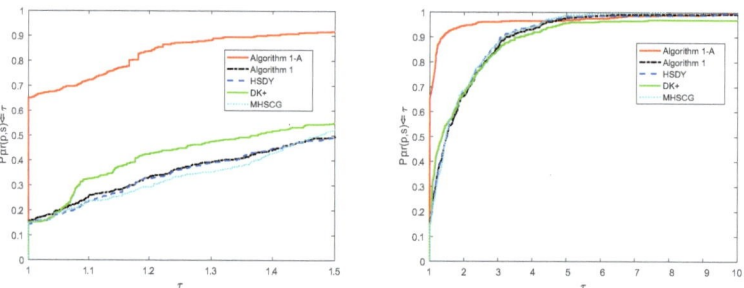

Figure 2. Performance profiles of the methods in the function and gradient case.

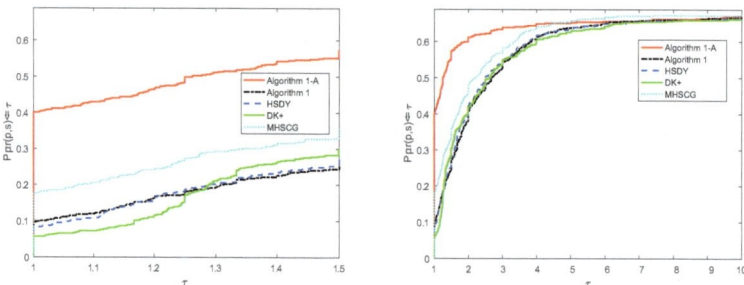

Figure 3. Performance profiles of the methods in the CPU time consumed case.

From Figures 1–3, we have that Algorithm 1 is comparable and a little more effective than the HSDY method, the DK+ method, and the MHSCG method for the above problems.

Meanwhile, Algorithm 1, with the accelerated strategy, is much effective and performs best in the experiment, which indicates that the accelerated technique indeed works and reduces the number of iterations and the number of function and gradient evaluations.

4.2. Comparison for Stability

In this subsection, we consider the numerical stability of Algorithm 1 for the ill-conditioned matrix problems and compare it with the MHSCG method in [26]. In fact, the quadratic objective function $f(x) = x^T \mathcal{I} x$ of (1) is ill-conditioned if matrix $\mathcal{I} \in \mathbb{R}^{n \times n}$ is in the form

$$\mathcal{I}_{i,j} = \frac{1}{i+j-1}, \quad i,j = 1,2,\ldots,n.$$

It is clear that the matrix $\mathcal{I}$ is ill-conditioned and positive definite [41], with different dimensions $n = 5, 6, \ldots, 50$. Furthermore, the authors in [42] show that the ℓ_∞ norm condition number of the Hessian matrix $\mathcal{I}$ gradually increases from 9.4366×10^5 for $n = 5$ to 6.9007×10^{20} for $n = 50$. In the following, we explore the numerical performance. The experimental environment, the parameter values, and the stop rule remain the same as in the above subsection. Meanwhile, the initial point is selected as $x_0 = (10, 10, \cdots, 10)$. The corresponding numerical results are presented in Tables 2 and 3, in which Dim is the dimension of x, NI means the number of iterations, NFG is the sum of the number of function and gradient evaluations, $Time$ means the CPU time consumed in seconds, and f^* denotes the optimal function obtained by the methods.

Table 2. Numerical results of the MHSCG method and Algorithm 1 in 5–40 dimensions.

	MHSCG Method				Algorithm 1			
Dim	NI	NFG	Time	f^*	NI	NFG	Time	f^*
5	5	22	0.000000	0.000000	5	22	0.000000	0.000000
6	13	48	0.031250	0.000000	13	48	0.000000	0.000000
7	21	72	0.000000	0.000000	21	72	0.000000	0.000000
8	21	72	0.000000	0.000000	21	72	0.015625	0.000000
9	27	92	0.000000	0.000006	24	82	0.000000	0.000000
10	41	143	0.000000	0.000007	29	97	0.000000	0.000000
11	75	246	0.000000	0.000009	55	192	0.000000	0.000000
12	58	203	0.000000	0.000003	70	249	0.000000	0.000008
13	57	190	0.000000	0.000004	70	246	0.000000	0.000000
14	86	276	0.031250	0.000008	123	429	0.000000	0.000000
15	75	264	0.031250	0.000009	89	314	0.000000	0.000009
16	98	330	0.000000	0.000008	52	177	0.000000	0.000001
17	24	82	0.000000	0.000002	66	232	0.000000	0.000002
18	65	215	0.031250	0.000009	28	97	0.000000	0.000000
19	31	105	0.000000	0.000007	27	94	0.000000	0.000000
20	111	373	0.031250	0.000009	131	452	0.000000	0.000010
21	117	379	0.031250	0.000008	31	108	0.000000	0.000000
22	96	333	0.000000	0.000010	66	236	0.000000	0.000000
23	68	233	0.000000	0.000009	85	303	0.031250	0.000000

Table 2. Cont.

	MHSCG Method				Algorithm 1			
Dim	NI	NFG	Time	f^*	NI	NFG	Time	f^*
24	50	175	0.031250	0.000000	43	151	0.000000	0.000000
25	96	318	0.000000	0.000009	103	377	0.000000	0.000000
26	113	370	0.000000	0.000009	112	410	0.000000	0.000004
27	22	78	0.000000	0.000000	129	473	0.031250	0.000001
28	104	372	0.000000	0.000009	24	87	0.000000	0.000000
29	156	513	0.000000	0.000010	130	449	0.000000	0.000001
30	54	185	0.000000	0.000001	121	446	0.000000	0.000007
31	39	144	0.000000	0.000003	97	341	0.000000	0.000008
32	26	97	0.000000	0.000001	79	292	0.031250	0.000001
33	87	309	0.000000	0.000010	66	234	0.031250	0.000002
34	58	213	0.000000	0.000006	60	217	0.031250	0.000000
35	97	327	0.000000	0.000009	25	95	0.000000	0.000002
36	24	86	0.000000	0.000000	132	481	0.000000	0.000003
37	23	84	0.000000	0.000004	55	192	0.000000	0.000001
38	93	312	0.046875	0.000010	40	142	0.000000	0.000003
39	148	487	0.046875	0.000005	124	442	0.140625	0.000010
40	66	231	0.000000	0.000007	136	496	0.031250	0.000007

Table 3. Numerical results of the MHSCG method and Algorithm 1 in 41–50 dimensions.

	MHSCG Method				Algorithm 1			
Dim	NI	NFG	Time	f^*	NI	NFG	Time	f^*
41	76	267	0.031250	0.000005	65	239	0.000000	0.000005
42	130	438	0.046875	0.000008	85	302	0.000000	0.000010
43	164	546	0.031250	0.000009	136	488	0.000000	0.000009
44	184	594	0.031250	0.000007	29	103	0.000000	0.000006
45	17	64	0.000000	0.000000	17	64	0.000000	0.000000
46	155	519	0.031250	0.000010	62	222	0.000000	0.000000
47	123	421	0.031250	0.000010	107	379	0.031250	0.000010
48	20	74	0.000000	0.000000	68	250	0.015625	0.000010
49	135	473	0.031250	0.000010	102	375	0.031250	0.000010
50	178	594	0.062500	0.000010	151	542	0.031250	0.000009

From Tables 2 and 3, it can be found that for the dimensions from 5 to 50, Algorithm 1 and the MHSCG method successfully solve all of them and obtain reasonable optimal function values, which are all not greater than 10^{-5}. For most problems, Algorithm 1 needed fewer iterations and function and gradient evaluations and obtained better optimal values. In order to show numerical performance intuitively, here we also adopt the performance profiles in [40] for the NI and NFG cases. The corresponding performance profiles are given in Figures 4 and 5.

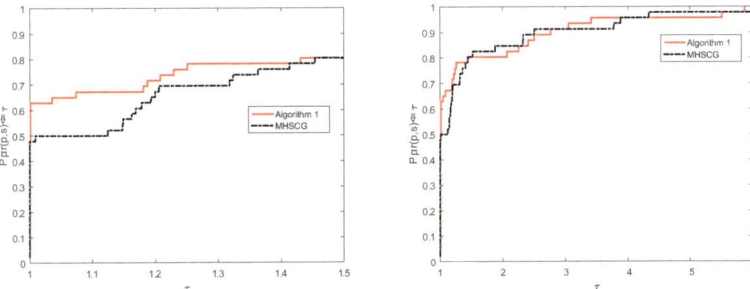

Figure 4. Performance profiles of Algorithm 1 and the MHSCG method in NI case.

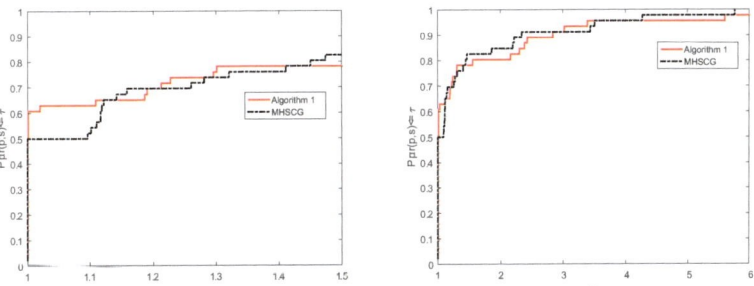

Figure 5. Performance profiles of Algorithm 1 and the MHSCG method in NFG case.

Figure 4 shows that Algorithm 1 and the MHSCG method solve these testing problems with the least total number of iterations in 63% and 48% of cases, respectively. Figure 5 indicates that Algorithm 1 and the MHSCG method solve these testing problems with the least total number of function and gradient evaluations in 61% and 50% of cases, respectively. All in all, the numerical results show that Algorithm 1 is more effective and stable than the MHSCG method for these ill-conditioned matrix problems.

4.3. Application to Image Restoration

In this subsection, we apply Algorithm 1 to some image restoration problems [43–45]. During the process, the normal Wolfe line search technique is adopted, the corresponding parameters remain unchanged, and two noise level cases for the Barbara.png (512 × 512) and Baboon.bmp (512 × 512) images are considered. In this part, we stop the process when the following criteria are both satisfied:

$$\frac{|f(x_{k+1}) - f(x_k)|}{|f(x_k)|} < 10^{-3}, \quad \|g(x_k)\| < 10^{-3}(1 + |f(x_k)|).$$

Meanwhile, to assess the restoration performance qualitatively, we also utilize the peak signal to noise ratio [45] (PSNR), which is defined by $PSNR = 10\log_{10}\frac{255^2}{\frac{1}{M\times N}\sum_{i,j}(u_{i,j}^r - u_{i,j}^*)^2}$, where M and N are the true image pixels, and $u_{i,j}^r$ and $u_{i,j}^*$ denote the pixel values of the restored image and the original image, respectively. For the noise level, we consider two cases: 20% (a low-level case) and 60% (a high-level case). The consumed CPU time and the corresponding PSNR values are given in Table 4. Meanwhile, the detailed performances are presented in Figures 6 and 7, respectively.

Table 4. Test results for Algorithm 1 and the MHSCG method.

Image	Noise Level	Algorithm 1		MHSCG Method	
		PSNR	CPU Time	PSNR	CPU Time
Barbara	20%	29.6638	2.265625	29.5831	2.578125
Baboon	20%	27.9223	2.609375	27.8455	3.250000
Barbara	60%	23.1256	3.593750	23.1103	3.765625
Baboon	60%	21.1836	3.484375	21.1582	3.671875

Figure 6. The noisy Barbara image, corrupted by salt-and pepper noise (**the first column**); the images restored via Algorithm 1 (**the second column**), and via the MHSCG method (**the third column**).

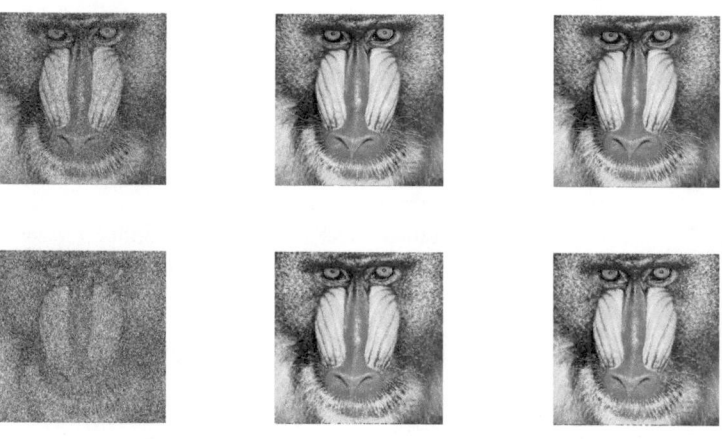

Figure 7. The noisy Baboon image, corrupted by salt-and pepper noise (**the first column**); the images restored via Algorithm 1 (**the second column**), and via the MHSCG method (**the third column**).

From Table 4 and Figures 6 and 7, we have that Algorithm 1 and the MHSCG method can all solve the image restoration problems successfully within a suitable time, and Algorithm 1 seems to perform a little better than the MHSCG method.

5. Conclusions

Conjugate gradient methods are attractive and effective for large-scale unconstrained optimization smooth problems due to their simple computation and low memory requirements. The Dai–Yuan conjugate gradient method has good theoretical properties and generates a descent direction in each iteration. Whereas, the Hestenes–Stiefel conjugate gradient method automatically satisfies the conjugate condition $y_k^T d_{k+1} = 0$ without any line search technique and performs well in practice. By the above discussions, we propose a new descent hybrid conjugate gradient method. The proposed method has a sufficient descent property independent of any line search technique. Under some mild conditions, the proposed method is globally convergent. In the experiments, we first consider 61 unconstrained problems with 9 different dimensions up to 90,000. Thereafter, 46 ill-conditioned matrix problems are also tested. The primary numerical results show that the proposed method is more effective and stable. Finally, we apply the hybrid method to some image restoration problems. The results indicate our method is attractive and reliable.

Author Contributions: Conceptualization, S.W., X.W., Y.T. and L.P.; methodology, S.W. and X.W.; software, X.W.; validation, X.W., L.P. and Y.T.; formal analysis, X.W., Y.T. and L.P. All authors have read and agreed to the published version of the manuscript.

Funding: This work was partially supported by Science Foundation of Zhejiang Sci-Tech University (ZSTU) under Grant No. 21062347-Y.

Data Availability Statement: All data included in this study are available upon reasonable request.

Conflicts of Interest: The authors declare no competing interests.

References

1. Li, D.; Fukushima, M. A global and superlinear convergent Gauss-Newton-based BFGS method for symmetric nonlinear equations. *SIAM J. Numer. Anal.* **1999**, *37*, 152–172. [CrossRef]
2. Yuan, G.; Wei, Z.; Wang, Z. Gradient trust region algorithm with limited memory BFGS update for nonsmooth convex minimization. *Comput. Optim. Appl.* **2013**, *54*, 45–64. [CrossRef]
3. Dai, Y.; Han, J.; Liu, G.; Sun, D.; Yin, H.; Yuan, Y. Convergence properties of nonlinear conjugate gradient methods. *SIAM J. Optim.* **2000**, *10*, 345–358. [CrossRef]
4. Hager, W.; Zhang, H. A new conjugate gradient method with guaranteed descent and an efficient line search. *SIAM J. Optim.* **2005**, *16*, 170–192. [CrossRef]
5. Fletcher, R.; Reeves, C.M. Function minimization by conjugate gradients. *Comput. J.* **1964**, *7*, 149–154. [CrossRef]
6. Dai, Y.; Yuan, Y. A nonlinear conjugate gradient method with a strong global convergence property. *SIAM J. Optim.* **1999**, *10*, 177–182. [CrossRef]
7. Fletcher, R. *Practical Methods of Optimization*; Unconstrained Optimization; John Wiley & Sons: New York, NY, UAS, 1987; Volume 1.
8. Hestenes, R.; Stiefel, L. Methods of conjugate gradients for solving linear systems. *J. Res. Natl. Bur. Stand.* **1952**, *49*, 409–436. [CrossRef]
9. Polyak, B.T. The conjugate gradient method in extreme problems. *USSR Comput. Math. Math. Phys.* **1969**, *9*, 94–112. [CrossRef]
10. Polak, E.; Ribière, G. Note sur la convergence de méthodes de directions conjuguées. *Rev. Fr. Informat Rech. Opér.* **1969**, *16*, 35–43. [CrossRef]
11. Liu, Y.; Storey, C. Efficient generalized conjugate gradient algorithms Part 1: Theory. *J. Optim. Theory Appl.* **1991**, *69*, 129–137. [CrossRef]
12. Xiang, Y.; Gong, X.G. Efficiency of generalized simulated annealing. *Phys. Rev. E* **2000**, *62*, 4473–4476. [CrossRef] [PubMed]
13. Yuan, Q.; Qian, F. A hybrid genetic algorithm for twice continuously differentiable NLP problems. *Comput. Chem. Eng.* **2010**, *34*, 36–41. [CrossRef]
14. Gao, F.C.; Han, L.X. Implementing the Nelder-Mead simplex algorithm with adaptive parameters. *Comput. Optim. Appl.* **2012**, *51*, 259–277. [CrossRef]
15. Yuan, G.; Wang, X.; Sheng, Z. The projection technique for two open problems of unconstrained optimization problems. *J. Optim. Theory Appl.* **2020**, *186*, 590–619. [CrossRef]
16. Yuan, G.; Wang, X.; Sheng, Z. Family weak conjugate gradient algorithms and their convergence analysis for nonconvex functions. *Numer. Algorithms* **2020**, *84*, 935–956. [CrossRef]
17. Mousavi, A.; Esmaeilpour, M.; Sheikhahmadi, A. A new family of Polak-Ribière-Polyak conjugate gradient method for impulse noise removal. *Soft Comput.* **2023**, *27*, 17515–17524. [CrossRef]
18. Polyak, B.T. *Introduction to Optimization*; Optimization Software Inc., Publications Division: New York, NY, USA, 1987.
19. Wang, X.; Yuan, G.; Pang, L. A class of new three-term descent conjugate gradient algorithms for large-scale unconstrained optimization and applications to image restoration problems. *Numer. Algorithms* **2023**, *93*, 949–970. [CrossRef]
20. Wang, X. A class of spectral three-term descent Hestenes-Stiefel conjugate gradient algorithms for large-scale unconstrained optimization and image restoration problems. *Appl. Numer. Math.* **2023**, *192*, 41–56. [CrossRef]

21. Touati-Ahmed, D.; Storey, C. Efficient hybrid conjugate gradient techniques. *J. Optim.Theory Appl.* **1990**, *64*, 379–397. [CrossRef]
22. Zhang, L.; Zhou, W. Two descent hybrid conjugate gradient methods for optimization. *J. Comput. Appl. Math.* **2008**, *216*, 251–264. [CrossRef]
23. Gilbert, J.; Nocedal, J. Global convergence properties of conjugate gradient methods for optimization. *SIAM J. Optim.* **1992**, *2*, 21–42. [CrossRef]
24. Dai, Y.; Yuan, Y. An efficient hybrid conjugate gradient method for unconstrained optimization. *Ann. Oper. Res.* **2001**, *103*, 33–47. [CrossRef]
25. Jiang, X.; Liao, W.; Yin, J.; Jian, J. A new family of hybrid three-term conjugate gradient methods with applications in image restoration. *Numer. Algorithms* **2022**, *91*, 161–191. [CrossRef]
26. Amini, K.; Faramarzi, P.; Pirfalah, N. A modified Hestenes-Stiefel conjugate gradient method with an optimal property. *Optim. Methods Softw.* **2019**, *34*, 770–782. [CrossRef]
27. Narushima, Y.; Yabe, H.; Ford, J. A three-term conjugate gradient method with sufficient descent property for unconstrained optimization. *SIAM J. Optim.* **2011**, *21*, 212–230. [CrossRef]
28. Dai, Y.; Kou, C. A nonlinear conjugate gradient algorithm with an optimal property and an improved Wolfe line search. *SIAM J. Optim.* **2013**, *23*, 296–320. [CrossRef]
29. Woldu, T.; Zhang, H.; Zhang, X.; Yemane, H. A modified nonlinear conjugate gradient algorithm for large-scale nonsmooth convex optimization. *J. Optim. Theory Appl.* **2020**, *185*, 223–238. [CrossRef]
30. Yuan, G.; Meng, Z.; Li, Y. A modified Hestenes and Stiefel conjugate gradient algorithm for large-scale nonsmooth minimizations and nonlinear equations. *J. Optim. Theory Appl.* **2016**, *168*, 129–152. [CrossRef]
31. Babaie-Kafaki, S.; Fatemi, M.; Mahdavi-Amiri, N. Two effective hybrid conjugate gradient algorithms based on modified BFGS updates. *Numer. Algorithms* **2011**, *58*, 315–331. [CrossRef]
32. Livieris, I.; Tampakas, V.; Pintelas, P. A descent hybrid conjugate gradient method based on the memoryless BFGS update. *Numer. Algorithms* **2018**, *79*, 1169–1185. [CrossRef]
33. Khoshgam, Z.; Ashrafi, A. A new hybrid conjugate gradient method for large-scale unconstrained optimization problem with non-convex objective function. *Comp. Appl. Math.* **2019**, *38*, 186. [CrossRef]
34. Narayanan, S.; Kaelo, P. A linear hybridization of Dai-Yuan and Hestenes-Stiefel conjugate gradient method for unconstrained optimization. *Numer.-Math.-Theory Methods Appl.* **2021**, *14*, 527–539.
35. Zoutendijk, G. *Nonlinear Programming, Computational Methods*; Integer & Nonlinear Programming: Amsterdam, The Netherlands, 1970; pp. 37–86.
36. Li, D.; Fukushima, M. A modified BFGS method and its global convergence in nonconvex minimization. *J. Comput. Appl. Math.* **2001**, *129*, 15–35. [CrossRef]
37. Babaie-Kafaki, S.; Ghanbari, R. A modified scaled conjugate gradient method with global convergence for nonconvex functions. *B Bull. Belg. Math. Soc. Simon Stevin* **2014**, *21*, 465–477. [CrossRef]
38. Andrei, N. An unconstrained optimization test functions collection. *Environ. Ence Technol.* **2008**, *10*, 6552–6558.
39. Andrei, N. An acceleration of gradient descent algorithm with backtracking for unconstrained optimization. *Numer. Algorithms* **2006**, *42*, 63–73. [CrossRef]
40. Dolan, E.; Moré, J. Benchmarking optimization software with performance profiles. *Math. Program* **2002**, *91*, 201–213. [CrossRef]
41. Watkins, S. *Fundamentals of Matrix Computations*; John Wiley and Sons: New York, NY, USA, 2002.
42. Babaie-Kafaki, S. A hybrid scaling parameter for the scaled memoryless BFGS method based on the ℓ_∞ matrix norm. *Int. J. Comput. Math.* **2019**, *96*, 1595–1602. [CrossRef]
43. Yu, G.; Huang, J.; Zhou, Y. A descent spectral conjugate gradient method for impulse noise removal. *Appl. Math. Lett.* **2010**, *23*, 555–560. [CrossRef]
44. Yuan, G.; Lu, J.; Wang, Z. The PRP conjugate gradient algorithm with a modified WWP line search and its application in the image restoration problems. *Appl. Numer. Math.* **2020**, *152*, 1–11. [CrossRef]
45. Bovik, A. *Handbook of Image and Video Processing*; Academic: New York, NY, USA, 2000.

Disclaimer/Publisher's Note: The statements, opinions and data contained in all publications are solely those of the individual author(s) and contributor(s) and not of MDPI and/or the editor(s). MDPI and/or the editor(s) disclaim responsibility for any injury to people or property resulting from any ideas, methods, instructions or products referred to in the content.

Article

Enhancing Parameters Tuning of Overlay Models with Ridge Regression: Addressing Multicollinearity in High-Dimensional Data

Aris Magklaras [1], Christos Gogos [2,*], Panayiotis Alefragis [3] and Alexios Birbas [1]

[1] Department of Electrical and Computer Engineering, University of Patras, 26504 Patras, Greece; a.magklaras@upnet.gr (A.M.); birbas@ece.upatras.gr (A.B.)
[2] Department of Informatics and Telecommunications, University of Ioannina, 47100 Arta, Greece
[3] Department of Electrical and Computer Engineering, University of Peloponnese, 26334 Patras, Greece; alefrag@uop.gr
* Correspondence: cgogos@uoi.gr; Tel.: +30-6977311944

Citation: Magklaras, A.; Gogos, C.; Alefragis, P.; Birbas, A. Enhancing Parameters Tuning of Overlay Models with Ridge Regression: Addressing Multicollinearity in High-Dimensional Data. *Mathematics* 2024, 12, 3179. https://doi.org/10.3390/math12203179

Academic Editor: David Greiner

Received: 12 September 2024
Revised: 4 October 2024
Accepted: 4 October 2024
Published: 11 October 2024

Correction Statement: This article has been republished with a minor change. The change does not affect the scientific content of the article and further details are available within the backmatter of the website version of this article.

Copyright: © 2024 by the authors. Licensee MDPI, Basel, Switzerland. This article is an open access article distributed under the terms and conditions of the Creative Commons Attribution (CC BY) license (https://creativecommons.org/licenses/by/4.0/).

Abstract: The extreme ultraviolet (EUV) photolithography process is a cornerstone of semiconductor manufacturing and operates under demanding precision standards realized via nanometer-level overlay (OVL) error modeling. This procedure allows the machine to anticipate and correct OVL errors before impacting the wafer, thereby facilitating near-optimal image exposure while simultaneously minimizing the overall OVL error. Such models are usually high dimensional and exhibit rigorous statistical phenomena such as collinearities that play a crucial role in the process of tuning their parameters. Ordinary least squares (OLS) is the most widely used method for parameters tuning of overlay models, but in most cases it fails to compensate for such phenomena. In this paper, we propose the usage of ridge regression, a widely known machine learning (ML) algorithm especially suitable for datasets that exhibit high multicollinearity. The proposed method was applied in perturbed data from a 300 mm wafer fab, and the results show reduced residuals when ridge regression is applied instead of OLS.

Keywords: overlay modeling; photolithography; parameters tuning; EUV lithography; semiconductor manufacturing; yield results

MSC: 37M05

1. Introduction

According to Moore's law, "the number of transistors that can be placed on a chip doubles every 24 months" [1]. Maintaining Moore's law is highly challenging, because it calls for continuous advancement in a very complex industry. Despite this, recent developments in the production of integrated circuits (ICs), particularly in photolithography, have enabled the industry to keep up with the high process standards. Owing to its role in transferring a desired pattern to a photosensitive material on the wafer surface (photocurable material; most frequently, commercial photo resist [2]) by exposing it to ultraviolet (UV) or extreme-UV (EUV) light, photolithography [3] is a crucial component of the entire process. Wafers with a high overlay (OVL) and small critical dimension (CD) are the result of a successful photolithography process. The smaller the exposed pattern and the smaller the exposed ICs on the wafer, the better the OVL and the smaller the CD. Therefore, photolithography is the most crucial step in the production of integrated circuits comprising the base mechanism that supports Moore's law.

In terms of hardware and software, photolithography machines rank among the most complex machines in the market. It is highly challenging to orchestrate and operate the machine in such a way that it satisfies the extremely stringent OVL and CD standards, given the machine's more than 50 million lines of code and thousands of hardware modules. This precision is impossible for the hardware alone. Software control techniques that cope with hardware imperfections are essential components of the machine. Software will enable the machine to meet the OVL and CD KPIs, which will confirm the machine's quality.

The fundamental premise underlying this is that the machine can precisely model anticipated wavefront aberrations at the nanoscale level. The software then adjusts the associated machine knobs, such as mirror locations, such that it compensates for the anticipated aberrations because it knows what to expect. The required pattern is then exposed to the fewest possible flaws because the predicted fingerprint is rectified before it reaches the wafer surface. Under these circumstances, we recognize that one of the most important and difficult responsibilities of the photolithography process is the ability to create precise models. These models are the primary tools for successful exposure.

The process of describing the spatial changes in the overlay (OVL) of the features being printed is known as OVL fingerprint estimation (FE) in photolithography. These discrepancies can be caused by several factors, including flaws in the mask or the lithography procedure itself. The OVL of the features at various positions on the wafer are often measured using specialized metrology instruments that can estimate fingerprints. Information regarding the spatial changes in the OVL is then extracted from the resulting data and utilized to generate a "fingerprint" of the lithography process. Modeling the OVL is an essential step in the FE process. OVL modeling is the process of creating mathematical and statistical models to forecast how various process parameters affect OVL. By modifying the lithography process parameters in real time to meet the necessary OVL criteria, these models can be used to improve the lithography process. To ensure a high yield and reliable performance of the lithography process, FE estimation is a crucial tool.

A polynomial model is a mathematical or statistical representation of a system or process and polynomial. The basis functions and parameters are the two main components of the model. The structure of the problem and the properties of the data being modeled influence the basis functions that are used. On the other hand, model parameters are the estimated values that are used to define the model and are derived from the data. The precise values of the basis functions that best suit the data are determined by the parameters. In our specific use case, we need to provide the model for OVL. A linear model for OVL is defined by

$$m(x,y) = \Phi \times p$$

Φ is the information matrix which consists of the basis function $\phi(x,y)$, and p are the parameters of our model. The OVL polynomial has p coefficients or parameters. As described above, the information matrix Φ is already known to us and, in that case, the goal of FE is to estimate the parameters p of our model.

Overlay control is a critical part that enables the exposure system to successfully imprint the complex patterns and meet the strict requirements of modern IC designs. The current photolithographic systems manage to successfully control overlay via a combination of advanced process control (APC) and metrology modules. Metrology contributes to defining and tuning the overlay models (so that they accurately describe the expected systematic and nonsystematic overlay errors [4–6]), as well as relating them to the corresponding controllable knobs of the exposure system [7]. The coupling of overlay error predictions, via overlay models, with machine knobs defines the so called run-to-run (R2R) paradigm of overlay control [8–10]. Obviously, for an R2R process to be successful, it is crucial that the overlay models can accurately estimate the expected overlay errors. Extensive research has been conducted in defining overlay models. In [11], multilevel state space models were defined based on existing physics models [12–14], where multilayer, stack up overlay error models were developed. Extensive research has been conducted for improving the overlay modeling process, with the focus being either on optimizing the wafer measurements ([15,16]) or on investigating different metrics and cost functions ([17] Zhang et al.).

However, it is not sufficient to define the overlay model based only on the underlying physics; it is equally important that the metrology system further tunes the parameters of the overlay model. The ordinary least squares optimization (OLS) method is the most employed regression technique by the current exposure systems. OLS finds the regression coefficients of the overlay model that minimize the residual sum of the squared errors of the difference between the measured and the predicted overlay [18]. In Figure 1, the process of FE is presented. Since the basis functions of the model $\phi(x, y)$ are already predefined, the goal of the FE process is to obtain the best estimation of the model parameters p.

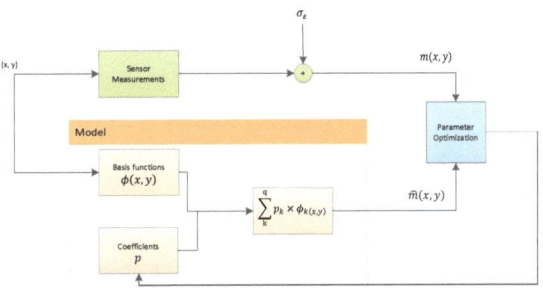

Figure 1. Fingerprint estimation as a block diagram.

Multicollinearity in high-dimensional datasets is a well-known challenge, particularly when multiple predictors are highly correlated. This can lead to unstable estimates in traditional regression models such as ordinary least squares (OLS), reducing their predictive power. To address this, alternative techniques such as principal component analysis (PCA), ridge regression, and lasso regression have been widely adopted. PCA is a dimensionality reduction technique that transforms the original variables into uncorrelated principal components, thereby eliminating multicollinearity by projecting the data into a lower-dimensional space where the principal components are orthogonal to each other [19]. Ridge regression adds an L2 regularization term to the OLS equation, which shrinks the coefficients of correlated variables, reducing their variance, and, thereby stabilizing the model [20,21]. Lasso regression, on the other hand, incorporates an L1 regularization term that not only shrinks the coefficients but can also set some of them exactly to zero, effectively performing variable selection while mitigating multicollinearity [22,23]. These methods are particularly useful when variable elimination is undesirable, as they allow the model to retain all the predictors while reducing the impact of multicollinearity on the predictive accuracy. Additionally, elastic net is an alternative approach particularly well suited for complex datasets. Elastic net combines both L1 (lasso) and L2 (ridge) penalties, making it highly effective in datasets that exhibit both multicollinearity and the need for variable selection. This hybrid approach balances the benefits of both ridge and lasso, allowing elastic net to handle correlated predictors and perform feature selection simultaneously [24]. When features in a dataset are highly correlated, the design matrix X in a linear regression model $Y = X\beta + \epsilon$ becomes nearly singular or ill-conditioned. This condition leads to large variances in the least squares estimates of the coefficients, β, because the inverse of $X^T X$ (which is needed to compute the OLS estimates $\hat{\beta} = (X^T X)^{-1} X^T Y$) will be unstable or significantly influenced by small changes in X or Y. Ridge regression minimizes $|Y - X\beta|_2^2 + \lambda |\beta|_2^2$, which shrinks coefficients smoothly and can handle collinearity better than lasso or PCA as it tends to reduce the coefficients proportionally, maintaining their relative influence on the outcome. Furthermore, ridge regression, by reducing the magnitude of all coefficients through its L2 penalty, tends to be more stable, although it does not reduce the model complexity by setting coefficients to zero.

A useful diagnostic tool to detect multicollinearity is the variance inflation factor (VIF), which quantifies how much the variance of a regression coefficient is inflated due to collinearity with other predictors. A high VIF value indicates that the parameter is highly collinear with others, making it problematic for reliable estimation. A general rule is that a VIF greater than 5 suggests moderate multicollinearity, while a VIF above 10 indicates a high level of multicollinearity [25]. By identifying variables that exhibit high variance inflation factor (VIF) values, we are able to determine which parameters induce multicollinearity. Subsequently, techniques such as principal component analysis (PCA), ridge, or lasso regression may be employed to address these issues, thereby enhancing the robustness of the model.

Importantly, the removal or combination of collinear parameters, while potentially reducing multicollinearity, is often undesirable because it can result in a significant loss of valuable information. Each predictor variable may carry unique and relevant aspects of the underlying data, and eliminating or combining them could obscure these nuances, leading to less precise and informative models [26]. Therefore, methods such as ridge or lasso regression, which allow for the retention of all variables while addressing the multicollinearity problem, are preferred in scenarios where preserving the integrity of the dataset is paramount.

In this paper, we are investigating the the fitness of the OLS algorithm for modeling highly dimensional overlay data. Among the aforementioned alternatives, we are proposing the usage of ridge regression over the classical OLS. The remainder of the paper is organized as follows: Section 2 describes the proposed method, and in Section 3 we show the results of applying the proposed method on an actual industrial process of 300 mm wafers. Finally, Section 4 presents the conclusions and potential future work.

2. Materials and Methods

In this paper, we propose to use ridge regression instead of the classic OLS method for tuning the parameters p of the overlay models. The overlay models, as mentioned above, consist of a set of basis functions $\phi(x,y)$ that are already predefined based on the physics and specific parameters of the process. Ridge regression, or Tikhonov regularization [21], is a statistical method for estimating the parameters of multiple regression models in scenarios where the independent variables are highly correlated.

Ridge regression is particularly useful in ill-posed problems which exhibit multicollinearity in their independent variables. In our case, we try to find the vector p of parameters such that

$$m = \Phi \times p$$

As mentioned before, the standard approach is to use the OLS method. OLS seeks to minimize the sum of the squared residuals:

$$||\Phi p - m||_2^2$$

However, if no p satisfies the equation or more p do, then the problem is ill-posed and OLS might lead to an over- or underdetermined system of equations.

Ridge regression adds a regularization term $||\Gamma x||_2^2$ for some suitable chosen matrix $\Gamma = \alpha I$. This is known as L_2 regularization. This ensures smoothness and improves the conditioning of the problem. The minimization problem to be solved, then, is

$$||\Phi p - m||_2^2 + ||\Gamma x||_2^2$$

And the corresponding parameter vector p:

$$p = (\Phi^T \Phi + \Gamma^T \Gamma)^{-1} \Phi^T m$$

To select the regularization parameter, we employed the 10-fold cross-validation method. The 30 layers were used as the training dataset, while the remaining 10 layers served as the test set. The cross-validation process determined that the optimal regularization parameter was $\alpha = 1.0$, which means that $\Gamma = I$. A value of $\alpha = 1.0$ means that the model benefits from a moderate amount of regularization, helping to stabilize the coefficient estimates and improve generalization without undermining the model's ability to accurately capture the relationships between the features and the target variable. Essentially, the regularization helps prevent overfitting by reducing the influence of less important or highly correlated features, but it does not overpenalize the model to the point where its predictions become too simplistic or inaccurate.

In Figure 2, the correlation matrix of the Overlay X and Overlay Y is presented. There seems to be high correlation between approximately 50 of the 161 parameters. This is an indication (a strong one, though) that there is significant collinearity in the parameters, and this needs to be further investigated.

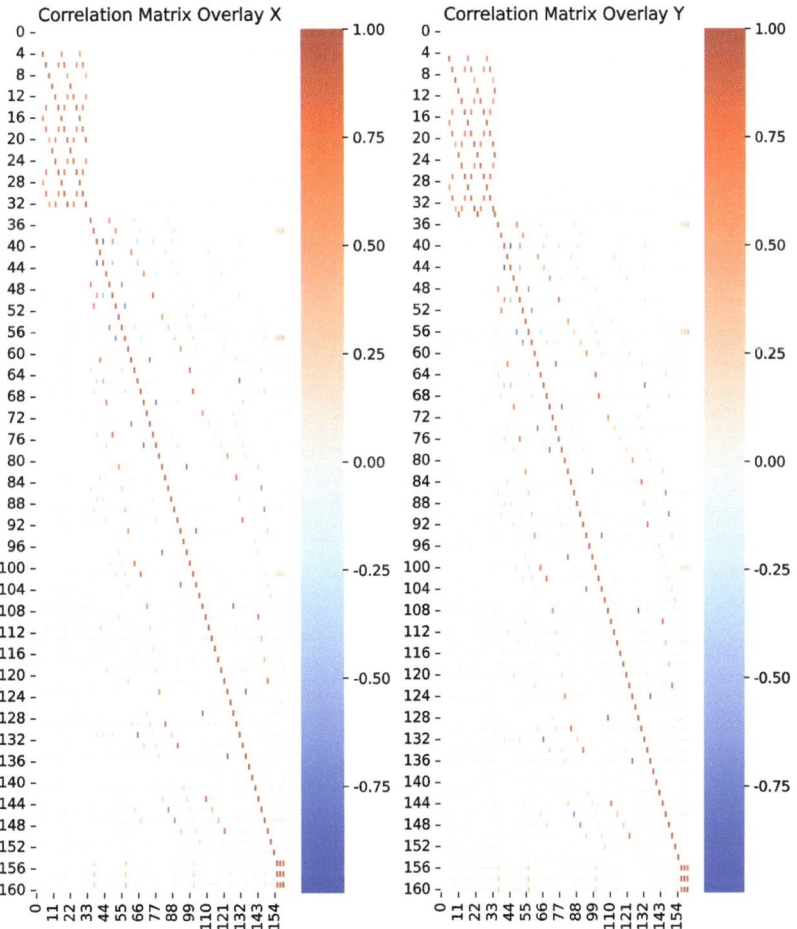

Figure 2. Correlation matrices for Overlay X and Overlay Y.

The variance inflation factor VIF is a statistical measure that quantifies the degree of multicollinearity for each independent variable. VIF is calculated as follows:

$$VIF = 1/(1 - R^2)$$

with R^2 being the square of the OLS solutions. A value of $VIF > 5$ indicates moderate multicollinearity, while $VIF > 10$ indicates high multicollinearity. Performing the VIF check in our OLS solutions for Overlay X and Y results in high mulitcollinearity in 62/161 parameters for Overlay X and in 109/161 parameters for Overlay Y. Therefore, the conclusion is that multicollinearity needs to be addressed. In this case, indeed, the ridge regression method should be able to address the issue and improve the parameter estimation method.

3. Results and Discussion

In our experiments, we compared the overlay residuals (in X and in Y) for both ridge regression and OLS methods. The expected overlay, per field point, is compared to the actual overlay. Next, a statistical analysis of the results is performed. In assessing the performance we use the 99.7th percentile and *max* residual metrics. Utilizing these metrics enables a comprehensive understanding of the overlay performance, providing insights into the extent of variability and the upper bounds of error dispersion.

The goal of our method is to accurately model the measured overlay and reproduce it with minimum error. In Figure 3, we can see the measured Overlay X on the left and the modeled Overlay X on the right, using the ridge regression method. In this visual representation, we can see that the modeled overlay is able to successfully capture the expected overlay. Also, in areas of the wafer where there seems to be abnormal behavior as on the edges of the wafer, the patterns seems to really match. Similarly, in Figure 4, ridge regression also performs well on Overlay Y.

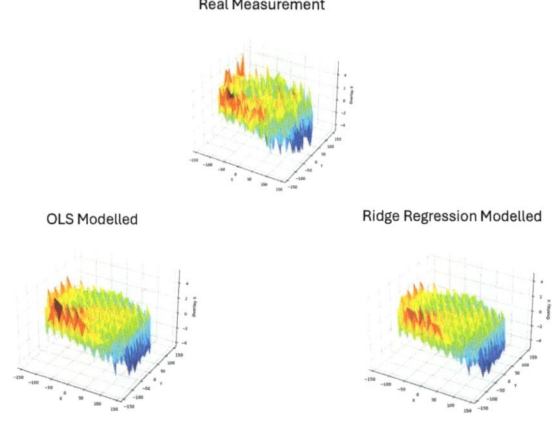

Figure 3. Overlay X—Comparing the modeling result of OLS vs. ridge regression for one of the exposed layers. The real measurement (that serves as a benchmark) is presented at the top of the figure.

The residuals vs. the predicted values for ridge regression and OLS are presented in Figures 5 and 6, respectively.

In Figure 7, the Overlay X residuals in 99.7 are presented for both OLS and ridge regression methods. For 8/12 layers, ridge regression outperforms the OLS method. Despite the overall model exhibiting certain statistical properties, such as multicollinearity, it is important to recognize that each layer in the process can behave differently. Several factors, particularly measurement noise, can significantly impact individual layers. In our case, this measurement noise plays a substantial role in the variability of the process. As a result, it is not surprising that OLS may outperform ridge regression in specific layers, such as layers 3, 5, and 6, where the unique characteristics of the exposure process may not benefit as much from regularization. In these cases, OLS may capitalize on the direct relationships between variables without the need for regularization, whereas ridge regression's penalty on coefficients may dampen the model's performance. However, it is important to focus on the overall performance of the model, rather than isolated instances. The broader trends across all layers indicate that ridge regression remains a robust choice, particularly in mitigating the effects of multicollinearity, even if OLS is favored in specific layers due to the unique "exposure specifics" that tend to influence the outcome.

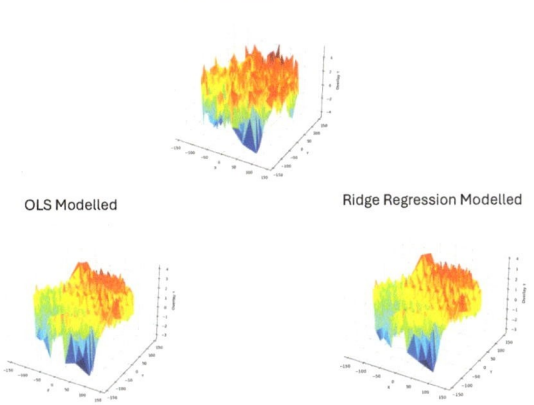

Figure 4. Overlay Y—Comparing the modeling result of OLS vs. ridge regression for one of the exposed layers. The real measurement (that serves as a benchmark) is presented at the top of the figure.

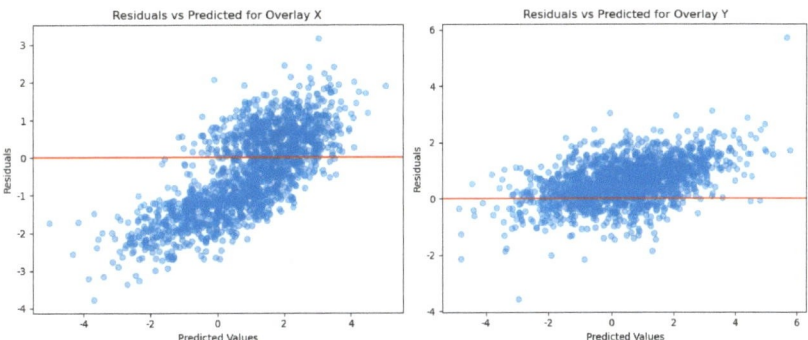

Figure 5. Residuals vs. predicted with ridge regression for one of the exposed layers.

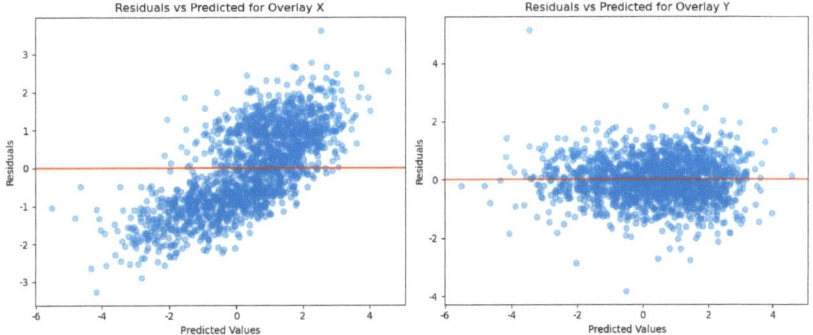

Figure 6. Residuals vs. predicted with OLS for one of the exposed layers.

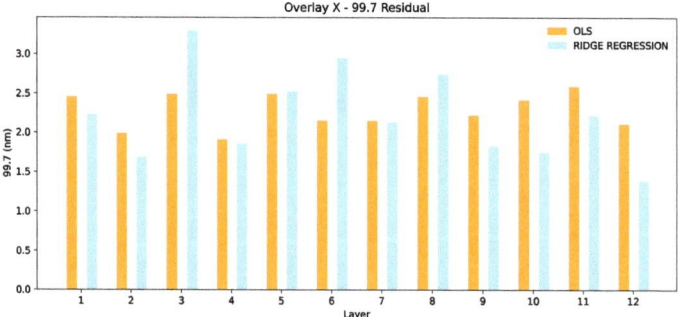

Figure 7. Overlay X—99.7 residual.

The max residuals in Overlay X are compared in Figure 8. Here, we observe a different pattern than in 99.7. OLS outperforms the ridge regression in 9/12 layers. From these results, we cannot yet draw a safe conclusion. It depends which metric we value most (99.7 vs. max), and this actually depends on the use case. However, the superiority of ridge regression in 99.7 only is an interesting conclusion already.

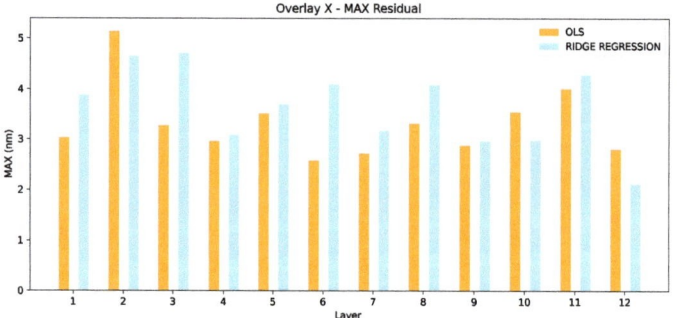

Figure 8. Overlay X—max residual.

When checking the Overlay in Y, we draw a more clear picture of the situation. As presented in Figure 9, ridge regression significantly outperforms the OLS in all 12 layers. On average, this is a 1.04 nm improvement. In this case, the superiority of ridge regression is clear.

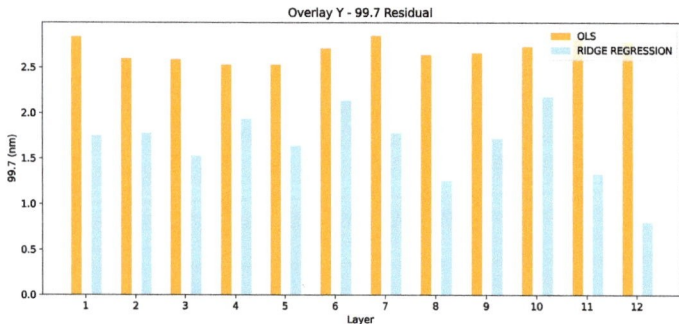

Figure 9. Overlay Y—99.7 residual.

Similarly, in Overlay max, Figure 10 shows ridge regression outperforming OLS in all wafers with an average improvement of 1.10 nm.

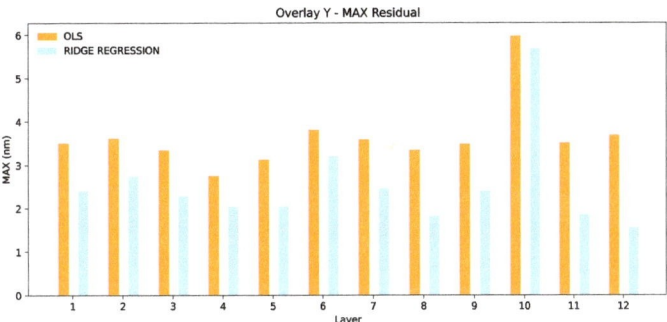

Figure 10. Overlay Y—max residual.

The results presented in Tables 1 and 2 illustrate the performance of ridge regression compared to ordinary least squares (OLS) across multiple layers in terms of the OVL X and OVL Y metrics, both for the 99.7th percentile residuals and the maximum residuals. In Table 1, which focuses on OVL X, ridge regression generally performs better than OLS, particularly in reducing the 99.7th percentile residuals. This is evident in most layers where the ridge regression residuals are consistently lower than those obtained using OLS. For instance, in layer 9, ridge regression produces a 99.7th percentile residual of 1.83 nm compared to 2.22 nm with OLS. Similarly, the max residuals also show improvement in many cases, such as in layer 8, where ridge regression results in a max residual of 4.08 nm compared to 3.31 nm for OLS. On average we can also see that Ridge Regression achieves smaller residuals in 99.7, however on MAX it performs worse than OLS on average. In Figure 11 we see the box plots for the Overlay X. For the metric 99.7, the OLS residuals exhibit a tight Interquartile Range (IQR) centered approximately around 2.4 nm, indicating a generally consistent performance across different samples. The Ridge residuals, while similar in median value, show a slightly wider IQR with values stretching from about 1.7 nm to nearly 2.7 nm. This suggests that while the Ridge model can occasionally offer a tighter fit, it might also produce more variable results in some instances. For the MAX residuals, both models demonstrate an increase in the spread of values compared to the 99.7 measurements. The OLS model displays an IQR from approximately 3.0 nm to 3.5 nm, with some outliers extending towards 4.0 nm, indicating a less consistent fit for maximum residual values. The Ridge model, while showing a lower starting point at around 2.0 nm, extends up to about 4.5 nm, matching the OLS model in variability. The presence of outliers in both models for the MAX residuals suggests that extreme values are a common occurrence, potentially indicating challenging scenarios where both models struggle to maintain a consistent performance.

In Table 2, which reports the Overlay Y residuals, ridge regression again shows superior performance over OLS. This is particularly noticeable in the max residuals, where ridge regression substantially outperforms OLS in most layers. For example, in layer 10, the OLS max residual is 5.98 nm, while ridge regression achieves a significantly lower value of 5.69 nm. The same trend is visible in the 99.7th percentile residuals, where ridge regression consistently yields lower residuals, such as in layer 3, where the residuals drop from 2.59 nm with OLS to 1.53 nm with ridge regression. In Figure 12 we see the box plots for Overlay Y. For the 99.7 metric, the OLS model exhibits a compact distribution with an IQR closely centered around 2.6 nm to 2.8 nm. This suggests a relatively stable and consistent model performance over the observed dataset. Ridge model demonstrates a significantly wider IQR, extending from 1.5 nm to 2.0 nm. The wider spread and lower minimum values may indicate a greater variability in model performance, potentially offering lower residuals but with less consistency compared to the OLS model. In the MAX nm residuals, the OLS residuals span from approximately 3.5 nm to 3.8 nm. Ridge residuals are slightly more spread ranging from 2 nm to approximately 2.8 nm.

Overall, the results clearly demonstrate that ridge regression provides better accuracy and robustness in reducing both 99.7th percentile and max residuals compared to OLS. This improvement is particularly beneficial in handling multicollinearity within the dataset, a well-known strength of ridge regression. The reduced variance in the ridge regression models contributes to more reliable and consistent predictions across all layers, making it the preferred method in this context.

Table 1. Overlay X residuals in nanometers.

Layer	OLS—99.7	Ridge—99.7	OLS—Max	Ridge—Max
1	2.46	2.23	3.03	3.88
2	1.99	1.69	5.14	4.65
3	2.49	3.3	3.27	4.71
4	1.91	1.86	2.96	3.09
5	2.49	2.53	3.51	3.7
6	2.15	2.95	2.58	4.09
7	2.15	2.13	2.72	3.17
8	2.46	2.74	3.31	4.08
9	2.22	1.83	2.88	2.96
10	2.42	1.75	3.54	2.98
11	2.59	2.22	4.01	4.28
12	2.11	1.39	2.81	2.12

Table 2. Overlay Y residuals in nanometers.

Layer	OLS—99.7	Ridge—99.7	OLS—Max	Ridge—Max
1	2.84	1.75	3.51	2.42
2	2.60	1.78	3.62	2.75
3	2.59	1.53	3.35	2.29
4	2.53	1.94	2.76	2.04
5	2.53	1.64	3.13	2.05
6	2.71	2.14	3.81	3.21
7	2.85	1.78	3.59	2.46
8	2.64	1.26	3.35	1.82
9	2.66	1.72	3.49	2.41
10	2.73	2.18	5.98	5.69
11	2.82	1.33	3.51	1.86
12	2.79	0.80	3.69	1.55

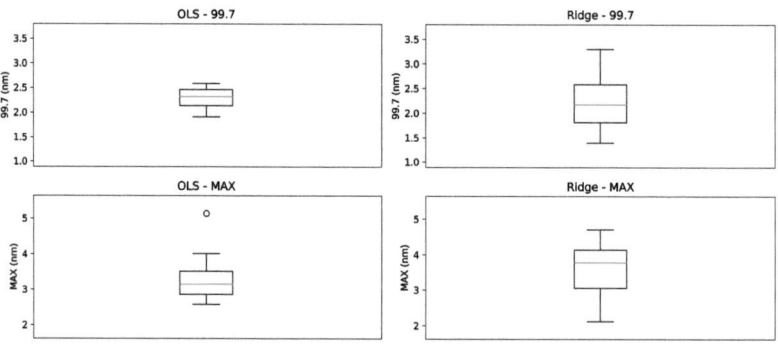

Figure 11. Box Plot Analysis for Overlay X Residuals.

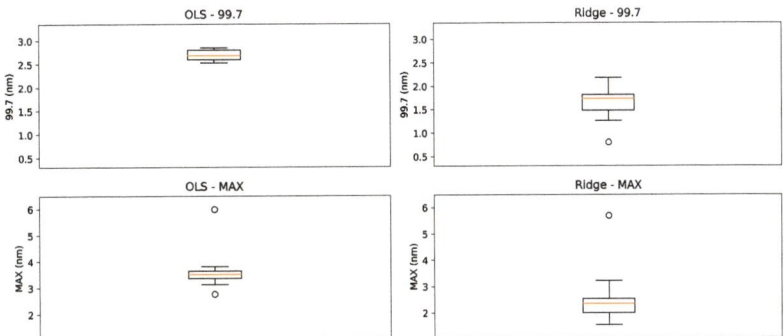

Figure 12. Box Plot Analysis for Overlay Y Residuals.

In Figures 13 and 14, we present the measured vs. modeled Overlay X and Y for all the 12 layers. The observed differences between the measured and modeled results can be attributed to several factors. First, despite the application of ridge regression to address multicollinearity, the strong collinearity between certain parameters may still impact the model's accuracy in specific cases, leading to discrepancies. Additionally, boundary effects at the edges of the wafer, where the photolithography process is more susceptible to physical limitations, may result in larger residuals, as these regions are often harder to model accurately. Moreover, while the polynomial model employed in this study is effective for many cases, it may not fully capture all the nonlinearities and complex interactions inherent in the photolithography process, particularly for edge cases. Lastly, measurement noise or inaccuracies in the metrology system may also contribute to the differences observed, as these errors can introduce additional variability that the model cannot entirely account for. Addressing these discrepancies may require further refinement of the model or adjustments to the regularization parameters used in the ridge regression approach. However, despite these discrepancies, the overall modeling performance remains satisfactory, as depicted by the residuals, which consistently show a good fit between the measured and modeled data across the majority of layers and regions. This indicates that the ridge regression approach still provides robust results in the context of overlay modeling.

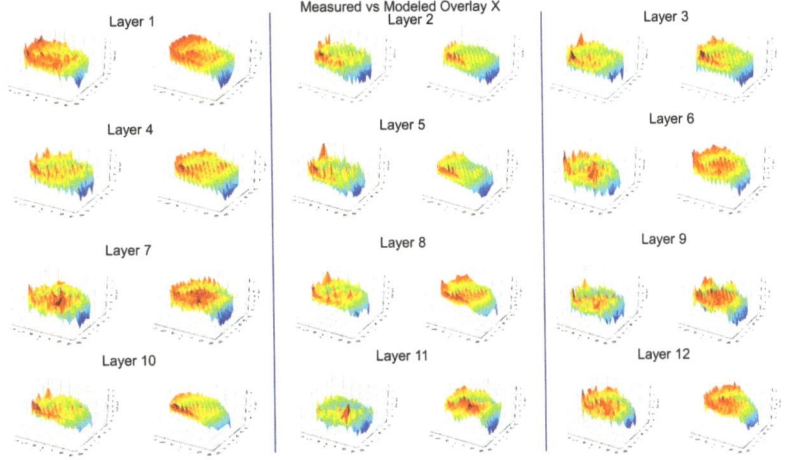

Figure 13. Measured vs. modeled Overlay X for all 12 layers.

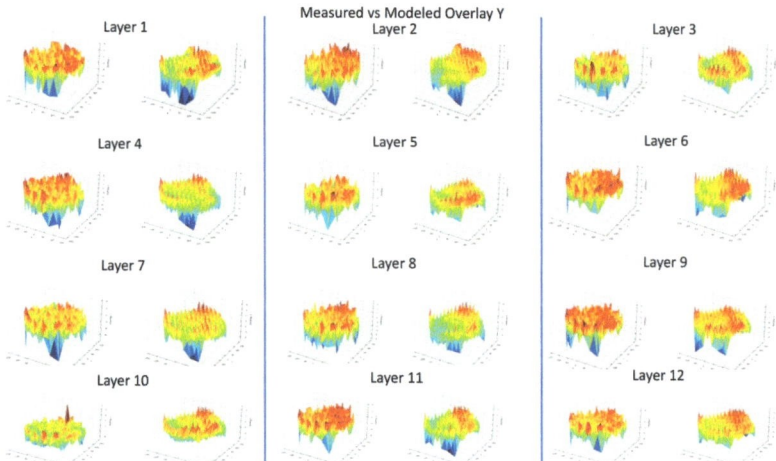

Figure 14. Measured vs. modeled Overlay Y for all 12 layers.

4. Conclusions and Future Work

Ridge regression results indicate an obvious superiority over OLS when the data exhibit multicollinearity. Especially in Overlay X, where this phenomenon is more intense, ridge regression outperforms OLS in every single layer. In the end, the overall improvement in 99.7 is 1.04 nm and in the max 1.10 nm. Such a performance improvement at the subnanometer level of precision cannot be ignored. It is clear that OLS needs to be enhanced for similar datasets. One potential direction for future work would be the investigation of improving the model itself, either by reducing the features or by dynamically, during wafer production, selecting the most informative ones depending on the state of the process.

Author Contributions: Conceptualization, A.M.; methodology, A.M., C.G. and P.A.; software, A.M.; writing—original draft preparation, A.M.; writing—review and editing, A.M., P.A. and C.G.; supervision, A.B. All authors have read and agreed to the published version of the manuscript.

Funding: This research received no external funding.

Data Availability Statement: The data presented in this study are not publicly available due to IP protection reasons.

Conflicts of Interest: The authors declare no conflicts of interest.

References

1. Moore's Law Inspires Intel Innovation. Available online: https://www.intel.com/content/www/us/en/history/museum-gordonmoore-law.html (accessed on 9 September 2024).
2. Jacobs, I.S. Fine particles, thin films and exchange anisotropy. *Magnetism* **1963**, *3*, 271–350.
3. Lee, K.Y.; LaBianca, N.; Rishton, S.A.; Zolgharnain, S.; Gelorme, J.D.; Shaw, J.; Chang, T.P. Micromachining applications of a high resolution ultrathick photoresist. *J. Vac. Sci. Technol. Microelectron. Nanometer Struct. Process. Meas. Phenom.* **1995**, *13*, 3012–3016. [CrossRef]
4. Hsueh, B.Y.; Huang, G.K.; Yu, C.C.; Hsu, J.K.; Huang, C.C.K.; Huang, C.J.; Tien, D. High order correction and sampling strategy for 45 nm immersion lithography overlay control. In *Metrology, Inspection, and Process Control for Microlithography XXII*; SPIE: San Jose, CA, USA, 2008; Volume 6922, p. 69222Q. [CrossRef]
5. Choi, D.; Lee, C.; Bang, C.; Cho, D.; Gil, M.; Izikson, P.; Yoon, S.; Lee, D. Optimization of high order control including overlay,alignment, and sampling. In *Metrology, Inspection, and Process Control for Microlithography XXII*; SPIE: San Jose, CA, USA, 2008; Volume 6922, p. 69220P. [CrossRef]
6. Lin, H.M.; Lin, B.; Wu, J.; Chiu, S.; Huang, C.C.K.; Manka, J.; Goh, D.; Huang, H.; Tien, D. Improve overlay control and scanner utilization through high order corrections. In *Metrology, Inspection, and Process Control for Microlithography XXII*; SPIE: San Jose, CA, USA, 2008; Volume 6922. [CrossRef]

7. Van Den Brink, M.A.; De Mol, C.G.M.; George, R.A. Matching performance for multiple wafer steppers using an advanced metrology procedure. In *Integrated Circuit Metrology, Inspection, and Process Control II*; SPIE: San Jose, CA, USA, 1988; Volume 0921, p. 180. [CrossRef]
8. Haq, A.U.; Djurdjanovic, D. Robust control of overlay errors in photolithography processes. *IEEE Trans. Semicond. Manuf.* **2019**, *32*, 320–333. [CrossRef]
9. Chien, C.-F.; Chen, Y.-J.; Hsu, C.-Y.; Wang, H.-K. Overlay error compensation using advanced process control with dynamically adjusted proportional-integral R2R controller. *IEEE Trans. Autom. Sci. Eng.* **2014**, *11*, 473–484. [CrossRef]
10. Tan, F.; Pan, T.; Li, Z.; Chen, S. Survey on run-to-run control algorithms in high-mix semiconductor manufacturing processes. *IEEE Trans. Industr. Inform.* **2015**, *11*, 1435–1444. [CrossRef]
11. Yu, J.; Qin, S. Variance component analysis based fault diagnosis of multi-layer overlay lithography processes. *IIE Trans.* **2009**, *41*, 764–775. [CrossRef]
12. He, F.; Zhang, Z. An empirical study-based state space model for multilayer overlay errors in the step-scan lithography process. *RSC Adv.* **2015**, *5*, 103901–103906. [CrossRef]
13. He, F.; Zhang, Z. State space model and numerical simulation of overlay error for multilayer overlay lithography processes. In Proceedings of the 2017 2nd International Conference on Image, Vision and Computing (ICIVC), Chengdu, China, 2–4 June 2017; pp. 1123–1127. [CrossRef]
14. Khaki, M.; Fathi, M.; Chien, C.-F. Partially observable Markov decision process for monitoring multilayer wafer fabrication. *IEEE Trans. Autom. Sci. Eng.* **2021**, *18*, 1742–1753. [CrossRef]
15. Magklaras, A.; Alefragis, P.; Gogos, C.; Valouxis, C.; Birbas, A. A Genetic Algorithm-Enhanced Sensor Marks Selection Algorithm for Wavefront Aberration Modeling in Extreme-UV (EUV) Photolithography. *Information* **2023**, *14*, 428. [CrossRef]
16. Magklaras, A.; Gogos, C.; Alefragis, P.; Valouxis, C.; Birbas, A. Sampling Points Selection Algorithm For Advanced Photolithography Process. In Proceedings of the 2022 7th South-East Europe Design Automation, Computer Engineering, Computer Networks and Social Media Conference (SEEDA-CECNSM), Ioannina, Greece, 23–25 September 2022; pp. 1–5. [CrossRef]
17. Zhang, H.; Feng, T.; Djurdjanovic, D. Dynamic Down Selection of Measurement Markers for Optimized Robust Control of Overlay Errors in Photolithography Processes. *IEEE Trans. Semicond. Manuf.* **2022**, *35*, 241–255. [CrossRef]
18. Horng, S.-C.; Wu, S.-Y. Compensating the overlay modeling errors in lithography process of wafer stepper. In Proceedings of the 2010 5th IEEE Conference on Industrial Electronics and Applications, Taichung, Taiwan, 15–17 June 2010; pp. 1399–1404.
19. Jolliffe, I.T. *Principal Component Analysis*; Springer Series in Statistics; Springer: Berlin/Heidelberg, Germany, 2002; ISBN 9780387954424.
20. Hoerl, A.E.; Kennard, R.W. Ridge Regression: Biased Estimation for Nonorthogonal Problems. *Technometrics* **1970**, *12*, 55–67. [CrossRef]
21. McDonald, G.C. Ridge Regression. In *Wiley Interdisciplinary Reviews: Computational Statistics*; Wiley: Hoboken, NJ, USA, 2009; pp. 93–100.
22. Tibshirani, R. Regression Shrinkage and Selection via the Lasso. *J. R. Stat. Soc. Ser. B (Methodol.)* **1996**, *58*, 267–288. [CrossRef]
23. Li, Z.; Shahrajabian, H.; Bagherzadeh, S.A.; Jadidi, H.; Karimipour, A.; Tlili, I. Effects of nano-clay content, foaming temperature and foaming time on density and cell size of PVC matrix foam by presented Least Absolute Shrinkage and Selection Operator statistical regression via suitable experiments as a function of MMT content. *Phys. A Stat. Mech. Its Appl.* **2020**, *537*, 122637. [CrossRef]
24. Zou, H.; Hastie, T. Regularization and Variable Selection via the Elastic Net. *J. R. Stat. Soc. Ser. B (Stat. Methodol.)* **2005**, *67*, 301–320. [CrossRef]
25. MKutner, H.; Nachtsheim, C.J.; Neter, J.; Li, W. *Applied Linear Statistical Models*, 5th ed.; McGraw-Hill/Irwin: New York, NY, USA, 2004.
26. Dormann, C.F.; Elith, J.; Bacher, S.; Buchmann, C.; Carl, G.; Carré, G.; Marquéz, J.R.G.; Gruber, B.; Lafourcade, B.; Leitão, P.J.; et al. Collinearity: A review of methods to deal with it and a simulation study evaluating their performance. *Ecography* **2013**, *36*, 27–46. [CrossRef]

Disclaimer/Publisher's Note: The statements, opinions and data contained in all publications are solely those of the individual author(s) and contributor(s) and not of MDPI and/or the editor(s). MDPI and/or the editor(s) disclaim responsibility for any injury to people or property resulting from any ideas, methods, instructions or products referred to in the content.

Article

Cyclic Structure, Vertex Degree and Number of Linear Vertices in Minimal Strong Digraphs

Miguel Arcos-Argudo [1,*,†], Jesús Lacalle [2,†] and Luis M. Pozo-Coronado [2,†]

1. Math Innovation Group, Universidad Politécnica Salesiana, Cuenca 010102, Ecuador
2. Departmento de MATIC, ETSI Sistemas Informáticos, Universidad Politécnica de Madrid, 28031 Madrid, Spain; jesus.glopezdelacalle@upm.es (J.L.); lm.pozo@upm.es (L.M.P.-C.)
* Correspondence: marcos@ups.edu.ec
† These authors contributed equally to this work.

Abstract: Minimal Strong Digraphs (MSDs) can be regarded as a generalization of the concept of tree to directed graphs. Their cyclic structure and some spectral properties have been studied in several articles. In this work, we further study some properties of MSDs that have to do with bounding the length of the longest cycle (regarding the number of linear vertices, or the maximal in- or outdegree of vertices); studying whatever consequences from the spectral point of view; and giving some insight about the circumstances in which an efficient algorithm to find the longest cycle contained in an MSD can be formulated. Among other properties, we show that the number of linear vertices contained in an MSD is greater than or equal to the maximal (respectively minimal) in- or outdegree of any vertex of the MSD and that the maximal length of a cycle contained in an MSD is lesser than or equal to $2n - m$ where n, m are the order and the size of the MSD, respectively; we find a bound for the coefficients of the characteristic polynomial of an MSD, and finally, we prove that computing the longest cycle contained in an MSD is an NP-hard problem.

Keywords: minimal strong digraphs; maximum length directed cycles; linear vertex; external chain; characteristic polynomial; NP-hard problem

MSC: 68R10

Citation: Arcos-Argudo, M.; Lacalle, J.; Pozo-Coronado, L.M. Cyclic Structure, Vertex Degree and Number of Linear Vertices in Minimal Strong Digraphs. *Mathematics* **2024**, *12*, 3657. https://doi.org/10.3390/math12233657

Academic Editor: Frank Werner

Received: 10 October 2024
Revised: 16 November 2024
Accepted: 19 November 2024
Published: 22 November 2024

Copyright: © 2024 by the authors. Licensee MDPI, Basel, Switzerland. This article is an open access article distributed under the terms and conditions of the Creative Commons Attribution (CC BY) license (https://creativecommons.org/licenses/by/4.0/).

1. Introduction

A Minimal Strong Digraph (MSD) is a strong digraph in which the deletion of any arc yields a non-strongly connected digraph. In [1,2] a compilation of the properties properties of MDSs can be found. Additionally, in [2] a comparative analysis between MSDs and non-directed trees, where a series of the analog properties of both types of graphs, is presented. In this sense, MSDs gain interest as a counterpart of trees in the context of directed graphs.

There are several other reasons to justify the interest in studying MSDs. One of them is the relationship between MSDs and nearly reducible $(0,1)$-matrices (via the adjacency matrix; see, for instance, [3,4]) and the non-negative inverse eigenvalue problem (see [5]): given real numbers $k_1, k_2, \ldots, k_n$, find the necessary and sufficient conditions for the existence of a non-negative matrix A of order n with characteristic polynomial $x^n + k_1 x^{n-1} + k_2 x^{n-2} + \cdots + k_n$. The coefficients of the characteristic polynomial are closely related to the cycle structure of the weighted digraph with adjacency matrix A by means of the theorem of the coefficients [6], and the irreducible matricial realizations of the polynomial (which are identified with strongly connected digraphs [3]) can easily be reduced to the class of Minimal Strong Digraphs. Hence, a better understanding of the cyclic structure of MSDs could lead to results on spectral theory.

Another goal for our work is trying to take advantage of the fact that minimality among SDs is a very restrictive condition. For instance, it is well known that the size of an MSD of order n is bounded by $2(n-1)$. We think that the fact that the class of MSDs is comparatively small, together with the properties obtained in [2], pointing out relationships between the size of the longest cycle in an MSD and the number of linear vertices, could lead to finding an algorithm of polynomial complexity to find the longest cycle in an MSD. Note that finding the longest cycle on a SD is an NP-hard problem.

Our work plan is, thus, to further study the properties of MSDs that could give a better understanding of their cyclic structure, especially those having to do with bounding the length of the longest cycle (regarding the number of linear vertices, or the maximal in- or outdegree of vertices); studying whatever consequences from the spectral point of view; and finally trying to devise an efficient algorithm to find the longest cycle in an MSD. The first steps are accomplished, but we have to accept that the restrictions we obtain to bound the length of cycles in an MSD are not enough to simplify the search of the longest cycle. In fact, we prove that finding the longest cycle in an MSD is NP-hard. Nevertheless, we think that the new properties of MSDs that we are able to prove are interesting in and of themselves, insofar as they progress the way of understanding the cyclic structure of MSDs, and hence they can lead to advances in spectral theory.

The outline of the article is as follows: In Section 2, we introduce some notations and review several results on MSDs. In Section 3, we study the relationship between the length of the longest cycle, the number of linear vertices, and the maximal in- or outdegree of vertices. We also state some MSD properties, regarding chains and its contraction, that arise from the ear decomposition. In Section 4, we state a bound for the coefficients of the characteristic polynomial of an MSD, extending the results of [2]. In Section 5, we prove that the problem of finding the longest cycle in an MSD is NP-hard. Finally, we draw some conclusions.

2. Notation and Basic Properties

In this paper, we use some concepts and basic results about graphs that are described below, in order to fix the notation [1,2,7–13].

Let $D = (V, A)$ be a digraph. If $(u, v) \in A$ is an arc of D, we say that u is the tail (or initial vertex) and v the head (or final vertex) of the arc, and we denote the arc by uv. We shall consider only directed paths and directed cycles. We shall denote by $n = |V|$ and by $m = |A|$ the order and the size of D, respectively.

In a strongly connected digraph, the indegree $d^-(v)$ and the outdegree $d^+(v)$ of every vertex v are greater than or equal to 1. We shall say that v is a linear vertex if it satisfies $d^+(v) = d^-(v) = 1$.

An arc uv in a digraph D is transitive if there exists another uv-path disjoint to the arc uv. A digraph is called a minimal digraph if it has no transitive arcs.

The contraction of a subdigraph consists in the reduction in the subdigraph to a unique vertex $\bar{v}$. Note that the contraction of a cycle of length q in an SD yields another SD. In such a process, $q - 1$ vertices and q arcs are eliminated. Given a cycle C_q, let $\bar{v}$ be the vertex corresponding to C_q after contraction. We shall denote by $d^-(C_q) = d^-(\bar{v})$ (respectively $d^+(C_q) = d^+(\bar{v})$). Note that $d^+(C_q) = \sum_{v \in C_q}(d^+(v) - 1)$ (and the same with $d^-(v)$).

Some basic properties concerning MSDs can be found in [1,2,8,14,15].

We summarize some of them: The size of an MSD digraph D of order $n \geq 2$ verifies $n \leq m \leq 2(n-1)$ [1]. The contraction of a cycle in an MSD preserves the minimality, that is, it produces another MSD; hence, if we contract a strongly connected subdigraph in a minimal digraph, the resulting digraph is also minimal, and each MSD of order $n \geq 2$ has at least two linear vertices.

If C_q is a cycle contained in an MSD D, then the number of linear vertices of D is greater than or equal to $\left\lfloor \frac{q+1}{2} \right\rfloor$. An MSD factors into a rooted spanning tree and a forest of reversed rooted trees (Theorem 20 [2]). Finally, we will use the next result.

Lemma 1 ([2]). *If an MSD contains a cycle C_2, then the vertices on the cycle are linear vertices or cut points.*

3. Lower Bounds of the Number of Linear Vertices of an MSD

Let D be an MSD and C_q a cycle contained in D.

In this section, we show some results obtained through the analysis of the degree of the vertices, especially those with a high degree.

Proposition 1. *Let $D = (V, A)$ be an MSD, λ the number of linear vertices of D, and $v \in V$ a vertex such that v is contained in each cycle of D. Then, $\lambda \geq max(d^-(v), d^+(v))$.*

Proof. If D is a cycle, then $d^-(v) = d^+(v) = 1$; therefore, $\lambda \geq 2 > max(d^-(v), d^+(v)) = 1$, and the proof is completed.

Otherwise, let $C_q = v, u_1, \ldots, u_{q-1}, v$ be a cycle contained in D. By definition of MSD, each arc of D is contained in at least one directed cycle of D, or else D would not be strongly connected. Since v is contained in each cycle of D, then each arc wu_i such that $w \notin C_q$ is contained in a cycle $v, \ldots, w, u_i, \ldots, v$ for $1 \leq i \leq q - 1$. In a similar way, each arc $u_i w$ such that $w \notin C_q$ is contained in a cycle $v, \ldots, u_i, w, \ldots, v$ for $1 \leq i \leq q - 1$.

We shall prove that in C_q, there must exist at least one linear vertex. Let us, in fact, suppose, by contradiction, that $u_i \in C_q$ is not a linear vertex for $1 \leq i \leq q - 1$. Hence, $d^-(u_1) = 1$ or else the arc vu_1 would be transitive in D. In fact, if $d^-(u_1) > 1$, since v is contained in each cycle, v is a vertex reached by walking in reverse direction from u_1 using an arc $u'_1 u_1$ different from vu_1 (such an arc exists because of $d^-(u_1) > 1$), and then a vu_1-path (not containing the arc vu_1) can be obtained by concatenation of a vu'_1-path with the arc $u'_1 u_1$.

Then, $d^+(u_1) > 1$ since $d^-(u_1) = 1$ and we are assuming that u_1 is not linear. Let $u''_1 \neq u_2$ be the vertex defined by the corresponding arc $u_1 u''_1 \in D$.

Now the following result will be proved for all u_i, $2 \leq i \leq q - 1$: $d^-(u_i) = 1$ and there is an arc $u_i u''_i$ with $u''_i \neq u_{i+1}$. To show this, the following reasoning is applied iteratively for each vertex, starting from u_2. First, we remark that $d^-(u_i) = 1$. Otherwise, the arc $u_{i-1} u_i$ would be transitive in D because an $u_{i-1} u_i$-path would exist, not containing the arc $u_{i-1} u_i$. In fact, since v is contained in each cycle, v is a vertex reached walking in reverse direction from u_i starting with an arc $u'_i u_i$ different from $u_{i-1} u_i$ (such an arc exists since $d^-(u_i) > 1$). Also, v is a vertex reached walking from u_{i-1} starting with the arc $u_{i-1} u''_{i-1}$. Then, a $u_{i-1} u_i$-path would be obtained by concatenation of the arc $u_{i-1} u''_{i-1}$ with the $u''_{i-1} v$-path, the vu'_i-path, and the arc $u'_i u_i$.

$d^+(u_i) > 1$ also holds because $d^-(u_i) = 1$ and, by hypothesis, u_i is not a linear vertex. Let $u''_i \neq u_{i+1}$ be the vertex defined by the arc $u_i u''_i$ belonging to D.

Finally, let us show that the arc $u_{q-1} v$ is transitive. In fact, since v is contained in each cycle, v is a vertex reached walking from u_{q-1}, starting with the arc $u_{q-1} u''_{q-1}$. The $u_{q-1} v$-path obtained by concatenation of the arc $u_{q-1} u''_{q-1}$ with the $u''_{q-1} v$-path proves that $u_{q-1} v$ is transitive. This fact contradicts the minimality of D.

We have still to prove that the linear vertices reached for each outgoing (respectively, incoming) arc from (respectively, to) v are all different. Let vu_1 and vu'_1 be two arcs in D. From vu_1, as we have seen, we can construct a path $v, u_1, \ldots, u_k$ such that $d^-(u_i) = 1$ for $1 \leq i \leq k$ and $d^+(u_i) > 1$ for $1 \leq i \leq k - 1$, and u_k is linear (note that k can be 1, but it must exist) as we have proved previously. Now, in a similar way, we construct a path $v, u'_1, \ldots, u'_l$ such that $d^-(u'_j) = 1$ for $1 \leq i \leq l$ and $d^+(u'_j) > 1$ for $1 \leq i \leq l - 1$ and u'_l is linear.

The paths $v, u_1, \ldots, u_k$ and $v, u'_1, \ldots, u'_l$ cannot rejoin after they leave v since all the indegrees of their vertices are 1. Hence, $u_k \neq u'_l$. The proof is completed. □

Proposition 2. *Let $D = (V, A)$ be an MSD of order $n \geq 2$, $v \in V$ a vertex of D, and λ the number of linear vertices contained in D. Then, $\lambda \geq max(d^-(v), d^+(v))$.*

Proof. If $D = C_n$ then $d^-(v) = d^+(v) = 1$, therefore $\lambda = q \geq 2$ and the proof is completed.

Otherwise, we obtain an MSD D' from D by the contraction of all cycles that do not contain the vertex v. Note that v is a vertex contained in each cycle of D'. Then, by

Proposition 1 $\lambda_{D'} \geq max(d^-(v), d^+(v))$ where $\lambda_{D'}$ is the number of linear vertices of D'. Note also that v preserves in D' all its incident arcs. Next we expand the cycles contracted previously. In this process, the linear vertices are maintained. Indeed, if we expand a linear vertex corresponding to a cycle of length greater than two, this fact is obvious. And, if we expand one corresponding to a cycle of length two, the result follows from Lemma 1, since for cycles of length two, the contracted vertex in D' will contain at least one existing linear vertex in D; hence, the number of linear vertices in D is not less than the number of linear vertices contained in D'. The proof is completed. □

Corollary 1. *Let $D = (V, A)$ be an MSD, C_q a cycle contained in D, and μ the number of linear vertices contained in D but not contained in C_q. Then, $\mu \geq max(d^-(C_q), d^+(C_q))$.*

Proof. If $D = C_q$, then $\mu = d^-(C_q) = d^+(C_q) = 0$, and the proof is completed.

Otherwise, we obtain an MSD D' from D by contracting C_q in a unique vertex v'. Note that the number of linear vertices of D' is precisely μ. The application of Proposition 2 then implies that $\mu \geq max(d^-(v'), d^+(v')) = max(d^-(C_q), d^+(C_q))$ and we are finished. □

As we mentioned in Section 2, if there is a cycle $C_q \in D$, the number of linear vertices of D is greater than or equal to $\left\lfloor \frac{q+1}{2} \right\rfloor$; see [8]. We ratify this result with a new, shorter proof, by using the previous properties.

Corollary 2. *Let $D = (V, A)$ be an MSD of order $n \geq 2$, C_q a cycle contained in D, and λ the number of linear vertices contained in D. Then, $\lambda \geq \left\lfloor \frac{q+1}{2} \right\rfloor$.*

Proof. Let v be the number of linear vertices contained in C_q, and μ the rest of linear vertices of D. Then, $\lambda = \mu + v$, and we know by Corollary 1 that $\mu \geq max(d^+(C_q), d^-(C_q))$. Since $d^+(C_q) + d^-(C_q) \geq q - v$, we have that

$$\mu \geq max(d^+(C_q), d^-(C_q)) \geq \left\lceil \frac{q-v}{2} \right\rceil, \qquad (1)$$

and then

$$\lambda = \mu + v \geq \left\lceil \frac{q-v}{2} \right\rceil + v = \left\lceil \frac{q+v}{2} \right\rceil \geq \left\lceil \frac{q}{2} \right\rceil = \left\lfloor \frac{q+1}{2} \right\rfloor. \qquad (2)$$

The proof is completed. □

As a consequence of Corollary 2, we obtain an upper bound for the maximum length of a cycle contained in an MSD.

Corollary 3. *Let $D = (V, A)$ be an MSD of order $n \geq 2$, C_l a cycle with maximal length l contained in D, and λ the number of linear vertices contained in D. Then, $l \leq 2\lambda$.*

Proof. By Corollary 2, we know that

$$\lambda \geq \left\lfloor \frac{l+1}{2} \right\rfloor, \qquad (3)$$

then

$$l \leq 2\lambda. \qquad (4)$$

The proof is completed. □

Since every vertex contained in an MSD must be contained in at least one directed cycle, we can obtain two different bounds for the number of linear vertices, one from the vertex degree and one from the cycle length. The next result somehow combines the two aforementioned bounds.

Corollary 4. Let $D = (V, A)$ be an MSD of order $n \geq 2$, C_q a directed cycle of length q contained in D, $u \in C_q$ a vertex of D, $d(u) = d^+(u) + d^-(u)$, and λ the number of linear vertices contained in D. Then,

$$\lambda \geq \left\lfloor \frac{q + d(u)}{2} \right\rfloor - 1. \tag{5}$$

Proof. As we did in the proof of Corollary 2, we call ν the number of linear vertices contained in C_q and μ the rest of linear vertices of D. The value of ν tends to be smaller, as there are more paths between the vertices contained in the cycle C_q. Then, for any vertex u contained in the cycle C_q, we obtain the following inequality:

$$\nu + (d^+(C_q) - (d^+(u) - 1)) + (d^-(C_q) - (d^-(u) - 1)) + 1 \geq q$$
$$\Rightarrow d^+(C_q) + d^-(C_q) \geq q - \nu + d(u) - 3. \tag{6}$$

Combining it with Corollary 1 ($\mu \geq max(d^+(C_q), d^-(C_q))$), we obtain

$$\mu \geq \max(d^+(C_q), d^-(C_q)) \geq \left\lceil \frac{q - \nu + d(u) - 3}{2} \right\rceil \tag{7}$$

and finally

$$\lambda = \mu + \nu \geq \left\lceil \frac{q - \nu + d(u) - 3}{2} \right\rceil + \nu = \left\lceil \frac{q + \nu + d(u) - 1}{2} \right\rceil - 1$$
$$\geq \left\lceil \frac{q + d(u) - 1}{2} \right\rceil - 1 = \left\lfloor \frac{q + d(u)}{2} \right\rfloor - 1. \tag{8}$$

The proof is completed. □

Corollary 4 can be useful when a vertex u with a high degree is contained in the cycle C_q (see examples in Figures 1 and 2). However, if the vertex u is not contained in the cycle, the number of linear vertices contained in the MSD could be much higher than the number of linear vertices obtained with this bound. For instance, in the examples in Figures 3 and 4), if $q = 10$ and the vertices in the cycle have degree 2 or less, the bound given by Corollary 4 would be 5, but the number of linear vertices would be at least 14; an analogous example is showed in Figure 5.

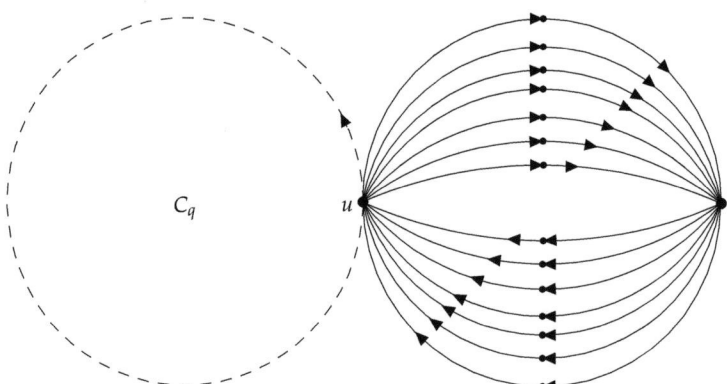

Figure 1. Example 1 for Corollary 4 where C_q contains a vertex u with high in- and out-degree.

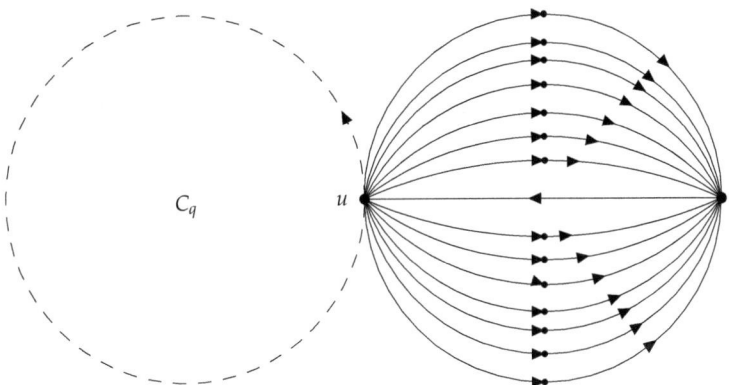

Figure 2. Example 2 for Corollary 4 where C_q contains a vertex u with high out-degree.

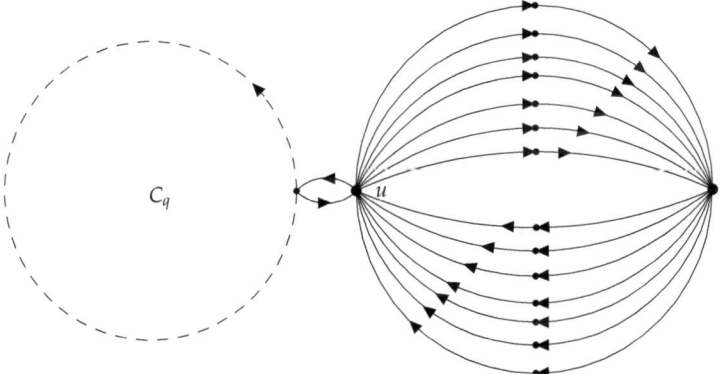

Figure 3. Example 1 of an MSD, in which there is a vertex with high degree (input and output) and is not contained in the cycle C_q.

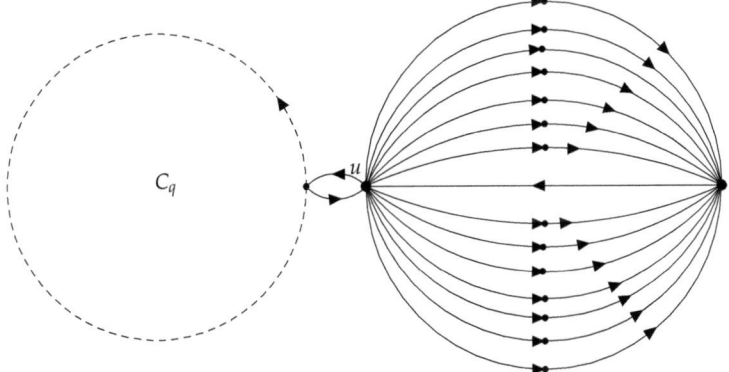

Figure 4. Example 2 of an MSD, in which there is a vertex with high output degree and is not contained in the cycle C_q.

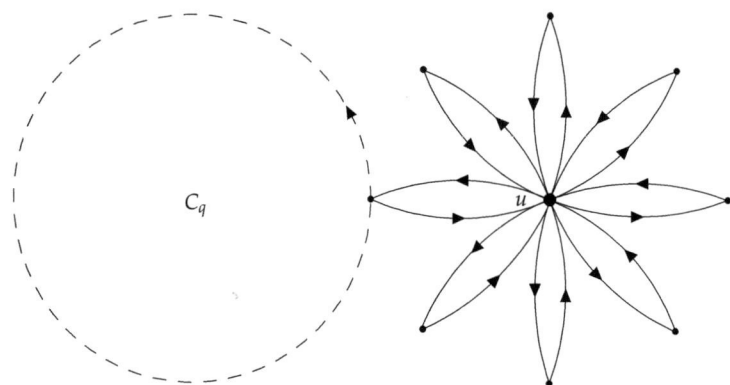

Figure 5. Example 3 of an MSD, in which there is a vertex with high degree (input and output) and is not contained in the cycle C_q.

Proposition 3. *Let $D = (V, A)$ be an MSD, and let C_q be a cycle of length q contained in D. Then, $q \leq 2n - m$.*

Proof. We obtain an MSD D' by contraction of C_q in a unique vertex v', and then $n' = n - q + 1$ and $m' = m - q$. Hence, since

$$m' \leq 2(n' - 1), \tag{9}$$

we obtain

$$m - q \leq 2(n - q), \tag{10}$$

and finally

$$q \leq 2n - m. \tag{11}$$

The proof is completed. □

Other Properties of MSDs

In [2,14], some results about ear decomposition are proved. We use these previous results to show the next properties of MSDs.

Definition 1. *Let $D = (V, A)$ be an MSD of order $n \geq 2$, and let $v_1, \ldots, v_l$ be a path contained in D. We say that the $v_1 v_l$-path is a* chain *with length l if $d^-(v_i) = d^+(v_i) = 1$ for all $1 \leq i \leq l$.*

Note that an isolated linear vertex is a chain of length 1.

Definition 2. *Let $D = (V, A)$ be an MSD of order $n \geq 2$, let $v_1, \ldots, v_l$ be a chain contained in D, and let D' be the digraph obtained from D by the elimination of the $v_1 v_l$-path. We say that the $v_1 v_l$-path is an* external chain *with length l if D' preserves the strong connection.*

Proposition 4. *Let $D = (V, A)$ be an MSD of order $n \geq 2$ and C_q a cycle contained in D such that $D \neq C_q$. Then, in D, there exists at least one external chain.*

Proof. We use the ear decomposition shown in Theorem 20 in [2] in a similar way to how it was used in the proof of the property that affirms that an MSD factors into a rooted spanning tree and a forest of reversed rooted trees.

Let us consider an ear decomposition of D, $\mathcal{E} = P_0, \ldots, P_k$. Since D is an MSD, each ear P_j ($0 \leq j \leq k$) contains at least one new vertex and two new arcs, with respect to $\bigcup_{i=0}^{j-1} V_i$ and $\bigcup_{i=0}^{j-1} A_i$, respectively.

Then, it is clear that the last ear $P_k = v_0^k \ldots v_{s_k}^k$ completes the construction of D, and $Q_k = v_1^k \ldots v_{s_k-1}^k$ is a chain of linear vertices, whose first and last vertex are joined to vertices of a minimal and strongly connected digraph D'. Hence, $D' = D - Q_k$ is an MSD, and therefore Q_k is an external chain of length $l = s_k - 1 \geq 1$. Trivially, we can say that if $D = C_q = P_0$, then there is no external chain contained in D. The proof is completed. □

Note that D' is an MSD with $n - l$ vertices and $m - l - 1$ arcs. Note also that if $P_0 = C_q$, with C_q as a maximal length cycle contained in D, and there exists any external chain with length $l \geq 1$ not contained in C_q, then $q \leq n - l$.

Proposition 5. *Let $D = (V, A)$ be an MSD, and let $v_1 v_l$-path be a chain contained in D with length $l < n$. Then, the contraction of all vertices of the $v_1 v_l$-path in a unique vertex preserves the minimality, that is, it produces another MSD D' with $n - l + 1$ vertices and $m - l + 1$ arcs.*

Proof. Let D' be the digraph obtained by the contraction of all vertices of the $v_1 v_l$-path in a unique vertex v'. Let n' be the number of vertices and m' the number of arcs of D'. In D', all vertices of the $v_1 v_l$-path are suppressed, but it contains the vertex $v' \notin D$, and then $n' = n - l + 1$. Since $d^-(v_i) = d^+(v_i) = 1$ for all $1 \leq i \leq l$, we have $m' = m - l + 1$. Now, let us assume that there are transitive arcs in D'. If we expand v', these transitive arcs would also exist in D, contradicting the minimality of D. Hence, D' is minimal. Since $n > l$, then a vertex $w \notin v_1 v_l$-path, exists also in D', and D' contains a wv'-path and a $v'w$-path. Therefore, D' is strongly connected. The proof is completed. □

Proposition 6. *Let $D = (V, A)$ be an MSD such that D is not a cycle. Then, there is not a cycle in D that contains all linear vertices of D.*

Proof. Let us suppose that C_q contains all linear vertices of D. We can obtain an MSD D' by contraction of C_q in a unique vertex v'. We know that D' must contain at least two linear vertices, and at least one of them is different from v'. Then, it is clear that there exists at least one linear vertex that is contained in D but is not contained in C_q. The proof is completed. □

Let D be an MSD such that D is not a cycle, and λ be the number of linear vertices contained in D. From the proposition above, it is trivial to see that a cycle C_q contained in D will contain at most $\lambda - 1$ linear vertices of D.

4. Upper Bounds for the Coefficients of the Characteristic Polynomial of MSDs

In [2], some results about bounds of the coefficients of the characteristic polynomial of an MSD are proved. In particular, it is shown that the independent term must be 1, 0, or -1. We follow the lines of that proof to generalize that bound.

Proposition 7. *Let $D = (V, A)$ be an MSD, and let $x^n + k_1 x^{n-1} + \cdots + k_i x^{n-i} + \cdots + k_{n-1} x + k_n$ be the characteristic polynomial of the adjacency matrix of D. Then,*

$$|k_i| \leq \binom{n}{i} \tag{12}$$

Proof. We claim that any subset of i vertices can be covered by disjoint cycles in at most one manner. In fact, take any subset $A \subset V$, with $|A| = i$, and consider the subdigraph D' to be generated by that A. Now, D' is a subdigraph of an MSD, so it has no transitive arcs. If it is not strongly connected, we can add arcs, one by one, until we obtain a strongly connected digraph D'' that would be minimal. Therefore, D'' would be an MSD, and the aforementioned result of [2] implies that there is at most one covering of the vertices of D'' (that is, of A) by disjoint cycles.

The coefficients theorem for digraphs allows us to finish the proof. □

5. MSD Properties Associated to Results of Algorithms Complexity

It was well known that minimality is a very strict condition in the family of strong digraphs implying, for instance, the size limitation $n \leq m \leq 2(n-1)$. As we have seen in previous sections, MSDs also exhibit strong constraints on the number of linear vertices and maximum in- and outdegrees of vertices, regarding the length of the longest directed cycle. Unfortunately, these constraints are not enough to construct an efficient algorithm finding the longest cycle in an MSD.

A proof that an MSD can be converted into a directed cycle by successively eliminating external chains is given in [16]. However, this process does not guarantee that the resulting directed cycle will have a maximum length. Figure 6 shows an MSD where the longest directed cycle is given by $u_1, u_2, u_3, u_4, u_5, u_1$, but this cycle will be obtained only in the case that the external chains eliminated are those formed by the u_6-path and u_7-path. Nevertheless, there is no an efficient algorithm that can determine the deletion of these chains and the non-deletion of the external chain formed by the vertex u_5-path because if this chain is deleted, then the longest cycle of the MSD will also have been eliminated.

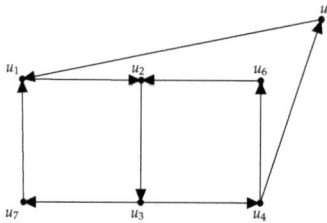

Figure 6. Example of an MSD that contains three external chains.

Theorem 1. *Computing a cycle with maximal length in an MSD is an NP-hard problem.*

Proof. We can reduce the problem of computing a cycle with maximal length in a strongly connected digraph to the problem of computing a cycle with maximal length in an MSD.

Let $D' = (V', A')$ be a strong digraph. We can build an MSD $D = (V, A)$ from D' as follows. For each arc $v'_i v'_j \in A'$, we add an intermediate vertex v_{ij}. We thus obtain

$$V = V' \cup \{v_{ij} \mid v'_i v'_j \in A'\} \quad (13)$$

$$A = \{v'_i v_{ij} \mid v'_i v'_j \in A'\} \cup \{v_{ij} v'_j \mid v'_i v'_j \in A'\} \quad (14)$$

Note that the strong connection of D' implies that D is trivially strongly connected. Note also that no arc of D can be transitive since every arc has a linear vertex v_{ij} as start- or endpoint. Hence, D is in fact an MSD.

Now, we remark that there is a one-to-one correspondence between cycles in D and cycles in D': for every cycle C'_q in D', a cycle C_{2q} arises in D, and all the cycles in D are generated in this way.

We conclude that any algorithm allowing us to compute the longest cycle of an MSD would then be able to compute the longest cycle of any SD, too. Since the problem of computing the longest cycle in a strongly connected digraph is NP-hard [14], then the theorem is proved. □

Theorem 2. *Let $D = (V, A)$ be an MSD. Finding a cycle contained in D with length $2n - m$ is an NP-complete problem.*

Proof. We can reduce the problem of determining if a digraph is Hamiltonian to the problem of determining if an MSD has a cycle of length $2n - m$.

Let $D' = (V', A')$ be a digraph. If D' is strongly connected, the same procedure used in the previous proof yields an MSD $D = (V, A)$ (if D' is not strongly connected, then it cannot be Hamiltonian). The order of D verifies $n = n' + m'$, and the size holds $m = 2m'$. Hence, finding a cycle in D with length $2n - m = 2(n' + m') - 2m' = 2n'$ would imply finding a n'-cycle in D', that is, determining if D is Hamiltonian. Since determining whether a digraph is Hamiltonian is an NP-complete problem, the theorem is proved. □

6. Conclusions

In this work, we have found some new properties regarding MSDs. The first set of properties has to do with the number of linear vertices in an MSD. We have seen that the existence of a vertex with a high in- or outdegree implies a high number of linear vertices. Furthermore, we have used this fact to give a simpler proof of the lower bound of linear vertices that we obtained in [8], where the existence of a q cycle implies at least $\lfloor (q+1)/2 \rfloor$ linear vertices. We have also proved that chains of consecutive linear vertices in an MSD can be contracted without loss of minimality. We feel that further research along these lines could give, from one side, a result linking maximal cycle lengths, maximal in- or outdegrees, and improved estimations of the number of linear vertices, as well as a better understanding of the cycle properties that can lead to spectral properties, such as the characterization of polynomials that can be realized as characteristic polynomials of MSDs. In this regard, we have proved a bound for the coefficients of such polynomials, advancing along the lines given in [2].

Since the number of linear vertices in an MSD is easily computed, we wanted to explore the possibility that the maximal length of a cycle could be bounded so as to allow to construct a polynomial complexity algorithm to find the longest cycle. Unfortunately, that is not the case, and we have proved that the search of a maximal length cycle in an MSD is NP-hard. Still, it can be interesting to look for a subset of MSDs for which the search for maximal length cycles can be performed efficiently. This kind of result could arise, also, by further study of the properties that we pointed out in the paragraph above.

Author Contributions: Conceptualization, M.A.-A., J.L. and L.M.P.-C.; investigation, M.A.-A., J.L. and L.M.P.-C.; writing—original draft preparation, M.A.-A.; writing—review and editing, J.L. and L.M.P.-C. All authors have read and agreed to the published version of the manuscript.

Funding: This research was funded by Universidad Politécnica Salesiana and supported by Math Innovation Group and Departamento de MATIC.

Data Availability Statement: No new data were created or analyzed in this study. Data sharing is not applicable to this article.

Conflicts of Interest: The authors declare no conflict of interest.

References

1. García-López, J.; Marijuán, C. Minimal strong digraphs. *Discrete Math.* **2012**, *312*, 737–744. [CrossRef]
2. García-López, J.; Marijuán, C.; Pozo-Coronado, L.M. Structural properties of minimal strong digraphs versus trees. *Linear Algebra Appl.* **2018**, *540*, 203–220. [CrossRef]
3. Brualdi, R.A.; Ryser, H.J. *Combinatorial Matrix Theory*; Cambridge University Press: New York, NY, USA, 1992.
4. Hedrick, M.; Sinkhorn, R. A special class of irreducible matrices—The nearly reducible matrices. *J. Algebra* **1970**, *16*, 143–150. [CrossRef]
5. Torre-Mayo, J.; Abril-Raymundo, M.R.; Alarcia-Estévez, E.; Marijuán, C.; Pisonero, M. The nonnegative inverse eigenvalue problem from the coefficients of the characteristic polynomial, EBL digraphs. *Linear Algebra Appl.* **2007**, *426*, 729–773. [CrossRef]
6. Cvetkovic, D.; Doob, M.; Sachs, H. *Spectra of Graphs: Theory and Application*; Academic Press: Cambridge, MA, USA, 1980.

7. Verstraete, J. *Introduction to Graph Theory*; Department of Mathematics of University of California at San Diego: San Diego, CA, USA, 2020.
8. Arcos-Argudo, M.; García-López, J.; Pozo-Coronado, L.M. Structure of cycles in Minimal Strong Digraphs. *Discret. Appl. Math.* **2019**, *263*, 35–41. [CrossRef]
9. Zverovich, V. *Modern Applications of Graph Theory*; Oxford University Press: New York, NY, USA, 2021.
10. Diestel, R. *Graph Theory*; Springer: Cham, Switzerland, 2024.
11. O'Regan, G. *Mathematical Foundations of Software Engineering—Chapter 7: Graph Theory*; Springer: Cham, Switzerland, 2023.
12. Kumar, Y.S. *Advanced Graph Theory*; Springer: Cham, Switzerland, 2023.
13. Lecca, P.; Carpentieri, B. *Introduction to Mathematics for Computational Biology*; Springer: Cham, Switzerland, 2023.
14. Bang-Jensen, J.; Gutin, G. *Digraphs: Theory, Algorithms and Applications*, 2nd. ed.; Springer: London, UK, 2009.
15. Berge, C. *Graphes*; North-Holland: Amsterdam, The Netherlands, 1991.
16. Chen, Z.B.; Zhang, F.J. Bounds of the longest directed cycle length for minimal strong digraphs. *Discret. Math.* **1988**, *68*, 9–13. [CrossRef]

Disclaimer/Publisher's Note: The statements, opinions and data contained in all publications are solely those of the individual author(s) and contributor(s) and not of MDPI and/or the editor(s). MDPI and/or the editor(s) disclaim responsibility for any injury to people or property resulting from any ideas, methods, instructions or products referred to in the content.

Article

Conceptual Framework for Adaptive Bacterial Memetic Algorithm Parameterization in Storage Location Assignment Problem

Kitti Udvardy [1], Polina Görbe [2], Tamás Bódis [2] and János Botzheim [3,*]

1. Multidisciplinary Doctoral School of Engineering, Széchenyi University, 9026 Győr, Hungary; udvardy.kitti@sze.hu
2. Department of Logistics and Forwarding, Széchenyi University, 9026 Győr, Hungary; gorbe.polina@sze.hu (P.G.); bodis.tamas@sze.hu (T.B.)
3. Department of Artificial Intelligence, Faculty of Informatics, ELTE Eötvös Loránd University, 1117 Budapest, Hungary
* Correspondence: botzheim@inf.elte.hu

Abstract: Recognized as an NP-hard combinatorial challenge, Storage Location Assignment Problem (SLAP) demands heuristic or algorithmic solutions for effective optimization. This paper specifically examines the enhancement of SLAP through the utilization of evolutionary algorithms, as they are particularly suitable for complex cases. Among others, the genetic algorithm (GA) is typically applied to solve this problem. This paper investigates the Bacterial Memetic Algorithm (BMA) as a possible solution for optimization. Though the comparative analysis of the BMA with the previously well-used GA algorithm under certain test parameters reveals that BMA is suitable for SLA optimization, BMA failed to achieve better results. We attribute the unsatisfactory results to the parameter settings, as illustrated by a few specific examples. However, the complexity of the problem and the parameterization does not allow for continuous manual parameter adjustment, which is why we have identified the need for a concept that automatically and adaptively adjusts the parameter settings based on the statistics and fitness values obtained during the execution. The novelty of this paper is to specify the concept of adaptive BMA parameterization and rules.

Keywords: storage location assignment problem; bacterial memetic algorithm; adaptive parameterization; evolutionary algorithms

MSC: 68W50; 68T05

Citation: Udvardy, K.; Görbe, P.; Bódis, T.; Botzheim, J. Conceptual Framework for Adaptive Bacterial Memetic Algorithm Parameterization in Storage Location Assignment Problem. *Mathematics* 2024, 12, 3688. https://doi.org/10.3390/math12233688

Academic Editor: Frank Werner

Received: 31 October 2024
Revised: 21 November 2024
Accepted: 22 November 2024
Published: 25 November 2024

Copyright: © 2024 by the authors. Licensee MDPI, Basel, Switzerland. This article is an open access article distributed under the terms and conditions of the Creative Commons Attribution (CC BY) license (https://creativecommons.org/licenses/by/4.0/).

1. Introduction

The efficiency of the warehouse operations is measured and assessed based on several factors. The low-level picker-to-parts systems involve pickers moving toward storage locations to retrieve products based on pick lists, with different generations evolving in terms of system setups and processes [1]. In these warehouses, efficiency is mostly measured by order picking. It is known that the picking process is very time- and cost-consuming due to the travel distances that the picker must cover during the process; moreover, efficiency is strongly influenced by the picking route and storage location assignment (SLA). If the lead time is reduced, more tasks can be completed, so efficiency can be improved. Travel time accounts for nearly 50% of the total picking time. The routing can be controlled by route optimization, and the lead time for picking tasks can be further improved by considering the SLA [2]. Rapidly changing demands—typical in the warehousing of products in the Fast-Moving Consumer Goods (FMCGs) sector—can upset previously optimized SLAs. An SLA is typically reviewed when order-picking efficiency has deteriorated significantly. The literature examined deals with the topic of the Storage Location Assignment Problem (SLAP).

SLAP is a huge combinatorial problem when hundreds or thousands of items need to be assigned to hundreds or thousands of locations, and on top of that, different criteria and storage methods increase the number of combinations. This type of problem is a NP-hard problem, and it is very difficult to solve using exclusively exact methods [3].

From the aforementioned, SLAP requires the use of heuristics or algorithms for SLA optimization due to the size of the combinations. There is a lot of research into optimizing SLA. There are solutions where heuristics are used to solve the problem [4–6]. Diefenbach et al. specifically examined the optimization of human-and-cost-centric storage assignment in picker-to-parts warehouses and solved it using a heuristic based on a custom opening procedure and a tabu search meta-heuristic [7]. Research has discovered that evolutionary algorithms are frequently employed to optimize SLA. Consequently, this paper primarily concentrates on these techniques. The Differential Evolution Algorithm was examined [8], and in another study, it was examined in conjunction with Global Local and Near-Neighbor Particle Swarm Optimization (GLNPSO) algorithm [9]. Particle swarm optimization was used to optimize SLA for outbound containers with a neighborhood-based mutation operator [10]. Moreover, in another research study, discrete evolutionary particle swarm optimization (DEPSO) was used [11]. Peng et al. examined and modified the Non-Dominated Sorting Genetic Algorithm III (NSGA-III) and compared it with Multi-objective Evolutionary Algorithm Based on Decomposition (MOEA/D). The goal in their study was to reduce the relocation tasks by optimizing SLA and crane scheduling [12]. The authors used their study's multi-objective evolutionary algorithm, called RP^2-NSGA-II, in a class-based storage warehouse. This algorithm was used to rank the set of alternatives based on the information contained in a valued outranking relation constructed by the ELECTRE III method [13]. Wan and Liu designed an optimization algorithm, which includes a design algorithm for a fishbone layout, SLA algorithm, and picker-routing algorithm. They compared the results of particle swarm optimization (PSO) and gravitational search algorithm (GSA) in solving storage location assignment and picker-routing problems [14]. In addition, the genetic approach was used in many studies. Zhou et al. used the genetic algorithm (GA) and its improvement with the simulated annealing algorithm (SA) and defined the genetic simulation annealing algorithm (SAGA) in an automated warehouse [15]. Xie et al. used genetic programming in their research [16,17]. The genetic algorithm was used with Pareto-optimization and a niche technique to find the Pareto-optimal solutions in Li et al.'s and Wu et al.'s research [18,19]. Ene and Öztürk used the genetic algorithm for a storage location assignment and order-picking optimization in the automotive industry [20]. Xu and Ren used genetic algorithms for a dynamic storage location assignment, which was based on a step-by-step process to optimize storage location gradually instead of a one-time optimization [21]. Saleet also used the genetic algorithm for a SLA in which the optimization process considered the parameter of items that are often ordered together to be stored close to each other in the warehouse [22].

This study focuses on warehouses that employ a low-level picker-to-parts system, where manual picking requires visits to multiple storage locations. Additionally, items in the FMCG or e-commerce sectors are characterized by rapidly changing demands, seasonality, and a broad product portfolio. These factors significantly influence the SLA more quickly, which is why this research specifically focuses on these items and their associated warehouses to solve SLAP and considering manual picking processes. A new approach was formulated to SLAP, whereby SLA should be continuously reviewed and optimized, and the near ideal state of the depleted picking locations should be replenished with the right item based on the new SLA proposal. In this way, we adaptively follow the near-ideal SLA and strive to avoid total warehouse repositioning. This is the Adaptive Storage Location Assignment, the concept and applicability of which the authors have previously published [23,24]. The first step of the Adaptive Storage Location Assignment (ASLA) is therefore the optimization of SLA, which requires an algorithm. So far, we have given a summary of what algorithms other researchers have applied to SLAP. Our focus was on evolutionary algorithms. The experience is that the genetic algorithm has been applied in many cases, and other evolutionary algorithms have been researched in this area, but the Bacterial Memetic Algorithm (BMA) has not been applied to SLA optimization thus far, so we started to investigate the applicability of BMA.

The BMA has been applied in many fields, such as continuous optimization, supervised machine learning, and combinatorial optimization problems, and its outstanding performance compared to other evolutionary algorithms has been highlighted [25]. Others also stated that the convergence of the BMA is theoretically more stable and faster than the genetic algorithm's is [26]. In this paper, we describe the development of the BMA for optimizing SLA and examine its suitability by comparing the results with those of the well-established GA. Preliminary findings classify the BMA as capable of assigning products effectively, and, based on previous experiences, better results are predicted in large combinatoric spaces. Upon examining the results of the GA, it was observed that the BMA's performance approaches that of the GA, yet it has not achieved as favorable a value for the objective function. It is assumed that the expected result cannot be achieved due to the large search space and complex parameterization. The BMA possesses more parameters than the GA, and numerous parameter settings were explored during the testing of the BMA. To enhance the performance of the BMA, following the initial static parameter settings, an investigation was conducted to determine the outcomes when certain operators are systematically applied during the optimization process. The manual modification of the BMA operator parameters during the optimization process showed that applying different operators or operator parameterization at the different stages of the optimization can improve the performance of BMA. Though it slightly enhanced the competitiveness of BMA, the vast number of combinations in parameter settings, when manually adjusted, have not yet produced satisfactory results. To achieve results comparable to or even better than those of the GA, based on the following research, this problem could potentially be resolved with an intelligent parameterization logic, such as a dynamic or self-adaptive parameter setup. The self-adaptive parameterization of evolutionary algorithms (EAs) is a long-researched yet still relevant topic. It addresses key challenges, such as the balance between exploration and exploitation, convergence speed, reduction in manual tuning, and enhancing solution diversity. As basics, O. Kramer's proposed a comprehensive survey on self-adaptation parameters in EA and defined several parameters which can be dynamically modified during the optimization process and identified possible key performance indicators [27]. The results of this study show that self-adaptation parameter control makes EAs highly effective for complex optimization challenges with enhancing the flexibility, efficiency, and robustness of the EA. H. Beyer et al. and S. Meyer-Nieberger et al. give an extensive overview of the methodology and the differences between self-adaptation and cumulative step-size adaptation in evolution strategies [28,29]. Both studies highlighted that self-adaptation parameterization enhances the robustness and efficiency of EAs. F. Ye et al. studied the effect of the self-adaptive mutation rates on Global Simple Evolutionary Multi-Objective Algorithm (GSEMO) [30]. The paper provides three techniques and uses several performance metrics. Results show that the algorithm performs better with self-adaptive parameters. J. Yao et al. compared a self-adaptive multifactorial evolutionary algorithm (SA_MFEA) to multifactorial evolutionary algorithm (MFEA) where self-adaptive parameterization led to a more robust and efficient optimization framework [31]. J. Cortez-González et al. presented a novel self-adaptive constraint-handling approach where the algorithm penalizes constraint violations dynamically. Due to this mechanism, the DE algorithm can tackle complicated, nonlinear, and multivariable optimization problems in chemical engineering [32]. S. Wang et al. created a self-parameter setup for DE, specifically in Self-Adaptive Ensemble-Based Differential Evolution (SAEDE). By defining the critical dynamic parameters, e.g., scaling factor, mutation strategy, population size, and crossover rate, and using an ensemble-learning mechanism to select the optimal parameters, more efficient convergence, higher success rates, and reduced manual tuning were achieved [33]. An improved differential evolution (DE) method with three separate mutation operators is presented by Xuming Wang and Xiaobing Yu, where six typical mutation operators were divided into three groups and a dynamic mutation and parameter selection method was applied. This strategy significantly improved the exploration and exploitation balance and resulted in a higher convergence speed and a more robust performance [34]. A multi-objective evolutionary algorithm with interval-based initialization and self-adaptive crossover operator for large-scale feature selection (FS) is proposed in the study of Y. Xue et al. in the field of personalized trip planning [35]. With the adaptive population size and self-adaptive crossover and mutation rates, the convergence efficiency of the Self-Adaptive Non-Dominated Sorting Genetic Algorithm II (SA-NSGA II) was improved, and the need for manual tuning was reduced. P. Karthikeyan presented a Self-Adaptive Immigrants Genetic Algorithm (SAI-GA) for virtual machine placement, whereas for self-adaptive parameterization, four immigrant strategies were defined with adaptive crossover and mutation [36]. As a result, the SAI-GA demonstrates, among other things, a great CPU performance and shows higher mean fitness value. On the topic of Flexible Job Shop Scheduling, the studies of L. Sun et al. [37] and Y. An et al. [38] show that the hCEA-MRF [37] improves solution robustness, quality, and adaptability, making it highly effective for complex, real-world scheduling challenges with variable processing times and makes the ACML-BCEA [38] both robust and versatile, capable of optimizing complex job-shop scheduling scenarios with minimal manual intervention.

Without aiming for completeness, based on the presented research, it can be stated that in the fields of genetic, multi-objective, multi-factorial, co-evolutionary, differential-evaluation, self-adaptive parameterization has led to significant improvements in algorithm performance. The demonstrated advantages of this logic are the improvement of the convergence speed, enhanced solution diversity, reduced manual tuning, and improved solution quality. During the State-of-the-Art review conducted for this paper, no self-adaptive parameterization concepts were found in the field of Bacterial Memetic Algorithm (BMA). However, since the studies examined highlight the benefits, we believe there is significant potential for this method in the BMA discussed in Section 2.

The aim of this paper is to demonstrate that the Bacterial Memetic Algorithm is suitable for solving the Storage Location Assignment Problem; however, static parameter settings restrict the attainment of satisfactory results. Therefore, we emphasize the need for adaptive parameterization, and we have formulated a concept for adaptive parameterization within the BMA algorithm. Future research will focus on developing the concept presented here, integrating it into the optimization process, and examining the extent of performance improvement compared to the genetic algorithm (GA).

2. Bacterial Memetic Algorithm for Storage Location Assignment Problem

As mentioned before, solving SLAP, a large combinatorial problem classified as NP-hard in the literature, requires a suitable algorithm for optimization.

So far, the authors have given a summary of what algorithms other researchers have applied to SLAP. The focus was on evolutionary algorithms. The experience is that the genetic algorithm (GA) has been applied in many cases, and other evolutionary algorithms have been researched in this area. The goal was to find an algorithm capable of handling more complex cases in warehouses and can be easily adapted to other warehouse environments by parameterization. The Bacterial Memetic Algorithm (BMA) is an evolutionary algorithm that models the behavior of bacteria based on its evolution [39]. The BMA has been successfully used in various optimization problems due to its fast operation, like the Order Picking Routing Problem [40], Traveling Salesman Problem [39], and flow shop scheduling problem [41]. Cs. M. Horváth et al. [25] also stated that numerous combinatorial optimization problems, continuous optimization tasks, and supervised machine-learning applications have been successfully solved using this technique. The paper summarizes that, in comparison to genetic algorithms (GAs), particle swarm optimization (PSO), and their respective memetic adaptations, BMA has shown a competitive performance in optimization and supervised machine learning [25]. As Á. Holló-Szabó [26] highlighted, every step in the BMA process contributes to the convergence in a unique way. Gene transfer is a global search subject that impacts the entire population; the goal of local search is to find the best individual, and bacterial mutation improves the solutions while decreasing the likelihood of remaining in a local minimum. They defined it as the primary distinction from GA, where mutation delays convergence by emphasizing gene pool diversity rather than rate of progress. As a result, BMA converges more quickly and steadily [26]. Based on previous research, we anticipate that these algorithms, particularly BMA, can efficiently optimize SLAP and potentially outperform GA. Therefore, our goal is to develop a BMA-based algorithm to provide an ideal SLA.

2.1. BMA Development and Parameterization

The BMA algorithm operates in four steps (Algorithm 1). The first step is to create an initial population with N_{ind} bacteria. Each bacteria represents a solution to the original problem. This can be performed randomly, or some rules can be defined. The following steps are bacterial mutation (BM) and local search (LS), performed on x % of the bacteria based on a given parameter. After ordering the population in ascending order by the objective function, the last step is gene transfer (GT). The steps of the BMA are repeated sequentially based on a specified number of generations.

Algorithm 1. BMA procedure.

1. Execute the initial population generation method
2. For i := 1 to N_{ind} do
3.   Evaluation of each bacterium and sort by defined objective function
4. End
5. For g := 1 to N_{gen} do
6.   For i := 1 to N_{ind} * BM_LS% do
7.   Execute bacterial mutation operator
8.   Execute local search operator
9.   End
10.   Order the population in ascending order by the objective function
11.   For i := 1 to N_{inf} do
12.   Execute gene transfer operator
13.   Order the population in ascending order by the objective function
14.   End
15. End

To examine the applicability of the BMA in solving the problem, it was necessary to define the evaluation method and objective function. In the studies discussed, picking lists were used to evaluate the optimization results. During the verification with these lists, the length of the picking route is examined to assess the efficiency of the SLA strategy. The primary goal of the optimization is to reduce either the picking route or the picking time. If the time taken to gather items from the lists or the distance of the route decreases, it indicates that the algorithm has succeeded in finding a better assignment. It is our opinion that this approach only examines a part of the SLA. In contrast, during the research, the entire state of SLA was considered. A novel evaluation method was formulated that is part of the developed BMA algorithm. The objective function is shown in Equation (1). The evaluation method and the objective function consider the value of the frequency of ordering items, items not allocated to a picking location, groups of items stored together, and items that are frequently ordered together [42]. Each of these is part of the objective function and can be set with a weighting parameter (w_n) based on the operation of the warehouse under examination. The items are provided with information needed for the objective function and support the steps of the algorithm.

The parameters of the objective function are as follows:

t is the time-period under examination,

p is a given picking location,
i is the item handled in the warehouse,
f_{pt} is the number of picking of the item on the p picking location at the t time-period,
l_p is the distance of the p picking location from the depot,
F_t is the summarized item order lines during the t time period,
j_t is the number of pickings of the item which is non-assigned on picking location at the t time period,
g_n is a given group of items,
lg_n is the distance between items (i_1, ..., i_n) within a group,
Ig_n is the number of items within a group,
o_{i_1,i_2} is the order frequency of two items ordered together (i_1, i_2) during the t time-period,
l_{i_1,i_2} is the distance between two items,
ω_n is the weight of the components.

$$\min \left(\frac{\omega_1 \cdot \sum_p (\frac{f_{pt}}{F_t} \cdot l_p)}{\omega_2 \cdot \frac{1}{\sum_i \frac{j_t}{F_t}}} + \omega_3 \cdot \sum_g \frac{\sum lg_n}{Ig_n} + \omega_4 \cdot \sum_i (\frac{o_{i_1,i_2}}{\sum_i o_{i_1,i_2}} \cdot l_{i_1,i_2}) \right) \quad (1)$$

Before creating the initial population, the encoding method is necessary for creating bacteria for the population. Each bacterium represents a possible SLA. The length of an individual is equal to the number of items handled in the warehouse. In the bacteria, the storage locations are assigned to the items. First, the items are ordered by the picking-frequency value, and then location data are assigned after. In the case when more items need to be assigned than the available picking location, the item is assigned the parameter "x". This item is a non-assigned item, which cannot be allocated to the picking location and must be collected by the picker from a distant or higher location. Buffer locations are also allocated and designed to support replenishing and repositioning tasks. The buffer locations fix the data and reduce the number of locations assigned for the items. Location data can be assigned to items using random and eugenic coding methods.

The random encoding method randomly sequences each picking location without any rule and assigns, and the eugenic encoding method sorts the picking locations based on the distance matrix before assigning them to the items. Figure 1 shows the encoding method with the non-assigned parameters. The parameters of the encoding method are i_n, which represents the item types that are ordered by the frequency value; PLs are the picking locations; and x is the non-assigned parameter.

The initial population generation steps are shown in Algorithm 2. The initial population can be generated with eugenic or random bacteria. After performing the necessary steps (assigning buffer locations), if eugenic bacteria are required, it assigns the locations in order; otherwise, locations are assigned randomly. A parameter defines how many bacteria are needed in the population, and parameterization helps generate the required number of bacteria. In this study, we perform the BMA steps on random initial bacteria. Our decision is based on the fact that we found it absolutely necessary to investigate the ability of the BMA to handle the SLAP problem and to sort the placement based on the parameters.

The BMA cycle starts with the bacterial mutation operator, according to Algorithm 3. Bacterial mutation is performed using clones for each bacterium in the population. The original bacterium is divided into segments. The length of the segment is a fixed parameter, and as many segments are created that can fit in the bacterium. The segments created are shuffled and sequenced, and mutation is carried out in the clones based on this order. The first segment is permutated in each clone. After the mutation, the clones are evaluated. The best clone segment is overwritten in each clone, and then the mutation steps are performed with each segment. After the last mutation, if the objective function value of the best clone is less than that of the original bacterium, it is overwritten and written back into the population.

A bacterium for SLA with random encoding	
i_1	PL8
i_2	PL6
i_3	PL1
i_4	x
i_5	PL13
i_6	PL17
i_7	x
i_8	PL19
i_9	PL4
i_{10}	PL2
i_{11}	PL14
i_{12}	PL11
i_{13}	x
i_{14}	PL9
i_{15}	x
i_{16}	PL16
i_{17}	PL5
i_{18}	PL12
i_{19}	PL7
i_{20}	PL20
...	

Selected buffer locations
PL3
PL10
PL15
PL18

i_n	item type
x	non-assigned parameter
PL	Picking location

Figure 1. Encoding method.

Algorithm 2. Initial population.

1. Order the locations in LocationTable in ascending order by Distance Matrix
2. For b := 1 to $N_{location}$ * Buffer percentage do
3.   Randomised permutation of buffer locations
4.   Overwrite the buffer locations in the LocationTable
5. End
6. For p := 1 to N_{ind} do
7.   If p <= N_{ind} * Eugenic percentage
8.   LocationTable
9.   Or else
10.   Randomized permutation of LocationTable
11.   End
12.   Copying bacteria into the population
13. End

After the BM operator, a local search (LS) is applied to improve the given bacterium. Genes are elements of the bacterium, and the local search involves swapping genes. To perform a local search, two groups are defined from which the genes to be swapped are selected. One collects those rapidly rotating items based on frequency data (i.e., category A products) that are located far from the depot point (Table1 in Algorithm 4). The other group (Table2 in Algorithm 4) contains the slowly rotating items that are located close to the depot point. The LS operator makes clones, and the process is repeated as often as defined by the parameter. In every repeat, the algorithm declares two independent genes in the given bacterium based on the defined groups and swaps the location data associated with the item types. The presented LS operator evaluates and sorts the clones after the modification. The LS operator runs for the current clone a specified number of times. If the best clone's objective function value at the end of the process is lower than the original bacterium value, the best clone overwrites the original bacterium. The LS is described in Algorithm 4.

Algorithm 3. Bacterial mutation.

1. For c := 1 to N_{clones} do
2.   Define clones c by copying the original bacterium
3. End
4. Declare integer variable Segment := 1
5. Declare integer variable SegmentLenght := 1
6. For i := 1 to N_{bac} do
7.   If SegmentLenght = $L_{clone} * L_{sgm}$ /100, then
8.   Define new segment
9.   Segment += 1
10.   SegmentLenght := 1
11.   Or else
12.   SegmentLenght += 1
13.   End
14.   Allocate i to the segment
15. End
16. Permutate the sequence of the segments
17. For s := 1 to Segment do
18.   for c := 1 to N_{clones} do
19.   Permutate the segment s of the clone c
20.   End
21.   Order the clones in ascending order by the objective function
22.   For s := 1 to N_{clones} do
23.   Copy the segment of BestClone to each clone
24.   End
25. End
26. If BestClone < initial bacterium, then
27.   Overwrite the original bacterium by the best clone
28. End

Algorithm 4. Local search.

1. For r := 1 to LS_{repeat} do
2.   Define clone by copying the original bacterium
3.   Define A items far from depot in Table1
4.   Define C items near to depot in Table2
5.   Repeat
6.   rnd1 := random integer number between 1 and L_{Table1}
7.   rnd2 := random integer number between 1 and L_{Table2}
8.   Until rnd1 ≠ rnd2
9.   Changing Locations on rnd1 and rnd2 records
10.   Evaluate clone by the objective function
11.   Order the clones in ascending order by the objective function
12. End
13. If the objective function of the best clone < objective function of the original bacterium, then
14.   Overwrite the original bacterium by the best clone
15. End

The final step in BMA is gene transfer (GT). GT allows for the recombination of genetic information between two bacteria in the steps described in Algorithm 5. A source and a destination bacteria need to be defined. A segment from the source bacterium is defined, and this segment is used in the destination bacterium. The source bacterium is randomly selected from the superior half of the population and is dedicated by the population percentage based on a specific parameter. Another bacterium is selected from the inferior half of the population, which will be the destination bacterium. These are the superior and inferior bacteria. The start of the segment is defined in the superior bacterium based on a specific parameter: how long the segment is and what percentage of the length of the bacterium it starts from. The information in the segment is deleted from the inferior bacterium to avoid duplication, and the segment is inserted in the same place from which it was extracted from the superior bacterium. The process is repeated for a number of infections times. After evaluation, if the transcription is successful, the inferior bacterium should be overwritten. The entire BMA cycle must be repeated as many times as the number of generations specified at the start of the process.

Algorithm 5. Gene transfer.

1. Define a random superior bacterium
2. Superior = RandomValue (1, N_{ind} * GT percentage)
3. Define a random inferior bacterium
4. Inferior = RandomValue (N_{ind} * GT_percentage + 1, N_{ind})
5. Copy the inferior bacterium into the Inferior_GT bacterium
6. Declare integer variable SegmentStart := (1, Lbac * GT_location_percentage)
7. Define a coherent L_{sgm} length segment from SegmentStart record from the superior bacterium
8. Delete the duplications within the Inferior_GT bacterium
9. Declare integer variable InsertStart := SegmentStart
10. Insert segment into the Inferior_GT bacterium
11. Evaluate the Inferior_GT bacterium
12. Overwrite the Inferior bacterium with the Inferior_GT bacterium

While describing the steps of the BMA algorithm, it was mentioned that the operator performs certain steps during optimization based on parameters. To operate the algorithm, several parameters are required, which are essential for its operation. These parameters are summarized in Table 1 for each operator. The scenarios generated with the basic parameters and their modifications were used to investigate the performance of the BMA.

Table 1. Initial operator parameters for BMA operation.

BMA Operator	Parameters
Initial population	Eugenic or random bacterium Number of bacteria Number of generations
Bacterial mutation	Number of clones Length of segment Percentage of the population
Local search	Number of clones Length of the segment Number of repetitions
Gene transfer	Size of the Superior bacterium group from the population Length of segment Start of the segment in the bacterium Number of infections

2.2. The Partial Results of the Development

The algorithms were developed, and the test environment was modeled with Tecnomatix Plant Simulation software version 2201.0010, which possesses its own programming language, called SimTalk. The executions were fulfilled in an ASUS TUF Dash F15

FX517ZE_FX517ZE hardware, with the following features: CPU 2th Gen Intel(R) Core(TM) x64 i7-12650H, 2.30 GHz, 10 cores, 16 logical processors, RAM 16 GB DDR5, and 4800 MHz.

Based on industry experience, an average warehouse size has been defined where the problem is realistic. A classic warehouse layout was chosen, with a single deep racking system, which is the most commonly used layout for picker-to-parts picking systems. In the test model, the specified warehouse had 1333 picking locations. The use of buffer locations was necessary for real warehouse operations. In this case, 10% of the total picking locations have been determined, reducing the total number of available picking locations to 1200. The model considered 1466 items that needed to be handled. The items are categorized by picking-frequency value for the A, B, and C categories. It is necessary to collect category A frequently and category C the least frequently. One item per location is allowed, so some items cannot be assigned to a picking location. These non-assigned items were physically collected but stored in locations that were not accessible for low-level picking. These specifications were implemented to the BMA for the assignment of items to picking locations.

The warehouse in the case study is responsible for storing and handling items such as e-commerce, where ordering patterns change and customer demands change rapidly, and item assortments are affected by seasonality.

We consider it a preliminary result that the BMA algorithm is functional and organizes the assignment on the layout according to categories. Figure 2 illustrates the changes in the assignment of each category relative to the initial state. Category A is marked in red, category B in green, and category C in blue. Figure 2a shows the initial state when the initial bacteria were generated. As mentioned before in this study, random initial population was generated and used. Figure 2b shows how the BMA algorithm organized the assignment according to categories. Category A items are close to the "x" depot point, and category C items are far from the "x" depot point.

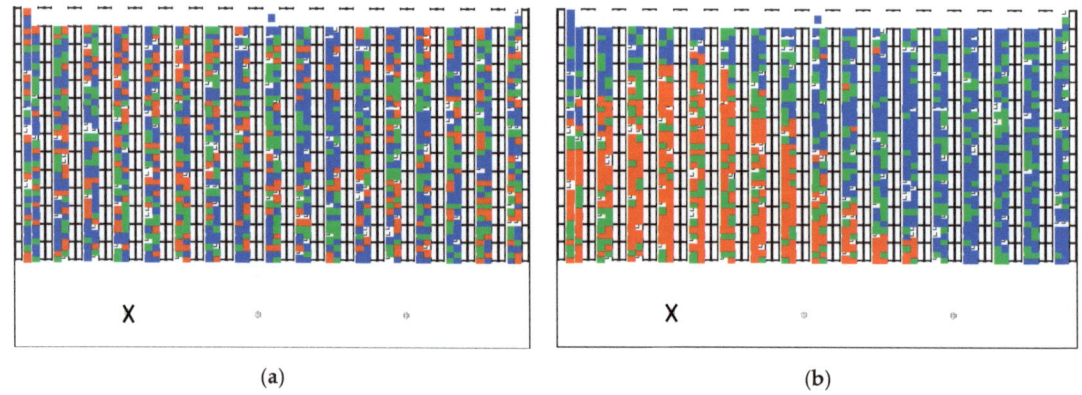

Figure 2. Change in the assignment during SLA optimization with BMA: (**a**) initial state and (**b**) assignment partial result.

During the study, a validation algorithm was used to verify the functioning of the algorithm. The genetic algorithm, most commonly used for solving SLAP, was chosen. This algorithm was programmed by implementing the described evaluation method. The same test environment was defined for the study. The operators of the BMA include the evaluation step significantly more often than the operators of the GA; hence, for comparison purposes, the evaluation value was considered to ensure comparisons were made on an equal-budget basis. Quantifying the running time will be the next step in the research.

During the testing of the BMA, numerous parameter settings were applied, and the effects of these settings were clearly observed throughout the process. These observations are summarized in Figure 3, alongside the results of the GA. The graph shows the change in the value of the objective function as a function of the evaluation number for different parameter settings. The x-axis shows the number of evaluations, and the y-axis the value of the objective function. Upon examining the evaluation value data, it was found that the GA achieved a more favorable fitness value than the BMA. A further examination of the algorithms highlighted the importance of incorporating parameter settings that can reduce the number of evaluations required by BMA operators. During the review of operators, it was observed that the LS operator contained many evaluation steps while making the smallest modifications within a bacterium. Parameters were integrated into the algorithm to specify when the LS operator should engage in the process and how often it should execute modifications across generations. The goal was to enable the algorithm to make significant improvements early in the generations with a higher random factor, building on the observed effectiveness of the GA in this aspect. Upon evaluating the outcomes after the parameter settings, it was determined that the improvement in fitness values quickly slows down during the initial phases of the generations. However, significant improvement occurs following the activation of the operator. Despite these gains, compared to other results, further modifications are necessary as satisfactory outcomes have not yet been achieved. Figure 3 shows the mentioned BMA results, the results obtained with the LS operator modification (BMA_LS_mod1 and BMA_LS_mod2) and the GA result.

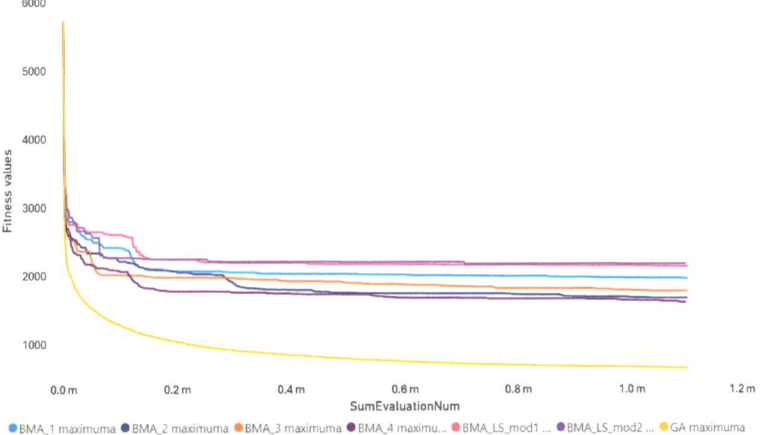

Figure 3. BMA parameterization results compared to GA results based on evaluation numbers.

As mentioned above, previous research has shown that BMA can achieve better results than GA, but based on the current state of our research, we have not yet been able to prove this for the SLAP problem. The next step of the research is an examination of whether it is indeed true that BMA also provides a better approach to solving SLAP. Due to the large number of combinations and limitations in parameterization, it is necessary to employ a different method for setting parameters during optimization. By examining options and other research, dynamic parameterization may offer a solution for adjusting BMA parameters during the optimization process to achieve favorable fitness values. This investigation led to the formulation of the concept of adaptive Bacterial Memetic Algorithm parameterization.

3. Concept of the Adaptive Bacterial Memetic Algorithm Parameterization

For evolutionary algorithms used in large-scale combinatorial problems, different parameterization may be ideal at different stages of optimization. The selection of the optimal adaptation strategy largely depends on the specific problem, the characteristics of the search space, and the goal of the algorithm.

For the presented problem, in this paper, three possible parameterization methods are examined:

Static: Static parameterization refers to when parameters are set before running the algorithm and remain unchanged during execution, regardless of time, generations, or the number of evaluations. As we presented, due to the high number of parameters and combinations, the manual static parameterization is not efficient int this case.

Dynamic: The parameters change according to a predefined rule or function, which adjusts them based on time or the number of generations. It can be efficient and enhance the effectiveness of the algorithm. The effectiveness of dynamic parameterization was tested, in which we set different parameters at various stages of the execution. One such setting was the delayed activation of the local search (after 5% of the generations). We found that it is important to allow more room for random search and mutation in the early stages of optimization, with local search taking precedence in later stages. While this approach helps, it still does not meet the expected results. We concluded that further adjustments to the parameters based on intermediate results are needed.

Self-adaptive: This method adjusts the parameters based on feedback from the algorithm's execution [25–27]. Depending on the problem, it is necessary to outline rules and equations that require extracting statistics during execution. These provide the basis for the algorithm to determine the need for parameter changes.

For the analysis, we need statistics like the following possible statics:

- Number of BM calls in one generation and the number of improvements of the BM;
- Number of LS calls in one generation and the number of improvements of the LS;
- Best value of the objective function in each generation;
- Objective function value of each bacterium in each generation;
- Amount of the Objective Function's progression through generations.

Based on the statistics, the proposed concept defines some problem-dependent rules for possible modifications, such as the following:

- Based on the BM's low-success statistics (e.g., there was no significant improvement in the last 20 generations), the BM frequency can be decreased for several BMA cycles, i.e., generations;
- Based on the BM's low success statistics (e.g., there was no significant improvement in the last e.g., 20 generations), the clones of the BM can be decreased with one clone, generation by generation, for several generations;
- Based on the LS low success statistics, we can pause the LS for several generations, and, simultaneously, we can increase the number of the BM clones;
- Based on the objective function progression statistics, e.g., in case of unsatisfactory progression, more frequent LS or more LS clones can be adjusted.

Based on these data and rules, the envisioned BMA process with self-adaptive parameterization is structured as follows (Figure 4).

Sure, we need a preliminary parameter setup whereby we start the BMA process. In this first cycle, the algorithm uses this configuration. Once BM, LS, and GT reach the end of the first generation, the adaptive parameter algorithm (APA) steps in and starts to analyze the results. Based on the previously mentioned statistics and rules used as examples, the APA decides over the need for parameter modification. The algorithm either modifies the parameters first or goes straightway forward to the next step of the BMA process. In this next step, the algorithm analyzes the number of generations, and if there are any left, then it starts the process again from the BM. If the algorithm has reached the maximum number of generations, then the optimization process ends. The BMA algorithm operates as follows with the integration of the APA module. Algorithm 6 shows the place of the APA module within the algorithm. APA examines whether parameter changes are required during execution; therefore, the algorithm itself stays the same, and just the parameterization can be modified (i.e., number of LS clones and BM frequency).

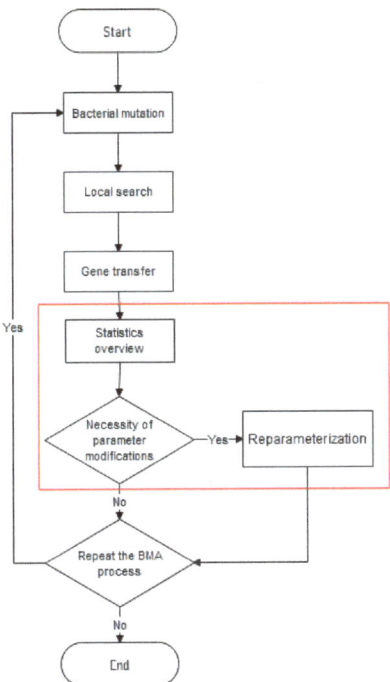

Figure 4. The BMA workflow based on the adaptive parameterization concept.

Algorithm 6. BMA procedure with APA module.
1. Execute the initial population generation method
2. For i := 1 to N_{ind} do
3.   Evaluation of each bacterium and sort by defined objective function
4. End
5. For g := 1 to N_{gen} do
6.   For i := 1 to N_{ind} * BM_LS% do
7.   Execute bacterial mutation operator
8.   Execute local search operator
9.   End
10.   Order the population in ascending order by the objective function
11.   For i := 1 to N_{inf} do
12.   Execute gene transfer operator
13.   Order the population in ascending order by the objective function
14.   End
15.   **Execute APA module**
16. End

Figure 4 shows where in the BMA workflow the APA module should be applied. Algorithm 6 shows the place of the APA module within the algorithm. APA examines whether parameter changes are required during execution. The algorithm itself stays the same; just the parameterization is modified.

As a following step of our research, the presented APA concept will be developed and built in the optimization process. With the examination of the improved optimization process results, the performance enhancement of the BMA can be defined, and the extended comparative study with the GA can be presented.

4. Conclusions

Recognizing SLAP as a substantial NP-hard combinatorial problem, this study explored advanced heuristic or algorithmic solutions for effective optimization. Traditionally, genetic algorithms (GAs) have been applied to SLAP, but recent investigations suggested potential in the application of the Bacterial Memetic Algorithm (BMA), primarily due to its versatility in tackling complex optimization challenges. Some research outlined that BMA could achieve an even better performance than GA. Based on these research results, a BMA was developed for SLA optimization and compared to the result of the GA. Contrary to expectations, the BMA did not yield as satisfactory results as expected. After examining this underperformance, the static nature of algorithmic parameters was defined as a notable challenge. It restricts the flexibility of BMA. With some manual modification, the results indicated that static parameterization, while occasionally effective, cannot respond to the complex warehouse storage conditions, leading to unsatisfactory results. It is required to achieve parity with or exceed the performance of the GA. Consequently, we explored the field of intelligent parameterization of evolutionary algorithms and formulated an adaptive parameterization concept for BMA. In this concept, the parameters are self-parameterized based on intermediate statistics and performance metrics. This adaptability allows the algorithm to dynamically shift its focus as the optimization processes. Adaptive parameterization represents a significant advancement in SLAP optimization, offering a novel framework for the dynamic optimization of evolutionary algorithms. By integrating adaptive mechanisms, our BMA model could leverage feedback from operational statistics, such as improvement rates of bacterial mutation and local search effectiveness to modify its approach dynamically. During the adaptive parameterization algorithm process, the BMA algorithm remains unchanged, and the module only changes the parameters of the BMA operators.

Our findings highlight the importance of adaptive parameterization in evolutionary algorithms—like in the BMA—particularly within warehouse management. Adaptive mechanisms can help bridge the performance gap between conventional static algorithms and the demands of modern storage location challenges. The research focused on a specific warehouse layout for FMCG goods with a low-level picker-to-parts system, which may limit generalizability to other environments. The ability of BMA to dynamically respond to changing storage demands makes it suitable for industries with high variability, such as e-commerce and FMCG sectors. By reducing picking times and improving storage efficiency, significant cost reductions and operational efficiencies can be achieved. This research expands the field of adaptive evolutionary algorithms by applying self-adaptive parameterization to the BMA framework, and, in practice, it provides a pathway for deploying advanced algorithms in real-world warehouses to solve combinatorial optimization problems. This research also highlights the potential for integrating machine learning to further refine parameter adjustments based on historical trends. Future research could explore adaptive controls or integrate machine-learning techniques that predict parameter adjustments based on historical data trends, further enhancing the robustness and efficiency of BMA for SLAP. While adaptive parameterization was conceptualized, its full implementation and testing and the presentation of a new comparative analysis with the GA remain as future research directions. The computational complexity of adaptive mechanisms may also pose challenges for large-scale applications, requiring further optimization.

Author Contributions: Conceptualization, K.U., P.G., and T.B.; methodology, K.U. and P.G.; software, P.G. and T.B.; investigation, P.G.; supervision, T.B. and J.B.; writing—original draft preparation, K.U. and P.G.; writing—review and editing, K.U., P.G., T.B., and J.B. All authors have read and agreed to the published version of the manuscript.

Funding: This research received no external funding.

Data Availability Statement: Dataset available upon request from the authors.

Conflicts of Interest: The authors declare no conflicts of interest.

References

1. Boysen, N.; de Koster, R. 50 years of warehousing research—An operations research perspective. *Eur. J. Oper. Res.* **2025**, *320*, 449–464. [CrossRef]
2. de Koster, R.; Le-Duc, T.; Roodbergen, K.J. Design and control of warehouse order picking: A literature review. *Eur. J. Oper. Res.* **2007**, *182*, 481–501. [CrossRef]
3. Leon, J.F.; Li, Y.; Peyman, M.; Calvet, L.; Juan, A.A. A Discrete-Event Simheuristic for Solving a Realistic Storage Location Assignment Problem. *Mathematics* **2023**, *11*, 1577. [CrossRef]
4. Quintanilla, S.; Pérez, Á.; Ballestín, F.; Lino, P. Heuristic algorithms for a storage location assignment problem in a chaotic warehouse. *Eng. Optim.* **2014**, *47*, 1405–1422. [CrossRef]
5. Liu, M.; Poh, K.L. E-commerce warehousing: An efficient scattered storage assignment algorithm with bulky locations. *Comput. Ind. Eng.* **2023**, *181*, 109236. [CrossRef]
6. Xie, J.; Mei, Y.; Ernst, A.T.; Li, X.; Song, A. A Restricted Neighbourhood Tabu Search for Storage Location Assignment Problem. In Proceedings of the 2015 IEEE Congress on Evolutionary Computation (CEC), Sendai, Japan, 25–28 May 2015. [CrossRef]
7. Diefenbach, H.; Grosse, E.H.; Glock, C.H. Human-and-cost-centric storage assignment optimization in picker-to-parts warehouses. *Eur. J. Oper. Res.* **2024**, *315*, 1049–1068. [CrossRef]
8. Wisittipanich, W.; Meesuk, P. Differential evolution algorithm for storage location assignment problem. *Lect. Notes Electr. Eng.* **2015**, *349*, 259–266. [CrossRef]
9. Wisittipanich, W.; Kasemset, C. Metaheuristics for warehouse storage location assignment problems. *Chiang Mai Univ. J. Nat. Sci.* **2015**, *14*, 361–377. [CrossRef]
10. He, Y.; Wang, A.; Su, H.; Wang, M. Particle Swarm Optimization Using Neighborhood-Based Mutation Operator and Intermediate Disturbance Strategy for Outbound Container Storage Location Assignment Problem. *Math. Probl. Eng.* **2019**, *2019*, 9132315. [CrossRef]
11. Kübler, P.; Glock, C.H.; Bauernhansl, T. A new iterative method for solving the joint dynamic storage location assignment, order batching and picker routing problem in manual picker-to-parts warehouses. *Comput. Ind. Eng.* **2020**, *147*, 106645. [CrossRef]
12. Peng, G.; Wu, Y.; Zhang, C.; Shen, W. Integrated optimization of storage location assignment and crane scheduling in an unmanned slab yard. *Comput. Ind. Eng.* **2021**, *161*, 107623. [CrossRef]
13. Fontana, M.E.; Lopez, J.C.L.; Cavalcante, C.A.V.; Noriega, J.J.S. Multi-Criteria Assignment Model to solve the Storage Location Assignment Problem. *Investig. Oper.* **2020**, *41*, 1019–1029. Available online: https://www.researchgate.net/publication/348518501 (accessed on 16 February 2024).
14. Wan, Y.; Liu, Y. Integrating Optimized Fishbone Warehouse Layout, Storage Location Assignment and Picker Routing. *IAENG Int. J. Comput. Sci.* **2022**, *49*, 957–974.
15. Zhou, L.; Yang, X.; Chen, L.; You, S.; Li, F.; Cao, Y. Effective storage location assignment model based on a genetic simulation annealing algorithm. *Int. J. Wirel. Mob. Comput.* **2020**, *19*, 9–17. [CrossRef]
16. Xie, J.; Mei, Y.; Ernst, A.T.; Li, X.; Song, A. A Genetic Programming-based Hyper-heuristicApproach for Storage Location Assignment Problem. In Proceedings of the IEEE Congress on Evolutionary Computation (CEC), Beijing, China, 6–11 July 2014. [CrossRef]
17. Xie, J.; Mei, Y.; Ernst, A.T.; Li, X.; Song, A. Scaling up solutions to storage location assignment problems by genetic programming. *Lect. Notes Comput. Sci.* **2014**, *8886*, 691–702. [CrossRef]
18. Li, M.; Chen, X.; Liu, C. Pareto and Niche Genetic Algorithm for Storage Location Assignment Optimization Problem. In Proceedings of the IEEE Innovative Computing Information and Control (ICICIC), Dalian, China, 18–20 June 2008. [CrossRef]
19. Wu, Q.; Zhang, Y.; Ma, Z. Optimization of Storage Location Assignment for Fixed Rack Systems. *Lect. Notes Comput. Sci.* **2010**, *6318*, 29–35. [CrossRef]
20. Ene, S.; Öztürk, N. Storage location assignment and order picking optimization in the automotive industry. *Int. J. Adv. Manuf. Technol.* **2012**, *60*, 787–797. [CrossRef]
21. Xu, X.; Ren, C. Research on dynamic storage location assignment of picker-to-parts picking systems under traversing routing method. *Complexity* **2020**, *2020*, 1621828. [CrossRef]
22. Saleet, H. Smart solution for enhancing storage location assignments in wms using genetic algorithm. *Int. J. Eng. Res. Technol.* **2020**, *13*, 3456–3463. [CrossRef]
23. Görbe, P.; Bódis, T.; Botzheim, J. A Conceptual Framework for Adaptive Storage Location Assignment Considering Order Characteristics. *Eur. J. Sci. Technol.* **2020**, 610–614. [CrossRef]
24. Görbe, P.; Bódis, T.; Földesi, P. Trade-offs in warehousing storage location reassignment. *Int. J. Logist. Syst. Manag.* **2023**. [CrossRef]
25. Horváth, C.M.; Botzheim, J. Bacterial Memetic Algorithm Trained Fuzzy System-Based Model of Single Weld Bead Geometry. *IEEE Access* **2020**, *8*, 164864–164881. [CrossRef]
26. Holló-Szabó, Á.; Botzheim, J. Comparison of Various Mutation Operators of the Bacterial Memetic Algorithm on the Traveling Salesman Problem. In *Communications in Computer and Information Science (ICCCI 2023)*; Springer: Cham, Switzerland, 2023; Volume 1864, pp. 508–520. [CrossRef]
27. Kramer, O. Evolutionary self-adaptation: A survey of operators and strategy parameters. *Evol. Intell.* **2010**, *3*, 51–65. [CrossRef]

28. Beyer, H.G.; Sendhoff, B. Robust optimization—A comprehensive survey. *Comput. Methods Appl. Mech. Eng.* **2007**, *196*, 3190–3218. [CrossRef]
29. Meyer-Nieberg, S.; Beyer, H.G. Self-adaptation in evolutionary algorithms. *Stud. Comput. Intell.* **2007**, *54*, 47–75. [CrossRef]
30. Ye, F.; Neumann, F.; de Nobel, J.; Neumann, A.; Bäck, T. What Performance Indicators to Use for Self-Adaptation in Multi-Objective Evolutionary Algorithms. In Proceedings of the GECCO '24: Proceedings of the Genetic and Evolutionary Computation Conference, Melbourne, Australia, 14–18 July 2024; pp. 787–795. [CrossRef]
31. Yao, J.; Nie, Y.; Zhao, Z.; Xue, X.; Zhang, K.; Yao, C.; Zhang, L.; Wang, J.; Yang, Y. Self-adaptive multifactorial evolutionary algorithm for multitasking production optimization. *J. Pet. Sci. Eng.* **2021**, *205*, 108900. [CrossRef]
32. Cortez-González, J.; Hernández-Aguirre, A.; Murrieta-Dueñas, R.; Gutiérrez-Guerra, R.; Hernández, S.; Segovia-Hernández, J.G. Process optimization using a dynamic self-adaptive constraint handling technique coupled to a Differential Evolution algorithm. *Chem. Eng. Res. Des.* **2023**, *189*, 98–116. [CrossRef]
33. Wang, S.L.; Morsidi, F.; Ng, T.F.; Budiman, H.; Neoh, S.C. Insights into the effects of control parameters and mutation strategy on self-adaptive ensemble-based differential evolution. *Inf. Sci.* **2020**, *514*, 203–233. [CrossRef]
34. Wang, X.; Yu, X. Differential Evolution Algorithm with Three Mutation Operators for Global Optimization. *Mathematics* **2024**, *12*, 2311. [CrossRef]
35. Xue, Y.; Cai, X.; Neri, F. A multi-objective evolutionary algorithm with interval based initialization and self-adaptive crossover operator for large-scale feature selection in classification. *Appl. Soft Comput.* **2022**, *127*, 109420. [CrossRef]
36. Karthikeyan, P. Genetic algorithm with self adaptive immigrants for effective virtual machine placement in cloud environment. *Int. J. Intell. Netw.* **2023**, *4*, 155–161. [CrossRef]
37. Sun, L.; Lin, L.; Li, H.; Gen, M. Cooperative co-evolution algorithm with an MRF-based decomposition strategy for stochastic flexible job shop scheduling. *Mathematics* **2019**, *7*, 318. [CrossRef]
38. An, Y.; Zhao, Z.; Gao, K.; Dong, Y.; Chen, X.; Zhou, B. A self-adaptive co-evolutionary algorithm for multi-objective flexible job-shop rescheduling problem with multi-phase processing speed selection, condition-based preventive maintenance and dynamic repairman assignment. *Swarm Evol. Comput.* **2024**, *89*, 101643. [CrossRef]
39. Kóczy, L.T.; Földesi, P.; Tüű-Szabó, B. Enhanced discrete bacterial memetic evolutionary algorithm—An efficacious metaheuristic for the traveling salesman optimization. *Inf. Sci.* **2018**, *460–461*, 389–400. [CrossRef]
40. Bódis, T.; Botzheim, J. Bacterial Memetic Algorithms for Order Picking Routing Problem with Loading Constraints. *Expert Syst. Appl.* **2018**, *105*, 196–220. [CrossRef]
41. Agárdi, A.; Nehéz, K.; Hornyák, O.; Kóczy, L.T. A hybrid discrete bacterial memetic algorithm with simulated annealing for optimization of the flow shop scheduling problem. *Symmetry* **2021**, *13*, 1131. [CrossRef]
42. Görbe, P.; Bódis, T. Generalized objective function to ensure robust evaluation for evolutionary storage location assignment algorithms. *Commun. Comput. Inf. Sci.* **2023**, *1864*, 546–559. [CrossRef]

Disclaimer/Publisher's Note: The statements, opinions and data contained in all publications are solely those of the individual author(s) and contributor(s) and not of MDPI and/or the editor(s). MDPI and/or the editor(s) disclaim responsibility for any injury to people or property resulting from any ideas, methods, instructions or products referred to in the content.

MDPI AG
Grosspeteranlage 5
4052 Basel
Switzerland
Tel.: +41 61 683 77 34

Mathematics Editorial Office
E-mail: mathematics@mdpi.com
www.mdpi.com/journal/mathematics

Disclaimer/Publisher's Note: The title and front matter of this reprint are at the discretion of the Guest Editor. The publisher is not responsible for their content or any associated concerns. The statements, opinions and data contained in all individual articles are solely those of the individual Editor and contributors and not of MDPI. MDPI disclaims responsibility for any injury to people or property resulting from any ideas, methods, instructions or products referred to in the content.

www.ingramcontent.com/pod-product-compliance
Lightning Source LLC
LaVergne TN
LVHW072333090526
838202LV00019B/2410